PC Magazine® Wireless Solutions

Neil Randall and Barrie Sosinsky

Wiley Publishing, Inc.

PC Magazine® Wireless Solutions

Published by
Wiley Publishing, Inc.
10475 Crosspoint Boulevard
Indianapolis, IN 46256-5774
www.wiley.com

ISBN: 0-7645-7438-8

Manufactured in the United States of America

10 9 8 7 6 5 4 3 2 1

1B/TQ/RR/QU/IN

For general information on our other products and services or to obtain technical support, please contact our Customer Care Department within the U.S. at (800) 762-2974, outside the U.S. at (317) 572-3993 or fax (317) 572-4002.

Wiley also publishes its books in a variety of electronic formats. Some content that appears in print may not be available in electronic books.

Library of Congress Control Number: 2004114968

Credits

EXECUTIVE EDITOR
Chris Webb

DEVELOPMENT EDITOR
Brian MacDonald

PRODUCTION EDITOR
Gabrielle Nabi

TECHNICAL EDITOR
Wiley-Dreamtech India Pvt Ltd

COPY EDITORS
Kim Cofer
Howard Jones

EDITORIAL MANAGER
Mary Beth Wakefield

VICE PRESIDENT & EXECUTIVE GROUP PUBLISHER
Richard Swadley

VICE PRESIDENT AND PUBLISHER
Joseph B. Wikert

PROJECT COORDINATOR
April Farling

GRAPHICS AND PRODUCTION SPECIALISTS
Jonelle Burns
Amanda Carter
Sean Decker
Lisa England
Jennifer Heleine

QUALITY CONTROL TECHNICIANS
John Greenough
Carl William Pierce
Charles Spencer
Robert Springer

PROOFREADING AND INDEXING
TECHBOOKS Production Services

About the Authors

Neil Randall teaches digital design and communication, as well as interface analysis, at the University of Waterloo (Canada). He is also an independent computer consultant, specializing in Windows applications and networking, and has contributed numerous features, reviews, and columns to a wide range of computer magazines, *PC Magazine* primary among them.

Barrie Sosinsky writes and consults on the computer industry, specializing in Windows, servers, and storage hardware and software technologies. He has written numerous white papers for Fortune 1000 corporate clients, nearly 30 computer trade books, and more than 400 magazine articles during his 25 years in the industry. He lives in Medfield, Massachusetts, approximately 21.79 miles from Fenway Park, 28.33 miles from the Fleet Center, and 6.82 miles from Gillette Stadium. He lives in a house that is getting smarter than he is, with two cats, two kids, a turtle, a frog, and several fish, and computers named after aircraft carriers (for the most part). Among his many hobbies are building computer systems, photography, and the acquisition and mastery of all types of electronic gizmos. He is currently working on launching an e-zine, to be called *TechnologyRoad.com*.

To Mary Elizabeth Lamont, for having faith in me. ~NR

To my wife Carol Westheimer, who makes it all worthwhile. ~BAS

Preface

One nice thing about the Internet is the ability to keep abreast of technology news on a daily—or even more frequent—basis. A few years ago, back before the bubble burst on tech stocks, sites such as news.com, newslinx.com, and their ilk ran story after story on the Internet itself, especially stories about the rise of Internet commerce. Starting about the year 2000, news stories started appearing in spades that talked about viruses, Trojan horses, denial of service attacks, hackers and crackers, and, of course, the Y2K scare.

Today, every time you open a tech news Web site, you're certain to read something about wireless.

Wireless is hot. It's everywhere. It's convenient, it's appealing, it's a new kind of magic. It promises the world, and in some ways it delivers on that promise. It fulfills a dream about communication technology we've had since communication technologies began: the dream of having technology come to us, instead of us going to it.

Wireless Is Now

Let's have a quick look at the two primary areas of wireless technology—cellular telephony and wireless (also called Wi-Fi) networking—and see what this means. Back in ye olden days, the only way to have a telephone conversation was over a telephone handset that was connected by wire to some location in that building. For homes, often this was the kitchen wall, or the small table in the hall that everybody in TV sitcoms always seemed to have. The telephone was almost always in a central location, so that when it rang it was easily accessible. Furthermore, it was part of a location, not part of a person. Phone numbers and postal addresses went hand in hand, as indeed they still do in the case of the standard phone service. You didn't phone a person, you phoned a place.

Cell phones have changed all that. When you phone someone's cell number and they answer, you have no idea where they are. They might be at home. They might be at work. They might be at church. They might be in another city, another country, anywhere. But the whole point is that their location isn't important: you aren't calling the person's house, you're calling the person. Where they are is wholly irrelevant. Cellular technology has changed the relationship between telephony and geography. But for anyone growing up at a time when phones were attached to buildings, not carried by people, the new relationship still jars.

For computers, wireless has done away with one of the least aesthetically pleasing—and most complicated to master—pieces of equipment imaginable: the wire. They're called cables, actually, not wires, but most people call them wires anyway. Either way, many people find them unsightly at best, dangerous at worst. String an Ethernet cable from the study upstairs all the way down the stairs to the family room in order to play your video games online, and not only have you shattered the house's chances of being featured in *Better Homes and Gardens* magazine, but you've also vastly increased the odds that someone will trip over the cable and fall down the stairs, possibly fracturing bones and certainly fracturing tempers. Now you can sit on the deck and surf the Web, or log in to your account at work, or take control of the PC in your office half-way across the world—without ever plugging a cable into your notebook. Using one wireless network, you can use a media player on the PC in your upstairs bedroom to view the videos stored on your PC in the basement; use a

notebook PC to research information on the World Wide Web and post the results to your personal document site; listen to Internet radio on your audio system; and play games on your Xbox against opponents on the Xbox Live network. And you can do these things simultaneously.

Before, you went to a PC that was wired into a network, or you brought a wire to your PC. Today, the network comes to you. Wherever you plunk your notebook down, or your Xbox or PlayStation 2, the network is ready to do whatever you need it to do. The technology, once again, has come to us. And that's as radical a change in the relationship between human beings and their communications technologies since — well, dare I say the printing press? Gutenberg's great invention not only lowered the cost of printed materials and made them infinitely faster to produce, but it also allowed people to take books with them rather than having to go elsewhere — monasteries, churches, palaces — to read them or, more likely, to hear them being read aloud. Next was the telegraph, which allowed fast communication over long distances. Then came the telephone, a truly revolutionary technology. And then television, which brought the motion picture concept into the home, and after that the personal computer — and then wireless.

Today, wireless technology has combined with computing technology to offer a range of communication and information options we've simply never had before. Wireless is at the hub of computer networking, telephonic communication, entertainment, and business, and has become the standard-bearer in that constantly upcoming thing called digital convergence. Our lives are in the process of transformation through technology — a process that ran throughout the twentieth century but has increased to a blinding speed over the past twenty years — and wireless technology now leads the way toward not only new technologies but also bringing older technologies together. To see it work — and the sheer effortlessness of it all — get yourself a combination cell phone/PDA (personal digital assistant) such as, say, the Handspring Treo 600 (from PalmOne), and use it to take a picture of the scenery outside your car and send it via e-mail to someone in your contact list. And then, just for good measure, upload it to your Web site and view the site on the Treo's display.

Five minutes, tops. And just try *that* 20 years ago.

What's fascinating about wireless technology, finally, is that although it's taking over the landscape, in many ways we barely notice it. It keeps coming to us in product after product, but it all seems so natural. The notebook computer still seems clunky, but the wireless Internet connection seems precisely as it should be. Sending photographs over a cell phone seems like something we should always have been able to do. Wireless text messaging — how could this not have existed before? Obvious, once you've tried it. And once again, in the case of your text messaging device, it's the device that seems awkward, the wireless connection that seems natural.

So here we are — a wireless world. This book helps you step into it.

About This Book

Why do you need a book to help you? You can, of course, learn to understand the growing world of wireless technology all on your own. Barrie Sosinsky and I, your two authors, know this very well, because that's how we've learned it. A bit at a time, piece by piece, figuring out how to work with each new technology as it appeared, and then watching as the next technology came along to show us that we were behind again. We did this over the years with computing technology of all kinds, and over the past half dozen years (and even more, in some cases) with wireless technology.

What we learned, aside from a whole lot of barely pronounceable technical terms, is that learning on your own is really, really inefficient. This book exists because, quite frankly, you don't need the hassle. You want this stuff to work for you, and you want it to work ***now***. And that's precisely as it should be.

What This Book Does

Anybody can buy and use a cell phone (well, as long as your eyes can see the little buttons and your fingers can press them). But cell phones have special features and special uses that few people know how to use, and new features and uses that keep appearing with each new generation of phone and each new addition to the cell phone services. This book helps you straighten out some of the potential confusion and, in the process, helps you troubleshoot cell phone use.

So yes, the book helps do that.

But this isn't a cell phone book — it's a wireless book. And the bulk of it is taken up with wireless connectivity of many kinds, starting with and focusing on wireless networks and what they can do for you. When designing the contents for this book, I took a long look at the wireless equipment I have lying around my office and asked myself questions such as:

- What good is all this stuff and how can people put it to good use?
- What can cause confusion?
- What can go wrong?
- What can people do to make the most of the wireless technologies they own?
- How can they avoid getting hacked?
- How can they stay abreast of all the changes and innovations?

And along with these questions came the one that should have come first: How can someone even get started with all of this?

If you've wondered about the answer to any of these questions — and in all likelihood you have, since you're reading this right now — this book will help you answer them. The book is designed as a series of solutions involving wireless technology — solutions for home users, small business users, and even anyone involved in setting up and maintaining wireless communication for larger businesses.

Each section of the book offers a look at a different range of solutions. For example, Part One is concerned with getting a wireless network up and running efficiently and usefully, and Part Two is all about making that network secure (a subject very near and dear to Wi-Fi's heart these days). By the time you've finished these two parts, you'll have a very good idea of how to make your wireless network function, what to do when it stops functioning (as it inevitably will), and how to make sure your neighbor, or a passing "war driver" (you'll learn about these), isn't accessing your wireless network and digging through the files on your notebook — or worse.

The rest of the book follows suit, but the topics range widely over the wireless map. From wireless entertainment centers to setting up and using Wi-Fi hotspots, the book offers ideas to make the most out of the burgeoning wireless field.

Who Should Read It?

This book provides useful ideas — sometimes sanity-preserving ideas — for anyone who works with wireless technologies. If you want a more particular list of people it will help, let's try this:

- Anyone who wants to set up a wireless network but doesn't quite know how
- Anyone who has set up a wireless network but wants to experiment with its configuration
- Anyone who wants to expand a wireless network to make it bigger and/or to include additional types of connections
- Anyone who has a wireless network but feels there must be more they can do with it
- Anyone who wants to secure a wireless network against intruders
- Anyone who has a secure wireless network but wants it even more secure
- Anyone whose small business needs a Wi-Fi hotspot for its customers
- Anyone who wants to log on to the Wi-Fi hotspot in the coffee shop but can't seem to do so
- Anyone who wants to set up a wireless media center in their house
- Anyone who wants to expand the usefulness of their cell phones
- Anyone who needs to understand the components of digital convergence

A long list, obviously. But this book touches on all these topics, and gives you hands-on examples of how to do the things you need to do to make your wireless equipment work for you. Work through part of it and you'll be able to use your devices more effectively. Work through all of it and you'll be able to start answering other people's questions, which, you'll quickly discover, is something of a mixed blessing, but extremely valuable.

One other thing you'll get from this book: a strong sense of what all those brain-mushing terms and abbreviations mean. You know the ones: 802.11b, 802.11g, Wireless-G, Wi-Fi, WEP, WPA, wireless broadband, and on and on and on. The computer world is filled with abbreviations, of course, but the wireless industry seems intent on giving us far more than we can handle. As you work through this book, you'll encounter numerous wireless terms, but in all cases you'll also find a comprehensible working definition for them, along with a readable explanation of what the technology behind each term actually does — not how it works, but what it means to *you*. And there's a good reason for this: Barrie Sosinksy and I had to figure these things out for ourselves over the course of the last several years, so we know what it's like to try to understand them. We figured we could help out a bit by passing what we know on to you.

The wireless future is fascinating, exciting, a little bit intimidating, and more than a little bit frightening. *PC Magazine Wireless Solutions* will help you get past the intimidating part, deal with the frightening part, and give you the skills and knowledge you need to keep the fascinating and exciting parts alive. And in the process, you'll end up with wireless networks and wireless gizmos that work better for you than you would have imagined.

Neil Randall, September 2004

Acknowledgments

First of all, let me acknowledge the gadget makers. These people keep inventing nifty thing after nifty thing, letting them join together in a kind of wireless wonderworld that not only lets people like me keep writing books, but really does promise a fascinating future.

I also acknowledge my editors at Wiley, Chris Webb and Brian MacDonald, who — let's just say — put up with a lot. I don't know if I would have.

And always, always, always — Heather. How she lives with the ups and downs of a book-writer I'll never know, but I'm not about to complain. I am, however, about to start buying way more flowers. Nobody on the planet deserves them more than she.

— Neil Randall

I would like to thank my co-author Neil Randall and acquisitions editor Chris Webb for allowing me to contribute to this project. The book benefited from the skilled efforts of its development editor Brian MacDonald, who kept the writing on track and in voice, as well as from the good work of technical editor Ankur Verma of Wiley Dreamtech. As always, I appreciate the help of my agent and friend Matt Wagner at Waterside in getting the project.

— Barrie Sosinsky

Contents at a Glance

Contents

Part I

Building and Using a Wireless Network

Chapter 1

Understanding Wireless

This chapter introduces wireless networking technology. Although you could certainly argue that you don't need to understand how wireless works to use it, as with all technologies, a basic understanding certainly helps when it comes to setup and troubleshooting. As an example, people who have trouble setting up their multi-component stereos also have difficulty figuring out why one component doesn't work with the group as a whole, even if the problem is only with which wire goes where. More significantly for computer users, not understanding even the most basic details of how computer viruses spread has ensured not only that viruses spread like wildfire, but also that virus hoax e-mail messages spread as well. One of the overarching solutions for technology use is understanding the technology you're using, at least to the degree that you can determine what might be going wrong.

We don't mean to suggest, of course, that you need to be an expert. Far from it. But when it comes to anything to do with computer networking — the subject much of this book deals with — knowing where to begin troubleshooting helps a great deal. In all our years of working with PCs, two things have always continued to astound us: the fact that PCs work at all, and the fact that you can get a group of them to work together. When you toss the concept of wireless into the bin, it goes beyond astonishment toward, well, magic. Arthur C. Clarke's great statement, "Any sufficiently advanced technology is indistinguishable from magic," applies quite nicely, for many people, to computers, networking, and wireless communication.

The Trend to Wireless

If the trend to wireless continues as it is, pretty soon you won't hear the word "wireless" at all, because there won't be any need for it. Once everything is wireless, and that does seem to be the direction in which we're heading, distinguishing between wireless and wired will no longer hold any useful meaning. Until that time, however, you're going to hear "wireless" more and more with each passing year, maybe even each passing month, so it makes sense to know exactly what the word entails.

Wireless means, of course, ***without wires***. All wireless communication takes place over radio waves, electromagnetic waves that carry signals. To be considered a wireless network, radio waves have to carry the signal at least part of the way. The greater the proportion of wireless to wired, the more wireless we consider the network. Take a pair of walkie-talkies, for example. Each walkie-talkie contains wires within its physical structure, but we consider walkie-talkie communication wholly wireless. Of course, many kids have experimented with a more primitive form of walkie-talkie,

joining two soup cans together with a piece of string (although metal wire works much better), and that, basically, demonstrates the difference. Take away the string and you need another way of sending the signal (beyond shouting). Radio waves do the trick. Keep in mind, in fact, that the radio itself was originally called a wireless.

The tin cans versus walkie-talkie comparison also helps convey the primary reason for the proliferation of wireless communications. You can expect even a cheap walkie-talkie to let you talk to someone a few rooms away, even further if you go outside. To accomplish the same effect with your soup cans, you need a longer and longer wire between them, and in some cases the wired connection becomes difficult. You are, in industry terms, ***tethered*** to the other communicator. In the same way, when you talk on a standard telephone set, you're tethered to the wall. Wires tether. One of the primary attractions to wireless technology is its ability to ***untether*** you, thereby giving you the freedom to move around. In industry terms, you gain ***mobility***; you are ***mobile***.

With all the obvious advantages to going wireless, you might be wondering why wireless solutions aren't even more pervasive than they already are. There are three answers: cost, reliability, and speed. Connecting through radio waves is simply more complex than connecting through wires, and without the physical connection, more problems can occur with the transmission. Very little interferes with a wired connection, but many sources of interference plague radio transmissions. With wireless, you're asking your signal to fly through the air and be picked up by another specific device, without any other device interfering with it in the meantime or stealing the signal right out of the air. Wires make the process significantly easier, with a clearer signal path and a more limited transmission. On top of all of these advantages, wired connections are faster and have better security.

Add it all up, and you have greater expense for development, greater expense for implementation, greater expense all around. Wireless costs. In fact, wireless has only one real advantage over wired: no wires. Its point, and a point that is absolutely beyond argument, is that wires restrict movement. More philosophically, for technology to perform its primary function of making people's lives better or easier or somehow richer, technology should strive to become more and more like a part of the person it's serving. You should be able to use it without having a wire hanging out of it.

To say nothing of aesthetics: Wires, according to some people, just don't look good when strung all over the house. Go figure.

From the standpoint of this book, and indeed from the standpoint of most news items you read today, wireless has two major streams: computer networking and telephony. Wireless computer networking refers to networks that rely in part on data transfers over a radio connection. Typically, the connection occurs at the user's device — laptop, PDA, and so on — with the network adapter card inside the device acting as a transmitter and receiver in an exchange of signals with the network. It's entirely possible to have a network that relies on wireless transfers in between wired components, but usually they're not set up in such a manner. Whenever the term ***wireless LAN*** or ***WLAN*** (LAN means ***local area network***) appears in this book, it is referring to a network in which the user device includes wireless adapter technology that connects to the network via radio waves. The primary standard for wireless LAN technology is IEEE 802.11, with 802.11g currently in the throes of rendering the venerable 802.11b yesterday's news. Well, venerable in computer terms, at least, where anything over two years old borders on the truly antique.

Wireless telephony takes two major forms: cordless phones and cellular phones. This book deals very little with cordless phones because they don't really do much that normal phones can't do, and they do a lot less than cell phones. Their primary interest in this discussion lies in whether or not they generate interference for other wireless signals, or vice versa.

Cell phone technology, on the other hand, does play a significant role in this book, just as it has, increasingly, out in the world. Cell phones represent the most significant release from tethered communications technology we've seen yet, and in fact have changed the very concept of telephony. Not long ago, telephones were associated with a place — an office, a street corner, a house, even a specific location in a house — but cell phones are associated with a *person*. Cell phones represent the first mass-market communications technology to go wherever its human owner takes it, remaining available for use at all times. Sociologists and psychologists have only begun to suggest the enormous difference this particular set of wireless technologies (cellular telephony is far more than just one) will have on its users. But you don't need experts to tell you some of the differences: Just watch teenagers with their cell phones, constantly checking for new voice or text messages, and you'll see how technology can dominate the day's activities. E-mail can do the same thing, of course, but the cell phone has the aura of even greater personal attachment.

Wireless networking and cellular telephony have been in the news as much as — perhaps more than — any other technology over the last half of 2003 and the first of 2004. That's unlikely to change because the charm of mobility has so far outstripped the fear of data theft and bandwidth intrusion. But as much as McDonald's, university campuses, and all those wireless coffee shops would like you to take advantage of the easy Internet access provided by wireless local area and wide area networks, problems await and threaten to derail everyone's best laid plans. Over the next two years, you're certain to see an increase in concerns about identity theft, corporate hacking, and every other type of illegal computer activity, and many of these concerns will relate specifically to wireless in all its forms. But so will some of the great changes and advances in how people connect to their networks, including and especially the Internet itself, and those things make all the effort worthwhile.

Transmissions, Channels, and Alphabet Soup

To understand fully how wireless local area networks (WLANs) function requires a complete understanding of computer networking and, for that matter, computers themselves, and this book wouldn't have enough room for such an explanation even if it dispensed with all other material. So we'll start from the premise that local area networks function just fine, and go from there. WLANs incorporate all the concepts of wired LANs, including data transfer (sending and receiving data), data throughput (the amount of data transmitted in any given chunk of time), and addressing (making sure the data gets to the right place). The only difference between a LAN and a WLAN, in fact, is the medium of transmission — wires for the former, radio waves for the latter.

When it comes to setting up and maintaining a WLAN, to say nothing of designing the technology behind it, the medium of transmission is a major difference. Wired networks provide more reliability than wireless, along with greater speed, in everything from establishing and maintaining a connection through transferring data and enforcing security. Wireless networks require a different degree of configuration, and an understanding of how the data gets from one PC to the next can help considerably when it comes to configuration and troubleshooting. Of course, the same is true to a degree of wired networks, but given the ubiquity of the Ethernet standard, under which the vast majority of smaller PC-based networks operate, wired networking at the small network level has become much easier to achieve than at any time in the past. Wireless, while getting easier, still demands more of both the network builder and the network user.

Wireless networks are based on the IEEE 802.11 standard, developed in 1997 to specify how to format and structure data for wireless transmission, and how devices will transmit and receive the data structures. 802.11 governs the three elements that constitute wireless networking: the network structure itself, the format and structure of the data that moves through the network, and the technical details of the radio signals over which the data structures travel. The standard determines how network adapters (everything from PC and USB cards to access points) convert computer data into radio signals and vice versa, outlining precisely what each byte of data needs to effect this conversion without data loss or corruption.

Although the 802.11 standard covers multiple types of wireless networking, you'll find only three of its subsequent standards in widespread use today: 802.11b, 802.11g, and the much less common 802.11a. These standards are outlined here only briefly because of their importance in understanding the workings of WLANs. 802.11b and 802.11g both transmit at 2.4 GHz, with 802.11a at 5 GHz. The higher the frequency, the greater the data transfer speed (theoretically, at least), and you can see the difference readily between 802.11b, the first common wireless standard, and 802.11a, which reached the market a couple years later. 802.11b possesses a maximum 11 Mb/sec (megabits per second), while 802.11a can reach 54 Mb/sec. 802.11g, the natural successor to 802.11b and the most popular standard in commonly available wireless products today, manages to achieve 802.11a's 54 Mbit/sec capability even on 802.11b's 2.4 Mhz frequency.

The result is a nice blend between 11a and 11b, with 11b's greater physical signal range and 11a's speed. For this reason, 11a devices have largely disappeared from the marketplace, while 11b products hang on primarily because they can be sold reasonably inexpensively. 802.11g is currently at the center of the wireless networking universe.

Today's wireless networks use a radio technology known as *Direct Sequence Spread Spectrum*, abbreviated to *DSSS*. DSSS divides radio transmissions into channels to avoid interference between channels and the multiple error connections caused by an older technology called *Frequency Hopping Spread Spectrum (FHSS)*. DSSS allows 802.11 protocols to take advantage of the 11 channels available in the range of frequencies near 2.4 GHz reserved throughout the world for unlicensed transmissions (that is, transmissions without need for regulation). The 802.11 technologies send messages, broken into tiny packets, through these channels with addressing information, initiating handshaking (communication) with devices along the way. The job of the network adapters in your PCs and the access points on your network is to ensure that the data flows into the PCs in the correct format and to the right locations.

Types of WLANs

From the minute you first get involved with setting up a wireless network, you'll find yourself confronted with the concept of network *mode*. Network mode, like network architecture (and other networking terms) means several different things in the Information Technology (IT) world, but wireless networks come in three major modes: ad hoc, infrastructure, and hybrid. The following list explains the differences:

- **Ad hoc** mode refers to a wireless peer-to-peer network: that is, a network in which each device (usually a PC) connects via wireless radio to every other PC directly. No central PC or device exists to act as a center of the network, or, in the terminology of computer networking, as a *server* for the rest of the PCs. The primary technical distinction between ad hoc and infrastructure networks is that infrastructure networks use an access point, while ad hoc networks do not, although ad hoc networks and infrastructure networks can certainly co-exist. Think of an ad hoc network precisely as its name suggests: you connect each PC as you require it, but in a completely non-centralized way. Figure 1-1 shows an ad hoc network of three PCs.

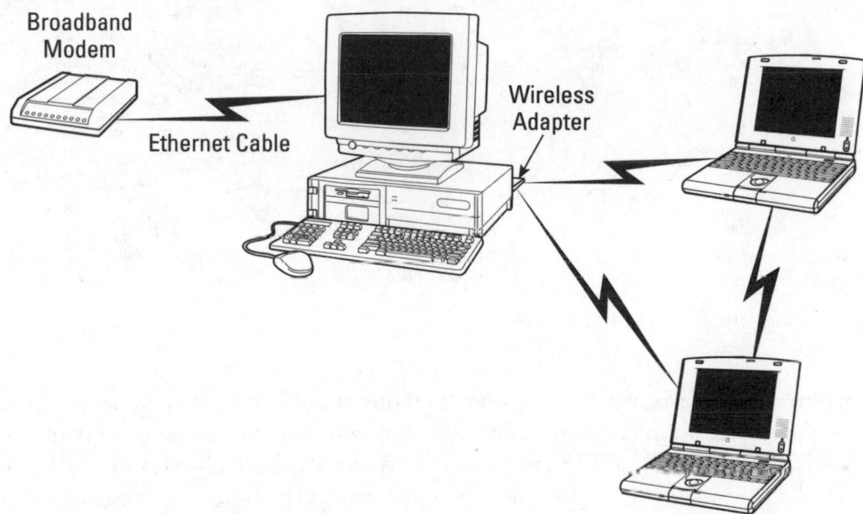

Figure 1-1: Several PCs joined together in an ad hoc network.

- **Infrastructure** mode refers to a wireless network controlled through a wireless access point that generates the signals for the individual devices to read through their wireless network adapters. The access point acts as a central traffic cop for the signals, and because you place it physically for the best possible reception, it provides more reliable connectivity than ad hoc networks. The access point also allows you to share your Internet connection without doing so through a PC (which you must do with an ad hoc network). This is a benefit first because you don't have to leave your PC on for network clients to connect to the Internet, and second because an access point can provide some firewall security. Most importantly, however, many access points also function as *bridges* between the WLAN and your wired LAN. In other words, if you already have a wired LAN, you can add the AP/bridge as another client to the wired network, and when you connect clients to the AP/bridge, you simultaneously add them to the network as a whole. Figure 1-2 shows a typical infrastructure network configuration:

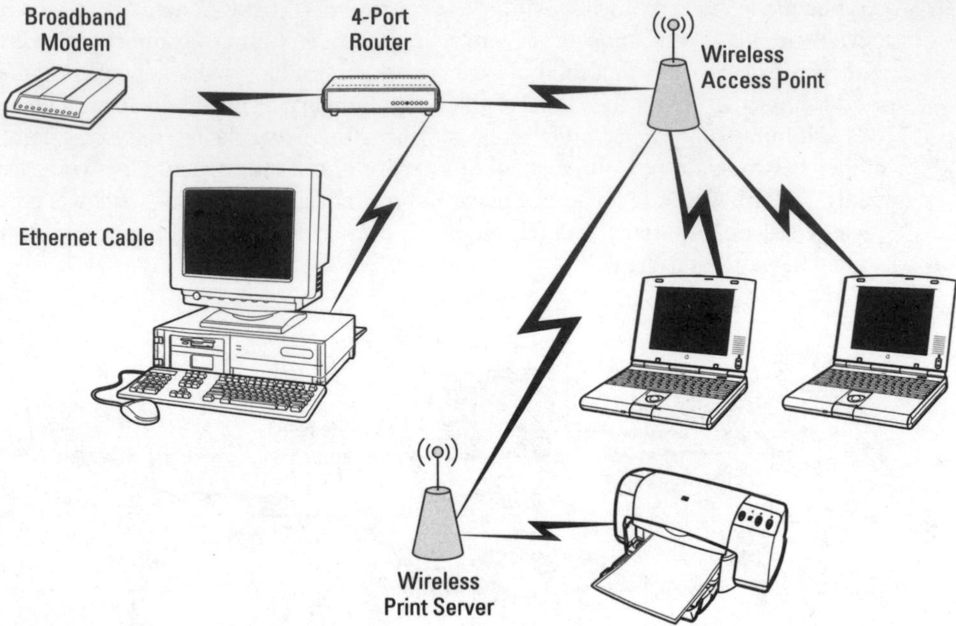

Figure 1-2: A small infrastructure network.

- **Hybrid** mode consists of a combination of ad hoc and infrastructure networks. In this mode, you create an infrastructure network, and you then create ad hoc networks among the devices connected to the infrastructure. In other words, the hybrid network adds WLANs to the larger WLAN, in much the same way as the bridged infrastructure network adds WLANs to a larger LAN. Hybrid mode maximizes the bandwidth of a wireless network by relieving the access point of the need to handle all traffic; instead, PCs transmit data to one another when possible, leaving the access point free to relay data to and from the wired LAN and to other access points. Figure 1-3 shows one kind of hybrid wireless network.

Each of these modes has its strengths and its weaknesses. An ad hoc network, quite obviously, works only when its PCs are physically close to each other, and only when limited in number. Furthermore, to share an Internet connection, one of the PCs must remain powered on. But communication is fast and connection is easy, a significant benefit for ad hoc groups of, say, students or employees. Infrastructure networks allow for a shared Internet connection with only the access point powered on, they centralize the network's connections (most access points also act as DHCP servers, providing network addresses for each device), and they bridge wireless and wired LANs. But large buildings require numerous access points for effective connectivity, and access points slow down considerably as more and more traffic is directed through them. Hybrid networks provide the ideal solution for smaller groups of people using a much larger network, but they run greater risks in uninvited connectivity and uncontrolled network activity.

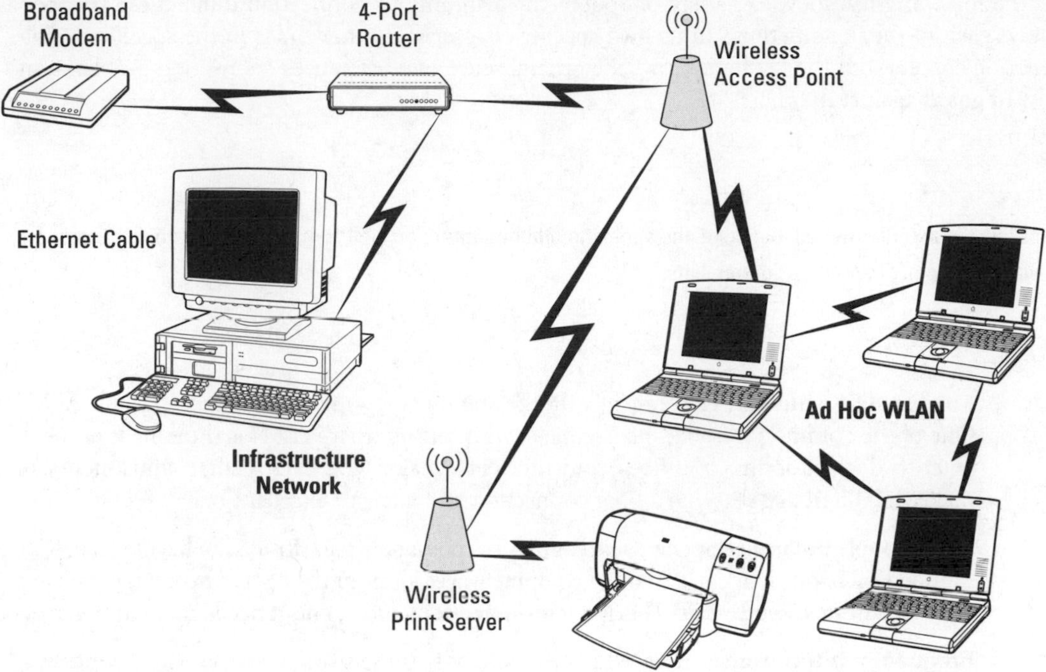

Figure 1-3: A hybrid wireless network.

Still, all these networking modes are available to you, and it's well worth the trouble to experiment with each to see which one (or ones) suits your purposes precisely. Chapters 3 and 4 cover a range of possible solutions for ad hoc and infrastructure networks respectively, with Chapter 4 also covering issues concerning hybrid networks.

Planning for Problems

You might have no problems whatsoever setting up, configuring, and maintaining your wireless network. Then again, George Steinbrenner might start voluntarily and cheerfully restricting the payroll of the New York Yankees so they compete more evenly with the Kansas City Royals. The fact is, wireless connections and the networks that depend on those connections sometimes go awry. You should begin your WLAN adventures by planning for problems.

Connection Planning

The greatest disappointment in setting up a wireless network occurs when it fails to work for the first time. Typically, wireless networks malfunction periodically for any number of reasons (most of which are covered in this book), but it's dispiriting to use your wireless-enabled laptop in one location one day, with network connections strong and reliable, only to use it in a slightly different location the next day with no connection at all, or a sporadic connection at best. You can't always stop this from happening, but you can make plans to better the situation.

The following list shows a variety of options for planning for connection difficulties. This book covers each of them, sometimes in its own specific chapter and other times in the specific troubleshooting chapter, but the list here shows the general sense of what causes connection problems and how to guard against them.

Cross-Ref

In particular, see Chapter 23, but solutions appear in other chapters as well, in conjunction with discussions of different types of wireless connections.

- **Misdirected Antenna:** Experiment with the antenna on your wireless access point (AP). One of the common mistakes people make with setting up a WLAN is thinking that the antenna doesn't do much. It does, sometimes in a major way. Even a small adjustment can make the difference between a poor connection and a fair to excellent one.
- **Not Enough Breathing Space:** Give your access point some air. Instead of having it surrounded by books, papers, and other equipment, get it out in the open where it has a chance to broadcast its radio signals. This is a transmitter, remember, and it needs room to transmit.
- **Frequency Interference:** Your WLAN isn't the only thing using your WLAN's frequency. In the same way that radio stations can interfere with each other on your car stereo, two wireless devices can interfere with each other in your house or office. Culprits typically include cordless phones, but microwave ovens, video beaming equipment, and baby monitors can also cut into your reception. Experiment with all your equipment to choose separate channels for each until you can have everything on at the same time with flawless reception.
- **Difficult Architecture:** No, not network architecture, but building architecture. Wireless signals often have trouble getting through walls, floors, and ceilings. They have even more trouble getting through multiple barriers. Sometimes you can solve the problem by placing the access point at a middle point of the floor or building and running an Ethernet cable from the router to the AP. Other times you have no choice but to add another AP, daisy-chaining them together to cover a larger area.
- **Malfunctioning Equipment:** Networking equipment can and does malfunction. Sometimes it's the wireless component of your router/access point. Sometimes it's the router port itself. Sometimes it's the network adapter card in your notebook. And sometimes it's a more complex network problem, such as failure to bridge the wireless network with the wired network. The best solution is always to have more than one of everything available for use (even if only a few lower-cost spare devices sitting in a cupboard available for emergencies), and if your business depends on your WLAN, you certainly want to establish that level of redundancy. For home users, the only solution is to track which part is going wrong and make adjustments accordingly. Planning for such problems often means nothing more than installing each component separately, and ensuring that it functions properly before installing the next component.

- **Altered Configurations:** Anyone with access to your WLAN's configuration screens, even legitimate access, can cause problems across the network simply by changing the configuration. Before attempting to fix anything, in fact, it's a good idea to open the configuration utility (which is often browser-based) and determine that nothing has been altered. Changed network names, channel numbers, even network names — all of these can render your wireless device unusable over the network. If you see changes, either change them back or, at the very least, write down the changes and then make precisely the same alterations to your device's configuration.

Security Planning

Ever heard of a war driver? One of the author's father was one — he was a dispatch rider in WWII — but that's not the kind of war driver we're talking about. War drivers are people who drive around cities and towns, their notebook (or PDA) and Wi-Fi access card in tow, looking for wireless networks they can access. As they pass businesses and houses, they click on a link in their browsers, or try to log on to a Windows network from Network Connections or Network Neighborhood, and see if the connection occurs. When it does, they stop and use that network as long as they feel like. If that network is yours, and you haven't taken precautions to secure your PC, you've just opened your computer to a total stranger.

This activity, of course, is unique to wireless. The only way to tap into a wired network is to plug a device physically into the network itself, usually into a router or switch. If you can't get to the physical linkage, you can't get onto the network. Tapping into WLANs is completely different because the only thing the hacker needs is a way to receive your radio signals. And many, many people do.

In fact, security lies at the core of most discussions about wireless networks today. Partly by their technological nature, and partly because of the way the components ship, WLANs seem to defy whatever security measures their owners put in place. It doesn't have to be that way, as you'll see elsewhere in this book, but currently it's a serious issue for everyone from IT professionals to home users. Put those radio waves out there, and somebody will want to steal them.

Cross-Ref

See Part II for detailed instructions on securing wireless networks, at least to the extent that easy uninvited access is no longer possible.

The following list outlines several ways to plan against security problems.

- **SSID Alert:** The SSID of a WLAN acts as the identifier for that WLAN. By default, most access points are set up to broadcast the SSID, so that anybody with a compatible network adapter can see the network and connect to it automatically. The easiest and perhaps most effective way to stop casual intruders is to configure your AP to stop broadcasting the SSID.
- **Password Protection:** Wireless LANs are no different from wired LANs in at least one respect: if you don't password-protect important data, you're simply asking to have it

stolen. Set up password protection for folders, disk drives, and any other resource on your network's PCs, and keep the passwords private.

- **WEP Security:** One of the two primary encryption technologies for wireless networking, WEP offers decent security and is readily available. Setting it up can be trying, especially for network cards that seem to insist on incompatibility, and there's no question that it can slow down your wireless transfers. But it's there, and it should be used.
- **WPA Security:** Still in its early days, WPA promises much stronger security than WEP. But incompatibilities with older wireless adapters make it a tough choice to make. You can take advantage of those incompatibilities, though, ensuring that most casual users won't be able to connect.
- **Turn It Off:** If you don't need 24/7 wireless connectivity, don't offer it to anyone else either. Unplug your access point when you have no use for it, and suddenly all other WLAN security issues disappear. Works for homes and small offices alike.
- **VPNs:** Virtual Private Networks, even when run over WLANs, can provide much more secure access than WLANs on their own. They're difficult to set up and administer, but if you're running a business LAN, you owe it to yourself to give it a try.

Summary

This chapter has introduced a range of issues surrounding wireless networking. Throughout the course of this book, you'll find all topics touched on here covered in detail, along with many other topics at all levels of wireless activity, all in a solutions-based format. In Chapter 3, for instance, you'll learn about the wide variety of equipment available for connecting in a wireless network, equipment ranging from the access points that form your network's base to the full range of network adapters that connect your PCs to your network. You'll also learn about other devices currently on the market, including such seemingly esoteric — but actually quite useful — items such as Ethernet adapters that take their power from the network itself so that you can place them in locations that do not have a power receptacle.

This is the kind of attention that wireless networking is receiving in the industry, with more solutions appearing every week to make your networking life easier. But all these devices offer their own peculiarities and idiosyncrasies, and working with and around those peculiarities and idiosyncrasies constitutes a large part of what this book is about.

Chapter 2

Sorting Through the Gear

Setting up a wireless network means configuring and using a variety of hardware products. These come in all shapes and sizes and from several vendors, each of whom offers their own particular promises and assurances that setup is so easy that even an engineer could do it. And while certainly that's more true today than it was in the early days of wireless LANs, true ease remains elusive. One of the problems is that companies differentiate their products by adding proprietary technology to them, technology that works with the 802.11 standard contained within the product that often hinders interoperability between similar products from competing vendors. For the most part, such technology has to do with increasing transfer speeds well beyond the capabilities of common 802.11, an obviously welcome feature, but one that can wreak a bit of havoc with products from other companies.

Although such a product development strategy is certainly understandable — otherwise products based exclusively on standards would all be the same as one another — it does mean you have to watch what you buy. So here are the first three rules about buying hardware for your WLAN:

- Unless you have a specific reason to purchase products from multiple vendors, stick with the same vendor for as many components as possible. Wireless products aren't the same as components for your stereo, after all; they haven't reached that level of standardization, and there's a good chance they never will.
- Even when you're buying from only one vendor, try to stick with the same product line from that vendor. Several vendors (D-Link and Linksys, for example) have more than one line of wireless products, and they design each product within each line to work flawlessly with all other products in that line. Other lines might work just fine with your chosen line, but to be completely certain — and assuming you're starting from scratch — just say no to divergent lines.
- If you come across a good deal from a different vendor, make sure the store has a return policy, and then buy the product anyway. There's an excellent chance you'll be able to make it work no matter how different its technologies may be. 802.11 is, after all, a standard.

This chapter introduces you to a wide range of wireless networking product categories, including wireless network adapters of three types (PC Card, USB, and PCI), wireless access points, wireless

media players, wireless print servers, and more. Most products are necessary to assembling a working, sophisticated WLAN. Others are nice to have, but not strictly needed. In all cases, we show recently released products, but we also point you to older products that offer similar solutions. The goal is to construct a WLAN that does what you need it to do, and as with any other construction product, getting the right tools is a crucial part of concluding the job satisfactorily.

Two Typical Scenarios

Before digging into the products themselves, let's take a look at two fairly typical situations for which a wireless LAN would come in handy. In the first, a family of four (two adults and two computer-savvy children) want to share a single broadband Internet connection to power three PCs, a video game console, and any notebooks the kids' friends bring over for homework or game-playing purposes. In the second, a small business sets up shop in a converted house, where stringing Ethernet cables up and down the stairs and along the baseboards simply isn't a practical idea. All employees need their own PCs, broadband Internet access, and constant access to a laser printer.

Note that here we simply discuss the type of equipment needed for each scenario; the equipment itself, along with commercially available examples, we describe throughout the remainder of this chapter.

Scenario 1: The Home Network

Assuming the three PCs are already in place, the next step is to subscribe to an Internet service provider for the broadband Internet connection. We'll also assume that this network will take the shape of what has become a standard in home networks, with one desktop PC connected to the network via Ethernet cable and the two notebook PCs through a wireless connection. To become fully functional as a wireless LAN with a shared Internet connection, this network needs the following:

- A broadband router/switch device and a wireless access point, or (more popularly) a combination broadband router/access point device. This unit (or these units, if they're separate) connects to the Internet service provider (via the broadband modem that service provides), directs traffic to and from the PCs on the network, and provides private Internet addresses to each PC on the network. It is the true hub of the network.
- An Ethernet adapter inside the desktop PC, which receives data from — and sends data to — the router/switch and the Internet.
- Wireless network adapters for each notebook PC, or notebook PCs with built-in Wi-Fi networking. These devices receive data from — and send data to — the access point and, from there, to the router/switch and the Internet.
- A wireless game adapter, which acts as a bridge between the access point and the game console, allowing the game console to access the Internet and the local network.
- An Ethernet port for the game console, either a separate unit, as in the case of the Sony PlayStation 2, or built-in, as in the case of the Microsoft Xbox. Also needed is networking

software for the game consoles and a user account to play online games (free for PlayStation 2, subscription for Xbox).

- Wireless network adapters for the notebook PCs brought into the house by the kids' friends, unless of course those notebooks already have adapters.

Scenario 2: The Small Business Network

Eight PCs need connectivity to each other and to the Internet in this scenario, and all need access to a networked printer as well. Assume that all of the PCs are to be connected wirelessly, because of the desire to avoid Ethernet cable completely. Once the company has broadband Internet access in place, this network requires the following in order to fill the company's needs:

- A wireless access point that accepts input from the broadband Internet modem. These access points have only one Ethernet port, where the cable from the modem goes. Because of the continually decreasing cost of broadband router/access points, however, it's probably a better idea to buy the combined device rather than just the access point (the combined device can also help with testing should the wireless connections fail), but only the access point is strictly necessary.
- Wireless network adapters for each notebook PC, or notebook PCs with built-in Wi-Fi networking. These devices receive data from — and send data to — the access point and thus the Internet.
- A wireless print server, which connects to the printer either by printer cable or (more typically) USB cable, and which takes its printing commands from the PCs on the network through the access point. Most wireless print server products have connections for two printers, so if you need two lasers, or a laser and, for instance, a color inkjet, one server does all. You can place the printer itself wherever the employees will find it convenient.

These scenarios play out through the remainder of the chapter.

Wireless Network Adapters

Your PC needs a way to connect to an Ethernet network, whether the network is wireless, or wired, or both. It makes that connection through a ***network adapter,*** a device that provides an interface for the computer to the network. Most PCs today ship with an adapter for ***wired*** networks installed at the factory, and increasingly these adapters are built directly onto the computer's motherboard. To date, only notebook and laptop PCs have had ***wireless*** adapters built in, but they're not yet a given. For the most part, to connect your notebook or desktop PC to a wireless network, you need to purchase and install a separate WLAN adapter. The majority of adapters come in one of three configurations: PC Card (CardBus), USB, or PCI, and these are the ones we cover in this chapter. However, new adapters have recently appeared using Compact Flash and Bluetooth technology, so the field continues to expand.

PC Card WLAN Adapters

PC Card components are those thin, rectangular products, shaped more or less like a thick credit card, that slide into the PC Card slots of notebook PCs (or desktop PCs that have a special adapter installed). Figure 2-1 shows an example of such a product, a Linksys adapter that handles both 802.11g and 802.11b wireless protocols. On the far right of the figure is the portion that stays outside the PC Card slot, and this portion bears the Linksys logo as well as indicator lights called Power and Link. The Power light, as you probably suspect, tells you that the adapter is getting power from the notebook (the card doesn't have a separate power supply). The Link light tells you if the card is receiving the wireless signal; as long as it shines a solid green, the card is communicating just fine. Keep your eye on this light, though; if it starts flashing, the card is no longer communicating with a wireless transmitter on your network (usually the access point), in which case you'll need to do some troubleshooting.

The more technically correct abbreviation for these components is PCMCIA (Personal Computer Memory Card International Association), but because nobody could come up with a decent way to pronounce that abbreviation, the industry understandably decided to adopt the phrase *PC Card* instead. In fact, as PCMCIA developed and took on 32-bit capabilities, it became known as *CardBus,* and the vast majority of WLAN products on the market today designed for notebook use are of the CardBus variety.

Figure 2-1: The Linksys Instant Wireless Wireless-G Notebook Adapter.

Because CardBus is a 32-bit interface, it's perfect for notebooks running 32-bit Windows platforms such as today's dominant version, Windows XP (Professional or Home Edition). Indeed, part of the success of wireless networking as a whole has been the ability of CardBus WLAN adapters to connect quickly and efficiently to the built-in wireless support offered in Windows XP. In the case of WLANs set up to broadcast their SSID, and not to enforce encryption (see Chapter 4 for details about SSID and other infrastructure configurations), connections from a Windows XP notebook with a CardBus adapter without proprietary protocols are practically automatic.

From a technical standpoint, the CardBus interface works nearly identically to the PCI (Peripheral Component Interconnect) interface common to today's PCs. The signaling protocols are almost the same, and the two interfaces interact with the PC very similarly as well. For WLAN equipment manufacturers, the similarities present the obvious advantage of being able to develop two types of component pretty well in parallel with one another. Indeed, if you watch the release schedules of WLAN hardware from these companies, you'll find that CardBus and PCI adapters come closely on the heels of one another (CardBus is usually first because its market is larger), while other types, such as USB adapters, come somewhat later.

Chapters 3 and 4 both deal extensively with PCMCIA and CardBus adapters because notebook adapters lie at the core of wireless networking. Although you can certainly create a WLAN that consists of desktop PCs connected wirelessly to each other (ad hoc) or to an access point (infrastructure), such an architecture is extremely uncommon (although it's certainly on the increase). Partly because most PCs now ship with adapters for wired Ethernet networks, partly because wired Ethernet adapters are a fraction of the price of wireless adapters, and primarily because people don't consider desktop PCs particularly portable, desktop PCs tend to find themselves wired to the network rather than beaming radio waves back and forth. Given the greater speed and reliability of wired networks, this approach obviously makes sense.

USB WLAN Adapters

USB has become the second most common WLAN adapter type in use, albeit a distant second to CardBus/PC Card. USB network adapters have the same reason for popularity as any PC peripheral with a USB connection: they set up easily, without opening the PC's case, and Windows versions starting with 98 Second Edition, especially Windows XP, typically recognize USB-based hardware without difficulty and help you step through the installation process. Furthermore, you can simply plug your USB-based hardware into the USB port, and unplug it, without any fuss and without any windows popping up on the screen warning you not to. USB works out of the box, and in the PC hardware world that's a major thing.

The only real problem with USB adapters is that, for notebook users, they don't offer the same effortless portability. PC Cards fit firmly in the PCMCIA slots and, from the standpoint of mobility, become part of the notebook itself. USB adapters are attached by a USB cable, so it dangles by a thread, as it were, if you try to carry it anywhere.

However, USB adapters work perfectly with desktop PCs, or with a notebook that you don't intend to move around very much. They tend to be less expensive than PC Cards, and they also tend to have something PC Cards rarely do: an antenna. Combine an access card's antenna with a USB adapter's antenna and you have a better chance of maintaining connectivity between devices than you do with PC cards. Being able to position and aim the antenna becomes even more apparent when you examine the difficulties of working with PCI wireless adapters, covered under the next heading.

USB WLAN adapters take different shapes. Figures 2-2 and 2-3 show two very different USB adapters from two different companies. The Linksys unit in Figure 2-2 offers a very small footprint — so you can put it practically anywhere — and an adjustable antenna; the design enables you to move it to the best possible location for receiving wireless signals, or to keep it close at hand and adjust the antenna to receive those signals. The D-Link adapter in Figure 2-3 gives you the convenience of closing up into a less breakable product when not in use, with the rectangular antenna folding down onto the main body of the unit, much like closing a small case with a hinged lid. How far you have the antenna raised, as well as how you face it, determines how well you receive the wireless signal.

Figure 2-2: The trim and fit design of the Linksys Wireless-G Portable Adapter.

Figure 2-3: The D-Link High-Speed 2.4 GHz Wireless USB Adapter with antenna raised.

PCI WLAN Adapters

Wireless adapters for the PCI interface, found in all PCs today, are much less plentiful than PC Card versions, and even less plentiful than USB adapters. The reason, once again, is that most desktops connect via Ethernet cable to an Ethernet adapter installed inside the PC. But as wireless networking becomes more pervasive, particularly in homes and in offices converted from homes, these adapters, along with USB versions, are taking on a more substantial role. Desktop PCs don't seem to be going away as the prognosticators once insisted they would (price and expandability being two major factors), so they remain in heavy use, but people want to connect them to LANs and the Internet without stringing cables along the baseboard or finding a way to run them through the walls. If you set up an access point and give each of your desktop PCs a PCI adapter, you can accomplish this quite readily.

PCI adapters have one major disadvantage when compared with USB adapters. Because of the way desktop PCs are constructed, anything installed in a PCI slot comes out of the back of the PC, precisely where you don't want a wireless adapter to reside. WLAN adapters need to communicate with other WLAN adapters (ad hoc) or with an access point (infrastructure), and the fewer physical obstacles between the wireless devices, the better. PCs tend to sit on the floor, often against walls or with other furniture surrounding them, and the chances of blocking the signal to and from the other wireless components of your network is high. However, see Figure 2-4, which shows a PCI WLAN adapter featuring an external antenna to counter the line-of-sight issues.

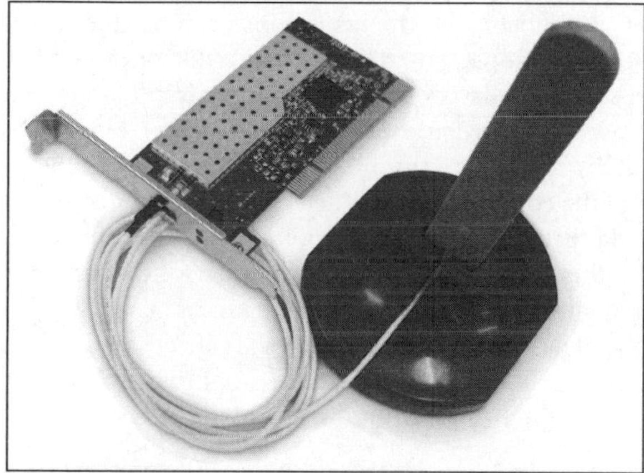

Figure 2-4: D-Link's Multimode Wireless PCI Adapter can be positioned to allow for better line-of-sight to the access point or other PCs.

For this reason, you should consider using PCI wireless adapters in only two situations:

- You have a clear "line-of-sight" from the back of your PC to the wireless adapter, and you have good reason to believe that the line-of-sight will remain uninterrupted in the future. A clear line-of-sight means an unhindered area in which the radio signals can move between the two devices, with of course walls, ceilings, and floors part of the unchangeable components. If

your desktop PC sits on the floor, make sure you keep a few feet (at least) between its WLAN adapter and any walls, bookshelves, file cabinets, boxes, briefcases, and anything else that sits on the floor as well. In other words, if you keep the PC in the open, you shouldn't have too much trouble connecting. Unless, of course, the PC itself blocks the signal path, in which case you can simply turn it sideways.

- You don't have any choice because your PC has PCI slots but no USB ports. If you have a PC purchased before roughly 2001, there's a good chance of this, although it's much less likely for PCs purchased in the past three years. Still, PCs without USB ports do exist, and many companies and homes keep PCs for more years than PC manufacturers would like. Of course, you can add USB adapter cards to an older PC, but if you add the cost of a USB adapter card to the cost of a USB wireless adapter, you're probably above the cost of a PCI wireless adapter anyway. Furthermore, if you're using Windows 95, Windows 98, or Windows NT, you don't have support for USB in your operating system. Windows 2000 support for USB is spotty at best, so if you use that OS, you're also better off with a PCI wireless adapter.

PCI WLAN adapters present one other major inconvenience. To install them, you most open the computer case, and most PC users don't like doing anything of the kind. Still, if this is your only choice, here are the steps to take.

1. **Open the case.** First, turn off the PC and remove the power cord from the case. If you can find the manual that came with your PC, it probably has the instructions you need for getting the case open. If, like the vast majority of people, you tossed it into a pile or put it somewhere you were sure would mean something later on, and therefore have no hope whatsoever of locating it, opening the case is usually fairly easy (but not always). Most cases have two side covers, held in place by screws or a thumb screw. After loosening the screws, slide the cover toward the rear of the computer until it detaches from the main structure of the case. Other cases demand that you remove the front plastic panel of the computer, which you can do either by lifting from the bottom (you'll find a kind of finger-hold at the base of the panel), or by prying the panel away from the main case using a screwdriver or butter knife. Once the panel has been removed, slide the side cover, or more frequently the single-piece top and sides of the case, toward the front (which is why you have to remove the front panel) until you've freed it from the rest of the case.
2. **Locate the PCI slots.** With the PC case open, look inside. You should see the motherboard, a large rectangular circuit board with various cables attached (one to the power supply and others to your hard drives). Figure 2-5 illustrates a typical motherboard layout, complete with its PCI slots (although yours aren't all likely to be empty). If you have a tower-style case (one in which the PC stands up rather than lying flat on your desk), lay it on its side so that the motherboard is parallel to the floor. Along the side where the external cords attach to the PC (your monitor cable, Ethernet cable, the phone cords to your modem), you'll find a row of long, narrow slots into which you can slide peripheral cards. Today's PCs typically have one AGP slot, usually occupied by the graphics card and five to eight PCI slots, many of which are also occupied. In fact, you might very well find only one PCI slot available for use.

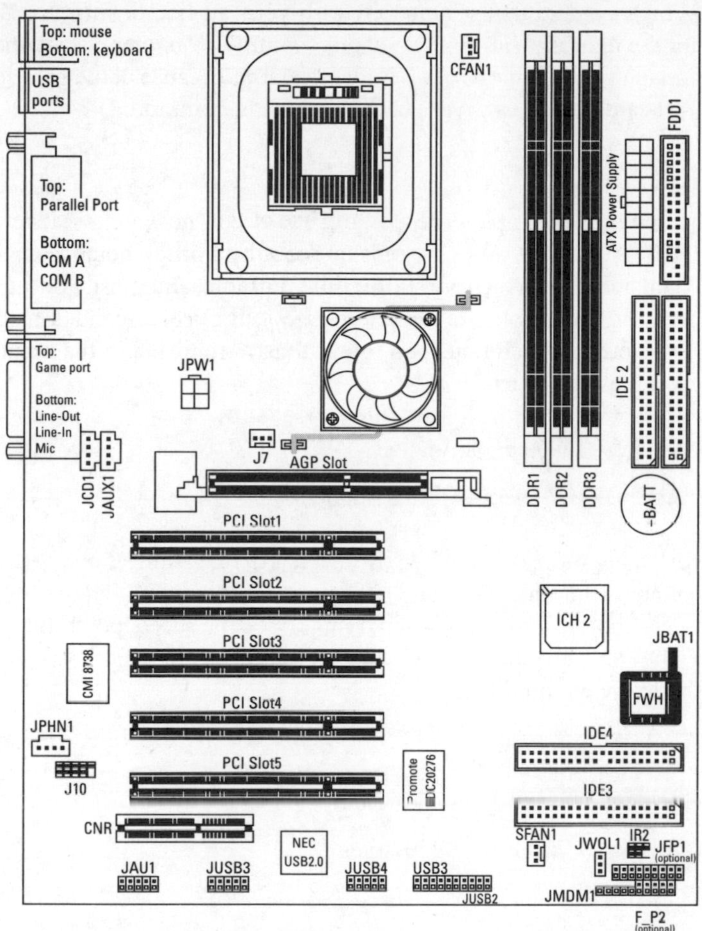

Figure 2-5: A typical PC motherboard, showing the PCI slots.

3. **Insert the WLAN adapter card.** Without forcing it, but using enough elbow grease to get the job done, push the PCI WLAN card into a vacant PCI slot. If necessary, rock it into place until it fits snugly into the slot. You know it's right when the small metal lip at the top of the card sits flush with the inside ridge of the case. Match up the slot on the metal lip with the screw-hole on the ridge and screw the card into place, or anchor it in place with whatever other mechanism your particular PC uses.
4. **Power on and install drivers.** Close the PC by reattaching the sides or the single-piece top/side component of the case along with the front panel. Replace the screws or set the thumbscrews. Attach any cables that came loose during your installation adventure and plug the power cord into the case. Power on the PC, wait for Windows to ask for a driver, and insert the CD that came with the PCI WLAN card. Windows typically locates the driver on the CD automatically and installs the necessary driver, but if it does not, you'll have to do so manually by using the directions found in the WLAN card's manual or quick-start card. If you can find neither, look for a Setup.exe file on the CD.

To configure your PCI WLAN card so that it functions with your ad hoc or infrastructure network, see the instructions for configuring USB WLAN adapters found in Chapter 3. Essentially, setting up any type of wireless adapters for wireless access is identical, but because of the presence of an antenna on most USB and PCI cards, these two types have the most in common.

Scenario Solutions

For the home network, the solution is simple. The desktop PC needs no wireless adapter at all because it connects to the LAN via Ethernet cable. It needs no mobility. For the notebooks, the most obvious solution lies in PC Card adapters, which are sturdy, fully portable, and mostly out of the way (they stick out from the side of the notebook, but not annoyingly). The recommended hardware is an identical PC Card WLAN adapter for each notebook (plus an extra to install in the friend's notebook), drawn from the following two products:

- Linksys WPC54G Wireless-G Notebook Adapter
- DLink DWL-G630 AirPlus G Wireless CardBus Adapter

The small business network takes more thought. On the one hand, PCI connections have a higher internal speed (because they are inside the PC) than USB connections. But PCI adapters can have connection problems with access points, especially when trying to see the access point through walls and floors. For that reason, the recommendation is to connect all PCs using USB WLAN adapters, using any combination of the following products:

- NetGear WG121 Wireless USB 2.0 Adapter
- Linksys WUSB54G Wireless-G USB Network Adapter
- DLink DWL-G120 AirPlus G Wireless USB Adapter

Access Points

Wireless *access points* (APs), also called ***wireless base stations***, have become a crucial component for any wireless network that goes beyond simple ad hoc status. The AP performs several important functions, but its primary task in its primary role is to act as a waystation for wireless traffic on the network. Indeed, many wireless networks use multiple APs, each one acting precisely as a waystation, extending the range of the WLAN by offering additional physical points of connection. In smaller networks, a single AP provides a centralized transmitter and receiver for all PCs on the network, routing traffic to and from the various wireless adapters while supplying all clients with access to one or more wired networks.

Access points come in many shapes, sizes, and configurations (as shown in Figures 2-6 and 2-7). However, no matter how else they might differ, all APs share the following components:

- **Antenna:** The primary function of the access point is to transmit and receive radio signals from other wireless devices on the network. To guarantee the best possibility of doing so, manufacturers attach at least one antenna to the case, and some APs are built with two. You can adjust the antennae according to your needs, to maintain connectivity with other wireless devices no matter where they might be and no matter what lies between them.
- **Ethernet Port:** The purpose of an access point is to create an infrastructure network, which means connecting to an existing Ethernet-based network. This wired network need not be a local area network (LAN); instead, it can be your broadband provider's wide area network (WAN). Many APs act as both network routers and Internet sharing devices, and this type offers Ethernet ports for both LAN and WAN connections. Others offer only one Ethernet port, which you can use to connect either to the broadband provider's modem or to an external router for your LAN. In the former case, the AP typically becomes the sole Internet access device for all the WLAN-connected devices you have (often one or more notebook PCs, each with its own PC Card WLAN adapter). In the latter case, it extends the LAN to any wireless devices, and as such operates similarly to a combined AP and router.
- **LED Indicators:** Like the vast majority of networking equipment, access points provide small lights (LEDs) that tell you what's going on at any given time. In fact, as you start to use your networking equipment together — broadband modem, router, and AP — you'll quickly discover that you can turn off the overhead lights in the room and have a light show of your own from all the flashing caused by the LEDs. These LEDs tell you a number of important details, such as whether the AP is making a connection with the wired network and whether it's transmitting and receiving data from wireless devices. Use the manual to learn how to read these LEDs, and remember how to do so. If your network doesn't seem to work, checking them often points to the problem. The same holds true of LEDs on your other networking devices.
- **Reset Button:** Sometimes you just can't get the access point functioning, typically after a power outage or after you've made significant changes to your network configuration (such as switching from a DSL provider to a cable provider). In these cases, once you've exhausted all configuration options, the reset button can become your best friend. Usually accessible with a pen, pencil, or other similarly shaped small point, you just press and hold it (often the LEDs tell you when you've held it long enough) and the access point reverts to its factory settings. Enter the configuration screens and start the process over.
- **Power Cord:** Believe it or not, this component matters quite a bit. Access points require their own power source, a fact that restricts the locations in which you can place them. This requirement usually presents no problem when positioning the primary AP, which especially in an infrastructure network tends to be near the primary PC (to run a networking cable from the AP's Ethernet ports to the PC's Ethernet port), but in many cases you'll want to place secondary APs in strategic locations for purposes of reception. Sometimes, this means high up on a wall, or even in the attic of a house.

Without power receptacles in those locations, you typically need to run extension cords to the AP, and extension cords pretty well negate the entire concept of wirelessness. Another option is to use Power Over Ethernet products, covered later in this chapter under the heading "Other Types of WLAN Equipment," but these have their own distinct disadvantages.

Figure 2-6: SMC's basic but highly functional EZ Connect SMC265W Wireless Access Point.

Cross-Ref

See Chapter 4 for details on setting up and configuring your access point(s), including the direction and adjustment of the antenna(e) and all software configurations.

Figure 2-7: Linksys's Access Points tend to look much like their AP Router/Switches.

Scenario Solutions

For the home network, the choice is a four-port router/access point. You don't actually need four Ethernet ports because you have only one desktop PC, but the ports can be useful when you want to download files to the notebook PCs (or upload from them) at high speed. Take the notebook to the router, plug it in to a vacant port, and your connection speed increases dramatically. Here are some recommended products, any of which fit the bill:

- DLink DI-624 AirPlusXtremeG Router
- Belkin High-Speed Mode Wireless G Router
- Linksys WRT54G Wireless-G Broadband Router

The same products apply to the small business network. In addition, however, we'll add an access point on each floor of the building to avoid connectivity problems between the PCs on different floors from the router/AP. The following access points will do the trick, although for the sake of ease of connection the small business should purchase two of the same access points, ideally from the same vendor (and even the same product line) as the router/AP. For that reason, the following list matches the preceding list of router/APs:

- DLink DWL-2100AP AirPlusXtremeG Access Point
- Belkin Wireless Network Access Point
- Linksys WAP54G Wireless-G Access Point

Routers and Switches

For the most part, routers, switches, and hubs are not actually wireless, but are included here because they nevertheless form the basis of the wired LANs that underlie infrastructure and hybrid networks. Furthermore, wireless access points frequently include router technology along with their wireless relay and addressing technology. Virtually all vendors of wireless networking equipment offer at least one product that combines an access point with a router, resulting in a single small box featuring three or four ports for Ethernet cables, another port for broadband modem hookup, and the wireless components required by the access point, including the antenna.

Routers and switches perform different functions. Today you'll hear the word ***router*** more often than ***switch*** when it comes to sales of home and small-office networking equipment, but in reality most cable/DSL routers also are switches. The difference is quite simple: routers connect two or more networks together and pass data between or among them, while switches provide interconnection among computers in a single network and isolate streams of traffic from each other so that signals make it from origin to destination without any other PC on the network having access to them. Another component, called a ***hub***, is an even simpler piece of equipment, functioning like a switch by allowing communication among the PCs on the network, but unlike a switch allowing only one communication stream at a time.

As mentioned, today's access point products often combine AP and router technology. Much less publicized is the fact that they also operate as network switches, even though the switch component is every bit as important as the router component. The main reason for this exclusion? Simply, in common language about computers, router and switch have begun to mean the same thing, although at even the first technical level they do not. When non-technical people start using computer terminology, the terminology tends to become less specific and therefore easier. Which, of course, is only natural. Even so, the official name of these products tends to include both elements: for example, Linksys offers a product called the "EtherFast Cable/DSL Router with 4-Port Switch." Then again, the company also offers a combination AP/router/switch that it calls, simply, the "Wireless-B Broadband Router" with no mention of either switch or AP in the name. Figure 2-8 shows a typical product combining all three technologies.

Figure 2-8: The D-Link Tri-Mode Dualband 4-Port Wireless Router combines support for 802.11a, 802.11b, and 802.11g.

Your fully constructed wireless infrastructure network consists of the following components:

- **Clients:** There's not much point having a network without computers to network together. In networking, these computers are called ***clients***. Your clients can be desktop PCs, notebook PCs, personal digital assistants (PDAs), and even devices such as printers, network hard drives, and hardware firewalls. Each device on the network gets its own unique network address, and the network hardware and software use that address to ensure that traffic destined for that device reaches it.
- **Network Adapters:** Any client connecting to the network through the wireless components needs a wireless LAN adapter. Any client connecting via cable needs an adapter with a port for that cable (typically Ethernet).
- **Internet Gateway:** Depending on the type of Internet connection you have, this component goes by different names. You can have high-speed dedicated lines (T3, for example), and various other access types at various costs. This book assumes that you have what has come to be called ***broadband*** Internet access, which currently comes in three forms: Cable, DSL, and Satellite (a fourth type, Wireless Broadband, is on the horizon). For these types, the Internet gateway is the modem to which you attach your incoming DSL, cable, or satellite signal. The modem receives signals through this connection and transmits them to your network through its Ethernet port, connected via Ethernet cable to the next component of your network. Here, that component is a router/switch or access point.
- **Router:** You can connect your PC directly to your Internet gateway, in which case it becomes part of the cable or DSL network. Users with only one computer typically do so. However, if you want to share the Internet connection with other computers, you must create a separate network. In such a case, you need a router to handle traffic between the two networks. You can buy a separate router, or you can set up a Windows PC to act as a router by engaging Windows' Internet Connection Sharing feature. This latter type of system has two disadvantages, however: you must leave it running to provide connectivity to other clients, and the PC itself is directly subject to intrusion (hackers, viruses, and other bad things) from the Internet. For those reasons, a separate router works better. Like access points, routers come in many shapes and sizes, but today's typical broadband router contains one Ethernet port for incoming cable or DSL traffic and four outgoing Ethernet ports (sometimes more, sometimes fewer), each of which can connect to a different client. These routers also act as switches, and many act as access points.
- **Switch:** You can buy a separate switch, but usually you would do so only if you add wired clients to your network to the point where you run out of Ethernet ports on the router/switch device. This book refers to routers and switches almost exclusively as routers, in keeping with the more common terminology today, and with the fact that switches and routers are often combined in a device sold as a router.
- **Access Point:** An access point is a client on your network. The access point (AP) enables wired communication on your network, and indeed operates as the starting point of your wireless LAN, but the AP connects to the rest of the network via Ethernet cable. It connects to the switch, which in turn connects to the router. In many cases today, however, the three components are combined in one, for the sake of convenience and usability. But

for configuration purposes it's important to realize that they still function as separate units. Think of an AP/router/switch product as the equivalent of a single-piece stereo system, as opposed to a multiple-component stereo that a network of separate router, switch, and AP would approximate, and you have the idea.

Other Types of WLAN Equipment

Given the growing popularity of wireless networks, you're unlikely to run out of products to buy to extend your network as far as you want. Many of these products are covered during the course of this book, each in its appropriate context, but this section outlines some of the range of products available today.

- **Wireless Media Players:** A number of these products have begun to appear, including the D-Link MediaLounge Wireless Media Player, the PRISMIQ MediaPlayer, and the LinkSys Wireless-B Media Adapter. These products let you stream video and audio to your TV or stereo system from your PC, by way of your wireless network. Companies hope that this product category will result in shared media resources throughout the house. You place a media player near your entertainment center, using its remote control and its on-screen interface to download and play video and audio files stored on your PC. As Figure 2-9 shows, the PRISMIQ enables you to connect to your network via Ethernet cable or wireless adapter, and offers standard RCA-style audio and video outputs as well as the higher-quality S-Video and Digital outputs. It's ready to hook directly to your TV and stereo system.

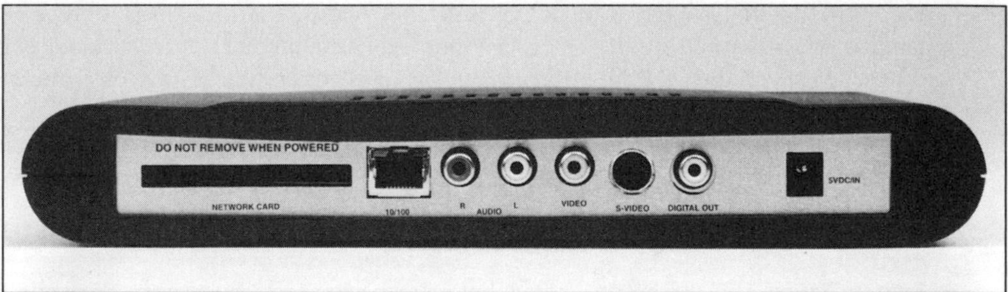

Figure 2-9: The back panel of the PRISMIQ MediaPlayer.

- **Wireless Cameras:** Wired video cameras are a dime a dozen, particularly the small USB webcams now tossed in to many PC bundles. Wireless cameras perform the same function, but they don't need to be plugged into a PC; you just beam the video signal over the wireless LAN. The Linksys Wireless-B Internet Video Camera even includes its own small Web server to provide effortless video display over the Internet. D-Link offers several wireless video solutions, including a wireless videophone for those who actually want to see the person they're talking to. D-Link targets its other wireless cameras for home security use.

- **Wireless Game Adapters:** If you want to play your PlayStation 2, Xbox, or GameCube online, you need a network connection. But nobody wants to run a big blue Ethernet cable into the family room, so D-Link and Linksys offer adapters that provide an Ethernet port for wired connection to the console and wireless technology for connection to the access point. Put the game adapter near the game, plug it in, and you're up and running with no unsightly cross-floor wires.
- **Wireless Presentation Players:** Linksys offers the Wireless-G Presentation Player for the purpose of using the wireless network for business presentations. You can plug a projector or monitor into the built-in VGA port and show the presentation directly from the device, using the wireless remote and the built-in laser pointer.
- **Wireless Antennae and Range Expanders:** If you want a wireless network with good connectivity over wide ranges, you need range extenders. Several options are available, including home-made antennae (covered in Chapter 12). If you want commercial products, however, they're available. D-Link offers an extensive range, including the Antennas Indoor 6dBi Microstrip Antenna (see Figure 2-10), the Antennas External Antenna Connector for its DWL-660 PC card, the Antennas Outdoor Omni-Directional Antenna, and more. Each of these antennae plugs into a connector on an access point. You can also buy simpler range extenders, which act as access points or wireless repeaters in order to increase the area of coverage for the WLAN.

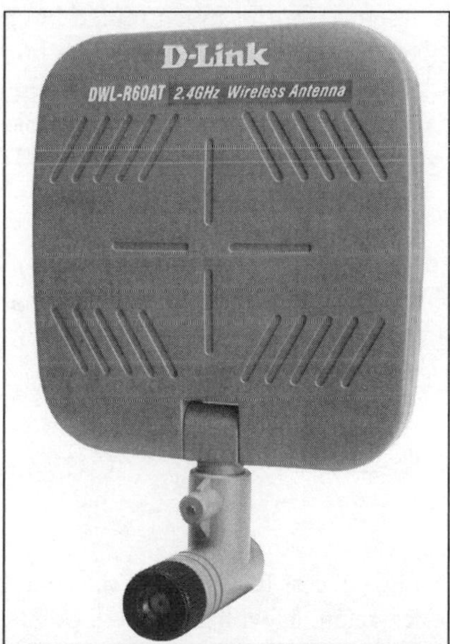

Figure 2-10: D-Link's DWL-R60AT wireless antenna.

- **Wireless Print Servers:** Print servers enable you to set up your printer to work directly over the network, instead of through a PC on the network. You don't need to leave a PC powered on; you simply plug the printer into a print server, connect the print server into the network, and print from the client. Wireless print servers use 802.11 technology to communicate with the

network, and provide USB or parallel ports for connection to the printer. D-Link offers the Air Wireless 2.4 GHz 3-Port Print Server, which features three parallel printer ports, as well as the Air Wireless 2.4 GHz Print Server with a single parallel port and a companion model with a USB port, for those with USB printers. The company also has a USB 2.0 model in their AirPlus G line, which compares with Linksys's Wireless-G PrintServer for USB 2.0. Linksys offers a comparable USB 1.1 print server as well, along with a small, efficient single-parallel port server model.

- **Ethernet-Wireless Bridges:** The typical direction of a network's construction is to move from wired to wireless. But sometimes you need to go the other way, connecting a wired network, or an item designed for a wired network, to an existing wireless network. Wireless game adapters do this, but so do standalone Ethernet to Wireless adapters. If you have a PC with a wired Ethernet card, for instance, you can run a cable from the PC to the adapter, and the adapter will connect it to the wireless network via the network's access point.
- **Wireless Power over Ethernet Adapters:** These adapters let you provide power to access points or extenders through an Ethernet cable, without the requirement of a power receptacle at that device's location. D-Link provides the Express EtherNetwork Power Over Ethernet Adapter, while Linksys offers its Power Over Ethernet Adapter Kit. They work similarly.
- **Wireless Bluetooth Products:** As Bluetooth becomes a more frequently used network standard, you can expect to see more products designed for this much-touted but as yet largely unfulfilled protocol. D-Link offers a range of products in its PersonalAir line at this stage, including the Wireless USB Bluetooth Adapter, the Bluetooth USB Printer Adapter, the Stereo Adapter Kit, and the USB Stereo Adapter Kit. You need Bluetooth-enabled products in order to use them, but these, too, are becoming increasingly available.

Scenario Solutions

The home network needs only one of these devices: the wireless game adapter for use with the video game console. Any of the following three products will work for this purpose:

- Linksys WGA54G Wireless-G Game Adapter
- DLink DWL-G820 High-Speed Gaming Adapter
- Microsoft Xbox Wireless Adapter (for Xbox users)

The small business requires a print server to allow all PCs access to the laser printer at all times. Any of the following products will fill this need, but once again, as with the access points, the list offers the same order as the list for router/AP devices. Products from the same vendor, and ideally even product lines from the same vendor, tend to connect more easily with one another. This list ups the ante a bit as well, providing multi-port print servers to enable the business to connect additional printers to the network, all of which are accessible to all PCs at any time:

- DLink DP-G321 AirPlus G Wireless Multi-Port Print Server (two USB and one parallel printer port)

- Belkin Wireless Print Server (two USB printer ports)
- Linksys WPS54GU2 Wireless-G Print Server for USB 2.0 (one USB and one parallel printer ports)

Summary

Wireless networks, like all computer networks, start with hardware rather than software. For this reason, this chapter focused on an introduction to the types of hardware you need for a functioning WLAN, with a nod toward equipment you don't need but might want to add anyway. Chapter 3 begins the process of setting up this equipment and putting it to actual use, a process continued in Chapter 4 and, indeed, throughout much of the remainder of this book.

You should keep one thing in mind, though. If you get seriously into the wireless game, you'll quickly find that you'll want more and more gear to perform an ever increasing number of functions. Wireless is fascinating, and its equipment is just as fascinating as its uses.

In the next chapter, you'll learn how to use some of this equipment to build the simpler of the two types of wireless network: the ad hoc network, a peer-to-peer wireless network that does not use an access point. Chapter 4 steps you through the process of implementing an infrastructure network, in which an access point controls all wireless connectivity.

Chapter 3

Building an Ad Hoc Network

In non-technical language, *ad hoc* refers to something created (such as an ad hoc committee) for a temporary period of time and without concern for its broader or more long-lasting implications. In computer networking language, an ad hoc wireless network is put together for a specific and usually temporary purpose, much like any ad hoc gathering. You start an ad hoc network by enabling a wireless network adapter on one PC, and you add PCs as you like by enabling wireless adapters in each of them and configuring all the adapters to the same wireless channel. Turn the PCs off, and the network disappears, hence its ad hoc nature.

In simpler terms, ad hoc wireless networks have one primary characteristic: They operate without access points (APs). The lack of an AP means that the computers can connect to one another, but they can't work in conjunction with a wired network. As a result, they have significantly less capability as a network, but they can still be quite useful. In particular, they operate well in a small home network or as an independent small network in an office where connecting to the larger network is difficult in certain situations. Think of ad hoc networks as their name suggests — temporary networks created for a specific purpose — and the possibilities multiply.

Note

Ad hoc networking also goes by the name *Independent Basic Service Set*, or IBSS. This name contrasts with the related term *Infrastructure Basic Service Set*, or BSS, from which the term *infrastructure network* derives.

Ad Hoc Topology

In computer networking terms, each network has a specific *topology*, or shape. Each computer or other device on the network is a *node* on that network, and the connections between the nodes are known as *links*. The topology describes the manner in which the nodes and the links interconnect. Although numerous topologies are possible, you'll find the following most frequently:

- **Bus:** All nodes on the network connect to a single central cable, called a ***bus*** (or backbone). The bus handles all traffic to and from the nodes.
- **Star:** A central computer (hub) controls all network traffic, with nodes communicating with each other through this hub.
- **Ring:** The network has the shape of a ring or circle, with each node connected to the two nodes on either side. Traffic moves around the ring to its appropriate destination.
- **Tree:** The core of the network is a bus topology, to which one or more star networks are attached.
- **Mesh:** All nodes are connected directly to all other nodes. In some meshes, not all interconnections exist, but the principle remains the same.

Ad hoc networks operate with a mesh topology. All PCs on the network connect to each other directly. All appear in the Network Neighborhood or My Network Places folders on each PC, and anyone can send data to — and receive data from — any node at any time. Looked at another way, ad hoc networks are *peer-to-peer* networks, so named in computer circles because all nodes are peers, all on the same hierarchical level with one another. No central computer (hub or server) controls the network and the traffic; each machine is as important as the next.

Tip

For your mesh network to work effectively, you should configure each PC to contain a shared folder, and then have each user save or copy files to be shared inside that folder. If you password-protect the shared resources, make sure that each user knows how to access them.

Setting Up an Ad Hoc Network

Getting an ad hoc network up and running requires three main steps: installing the wireless LAN adapters in your computers, configuring the adapters so they can find and connect to one another, and establishing the network on your PCs so they can share resources. With all three steps completed, your ad hoc network is ready for use.

Before going any further, however, let us warn you that wireless networks, for all their advances over the past few years, can still provide some of the most frustrating moments in computing. Actually, that statement applies to computer networking in general, which can be filled with problem after problem, but wireless networking seems especially susceptible to difficulties in configuration and sustained connectivity. Despite the best efforts of Microsoft, the Linux initiative, and all the network equipment vendors, it remains safe to say, as it did ten years ago, that networking is the black hole of computing. Nor should this come as much of a surprise: given the trouble many people have keeping *one* computer working properly, it makes sense that getting two or more computers talking to each other is simply asking for problems.

That said, Windows helps, especially Windows XP, the most network-savvy version of Windows yet released. Its Network Setup Wizard, covered in this chapter, can create a functioning network quickly and, for the most part, reliably. The problem with setting up networks is this: What do you do if it ***doesn't*** work? And that's where the frustrations lie.

Here's an example. While writing this chapter, we needed to set up our own ad hoc network and connect the entire thing to the Internet. We don't usually work with ad hoc networks because — as you'll discover in Chapter 4 — infrastructure networks are both more common and more useful. But we've installed and configured numerous ad hoc networks in the past, so this should have been the proverbial piece of cake. Take apart the infrastructure network, install the WLAN adapters in all the PCs, tell everybody where to find each other, and presto. Instant network.

Well, not so much. After many frustrating hours, we discovered that one of the USB adapters was slightly malfunctioning. Slightly, not fully. If something doesn't work at all, it's easy to deal with. But when something ***almost*** works, it simply frustrates, because you don't know where to look. The adapter appeared to be working, so we spent a great deal of time digging through Properties dialog boxes, reconnecting and reconfiguring adapters, and generally rebuilding the entire network structure. By the time we eventually discovered the true culprit, we had reconfigured everything on all the PCs so completely that we essentially had to start over.

Why are we telling you this? Simply to demonstrate that although setting up a network ***can*** be quick, easy, and painless, don't be surprised, upset, or discouraged if it proves otherwise. Networking problems can happen to anyone, no matter how experienced. Just ask any IT professional.

Installing the Wireless Adapters

Every PC on your wireless network needs a WLAN adapter to connect to the network's other devices. While you can choose from several different types of adapters, including Compact Flash versions for the growing number of laptop PCs that contain Compact Flash ports, this chapter covers only the two primary types, USB and, in particular, PCMCIA (PC Card/CardBus). Configuring any of these cards requires stepping through the same basic process.

Installing your WLAN adapter is much like installing any other piece of hardware on a PC, period. Believe it or not — and many users frequently do not — reading the installation guide that came with your hardware actually matters. Primarily it matters for only one reason: to determine whether or not to install the drivers first or to plug the card in first.

When you install any hardware on a PC, ultimately you need both the hardware and its drivers in place to have the PC recognize the hardware and for the hardware to operate correctly. In some cases, Windows already stores the drivers — this is especially true of Windows XP, and even more true if you install the drivers first — and in that case your driver concerns are over, or at least put on hold, because Windows installs the drivers as soon as it recognizes the device. If Windows does not install its own drivers, then you need to use the drivers included on the CD-ROM that shipped with the hardware. But even if Windows does install its own drivers, you should install (eventually if not immediately) the latest drivers for your adapter, available from the manufacturer's Web site.

As mentioned previously, the order of installation can matter. For whatever reasons, order is more important for USB devices, but it can matter for PC Card and PCI adapters as well. Indeed, this is one of the long-standing bugaboos of USB equipment in particular: sometimes it's simply better to install the drivers first, and there seems to be no consistency about the requirement.

One thing is certain. Although you might be wrong to install the device before the drivers, the reverse is never true. So you might as well just install the drivers first. Insert the CD (or floppy disk, if you have a much older adapter) into your PC's drive and either wait for Autorun to launch the installation utility or, if the installation utility doesn't launch, locate the Setup file on the CD (often in a folder called drivers, but sometimes in the CD's root folder) and launch it from there. You'll be greeted with one of the standard Windows installation programs, and you need only follow the defaults or, if you wish, change elements such as the drive location to suit your needs.

With the drivers installed, you may or may not be asked to restart the PC. If you are, restart. This allows the drivers to load into system memory, ready for you to insert the PC Card or USB cable. Once Windows has restarted — give it enough time to perform its usual automatic software loads — plug in the USB adapter or insert the PC Card adapter, and watch as Windows XP recognizes the hardware and associates its drivers. In the case of a PCI adapter, you can shut down the PC instead of restarting it, open the desktop case, and install the adapter before booting it back up.

Note

Surely, very little about a PC is as annoying as the requirement for rebooting after installing something. Software developers have reasons for doing it this way — drivers need to load into memory, for example — but it almost always seems a disruptive procedure. You're in the middle of doing a number of other things on your PC when you realize you have to install that new USB device (for instance), so you pop the CD in the drive and let Autorun perform its duties. Two or three clicks later and everything's ready to go, except for that window telling you the PC needs rebooting to complete the installation. Sometimes you don't actually have to do so, but it's almost impossible to tell. So you close everything down and go along with the process, disrupting the flow of thought, energy, and time. All of this said (and thanks for listening), do yourself a favor and close all open programs before installing *anything* on your computer; in addition, run the System Restore utility from Windows' System Tools folder (Start → All Folders → Accessories) immediately before the install, so that if anything goes wrong you can turn back the clock to Windows as it was before you installed.

If you choose to install the adapter before the drivers, Windows steps you through the installation process. In the case of Windows XP Service Pack 2 (SP2), you begin with the dialog box shown in Figure 3-1. The Windows Update component of Windows XP (and other Windows versions) has always had a certain number of device drivers available for download, but SP2 represents the first time the initial driver installation has prompted for an immediate search of the site.

If you know your equipment is brand new, with little likelihood of the latest drivers being on the Update site, choose "No, not this time." But it never hurts to check, so you might as well start the installation process with "Yes, this time only" and see what transpires. If Windows can't locate a driver, click the Back button on the subsequent dialog box and proceed with the installation from there, choosing to "Install from a list or specific location" as shown in Figure 3-2.

Figure 3-1: Giving permission to search Windows Update for drivers.

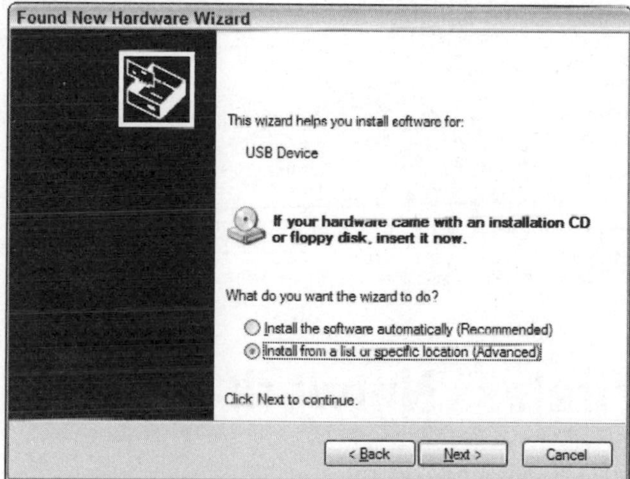

Figure 3-2: Specifying the location of the WLAN adapter driver.

The default radio button for this screen is for Windows to install the software automatically, a selection that works perfectly if you install the drivers before the hardware. But in this case, Windows doesn't know where to find the driver, so you need to specify. Actually, it's not even that difficult because if you put the CD-ROM in the CD/DVD drive and then choose automatic installation, Windows will almost certainly find the appropriate driver files.

After installing the driver, you might well come across the dialog box shown in Figure 3-3, in which you instruct Windows to use the driver even though it has not been "signed." To place the Windows logo on their products, hardware vendors must pass a set of tests designed by Microsoft, ensuring that the driver will function in Windows without danger of upsetting any of the delicate Windows apple carts. You'll see this dialog box in particular with new hardware, because nobody waits for Microsoft to complete the logo testing before releasing the product. When you see the dialog box shown in Figure 3-3, click Continue Anyway to finish the driver installation.

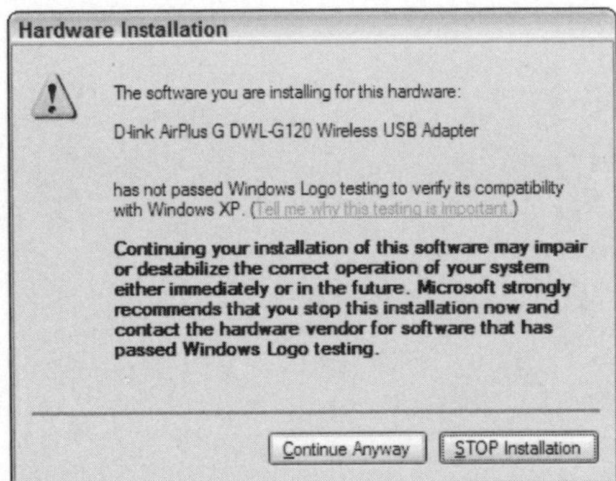

Figure 3-3: Just say yes. No major vendor is going to release a dangerous driver.

Once the drivers are installed and the WLAN adapter is in place — in not just one but in *all* the PCs you want to join together in an ad hoc network — you can proceed to the configuration of the network itself.

Configuring Your Wireless Network

Configuring a WLAN means getting the WLAN adapters to communicate with one another, and getting them to work together as a Windows-based network. Think of the two procedures like a phone call: the telephone provides the technology for communication, so you can simply dial the number and the other person will answer, but actual communication, in the sense of meaningful sharing of information, is a completely different proposition. Drawing the analogy further, if you've ever made a phone call where the connection goes awry (static, long delays, or even a disconnection), you've experienced what in wireless networking terms would be an inability for the adapters to perform their technical function. On the other hand, if your phone call consists of the two of you fuming at each other in silence and not actually saying anything, then the connection works but the communication doesn't.

Letting Windows Handle Everything

As with everything else network-related, Windows XP can handle all the details if you wish. Support for wireless networking is built directly into the operating system, which is obviously a help when it comes to establishing WLANs. If all your PCs operate under Windows XP, by all means start with this option and see if your ad hoc network pops up on its own, fully functional and ready to roll.

To do so, simply install the WLAN adapters and turn on your PCs. Windows automatically creates a network called "default" that all adapters can locate and connect to. However, Windows XP is also security-conscious, and by default it does not automatically connect to networks on which WEP or WPA encryption is disabled. You can see the wireless networks that you can connect to by right-clicking the wireless network icon in the icon tray or in the Network Connections folder and selecting View Available Wireless Networks from the context menu. Figure 3-4 shows the Wireless Network Connection dialog box from Windows XP with the Connect button grayed out. To make this button available for use (and thus connect to the network), click the checkbox labeled "Allow me to connect to the selected wireless network, even though it is not secure."

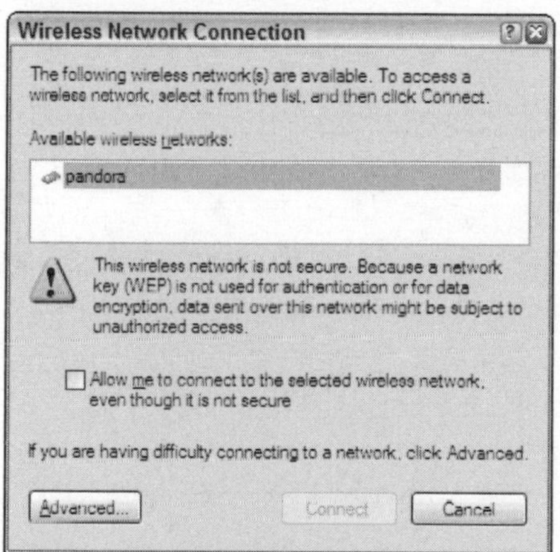

Figure 3-4: Connecting to a specific wireless network.

Figure 3-5 shows a significantly different dialog box. This item appears when you select View Available Wireless Networks in Windows XP SP2. Click the network name and then the Connect button, or, if you prefer, choose Change Advanced Settings from the Related Tasks menu, an action that takes you to the dialog box shown in Figure 3-4.

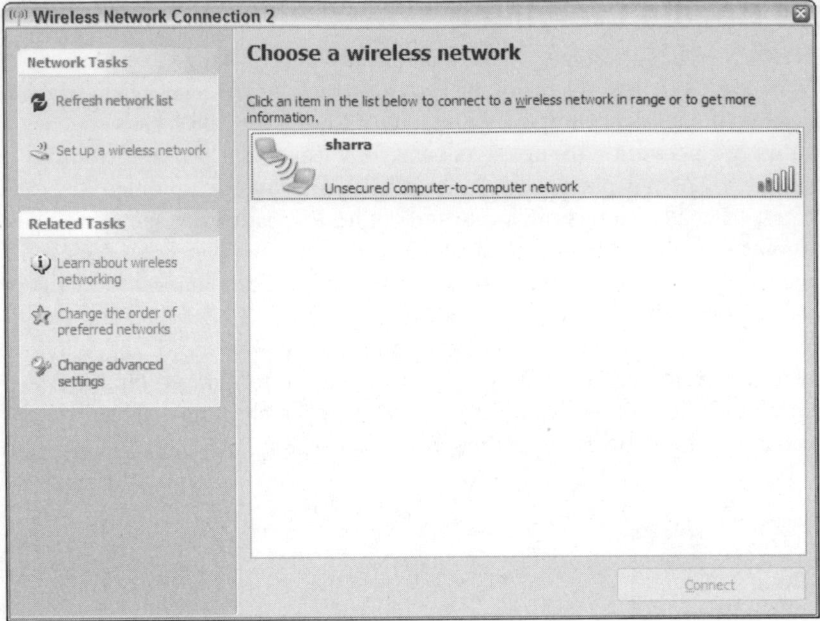

Figure 3-5: Connecting to a wireless network in Windows XP Service Pack 2.

If you know a wireless network exists, but you don't see it in the list, you can add it manually. In fact, this is the way to create a new network from scratch as well. To do so, follow these steps:

1. Open the Wireless Network Connection Properties dialog box and click the Wireless Networks tab.
2. In the Preferred Networks region of the dialog box, click Add. See Figure 3-6 for the result.
3. In the Network Name (SSID) field, type the name of the network you know exists (or a new name if you wish to create a new connection). The name is freeform; you can call it whatever you wish.
4. For the time being, select Disabled on the Data Encryption drop-down menu. It is *always* better to set up and troubleshoot a wireless network first and then add encryption afterward. Otherwise, if you have difficulty connecting, you'll have trouble determining if the network itself or the encryption is causing the problem.
5. If you want to restrict connections to an ad hoc network (as is the case for this chapter), be sure to check the box at the bottom of the dialog box, "This is a computer-to-computer (ad hoc) network; wireless access points are not used." You can use this feature to prevent the network from connecting to an AP-based network if one of these exists as well.
6. Click OK to close the box and choose the network you just added.

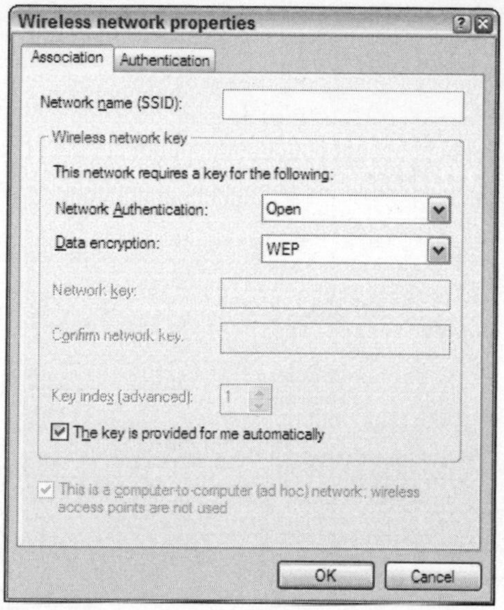

Figure 3-6: Adding a network to the available networks list.

Configuring the Network Yourself

If you prefer to configure the network yourself, use the configuration utility that (in all likelihood) installed with your drivers. Actually, this is one reason to install the drivers using the installation utility on the CD instead of locating them using the hardware installation procedure in Windows; not only do you get the drivers, but you install any supporting programs as well. You can typically launch the configuration utility from the All Programs menu in Windows XP, but usually it loads automatically with Windows and its icon appears in the icon tray in the bottom-right corner of the screen.

Figures 3-7 and 3-8 show two screens from the configuration utility for the D-Link AirPlus XtremeG PCI wireless adapter. Your utility will almost certainly offer similar configuration options. As you can see, the options here closely resemble those on the Wireless Network Properties dialog box for Windows XP. You give the network a name (SSID), choose the mode — ad hoc or infrastructure — and enable or disable encryption. If you enable encryption, you choose a key length and either have the keys automatically generated or type them yourself. See Part II for a full discussion on configuring WLAN security. You can leave the network unencrypted until you reach that point.

Figure 3-8 shows the Advanced screen of the D-Link utility. Here, several choices present themselves. The most significant option is the Channel: you can choose any channel from 1 through 11. For the ad hoc network to function, you must set all WLAN adapters to the same channel. Otherwise, they have no way of communicating with one another.

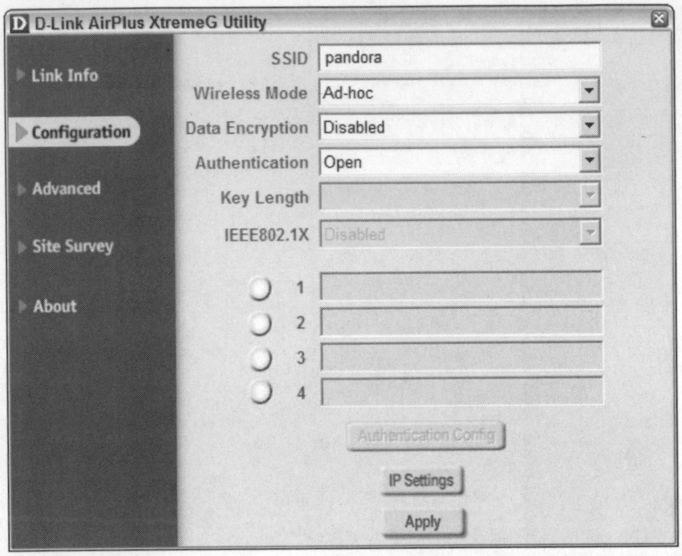

Figure 3-7: The Configuration dialog box for a D-Link WLAN adapter.

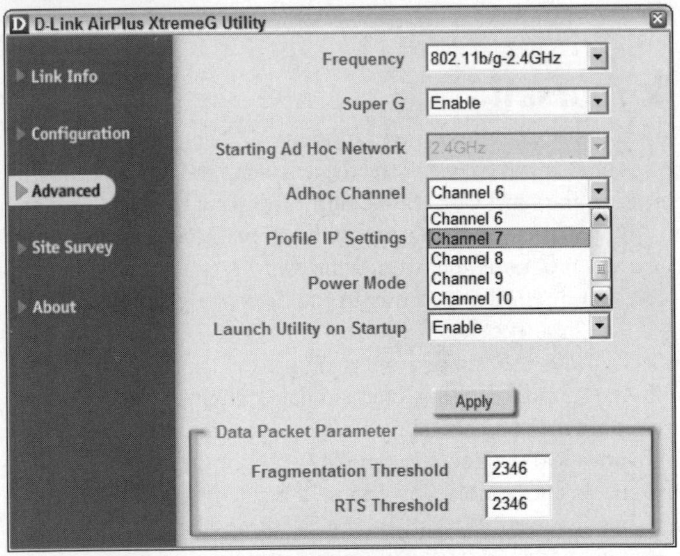

Figure 3-8: Advanced configuration options.

Tip

If you have trouble with sporadic loss of connectivity for your WLAN, try changing the channel on which it operates. You might be experiencing interference from another radio-based device in your house or office. Be sure to change the channel setting on *all* WLANs on the network.

In this particular case, D-Link offers a variety of additional options. You can choose support for both 802.11b and 802.11g protocols, or, if you wish to ensure connectivity with older WLAN adapters, 802.11b only. You also can choose D-Link's Super G mode from here, or disable it. Super G is D-Link's technology for enhancing the 802.11g connection, and it works best only when all WLANs on the network operate with it. Several WLAN adapter vendors have a similar proprietary technology for offering enhancements to their wireless equipment.

Cross-Ref

To learn about setting the security options for your WLAN, see Part II.

At this point, you've finished the majority of work needed to get a fully functioning wireless LAN up and running. In fact, you *have* a wireless LAN up and running, and without going any further you can start sending files back and forth between your PCs, share the printer that's connected to one of those machines, play games across the LAN, and even control one PC from another using Windows XP Professional's Remote Desktop feature.

The only thing missing from your network is the ability to share an Internet connection, one of the primary reasons behind creating a LAN in the first place, especially in homes and small offices. So let's turn to that task now, after which you'll be ready to take full advantage of the network you've built.

Sharing an Internet Connection

You don't need an Internet connection to have an ad hoc network. For that matter, you don't need an Internet connection to have *any* computer network. Computer networks existed long before widely available Internet connectivity, indeed long before the Internet itself. And remember that the Internet is simply another network, special only in the fact that it operates as a network of networks (hence the *inter* portion of its name), and the fact that the world has adopted it. But many networks continue to exist that offer full connectivity internally without external Internet access.

That said, in the case of pretty much all non-business LANs, Internet connectivity has become the norm. In fact, you could argue that it's become the entire purpose for creating the LAN in the first place. In homes and many small offices, particularly homes, users rarely need their PCs to connect to one another; instead they need them — or at least want them — to connect to the Internet. E-mail and the Web, for these users, are far more important than sharing files, printers, or other resources, or even playing networked games.

If you want to share an Internet connection most reliably and conveniently with your wirelessly-connected PCs, buy an access point and build an infrastructure network (for details, see Chapter 4). However, you can most certainly share an Internet connection among the PCs on an ad hoc network. You simply need to designate one of those PCs the sharing computer, connect it to the Internet, and use the Internet Connection Sharing (ICS) feature of Windows to make the Internet available to all the other networked PCs.

Internet Connection Sharing works by fooling the Internet into thinking that only one computer is performing Internet requests, uploads, and downloads. The sharing machine acts as a focal point for the entire LAN, with all incoming and outgoing data passing through it. In effect, the sharing computer acts as a proxy server, and in fact Windows ICS is a kind of simplified proxy server. Full proxy servers control, secure, and cache all incoming and outgoing data, and offer control over individual machines on the LAN, whereas Windows ICS just routes data and offers minimal security.

With Windows ICS, each computer on the LAN is given its own unique IP (Internet Protocol) address, just like all other computers on the Internet. However, the LAN's IP addresses are private to that LAN, and do not provide direct Internet access. The only computer with a public Internet IP address is the sharing machine, and it has two IP addresses: one private, one public. The public IP number is assigned by the Internet service provider at the time of connection, while the private IP number is assigned through the Network applet in Windows Control Panel, either manually or via the ICS wizard.

For the remainder of this discussion, let's give the computers names to avoid confusion. We'll call the sharing machine Computer A and the other PCs on the LAN Computer X, Y, and Z (as needed).

The private IP address for Computer A is 192.168.0.1 — the 192 series is restricted to private LAN use (the Internet doesn't recognize the 192 numbers). The ICS wizard sets this IP automatically, or you can set it yourself using Control Panel's Network app. Computers X, Y, and Z (and all others on the LAN) require IP numbers in the range 192.168.0.2 through 192.168.0.253. You can assign these numbers through the Network app, or you can have the sharing computer assign them through its built-in DHCP (Dynamic Host Configuration Protocol) routine. The latter is easier, simply because it eliminates the need to dig into each machine's Network app manually. Indeed, nearly all cable/DSL routers and other Internet sharing devices, including server computers, use DHCP as the basis for address assigning, although not all begin the counting with 192.168.0.1 as Windows itself does. The Microsoft Wireless Base Station, for example, takes the address 192.168.2.1 and assigns from there, and other routers use other private-range addresses.

When Computer X makes a request to the Internet, such as sending e-mail to an Internet address or clicking an external hyperlink in a browser, Computer X's private IP address is sent to Computer A. There, the private IP address is translated to Computer A's public IP address — with Computer X's IP address retained in conjunction with the request by the sharing computer — so that the requested Internet server can respond. The response from the Internet comes back to Computer A's public IP address, and Computer A recalls the original IP address and sends the response to Computer X.

Computer A works the same way as all other machines on the LAN, translating all interactions from the 192.168.0.1 address to the public IP address. But because the data doesn't need to flow between machines in this case, the process is faster than one in which the data traverses the LAN wires. Computer A *will* be affected by network slowdowns, however, just like any other computer on the LAN.

Caution

To share an Internet connection with a PC acting as the ICS host, you must leave the host machine powered on if you want other PCs on the network to access the Internet. Because the host receives and transmits all incoming and outgoing Internet traffic, as soon as you power it down, you remove the point of connection with the Internet.

This fact provides one of the two primary reasons for choosing an access point or a router/switch combination for providing Internet access: you can leave the AP or router powered on while consuming very little electrical power, allowing you to power down other computers on the network as you wish. The other reason is even more important. With the AP or router providing the initial access to the LAN, it appears to anyone on the Internet as the *only* node on your network. Automatically, you have a built-in safeguard against intrusion from the Net.

Although ICS setups typically use a router or switch, with or without the access point, for the sake of establishing a more purely ad hoc network, we dispense with the AP/router/switch here to work solely with one PC acting as an ICS host, and however many node PCs as you wish forming an ad hoc network with one another and receiving an Internet connection from the ICS host. What you get in the end is a network with each node wirelessly connected to each other node, and each one capable of accessing the Internet as well. Call it ad hoc–plus, if you will.

Configuring the ICS Host

The network in this demonstration (a typical such network) has a desktop PC as a host PC and three notebook PCs constituting the ad hoc WLAN. Certainly you could start with a notebook PC instead, but we've chosen a desktop for the simple reason that it will be the only node on the WLAN without a PC Card wireless adapter. Instead, it can use either a PCI or a USB adapter, and the example here uses the latter.

To share a broadband connection, the ICS host needs an Ethernet LAN adapter, typically a PCI card inside the computer or an adapter build right onto the mainboard. In either case, you connect the ICS host to the Internet by running an Ethernet cable from a cable or DSL modem (typically) into the Ethernet card. You then set up the Internet connection according to the instructions you receive from your Internet provider. In the case of virtually all cable and DSL providers, this means first configuring the Network Properties dialog box to obtain an IP address automatically and to obtain the DNS (Domain Name System) server addresses automatically, as shown in Figure 3-9.

DSL customers need to create a login script as well, a process you can perform either via the New Connection Wizard or the Network Setup Wizard. This login script consists only of the username and password your ISP has assigned to you, and the wizard not only gives you a screen with fields for both of the entries, it also stores the entries for future logins. To sign into your DSL account, you launch the Connect dialog box from the desktop or from the Network Connections dialog box, and on this box you'll see the username in the appropriate field, along with a password field that says, "*[To change the saved password, click here.]*." The password you typed in the wizard is the one already in force, so there's no need to change it unless you do so with your ISP.

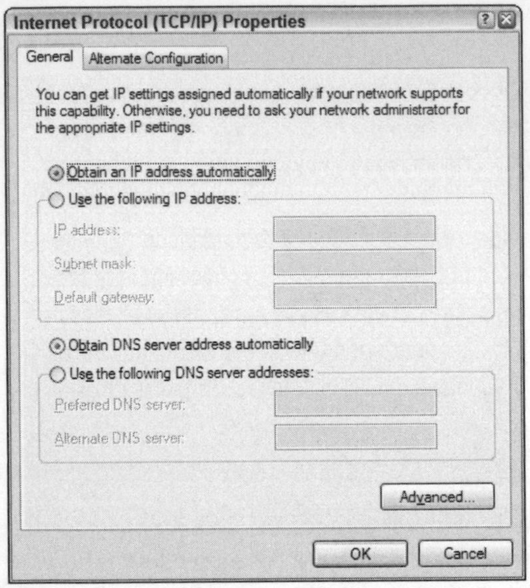

Figure 3-9: Configuring the TCP/IP settings.

Note

You don't actually need a high-speed Internet connection for Windows ICS. Instead, you can share a dial-up connection with full reliability. But if more than two nodes start using a dial-up connection simultaneously, you'll notice some very definite slowdown. For that reason, this example uses a broadband connection.

Unless you've used the Network Setup Wizard, during which Windows configures your PC to share the Internet connection, you must tell Windows that you wish to do so. Open the Network Connections folder by first opening My Network Places and then clicking the View Network Connections link in the Network Tasks pane. Right-click the icon for the network resource (LAN or Internet connection) you are using to connect to the Internet and choose Properties. Under the Advanced tab you'll find the checkbox, "Allow other network users to connect through this computer's Internet connection." Check this box, and unless you have a specific reason to uncheck the other boxes — "Establish a dial-up connection whenever a computer on my network attempts to access the Internet" and "Allow other network users to control or disable the shared Internet connection" — leave them selected. If you're using DSL or cable, feel free to uncheck the former, and if you want to ensure nobody else disconnects, uncheck the latter, but typically neither option presents any problem.

If you want to use the Network Setup Wizard to configure ICS instead of doing so manually, launch it from the Network Tasks pane, by clicking the "Set up a home or small office network" link, and follow these steps:

1. Step through the wizard to the question, "Do you want to share an Internet connection?" With your cable/DSL connection already established, the appropriate response is "Yes." If you have more than one possible connection and you don't want to use the default suggestion, click "No, let me choose another way to connect to the Internet."

2. On the "Select a connection method" screen, choose "This computer connects directly to the Internet. The other computers on my network connect to the Internet through this computer." Note that if you have already established a LAN with the Internet connection shared through a cable/DSL router or a separate router, choose the second option, "This computer connects to the Internet through a residential gateway or through another computer on my intranet." If you do so, however, your PC no longer acts as host; the router does. For this example, therefore, the first choice is correct.

Note

Other options are available from the "Select a connection method" screen as well, depending on your current setup. Click the Other radio button, and then Next, to see these choices. One option is, "This computer connects to the Internet directly or through a network hub. Other computers on my network also connect to the Internet directly or through a hub." If you have an Internet connection but no network, or the reverse, you will see either "This computer connects directly to the Internet. I do not have a network yet" or "This computer belongs to a network that does not have an Internet connection." Obviously this last possibility is irrelevant for this particular section of this chapter—which expressly discusses connecting to the Internet—but keep in mind its availability in case you wish to create a network without Internet access.

3. Choose the Internet connection you wish to share. Windows takes its best guess at it for the sake of automation, and this guess is usually right. You want to share the broadband connection, which in turn provides Internet access to all machines. See Figure 3-10.

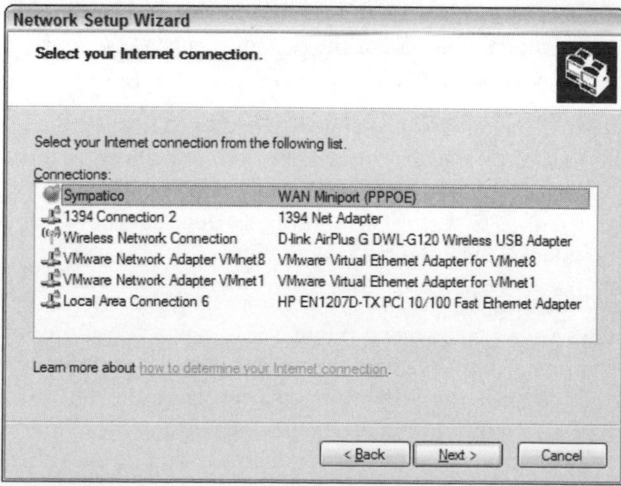

Figure 3-10: Choosing the source of the Internet connection.

4. On the next screen, "Select your private connection" (see Figure 3-11), you choose the connection that will provide Internet connectivity for the ad hoc WLAN (refer to Figure 3-10). Here's where difficulties can result. The answer, in our sample case, is the Local Area Connection belonging to the Ethernet card in your PC — not the Wireless Network Connection option, if it appears in this list. In other words, Steps 3 and 4 have you establish the broadband connection as sharing the Internet connection, and the Ethernet card (Local Area Connection) as acting as the hub for the WLAN.

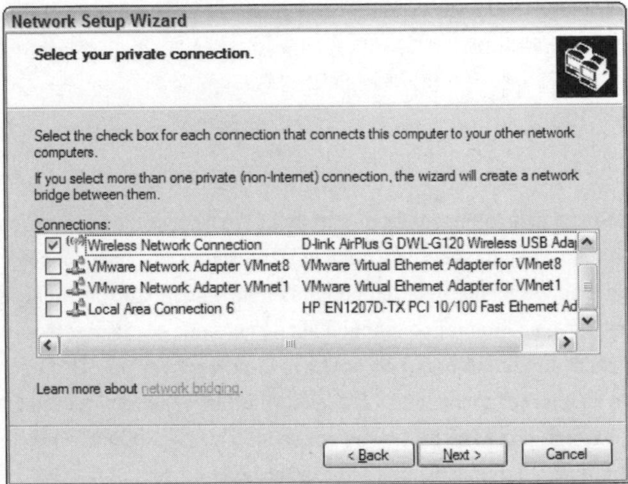

Figure 3-11: Choosing the network for distribution of the Internet connection.

5. The next screen has you giving the ICS host computer a name and an optional description, and naming the workgroup whatever you choose. Windows standardizes on MSHOME for the network name, but not only can you change it, you should. Anyone looking to break into your network has an easier time if you opt for the default name, so personalize it and simultaneously get rid of some casual hacking.

6. On the "File and printer sharing" screen, you can choose whether to turn on the file and print sharing option. If you do turn on file or print sharing, you risk allowing intruders easier access to your files. In fact, if you don't have a firewall program, don't even consider turning this option on. The default is to turn it off, and that's a good idea for now. You can always reverse your decision later by reconfiguring the network.

7. After clicking Next twice (the first time to confirm your choices), Windows sets up your network. The first time it does so can take several minutes, but if you re-run the wizard later it takes significantly less time. After finishing, the wizard presents you with the choice of creating a network setup floppy disk for use on the other nodes on the network, using an already created network setup floppy, setting up the nodes by using the Windows XP installation CD, or finishing the wizard without creating media to run on the other nodes.

If all your nodes are running Windows XP, as this chapter assumes, you don't need to do anything. For PCs with any other version of Windows, create the setup floppy as assurance of getting the network up and running on all your machines.

Tip

To make changes at any time to your Windows XP network, you don't need to fiddle with the network connections settings. Instead, simply relaunch the Network Setup Wizard and choose different options. If you've made numerous specific changes to your network settings, this wizard will probably reset most of them, in which case running the wizard might be the wrong idea, but for most users the wizard provides the easiest and most foolproof method of ensuring a functioning, correctly configured network.

Providing Internet Connectivity to the Ad Hoc WLAN

At this stage, you have an ICS host ready to roll, but you have no way for the other nodes on the network to connect to it. For this, you need to install a WLAN adapter into the host. If your host PC contains a PC Card adapter (most desktop PCs do not), you can simply use an adapter identical to those in your notebook PCs. In the vast majority of cases, however, you need a PCI or USB adapter. This example uses USB, simply because it's easier to install and set up, although we've become aware through testing a variety of products that both PCI adapters and PC Card adapters tend to connect — and maintain the wireless connection — on a more consistently reliable basis. If you intend to share your Internet connection with a WLAN in the manner described in this chapter, you should consider using a PCI WLAN adapter if your ICS host is a desktop PC or a PC Card WLAN adapter if your host PC is a laptop.

Note

As you've undoubtedly noticed by now, the machine that hosts the Internet connection needs two separate network adapters — one for the host to connect to the Internet, and the other to allow the other network devices to connect to the host. If you were to set up ICS for wired access only, you would need two Ethernet LAN adapters inside the PC, but that would provide a connection for only one external device. To split the signal, you would need a switch or a hub, with a cable connecting each PC to that switch or hub. For this reason alone, a wireless setup is often more convenient. A single wireless adapter can accommodate as many WLAN nodes as you wish.

Here, too, the Network Setup Wizard can help you. Install the drivers for your WLAN adapter on the desktop, plug in the adapter itself (PCI slot or USB port), and connect the adapter to the ad hoc network you've already created. With the ad hoc network fully in place, run the Network Setup Wizard once more. This time, Windows will bridge the Ethernet connection to the Internet with the wireless connection to the other nodes on the WLAN, while simultaneously configuring the ICS

host's WLAN adapter to provide IP and DNS addresses to those nodes. The node PCs require this addressing information to connect to the Internet and receive and send traffic beyond the ad hoc network.

If you don't want to use the Network Setup Wizard, you can configure the ICS host's WLAN adapter manually to perform the same addressing function. To do so, configure all WLAN adapters, including the one installed in the ICS host, to obtain IP and DNS server addresses automatically. Open the Network Connections folder, right-click the icon for that connection, and, on the General tab of the resulting Properties dialog box, select the Internet Protocol (TCP/IP) item in the list of items and then click the Properties button. On the General tab of the Internet Protocol (TCP/IP) Properties dialog box, choose the top radio button in each section — "Obtain an IP address automatically" and "Obtain DNS server address automatically" — and then click OK until you've closed all the dialog boxes. Because the ICS host is configured to share an Internet connection, and because the host's WLAN adapter receives its IP and DNS addresses automatically and communicates with the rest of the ad hoc network, the nodes on the WLAN will also receive Internet connectivity information.

Again, if you have difficulties with the manual setup, run the Network Setup Wizard and let Windows do the job for you. Indeed, often this is the most efficient method to use.

Summary

This chapter has taken you through the steps needed to create an ad hoc wireless network. You've installed your wireless LAN adapters on your desktop and notebook PCs, you've configured them to communicate through one specific Wi-Fi channel, and you've used them to share resources (files and printers, for example) across the ad hoc LAN. You've also seen how to configure one of your PCs to act as an Internet host, sharing a single Internet connection among all your PCs through the seeming magic of DHCP. You have a fully functional WLAN up and running, and if it serves your needs, you can leave it at that.

More likely, though, you've already begun to notice one of the major limitations of ad hoc networking. To keep the Internet connection available for all your machines, you have to keep the host PC running. As soon as you shut it off, its connection to the Internet disappears, so obviously it can no longer share it. Less noticeable, but equally important, is a second limitation: security. Ad hoc WLANs don't offer much security against Internet intruders at all.

Chapter 4 introduces you to the standard form of Wi-Fi connectivity, the infrastructure LAN. You'll learn how to use a wireless access point (AP), in combination with a router/switch device, to create a wireless network that shares the Internet connection without leaving one of your PCs powered on, and that provides at least some degree of security through the built-in firewall capabilities of the router/AP itself.

Chapter 4

Building an Infrastructure Network

Technically, an infrastructure network has one distinguishing characteristic: a wireless access point (AP). However, the true power of infrastructure networks lies in their ability to bridge wired and wireless networks, with both networks functioning as one larger network in a thoroughly seamless fashion. If you've ever worked with a wired network, and you suddenly move to an infrastructure network, accessing your wired PCs directly from your wireless-only notebooks, the whole thing seems like something approaching magic. It's not, of course, but as you sit wherever you want in your home or at your office, transferring files from your desktop PC or simply using the AP/router to access the Internet, you can experience a sense of freedom that almost overwhelms. As with all computer technology, the gee-whiz factor passes fairly quickly, but the combination of wired and wireless networks remains one of the more fascinating computer technology combinations of the past several years.

In this chapter, we take you through the process of setting up a wireless-to-wired infrastructure network using Windows PCs and a combination AP/router hardware device. In this four-PC network, one PC connects to the router via Ethernet cable while the other three use a combination of different types of wireless network adapters.

Start with a Wired LAN

To create an infrastructure wired-to-wireless network, you start with a functioning wired Ethernet LAN. That might seem blatantly obvious, but you can run into some very real problems if you don't have the wired LAN working properly before adding the wireless components. None of which is to suggest that you can't put the pieces in place one at a time and make them cooperate as you do so, reconfiguring the LAN repeatedly in the process. But for your first combined LAN (and from our experience, your second and third as well), you'll find the going much smoother if you start with a working LAN and then add the WLAN portion.

Note

Even though this section covers setting up a wired LAN, the procedures for establishing workgroup membership and Internet connection sharing apply equally to wireless LAN configuration as well — just in case you needed any further statement of relevance here.

So what do we mean by a working LAN? In fact, your wired LAN need not consist of multiple computers at all. A single PC connected to the router constitutes a network for these purposes; the WLAN bridges to that PC and creates a wired-wireless combination. Mostly, though, a LAN consists of more than one PC, so for the purposes of this chapter we'll include two, as well as two notebook PCs with wireless connections. Still, if you have only one PC with a WLAN adapter , and a second PC with an Ethernet adapter, and you connect them both through an AP/router, you have a two-PC infrastructure LAN.

Configuring the Workgroup

Creating an Ethernet LAN begins with installing of Ethernet adapters in or (in the case of USB adapters) on the PCs you wish to connect to the LAN via Ethernet. If you recently purchased a PC, you'll probably find a network card already in place. Examine the back of the case (or the back or side of the notebook PC) for an Ethernet port — it looks a lot like a phone jack, except that it's a bit wider. If the connector on the Ethernet cable fits into it, then you have the adapter.

Tip

It's possible, but highly unlikely, that the Ethernet adapter is installed but disabled. If the PC does not establish a connection with the network, right-click My Computer, choose Properties, click the Hardware tab, and open Device Manager. Expand the Network Adapters category, right-click the name of the adapter in your PC (it might bear a different name from its brand name), and choose Properties. The Properties dialog box tells you if the adapter is functioning properly.

With the Ethernet adapter in place, you can configure a workgroup. The term ***workgroup*** simply means ***network***, but in computer networking terminology it has a more specific meaning. A workgroup consists of a group of computers linked to one another without the presence of a ***domain***. Any PC configured with the workgroup's name can join the workgroup and take advantage of file and printer sharing as well as other network capabilities. A domain, by contrast, is a group of computers connected through and controlled by a central computer (or group of computers) called a ***domain controller***. The domain controller takes care of all issues involving authentication and permissions, with only the domain administrator able to make changes to these configurations. As you might expect, domains tend to exist only in larger organizations, with workgroups the primary network type in homes and small offices.

This book deals with workgroups rather than domains. Although wireless networking is certainly possible — and practiced — in conjunction with domains, most readers of this book will almost certainly have a stronger need for details on connecting home PCs or, at most, SOHO (Small Office, Home Office) or SMB (Small to Medium Business) networks to wireless LANs, with domains well out of range. Indeed, the Network Setup Wizard in Windows XP focuses largely on workgroups, as does much of the documentation that ships with wireless adapters and access points.

You need only one computer to configure a workgroup. In fact, when you install Windows XP, you automatically configure a workgroup during the Setup process. By default, Windows XP sets up a workgroup called MSHOME, but Setup lets you change that name to whatever you wish.

CHANGING THE WORKGROUP NAME: METHOD 1

To determine the current workgroup to which your PC belongs, right-click My Computer and choose Properties. Click the Computer Name tab and look for the Workgroup heading. Beside it you can see the workgroup name.

To change the name of the workgroup to which your PC belongs, click the Change button. In the Member Of section at the bottom of the resulting Computer Name Changes dialog box, shown in Figure 4-1, ensure that the Workgroup radio button is selected, and type whatever name you wish in the corresponding field. Click OK to make the change.

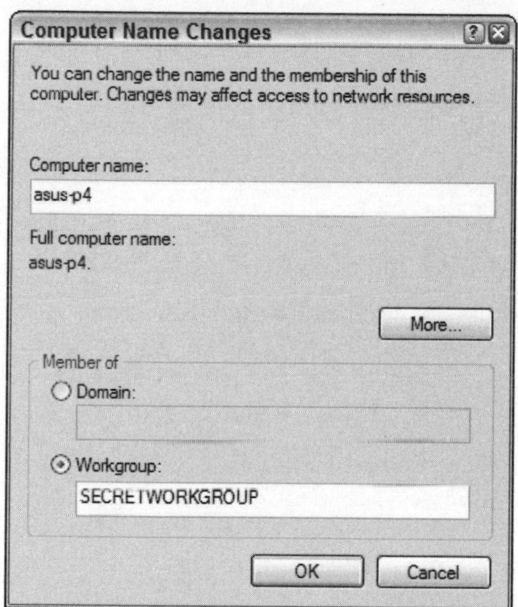

Figure 4-1: Changing your workgroup name.

Note

You can also change your PC's name from the Computer Name Changes dialog box. Unlike changing the workgroup name, changing the PC's name has no effect on the ability of your PC to access the network, nor the ability of other network members to access your PC. The only change for other network users will be seeing a new computer name in the Network folder.

CHANGING THE WORKGROUP NAME: METHOD 2

The Computer Name tab of the System Properties dialog box offers a second method of changing the workgroup name. To do so, click the Network ID button followed by the Next button. This takes you to the screen shown in Figure 4-2, a confusing interface design that seems to simply invite people to make configuration errors.

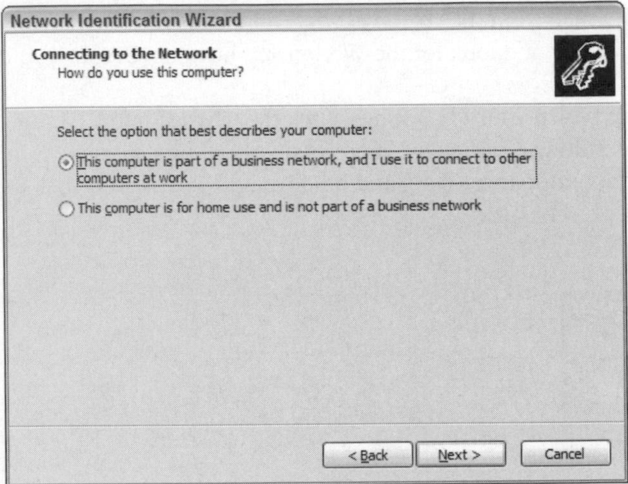

Figure 4-2: Which network do you choose?

Why is it confusing? You have only two options on the Connecting to the Network screen:

- This computer is part of a business network, and I use it to connect to other computers at work.
- This computer is for home use and is not part of a business network.

Hmmm. Which to choose? What exactly does "a business network" consist of? What if you have a four-PC office that you run from your converted basement? Does that count? Or does this mean a big, domain-oriented business network? Doesn't the second option mean that your computer will end up without a network setting at all?

If you take the wizard a step further, it doesn't get a whole lot clearer. To show why this confuses, try clicking the second option; you immediately set the wizard in motion, forcing you to wait while it does something the wizard never actually specifies. In fact, you pretty well have to assume that you've simply removed your PC from any kind of networking whatsoever. This assumption seems even more evident if you click the Back button instead of the Finish button after the wizard reaches its final screen, and then click the first option, "This computer is part of a business network . . ."

From this option, you're presented with two sub-options:

- My company uses a network with a domain.
- My company uses a network without a domain.

No problem with this selection: if you don't have a domain (as the configuration in this chapter assumes), click option 2. Furthermore, this two-item menu would seem to confirm that the original option 2, "This computer is for home use and is not part of a business network," would result in no network configuration because otherwise why have a second option for connecting to a workgroup, i.e., "a network without a domain." There. Confusion solved.

Not so fast. As it turns out, both main options for the Network Identification Wizard let you configure your PC for a workgroup. The difference is that option 2, "home use," sets up the PC on a workgroup automatically, specifically a workgroup called, creatively enough, Workgroup. The second option, "business network," lets you name the workgroup from within the wizard. How obtuse can you get?

In fact, the primary function of the Network Identification Wizard is to let you connect easily to a domain. Stepping through the wizard after making this selection, you fill in your username and password, as well as the name of the domain and possibly more. For connecting to a workgroup, manually changing the Workgroup name, as in Method 1 above, or using the Network Setup Wizard, outlined in Method 3 in the next section, accomplishes everything you need.

CHANGING THE WORKGROUP NAME: METHOD 3

As discussed in Chapter 3, Windows XP contains an extremely useful tool for configuring a workgroup: the Network Setup Wizard. Available directly from Control Panel, or as the link labeled "Set up a home or small office network" in the Network Tasks area of the Network Connections folder (which is available from Control Panel or My Network Places), the Network Setup Wizard takes you through a variety of options and finishes with a fully configured workgroup-based network.

After working with the other two methods for setting up your network, we encourage you to use the Network Setup Wizard every time you need a new workgroup, and indeed every time you add a PC to your existing network. The wizard works, and it leaves nothing to chance. It takes your PC through the process of activating its network components, locating the network to which you assign it, and adding that network to the appropriate access folders. When you have the network configured on the new PC, it should appear automatically in the My Network Places folder of all other PCs in the workgroup, but if not, you need only run the same wizard on any PCs where it does not.

To set up your PC on a workgroup using this wizard, follow these steps:

1. Open the Network Setup Wizard from Control Panel.
2. Click Next until you arrive at the screen labeled "Do you want to use the shared connection?" If you have already established an Internet connection, Windows presents this screen with the default selection, "Yes, use the existing shared connection for this computer's Internet access (recommended)." You may choose another Internet connection if you wish, but in all likelihood the recognized connection is the one you want. Continue with the wizard, accepting its default.

Tip

On the third screen, the wizard informs you if it has located any disconnected network hardware (usually a network adapter), as shown in Figure 4-3. If you need that hardware recognized for your LAN, stop at this point, open the Network Connections folder, and use the Properties dialog boxes to determine why Windows does not see the connection. If you do not require the connection, as in the case of a secondary LAN adapter inside your PC, click the "Ignore disconnected network hardware" checkbox and click Next to continue.

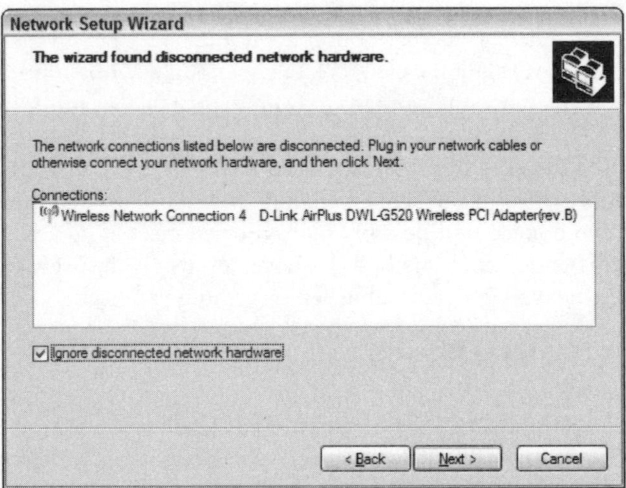

Figure 4-3: Windows has found a disconnected LAN adapter.

3. On the subsequent screen, you can name or rename the computer and give it a description. After completing the wizard, the name you choose identifies this PC in My Network Places, while the description appears as a subtitle for that name. If you have more than four or five PCs, the name and description can help you locate and access the correct one at a glance.

4. Figure 4-4 shows the "Name your network" screen. Here, as in the Network Identification Wizard, you can provide a name for your workgroup. The wizard always supplies MSHOME for its default, but you need not accept that name. Type the workgroup name you want — it will accept anything you type — and click Next.

5. The next screen lets you turn file and printer sharing on or off. If you want your network nodes to share your printer or have access to your files, turn this option on, but your stronger security choice is to leave it off. Remember that anyone gaining unauthorized access to your PC can share your files by connecting to your PC, if this option is on. That said, one of the primary reasons for creating a network is to provide a shared location for files, and to share resources such as a printer, so if that's what you want, you have no real choice.

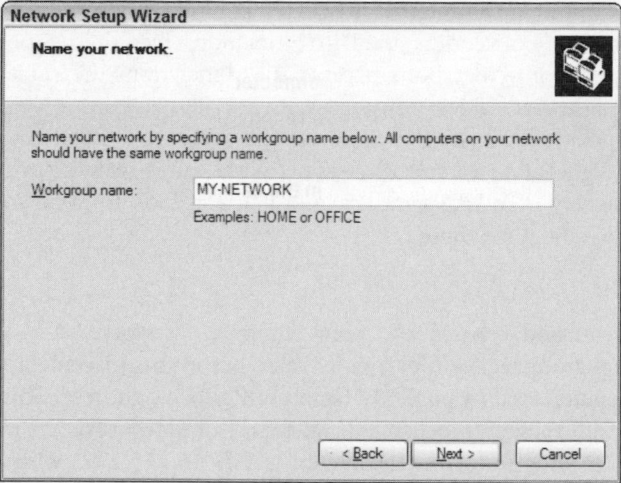

Figure 4-4: Giving your workgroup a recognizable label.

Tip

If you're concerned about sharing files but you want a shared printer, consider purchasing a print server device. These devices provide either a parallel port or a USB port for connecting a printer directly, without having it attached to one of your network PCs. The printer is available at all times to any network node, no matter which PCs are powered on or off. You can even add a wireless print server, as shown in Chapter 13.

6. With these choices made, click Next twice to complete the wizard. At this point, Windows configures your PC according to your choices, and ends with a Finish button that takes you back (without rebooting) to your desktop.

Congratulations. You have a network for your PC. Now it's time to give your computer some comrades.

Adding the Router/AP

With the network adapters in place inside the PCs designated for the wired LAN, it's time to add the single most important member of your network: the router/access point (router/AP) combination device. This invaluable piece of hardware controls both your incoming and your outgoing network traffic, from both the wired and wireless nodes, provides local addresses for all your network nodes, lets you connect your wireless nodes to the network, ensures that the incoming traffic gets to the PC that requests it, and even gives your network a firewall. In other words, it's the traffic cop, the postman, and the security guard all rolled up in one. Given the cost of these devices (often under $100), you'd be hard-pressed to find another device of any kind that so convincingly earns its keep.

For this chapter, to demonstrate setting up a router/AP, we used a D-Link DI-624 Wireless Router. Like many similar products from a variety of vendors, the DI-624 includes five Ethernet ports and a wireless access point. One of the five Ethernet ports accepts the signal from the cable or DSL modem, while the others accept Ethernet cables from any network PC containing an Ethernet (wired) LAN adapter. The access point allows any PCs with wireless adapters to share the Internet connection and simultaneously bridges the wired and wireless networks into a seamless whole. This configuration is typical of this category of WLAN product, and you can look to Microsoft, SMC, Linksys, and other vendors for much the same thing.

CONNECTING THE ROUTER

The router sits between your broadband modem and your computer network, or, if you will, between the Internet and your workgroup. Indeed, part of its value lies in this placement. To communicate with the Internet, a computer needs a public IP (Internet Protocol) address. This address takes a four-part numerical form, with each part focusing the address further towards the individual machine itself. For example, the IP address for microsoft.com is 207.46.245.222, with the final number belonging to a specific computer within a broader range of addresses.

The Internet can function because of this addressing system. But three problems emerge from the system, all of which a cable/DSL router is designed to help solve. First, every single computer connected to the Internet requires a unique public IP address, and if each computer on each network in each organization in each country of the world had its own, there wouldn't be enough addresses to go around. Second, for each of your own network PCs to have its own public address, you'd need a separate Internet connection for each. Finally, because the IP address is public, not only is the Internet visible to your machine, your machine is visible to the Internet. Intruders know this and take advantage of it.

A cable/DSL router helps solve the last of these issues by providing firewall software that intercepts incoming Internet traffic of the type typically used by hackers to break into systems. To be sure, no firewall is completely foolproof; a dedicated intruder will likely find a way in. But your router's firewall, especially when combined with an additional firewall at the operating system level, such as Windows XP's built-in firewall or a commercially available software firewall product such as Zone Alarm Pro, goes a long way to thwarting casual intruders and even some more advanced efforts.

The cable/DSL router solves the two addressing problems together, by acting as a DHCP server. As explained in Chapter 3, a DHCP server takes a single public IP address and allows a range of private IP addresses to connect through it to the Internet. The private address is typically in the range 192.168.x.x., a range reserved in Internet standards for precisely this purpose. Cable/DSL routers can provide well over 200 private addresses, so unless you have a large office (or an incredibly big house), you aren't likely to use all of them at once. Besides, if you did so, your poor old cable or DSL connection would probably start suffering a bit of lag because of all the nodes hitting on it.

To connect the router to your network, do the following:

1. Power off all PCs.
2. Power off your broadband modem.
3. Disconnect your PC's Ethernet cable from your cable/DSL modem.

4. Run a cable from the Ethernet port on your cable/DSL modem to the WAN (wide area network) port on the router. This port goes by various names, including Internet port, depending on the brand and model.
5. Run cables from the Ethernet adapter on each PC into the Ethernet ports on the router.
6. Power on your cable/DSL modem and wait a few minutes for it to negotiate communications with your Internet provider.
7. Power on your router, waiting another few minutes for it to negotiate communications with your broadband modem.
8. Power on one PC. Enter the router's administrative screens to make any necessary configuration changes.
9. Power on your remaining PCs.
10. If the PCs can't see each other, run the Network Setup Wizard on each, making sure to give them all the same workgroup name.

There. You've created the essentials for an infrastructure network. You have multiple PCs connected through a router/AP, and you have your router/AP ready to connect to the Internet and share a broadband connection among all the networked PCs. There's a good chance your PCs are already on the Internet, in fact — fire up a Web browser and find out. If not, then you need to configure the router, and we turn to that step now.

CONFIGURING THE ROUTER

In most cases, your router/AP will function just fine straight out of the box. Manufacturers configure them with the most commonly used settings, with DHCP service enabled and Dynamic addressing in place. If you connect to the Internet via cable modem, you probably won't need to reconfigure the router at all. Just turn everything on, open a browser window on one of the connected PCs, and see if you're on the Net. Then, open My Network Places and determine if all members of the workgroup can see one another. If both types of connection work, you don't even need to touch the settings.

However, in two specific cases you'll need to adjust the Internet settings of your router, while in all cases you should change the default password and check to make sure the firewall is enabled. The remainder of this section focuses on those issues, as well as providing an overview to other options available for configuration.

In the case of practically all router/APs today, you open the configuration screens in a Web browser. Read the instructions that came with your router to determine the address to type in the browser's Address or Location field. It always starts with 192.168., but vendors tend to use different address completions. Microsoft uses 192.168.2.1 for its broadband router, for example, while Linksys uses 192.168.1.1. As Figure 4-5 shows, D-Link's administrative screens open with the address 192.168.0.1.

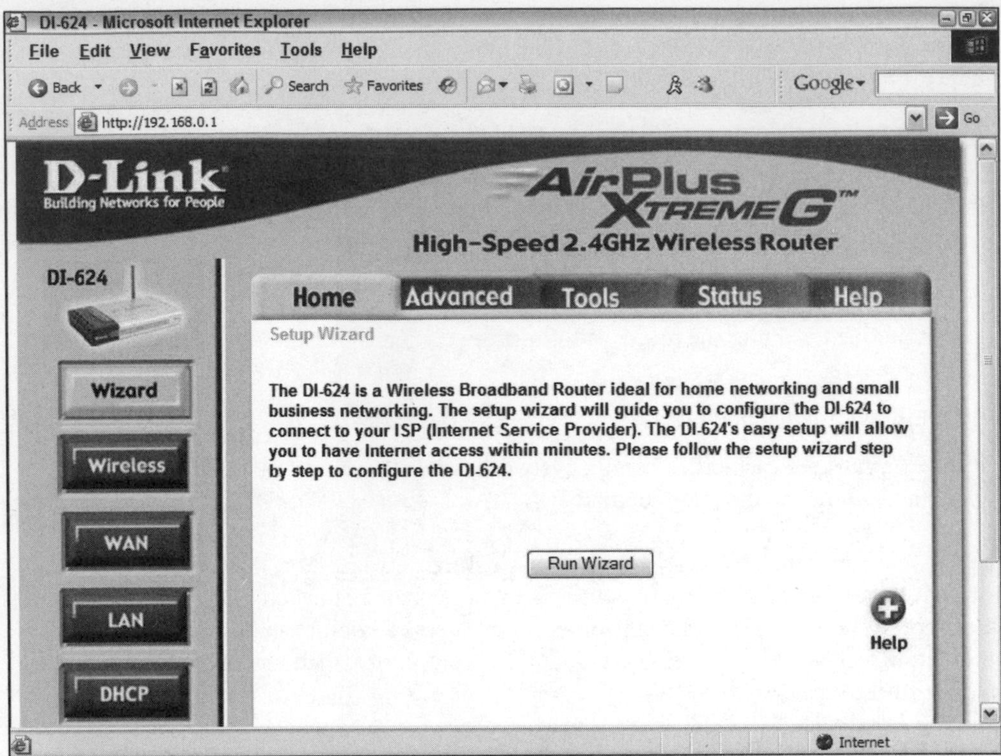

Figure 4-5: The opening screen for the DI-624's configuration utility.

This screen shows some of the numerous configuration options available. A wizard takes you through the primary settings, but you should take some time to tour around the utility to get a sense of the range of possibilities. On the D-Link screens, each tab leads to an additional set of configuration options, as shown along the left-hand side in Figure 4-6.

Figure 4-6 also shows the area you should go to first, the password change option. Out of the box, all routers tend to open with some version of the *admin* username and/or password, and even if nobody else uses your network you should change the password to prevent intruders from breaking into your PC and setting the options themselves. Change the administrator's name and password, and be sure to write them down and keep them so you can get into the utility when necessary.

Tip

If you can no longer remember the username/password combination, use the router's reset button to restore the factory settings. The reset button is typically at the back of the router and requires a pencil or similar object to press it in (to prevent accidental resets). Usually you have to hold the button in for a few seconds to get the router to respond to the reset (again, to prevent accidents).

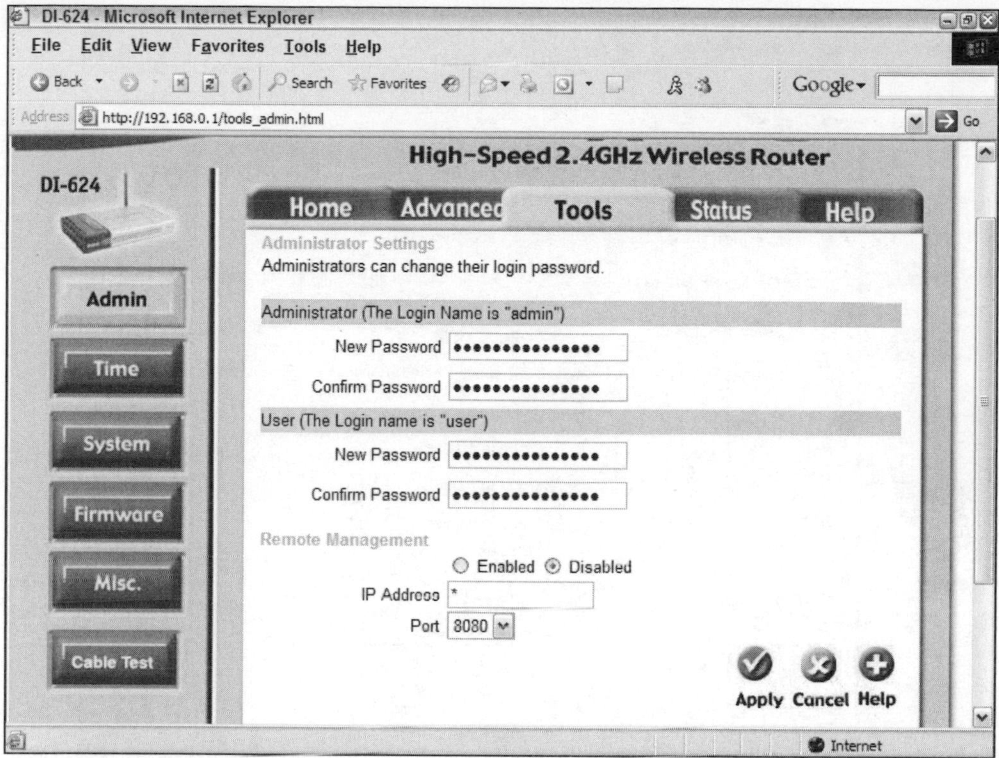

Figure 4-6: The configuration topics on D-Link's Tools tab.

If you connect to the Internet via cable modem, you probably require no further configuration. However, some cable providers require that you enter a Host Name to complete the connection. You'll typically find this setting under a screen for WAN or Internet settings, WAN in the case of the D-Link router. Figure 4-7 shows the results of clicking the WAN button on the left side of the opening screen, followed by selecting the Dynamic IP Address radio button at the top of the resulting display.

The Host Name field appears under the Dynamic IP heading, along with the computer's MAC Address. You don't need the MAC address information, but your network most certainly does; the MAC address plus the private IP address, along with the public IP address, constitutes the full network address of the PC.

If your Internet connection comes through a static IP address, as might be the case if you set up your router at your company office (in which case be sure to check with your systems administrators), click the Static IP Address radio button. The resulting screen lets you manually set the IP address, the subnet mask, the gateway address, and the two DNS server addresses, all addresses required to complete the connection to the Internet. You might also need this configuration screen if you have purchased a business account through your ISP. Some ISPs offers static IP addresses to facilitate the setup of Web servers and other servers, for which public access depends on an unchanging IP number.

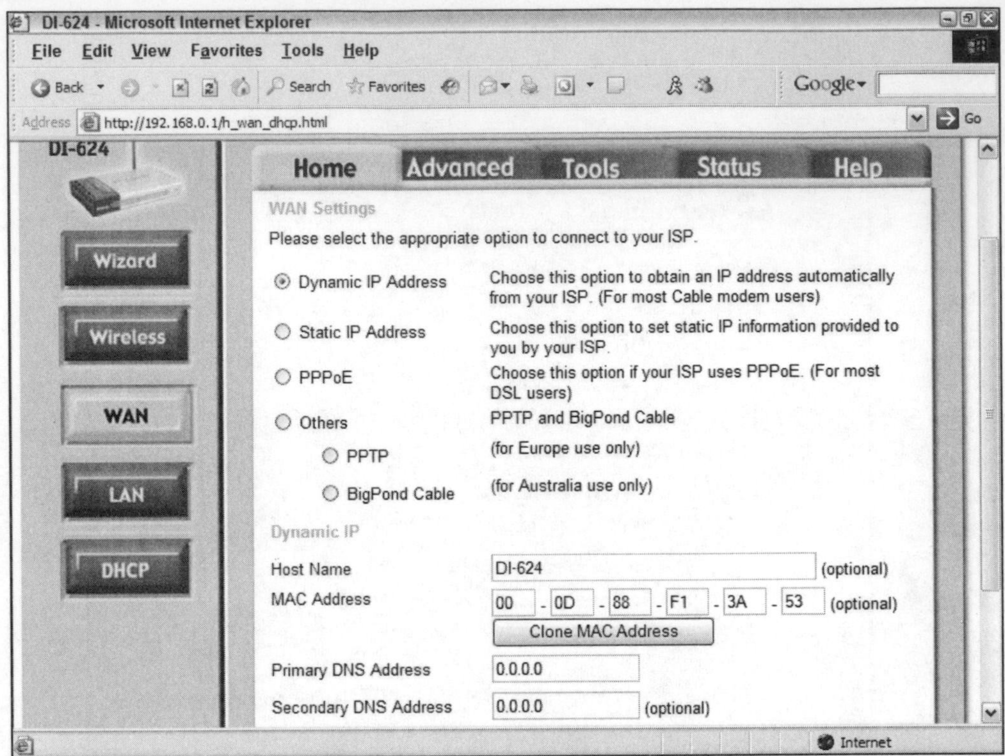

Figure 4-7: The Dynamic IP Address configuration screen.

The most extensive change most home or small office users need to make occurs in the case of DSL Internet access. If you have a DSL connection, you also have a username and password required to dial in to the provider. In fact, if you've been connecting through a single PC, you already have this information stored to allow you to connect on demand. But because your PC no longer connects directly, you have to tell the router how to log on. To do so, click the PPPoE option, as shown in Figure 4-8.

PPPoE stands for Point-to-Point Protocol over Ethernet. When you connected to the Internet through your older dial-up modem, in all probability you did so through a PPP connection, or Point-to-Point Protocol. PPPoE is simply an extension of PPP, using the higher speed of Ethernet in conjunction with the higher speed of DSL telephony to give you broadband speeds. Hence the name PPPoE, and the need to configure it for connection to your DSL provider.

Once you've made your changes, save them for the router to use them. You might have to reboot your PC to make use of the changes, but typically you do not. Wait for a minute or so while the router reconfigures itself, and then try to connect to the Internet with your new settings. If it works, you're done. If it does not, check the username and password for your PPPoE setting (DSL providers tend to make passwords pretty obscure and hard to type), and see if that makes the change you need.

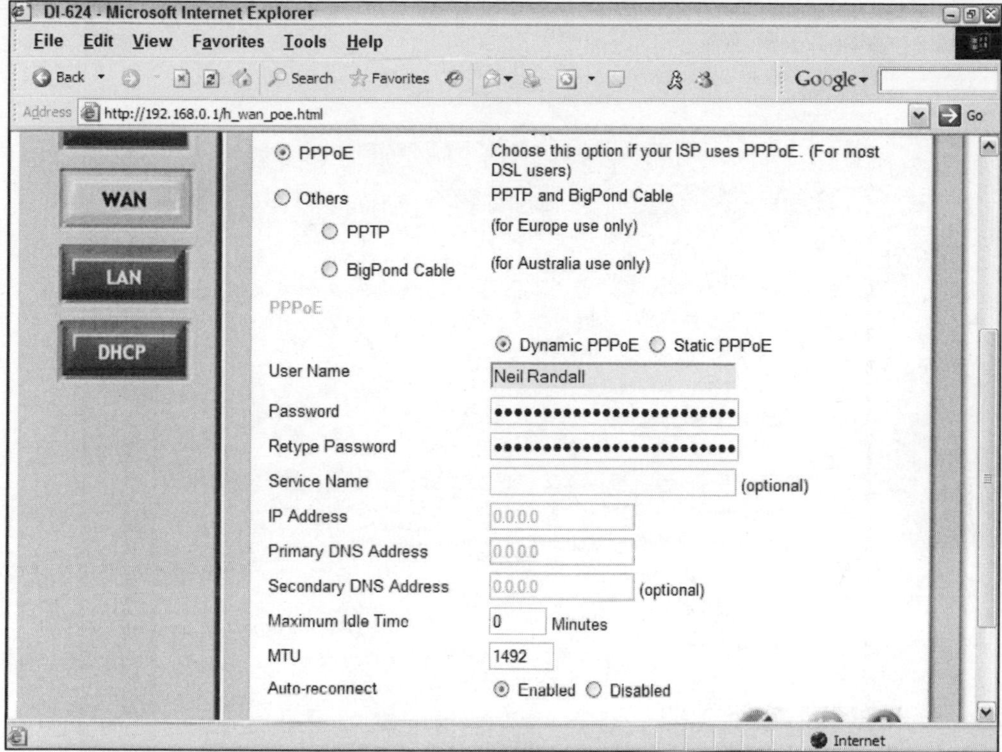

Figure 4-8: Configuring a DSL connection.

With everything in place, check your router's status. Sometimes this option is called Connection, but usually you'll find it by clicking Status. The D-Link router used for this example features the Status screen shown in Figure 4-9. At the top is the LAN information, including the private IP address of the router and the MAC address it provides to the Internet, along with a statement about whether or not the DHCP service is running. Under the WAN heading you can see the MAC Address of the PC on which the browser is running, along with the public IP address through which the router is connected to the Internet, and the gateway and DNS server addresses.

Tip

If you find yourself unable to get a functioning Web page or e-mail connection, check the PPPoE status screen to see if your modem is connected. If not, press the Connect button to connect it manually.

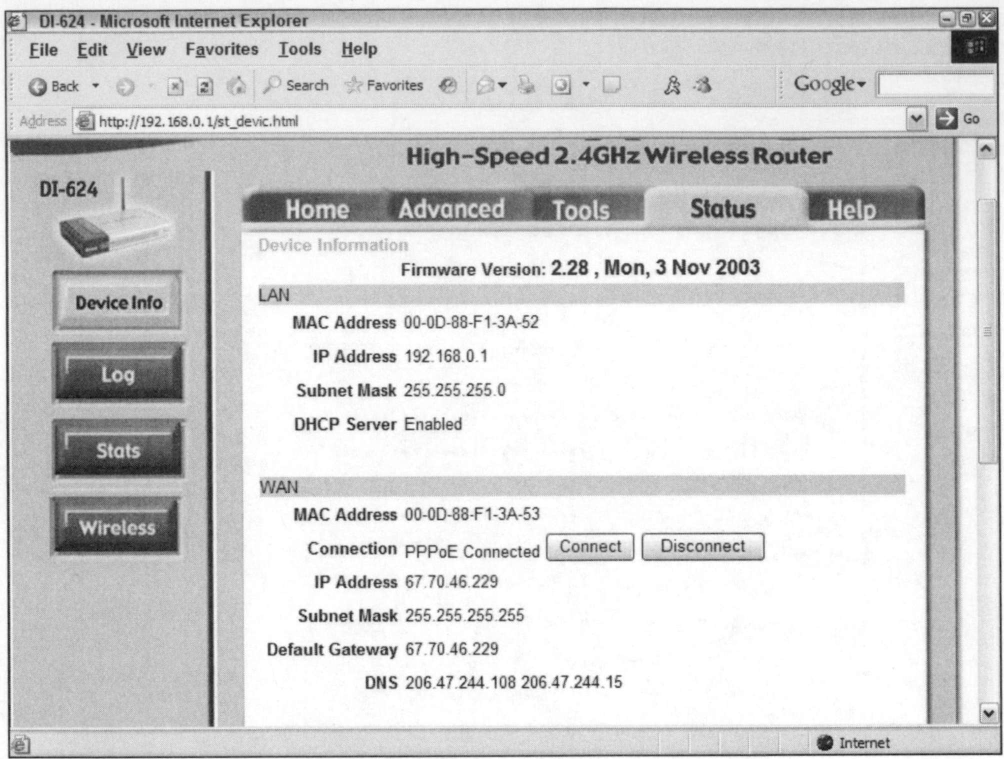

Figure 4-9: The connection details of the D-Link router.

A wide range of additional items is available through the configuration screens. On the D-Link screens, the Misc button under the Tools tab lets you reboot the router, perform a Ping test to make sure the router is connected to the Internet, block Ping requests from outside (to prevent intruders knowing about your machine), and enabling Universal Plug 'n Play as well as a special feature called *gaming mode* (which allows networked PCs to connect to each other through the firewall). The Firmware button lets you check the D-Link site for a firmware update to the router, downloading and installing it if available (all manufacturers provide firmware updates periodically). You also can configure firewall rules, traffic filters, and application behavior, all of which reach far beyond the scope of this book. Suffice it to say that any router/AP you purchase today will provide any number of configuration options, and that you're unlikely ever to need most of them for daily network use. But if you do need them, rest assured you'll find them among these screens.

Add a Wireless LAN

With the wired network set up and the router/AP configured, it's time to complete the infrastructure network by adding a wireless LAN. The process begins in a manner similar to the ad hoc network setup described in Chapter 3, with the installation of the wireless LAN adapters in each of the PCs you wish to connect to the wireless network. The primarily difference lies with the addition of the access point, and the remainder of this chapter focuses on configuring and using the access point to allow the infrastructure network to come into play.

The beauty of an access point is the degree of flexibility it gives you in adding nodes to the network. On a wired Ethernet network, you can add only as many PCs as you have available ports on the router/switch device, or alternatively you can add additional switches to extend the network. With an access point, you can simply keep adding additional nodes, configuring each one to connect to the access point to send and receive network traffic and connect to the Internet. If you configure your access point to broadcast its SSID, anyone in range of the AP can connect to the infrastructure network as long as you provide them with the necessary WEP or WPA encryption settings. If you leave your AP unencrypted, any PC within range that can see the AP can connect to it. This is the most unsecure way to configure a network, but it is also the primary configuration for home or small office infrastructure networks. As discussed in Chapter 1, such a setup allows intrusion from anyone passing nearby.

That said, this chapter takes you through the process of configuring an infrastructure network without getting into encryption technologies at all. Part II of this book covers encryption in detail, so for the time being, the goal is to have a functioning infrastructure LAN, with wired and wireless nodes communicating with each other freely and easily. We'll add security in a short while.

Configuring the Access Point

This chapter assumes that you have a combined router/access point device, of the type available from a number of hardware vendors and on the shelves of any computer store. Typically, such a device features an Ethernet port that connects to the broadband modem, four additional ports for connecting up to four nodes with Ethernet cable, and an access point built into the device with one or more antennae for effectively transmitting and receiving radio signals. As with the rest of this chapter, the demonstration device here is the D-Link DI-624, but you can buy similar devices from vendors such as Linksys, SMC, USR, Microsoft, and more.

Note

You can also get access points without the combined router/switch. These units provide an Ethernet port for the cable or DSL modem, and often a USB port to connect to a PC in order to configure it so that the WLAN adapters can connect. The principle is the same, but obviously such a device assumes a wireless LAN only, unless you connect it to another router via Ethernet cable and after that to the WLAN adapters.

To configure the access point in the DI-624 requires a visit to two configuration locations: the Wireless Settings screen and the Wireless Performance screen. You can reach the Wireless Settings screen by clicking the Wireless button under the Home tab, which takes you to a screen that looks like that shown in Figure 4-10.

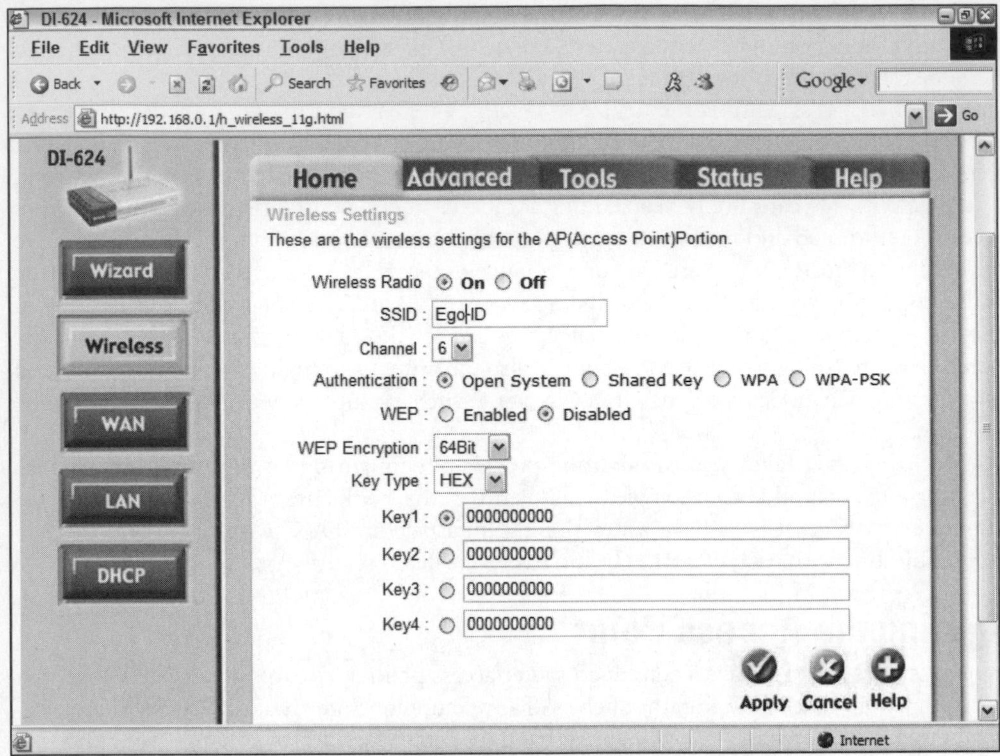

Figure 4-10: D-Link's Wireless Settings options.

The Wireless Radio option simply lets you turn the access point on or off (something that isn't even mentioned in D-Link's less-than-optimal Help system). The most important settings on the screen are the SSID field and the authentication/encryption areas. The D-Link router ships with an SSID called "default", and your first task is to change this name so that anyone trying to break into the AP won't have quite as easy a task. Give it a name you'll remember, but make it yours. The channel information is less important, although do jot it down so that you'll remember it should anyone be unable to connect. All WLANs on the network must be set to the same channel.

The remainder of this screen deals with authentication and encryption settings. Part II treats these topics in detail, so we won't work through these settings here. In fact, when you're first configuring your WLAN, leave authentication open and encryption disabled; any problems you might have with connectivity become even more complex with these mechanisms in place. Get the WLAN working first, and then come back and make it secure.

One of the single most important security decisions you can make is to prevent the AP from broadcasting the SSID. SSID broadcasts allow any PC with a network card to see the network and, especially with the wireless support built into Windows XP, connect automatically to it. For reasons of ease of use, manufacturers tend to ship their access points with SSID Broadcasting enabled, reasoning that many of these devices will be used in homes and small offices, where instant, transparent access solves problems. However, if you're sitting in your family room some evening and just happen to discover that you can connect to the wireless LANs run by your neighbors to the left and right, with full access to their Shared Folders, you quickly realize that SSID broadcasting is a bad idea if you have any desire for privacy.

You might have to search the configuration screens to figure out how to disable SSID broadcasting. On the DI-624, to cite one example, you need to click the Advanced tab and then, on the left-hand side, the Performance button, yielding the screen shown in Figure 4-11. Four lines from the bottom, the option appears. Click the Disabled radio button, click Apply, and your SSID is no longer broadcast.

Your access point is ready to go. At this point, it's time to tell the wireless LAN adapters how to connect to it.

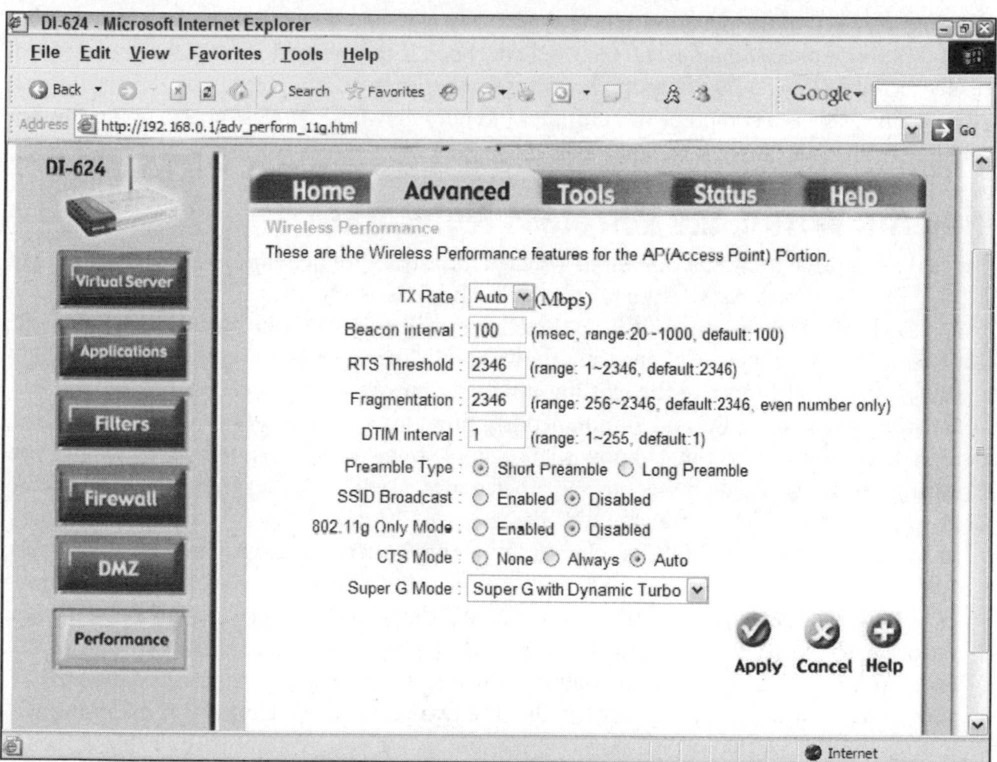

Figure 4-11: The Wireless Performance screen on the D-Link router/AP.

Configuring the WLAN Adapters

Setting up your WLAN adapters to see your network is no different through an access point than for the ad hoc networks discussed in Chapter 3. If you're using an older version of Windows than Windows XP, open the configuration utility provided by the manufacturer of your WLAN adapter and set the SSID and the channel to match the settings of the AP. If you're using Windows XP, right-click the icon for the WLAN Adapter and choose View Available Wireless Networks.

The resulting Wireless Network Connection dialog box lists the wireless networks available and lets you connect to them by clicking the network name and then the Connect button. Windows XP automatically safeguards you from connecting to an unsecured WLAN — one for which authentication and/or encryption settings are not in place — by first forcing you to click a checkbox labeled "Allow me to connect to the selected wireless network, even though it is not secure." When you do so, the Connect button becomes available, and you can join the network.

If Windows XP does not see the network, of if another one is available for use, you can add it to the list of networks via the Wireless Networks tab of the Wireless Network Connection dialog box. Click Add, type the SSID of the network, and click OK. You can then select this network from the list and connect to it, once again filling in the required checkbox if the network is unsecured. Windows automatically recognizes the network as infrastructure rather than ad hoc, removing the checkmark from the statement "This is a computer-to-computer (ad hoc) network; wireless access points are not used," a statement that appeared in the examples in Chapter 3.

Bridging the Wired and Wireless Networks

Everything is now in place to finish your wired-wireless infrastructure network. All that remains is to bridge them, a process Windows XP does for you through its Network Setup Wizard.

Run the wizard from Control Panel or from the Network Tasks area of the Network Connections folder, from each PC on the network, ensuring that you give the same Workgroup name to all PCs and that you tell the wizard to share the existing Internet connection. This process bridges the network connections on the local PC and simultaneously provides a bridge between the wireless and wired components of your LAN. You can now share a single Internet connection and, as long as you have file sharing set up, you can connect to the other nodes at will, whether they are connected to the network via Ethernet cable or wireless LAN adapter.

Note that Windows Millennium Edition offers a similar network configuration process, but earlier versions of Windows, such as Windows 2000 and Windows 98 (and Windows 98 Second Edition) do not. In many cases, PCs running older versions of Windows will connect to your network just fine, but if not, you'll need to configure their network settings using the Networking utility in Control Panel. Although we make the assumption in this book that you're using Windows XP, primarily because virtually all computers sold in the past two years have included this operating system, configuring Windows 2000 or Windows 98 computers for your WLAN isn't all that difficult. Open the Networking utility and launch the Properties dialog for the TCP/IP protocol. In that dialog box, make sure that all options are configured to automatic rather than manual settings. For example, tell Networking to acquire an Internet address (IP number) automatically from a DHCP server, and to acquire DNS connections automatically as well.

When you first create such a network, the effect seems nothing short of magical, but of course after a few file transfers, network communications sessions, and the odd network game, it all

becomes old hat. But you have, in fact, merged two networking technologies that not long ago would have seemed too disparate to combine at all, and without an overwhelming degree of effort. All in all, not bad.

Summary

You now have a fully functioning, sophisticated wireless network completely in place. You have multiple PCs all connecting either via wireless network adapters through an access point, or via standard Ethernet cable to a router, with all PCs sharing a single broadband Internet connection and taking advantage of any built-in security software — in the form of a firewall — that might be enabled by default inside your router/AP. You can now use your wireless PCs (and other wireless devices) anywhere within range of your access point, sharing resources among them.

In fact, you have the basis here for as large a network as you need. Your AP enables you to connect hundreds of devices, and you can add additional APs to extend the range of your WLAN. You can add additional switches to handle more wired PCs as well, with all wired and wireless machines bridged to the same network for the sake of resource sharing. These expandability is an extremely useful feature for anyone building a WLAN in an office setting, but even a home network can grow as you add notebooks, PDAs, game consoles, and wireless media players. The point is that, with an infrastructure network in place, the sky's the limit.

Next up: making use of the network you've just put in place.

Chapter 5

Using Your Wireless Network

The preliminaries are out of the way. You've created both an ad hoc and an infrastructure network, you've configured your router and your access point, and you're ready to move to the next stage. Well, the next stage is actually using what you've put in place. This chapter is all about using your new infrastructure network as a network, and in that sense the instructions here cover not just wireless network procedures, but network procedures in general. We have designed this chapter for those new to setting up, configuring, and wringing the full potential from a functioning network, no matter how small that network may be. If you are already familiar with networks and their workings, we encourage you to skip to Chapter 6 and begin to examine wireless security. We can't promise that you won't miss something—this chapter does cover some wireless specifics—but the choice is yours.

Computer networking is all about sharing resources. With your wired-wireless infrastructure network, not only can you share a single Internet connection among several PCs, you can share printers, scanners, hard drives, and other devices you use every day. If the network is sophisticated enough, you can even share applications. The result can be a significant savings in the cost of computer hardware and software, especially hardware, to the degree that the equipment you need to buy to build the network in the first place quickly pays for itself.

Computer networking is also all about security. On a network, you can create users and accounts, and you can restrict these accounts to specific functions. Not everyone needs access to everything, and in many cases you don't want anyone other than a single administrator, or perhaps two, to be able to perform specific tasks. Of course, nothing is more secure than a standalone PC connected to nothing at all, including the Internet, but such a configuration is growing increasingly rare (good thing, too, or this book wouldn't have much of a shelf life). Running a network today, even a two-PC home network with a shared Internet connection, requires at least some knowledge of network security. Otherwise, you run the risk of viruses, stolen data, and worse.

The Simple Network: Sharing Files and Printers

Most two- or three-node networks have simple needs. They share an Internet connection and possibly a printer, and they have access to a set of shared folders for easy transfer of files among them. Windows XP sets up such a network straight out of the box. As soon as you install the networking components during Windows setup, you create a Shared Documents folder specifically designed for availability to all network users. When you install Windows XP, you also create one or, typically, two or three user accounts. Every Windows XP installation includes an Administrator account, established early in Setup, and towards the end of the Setup process you can set up five additional accounts, before you fully launch Windows itself (at which point you can create many more). Each account contains a set of folders unique to that account, all of which are shareable across the network. Later in this chapter we outline the uses of user accounts; for now the point is that they exist, and they can share specific resources according to the specific needs of each user.

Figure 5-1 shows the My Network Places folder for a computer with several available shared resources. This folder has two parts: Local Network and The Internet. Folders in The Internet area refer to Web sites and FTP sites to which this PC has connected for the sake of downloading or editing Web sites. In this case the addresses appear courtesy of Microsoft FrontPage, which counts each edited Web site as a Network Place. Although these folders are most certainly valid for listing here, the folders in the Local Network area are commonly considered shared network folders in the more standard sense of the term. In this area you see all available shared folders. In this case, two of those folders are actually on different PCs. Those listed as belonging to ICS Host are in fact located on the PC where we took the screenshot; Windows considers those folders as network folders, even though they reside on this PC, because they are simultaneously local resources and local network resources. Understanding this feature becomes crucial when understanding how Windows creates and configures networks. To Windows, unless otherwise stated, everything belongs to the network.

A much less populated network folder appears in Figure 5-2. Here, the only two network locations available to the PC are itself and a desktop PC called ICS Host. In this particular case, the PC belongs to a network of only two nodes. Only the local folders are available at all; the second PC is visible on the network but has no shared folders.

The two situations shown in Figures 5-1 and 5-2 demonstrate Windows XP's ability to restrict network access to specific PCs. This feature becomes increasingly important as your network grows. If you don't configure the restrictions, you can end up with lost files and other problems, often innocently caused by users trying to manipulate files without realizing their shared status. This chapter is concerned in part with creating these restrictions to make the network behave precisely as you need it to, but also with ensuring that each user has access to precisely the necessary resources.

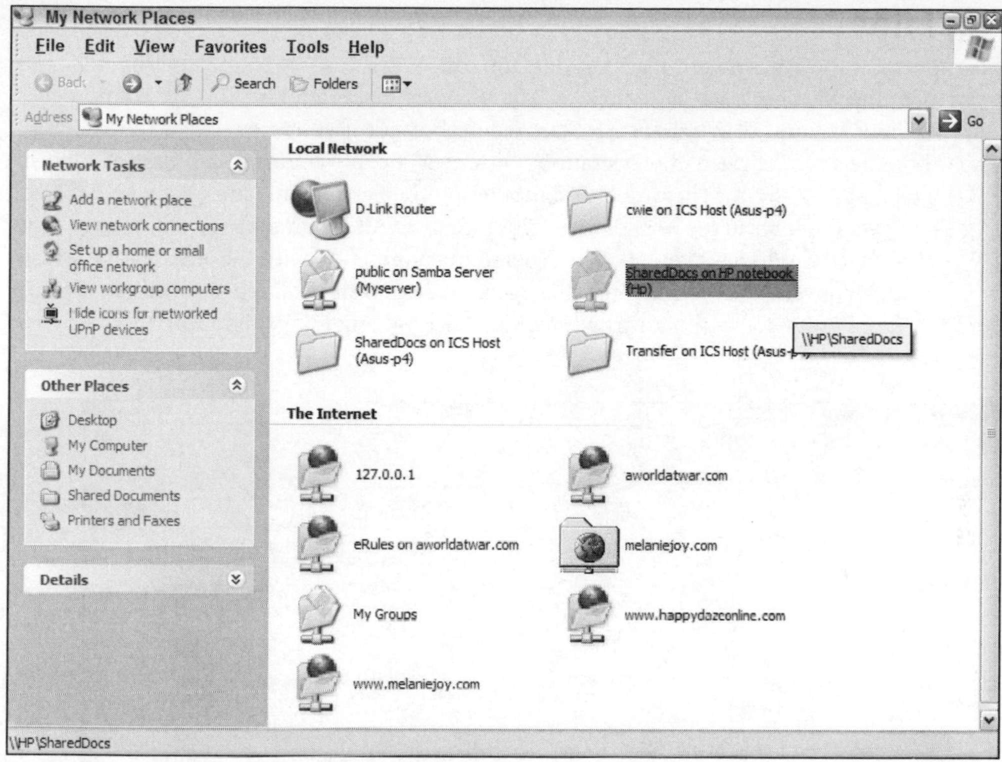

Figure 5-1: A crowded My Network Places folder.

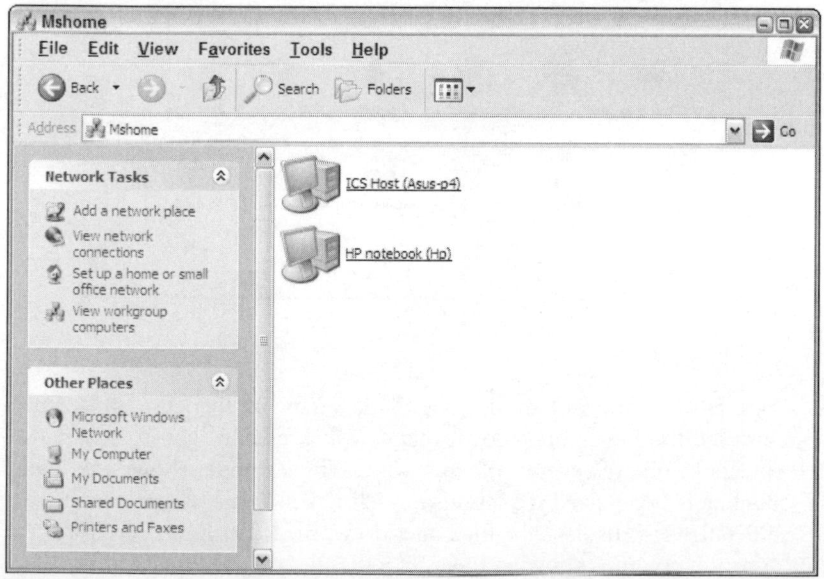

Figure 5-2: A typically sparse My Network Places folder on a newly added machine.

Sharing Files

Shared files appear in the My Network Places folder. You can access this folder directly from the Start menu, or by opening My Computer and clicking My Network Places on the left (My Computer is available in the right column of Windows XP Start menu, but not if you've switched to the classic Start menu). For the most efficient file operations, however, open Windows Explorer, shown in Figure 5-3, by clicking Start, right-clicking My Computer on the Start menu, and choosing Explore; by clicking Windows Explorer in the Accessories folder (Start → All Programs → Accessories); or by pressing Windows+E (the Windows key on the keyboard in conjunction with the letter E). Windows Explorer gives you a convenient two-panel file management system from which you can manipulate files and folders in any way you wish: copying, moving, deleting, renaming, and more.

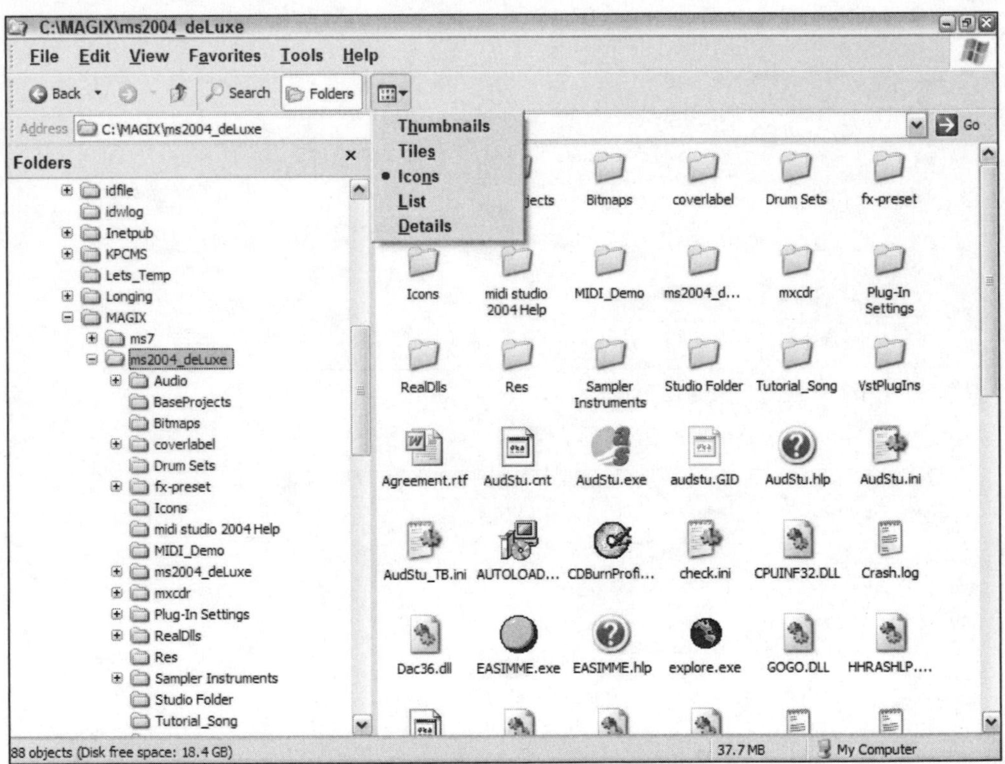

Figure 5-3: The Windows Explorer File view.

Figure 5-3 shows the two panes of Windows Explorer, the Folders pane on the left and the Files pane on the right. You can also see the Views drop-down menu, which enables you to adjust the Files pane to display the contents in one of several different ways. This example shows the Icons view, but you can choose Thumbnails (icon-sized reductions of picture files), Tiles (large icons), List (small icons), or Details. The Details view displays the filenames down the left column, along with a small icon for each, and information columns showing the size of the file, the file type, and the date last modified. By right-clicking the headings row, you can add or delete information columns until you have the Details view customized to your tastes.

Of course, any folder view in Windows offers the same multiple Views options, so this by itself offers no reason to open Windows Explorer in particular. Having the two side-by-side panes, however, does. Unless you establish a practice in which you want users to work directly from shared folders, opening and saving their documents to these folders, users will want to transfer the files they need to their own PCs, work with them, and transfer them back to the shared folder. They could open two separate folders and drag files from one to the other, but using the two panes of Windows Explorer speeds up the process and offers better control overall. Furthermore, and despite Microsoft's seeming insistence to the contrary, using the two panes for transfer among folders is far more intuitive than using standard single-pane folders.

All of which raises the question of how to share a folder in the first place. It's simple, actually. Just open either Windows Explorer or My Computer, navigate to the folder you wish to share, right-click the folder name, and choose Sharing and Security from the pop-up menu. Alternatively, choose Properties from the menu and then click the Sharing tab on the dialog box that appears. Next, click the "Share this folder" checkbox. Figure 5-4 shows the dialog box after clicking the checkbox for sharing the folder on the network. Windows fills in the Share Name field with the existing name of the folder, but you can rename it to make its function more apparent to anyone who locates the folder for use.

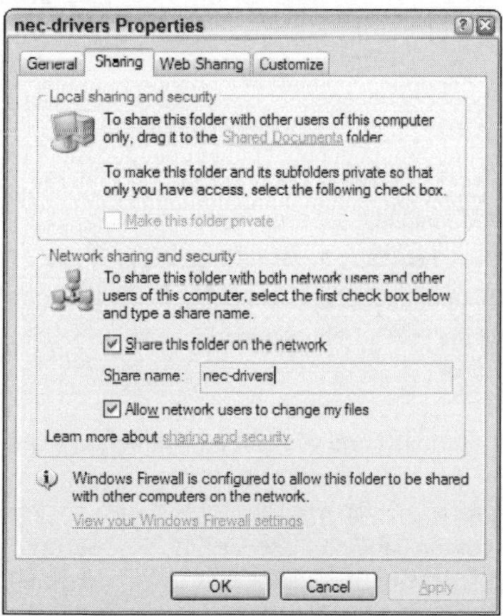

Figure 5-4: Sharing a folder.

Several other points of interest appear on this dialog box. First, users accessing the folder from the network cannot alter any of the files, unless you click the checkbox allowing them to do so ("Allow users to change my files"). Don't confuse this feature with actual security, though. Although users

can't change the files, they can copy them without restriction. Think of this feature as a safeguard against important files being edited, and you have the right perspective.

At the top of the dialog box you can see the settings for local sharing and security. The dialog box instructs you to share the folder by dragging it into the Shared Documents folder, which of course is already available to all users, so the instruction seems rather redundant. What makes Local Sharing and Security interesting is the box labeled, "Make this folder private," a powerful feature that you'll frequently find grayed out, as it is in this figure. Each user can make a folder private only if it's located inside that user's specific file structure, within Windows XP's Documents and Settings folder. In the Documents and Settings folder (located on the same drive as Windows XP) exists a set of subfolders under each user's parent folder (which bears each user's username), and only those folders are available for privatizing.

Functionally, this feature means that anyone can block access to his specific Documents and Settings folder, and its subfolders, by making his files private and password protecting his account. Furthermore, even though the dialog box does not say so, nobody on the network can access that folder either.

The difference between the two sections of the dialog box is this: Except for folders made private (and only those within your account name in the Documents and Settings folder can be private), anyone logging on to a specific PC can access all folders on that PC. By contrast, to allow people on the *network* to access a folder, no matter where it resides, you have to share it using the Network Sharing and Security section of the dialog box. The upshot of this is that a folder made private is available to no one at all, whether on the network or on that PC, and is thus the most effective privacy setting of all. Denying access, of course, is the other side of sharing.

Note

Even a user with a Limited account type in Windows XP can block access to the user-specific folders through the "Make this folder private" option. Neither other Limited accounts nor even Administrator types can get into that user's folders. Administrators can circumvent the restriction by taking ownership of the folders, but doing so is a relatively difficult process and requires access to standard file sharing, available by unchecking the option "Use simple file sharing" on the View tab of the Folder Options menu.

Windows XP actually offers two file sharing interfaces, Standard and Simplified. By default, the operating system uses Simple File Sharing, but you can switch to the more powerful Standard system by opening the Folder Properties dialog box (from Control Panel or via the Tools menu in My Computer), choosing the View tab, and unchecking the option labeled "Use simple file sharing." Figure 5-5 shows the Sharing tab on Windows XP's alternative Properties dialog box, which appears when Simple File Sharing is toggled off. The Standard file sharing options aren't quite as easy to use, but they do offer a significantly greater range of options. Here a folder named ASUS-files is being shared with the network, and a description of the folder has been typed into the Comment field. Oddly enough, this comment doesn't do anything for anyone else on the network; you would think it would appear in the My Network Places folder on all other machines, to help people know what the folder contains, but no such luck. Apparently, it exists solely for the benefit of the sharer of the file, surely the person who needs the comment least.

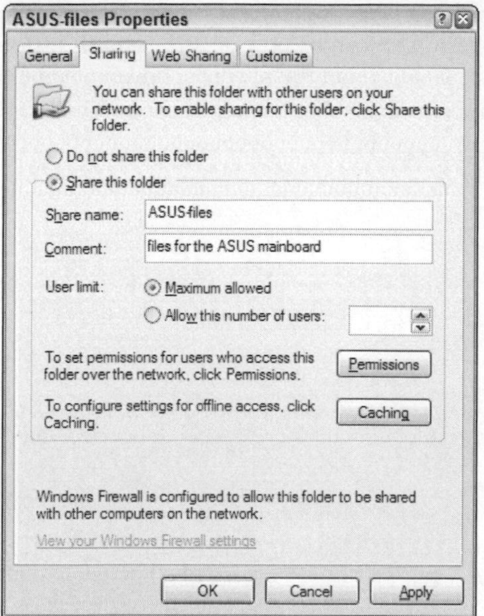

Figure 5-5: The standard file sharing dialog box.

The primary difference between this Properties dialog box and that for simple file sharing is the ability to control access by user. We cover this feature later in this chapter, under the heading "The Standard Network: Users, Groups, and Permissions."

Other options, also visible in Figure 5-5, enable you to restrict the number of users who can get access to that folder at any given time, and also let you configure the way the folder works for users using Windows' offline access feature. To restrict the number of users, click the "Allow this number of users" radio button and use the arrow keys to choose the number you want (or type it in). Configuring caching settings is well beyond the scope of this book, but in effect enables you to determine whether or not you will allow the users on your network to store local copies of files they retrieve from shared folders. The benefit of caching is speed of access each time the user loads the file; the disadvantages, as you've no doubt guessed, are lessened security and possible confusion. Not only do you suddenly have a shared file on another PC, an obvious security risk, you also have users potentially working with outdated versions of important files.

As soon as you click OK to enable the sharing of a folder, its icon appears in the My Network Places folder of all PCs connected to the workgroup.

Sharing a Printer

Most small networks consider printer sharing even more important than file sharing. Indeed, for a home network or a small office network, sharing a printer can save a considerable amount of money, especially when more than one user requires more than one kind of printer. Even on a home network of three PCs, with each person needing color inkjet printouts for some purposes and black and white laser printouts for others, being able to let all users print on both printers without the need for moving the printers or transferring the files becomes, at the very least, a major convenience.

To share a printer, open the Printers and Faxes folder from the Start Menu or Control Panel. Highlight the printer you wish to share, and click the Share this Printer link on the Printer Tasks menu. You can also right-click the printer's icon and choose Sharing. On the resulting Properties dialog box (shown in Figure 5-6), select the radio button labeled "Share this printer" and, if Windows does not supply an easily recognizable name, edit the Share Name field.

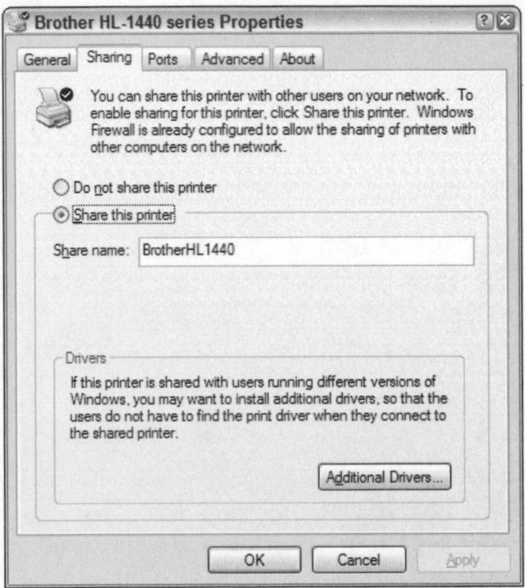

Figure 5-6: The sharing dialog box for printers.

After clicking OK, the printer becomes available to anyone on the workgroup. Before you click, however, determine if any workgroup PCs are running an earlier version of Windows, such as Windows 98, Me, or 2000. If so, you can install drivers for that operating system on the printer host PC (the one to which the shared printer is physically connected), so that users attempting to print from their PCs do not encounter a "driver not found" error, and instead download the drivers from the host automatically. This option, as seen in Figure 5-7, can prove extremely useful on small office networks with mixed operating systems, a fairly typical scenario. You get to this dialog box by clicking the Additional Drivers button on the Sharing tab; you can see this button in Figure 5-6.

Choose the operating systems that has the printer driver you wish to make available and click OK. Windows prompts you for the location of the driver and, once you have located it, installs it on your PC.

Tip

It would have been a nice touch for the Additional Printers dialog box to tell you in advance that you'd need the actual driver for this operation — the instructions imply that you simply need to choose the OS and click OK. Before accessing the dialog box, visit the printer manufacturer's Web site and download the drivers you need, saving them to a folder you can easily locate when you access this feature.

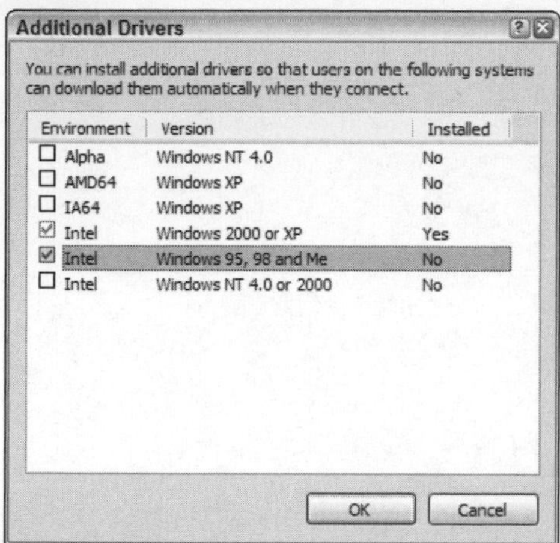

Figure 5-7: Installing printer drivers for other Windows versions.

Sharing the printer does not automatically make it available to the workgroup users; they still have to install the printer on their systems on their PCs via the Add Printer Wizard. To do so, access a network PC and open the Printers and Faxes folder. Click Add a Printer and click the radio button labeled "A network printer, or a printer attached to another computer." Clicking Next takes you to the Specify a Printer screen, on which you have three choices: browse for a printer, type the name of a printer on the network, or type the URL of a printer connected to the Internet or your local intranet. For small networks, browsing works perfectly fine, so select it and click Next.

On the resulting Browse for Printer screen (see Figure 5-8), choose the appropriate printer and click Next. Windows warns you about the security dangers of downloading drivers, and when you click Yes, locates the driver for that printer, either on its own hard drives or the network (assuming you've made the driver available through the printer sharing process outlined above). After installing the driver, the printer is ready for use from the network PC.

Tip

To get the most consistent and usable printer sharing, invest in either a network printer or a print server. A network printer contains its own Ethernet adapter, and you connect it to your router as you would any other PC. A print server works essentially the same way, providing a network adapter for printers that do not already have one (which is the case for most printers). In both instances, the printer takes on a network name of its own, and you can use it from any PC on the network at any time. With PC-based printer sharing, by contrast, workgroup users can print only if the PC to which you have connected the printer is powered on. Chapter 13 covers wireless print servers, but you can purchase wired versions even more readily, often as part of a router/access point combination.

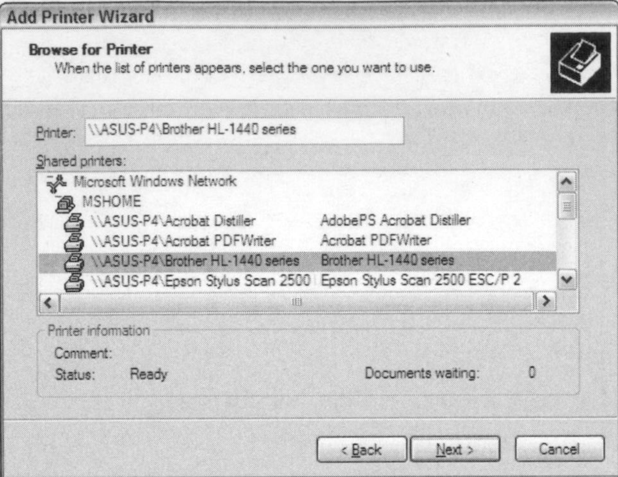

Figure 5-8: Browsing the network for a printer.

The Standard Network: Users, Groups, and Permissions

Windows XP offers three fundamental types of resource sharing on networks: simple, standard, and advanced. These aren't official names for the three types, except in the case of Simple File Sharing. But we use the terms here because they work well enough for distinguishing among the possibilities for networking in the Windows XP environment. Indeed, working with Windows XP networks requires a solid understanding of all three.

While certainly not set in stone, and without denying that this categorization offers its own over-simplification, here are the distinctions among the three:

- **Simple Networking**—Uses the Simple File Sharing option in Windows XP, available via the View tab on the Folder Options dialog box. This option lets you share files and folders among the members of the workgroup, without specifying precisely which users can access which resources, and it also lets each user make their user-specific folders private, and therefore inaccessible to all other users. Simple networking also includes the use of the User Accounts applet on the Control Panel for creating accounts, as opposed to the user and group dialog boxes in Administrative Tools.
- **Standard Networking**— Turns off Simple File Sharing, permitting a more precise determination of who gets to access specific resources. To make this distinction possible, it also includes (usually) the users and groups in the networking decisions. Simple networking

also includes users and groups, but the network administrator doesn't really need to do anything special to incorporate their use. With standard networking, resource sharing becomes much more specific, and therefore the tools with which to accomplish that sharing also need more specificity. In addition, in standard networking, users and groups are typically created via the Administrative Tools group instead of the User Accounts applet in Control Panel.

- **Advanced Networking**—Includes the use of domains. Domains offer network administrators extensive control over resources and their users and groups, and allow for networking activities well beyond the ability of workgroup networking. This book does not cover domain networking, except to note that wireless networking is as much a part of domain networking as it is of workgroup networking. If you want to explore the world of domains, check out *Windows Server 2003 Bible*, also from Wiley.

In this section, we introduce the elements of Windows XP standard networking that you can use to your benefit in setting up an infrastructure network. Once again, the focus lies with the sharing of resources, specifically files and folders. Printers share in much the same way as with simple networking, so there's no new ground to cover in that regard. Primarily, this section covers how to specify user-level and group-level access to network resources, and for that reason it begins with a look at users and groups themselves.

Setting up Users and Groups

You can create users through the User Accounts applet in Control Panel, but for full control over users, and to create groups of users, you must use the Computer Management console in Administrative Tools. Open Control Panel, double-click the Administrative Tools icon, and launch the Computer Management console. Expand the Local Users and Groups item in the left pane on of the console and click users to reveal the list of users already on your PC.

Note

If your PC is already part of a network maintained by a professional systems administrator or IT staff, you might not have access to the Local Users and Groups item (and possibly not any Administrative Tools applets). Assuming you do have this access, however, the Computer Management console shows a list of user accounts well beyond the number of accounts you see on the Welcome screen when you launch Windows. Primarily, the extra accounts represent system accounts, necessary for specific functions but not designed as user accounts in the way you normally think of them. For example, the HelpAssistant account exists to enable Remote Assistance procedures on the PC, and the IWAM_ account functions only in conjunction with the Internet Information Services Web server. One account you will find here is Administrator, the account created when you installed Windows.

Figure 5-9 shows the result of right-clicking a user account and choosing Properties. The Properties dialog contains three tabs, each of which performs a specific and important function:

- **General.** On the General tab you can provide the full name of the user if you have an abbreviated or nickname-like username. You can also provide a description of the user, to help other users identify that person. Most importantly, you can specify how you want Windows to handle the password. You can configure it so that it never expires or for mandatory change at next logon. You can also disable or lock out the user from here.
- **Member Of.** At first glance, this tab offers very little information. In fact, only the user groups to which this user account belongs show on the screen. Clicking the Add button demonstrates its usefulness, however, revealing (once you've clicked the Advanced button) the Select Groups dialog box. Click the Find Now button to reveal the list of groups to which you can assign this user (see Figure 5-10).
- **Profile.** For the most part, you won't need to use the Profile screen, but it can be useful for a variety of purposes. The User Profile fields let you specify a script to activate when the user logs on to the network, with scripts launching programs, setting defaults, and in any other way you wish configuring the PC to that user. The Home Folder fields let you define the folder that the user automatically enters when joining the network, as well as a network drive location if applicable. This book deals with none of these possibilities, and in fact these options tend to be reserved for more advanced networking management. Some also apply more readily to older versions of Windows, in which workgroup networking required different kinds of network configurations.

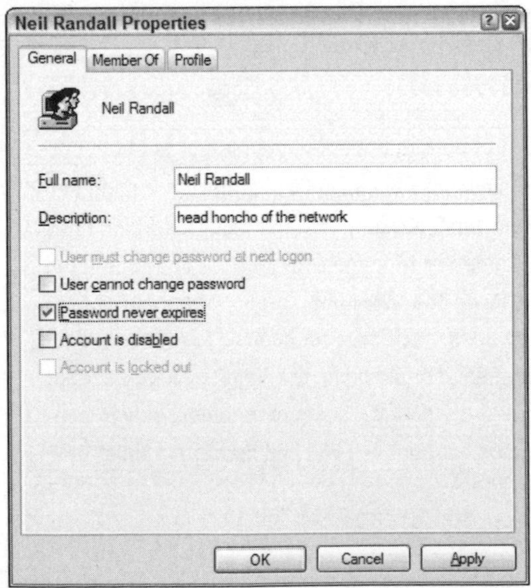

Figure 5-9: The User Properties dialog box.

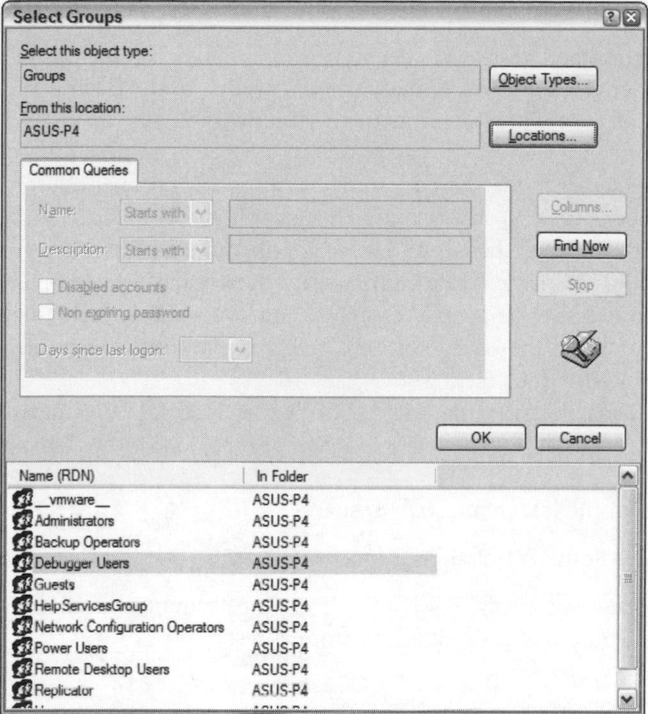

Figure 5-10: The Select Groups dialog box.

For the purposes of this chapter, the most significant tab is the middle one, Member Of. Here you can distinguish among your users by placing them in groups, for the purpose of then assigning groups, instead of individual users, to network resources. On a small network, for example a network of fewer than ten users, this process is unnecessary because you can almost as quickly assign individual users to network resources, but even here you might find the Groups feature useful. One of the benefits is that if you decide to change the location of a resource (for example), and you have, say, eight users working from that resource, you need only change the assignment of the group and all users will automatically change as well.

Tip

While not strictly necessary, you can improve the specificity of your network further by changing the method by which users log on to their PCs. The Windows XP Welcome screen offers usability advantages, but it causes potential security problems by revealing all available usernames, something no professional network should do. To change to the classic Windows 2000 logon screen, open the User Accounts applet from Control Panel and click the option labeled "Change the way users log on or off." Uncheck the option "Use the Welcome Screen," and click Apply Options. Next time you log on, the users will see the classic logon screen, with the requirement that they type their username and password in the dialog box.

Standard File Sharing

Figure 5-5 earlier in this chapter shows the standard sharing dialog box, available when the Simple File Sharing option is unchecked in Folder Options. Two primary elements come to the fore for the purposes of creating a more secure and user-specific infrastructure network: User Limit and Permissions.

The User Limit feature lets you restrict access to the shared resource to a specific number of users at one time. For example, if you want to ensure that only one person can edit a document file or a graphics file at any one time, click the radio button labeled "Allow this number of users" and use the arrow buttons to set the number to 1 (or just click the arrow button, which automatically selects the radio button). If you have a group of employees working on a document and you want no more than four to be able to access it during a meeting, set the User Limit to 4 before the meeting begins and reset it to Maximum (or the previous limit) after the meeting.

The problem with this approach is that it restricts the number of people accessing the shared resource, but it does not specify who. To restrict access to specific users or groups, follow these steps:

1. Open the Properties dialog box for the folder you wish to share.
2. Click the Sharing tab, and then click the Permissions button.
3. On the resulting Permissions dialog box, check to see if the Everyone account is listed. If so, select it and click the Remove button to prevent access from all users.
4. Click the Add button.
5. On the resulting Select Users or Groups dialog box, click the Advanced button.
6. Click the Find Now button.
7. Highlight the users and/or groups to whom you wish to grant access and click OK. Note that you can select multiple entries by holding the Ctrl key as you click on each one.
8. Click OK to add those Users/Groups to the list.
9. Click OK again to return to the Permissions dialog box.
10. Select a user from the Group or User Name list and check the appropriate boxes in the Permissions list at the bottom of the dialog box (see Figure 5-11). You can enable each user to read the item only, change it, or have full control over it (which allows deletions as well). Be careful here, because this is your primary form of control over who gets to do what to each resource.

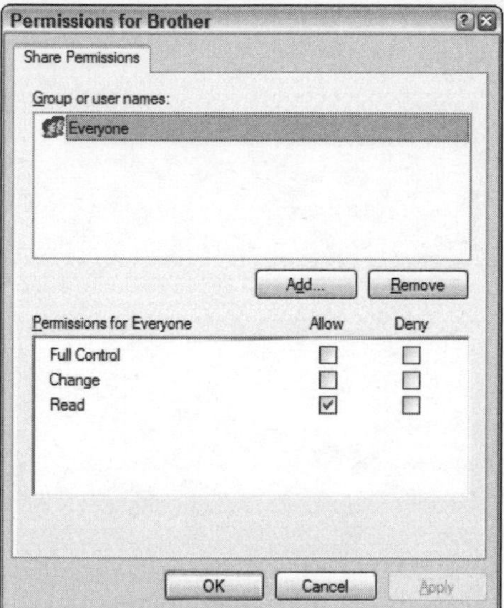

Figure 5-11: Specifying permissible actions for each user.

Summary

Your network is now fully available for use. As you build it, you can perform a virtually unlimited number of additional configurations, but for the most part, let simplicity be your guide. The more complex the network, the more difficult it becomes to manage, both for yourself and for anyone who might later take it over.

So where do you go from here? Believe it or not, you don't have to go anywhere. You have a complete, functioning, and highly impressive infrastructure network in place, complete with shared broadband Internet connection, shared printers, shared folders, and the ability to engage in any networking activity available, including many not covered in this chapter: collaboration, whiteboarding, playing games, and more. You could stop right here and do nothing more than enjoy your network and make the most of it.

But the wireless world is filled with many other possible uses, and a host of possible problems as well. Part II of this book deals with possibly the most critical issue surrounding wireless communications: security. Here you'll learn how to establish the two most widely used types of encryption in Wi-Fi today, and how to ensure — as much as possible — that only the people you *want* to have access actually *do* have access.

Part II

Wireless Security Solutions

Chapter 6

Configuring WEP

Security dominates discussions about wireless communication. Sure, the whole wireless phenomenon still makes all the news stories, especially when it comes to high-tech news, with Wi-Fi becoming the catch-all term of this decade the way Web dominated the '90s, but no matter how innovative, how exciting, how flat-out cool journalists and marketers paint the wireless landscape, questions about security follow close behind and, in many cases, even lead the way. The reason is simple: remove the wires and you simultaneously remove the access restrictions. Wireless networks provide less built-in security than any type of network in computing history.

In fact, many wireless networks begin life completely unsecured because vendors design APs and WLAN cards with ease of use in mind, and configuring security settings almost never equates to ease of use, at least not in the minds of home or small office purchasers. For this reason, the vast majority of Wi-Fi equipment ships with security disabled. If you want a secure network, you have to set it up intentionally and consciously because the equipment won't do it for you.

Why not?

First, wireless security has proven difficult to implement. For that matter, electronic security of any kind has proven exceedingly difficult to guarantee to any degree whatsoever. If you don't believe that, look at all the critical updates Microsoft makes available, for all flavors of Windows, as downloads from their Web site or via Windows Update. The vast majority of these updates deal with issues surrounding intruders from the Internet, and the Internet remains primarily wired, not wireless. If a company with Microsoft's resources, and with Microsoft's control of its product, can't protect your PC from intruders that enter through wired communication, what chance does anyone have of securing communication through much more accessible radio waves between much less controllable technologies?

Secondly, wireless and convenience go hand in hand. Cellular phones and Wi-Fi networks sell themselves because they do away with tethering, with the need to do your computer work, or your phone calling, with a wire restricting your motion and creating unsightly or even dangerous obstacles across your floor. For a product to sell its convenience, it has to follow the sale with a performance emphasizing convenience, something a requirement for encryption and authentication configuration would do little but dispel. To be sure, the recent expansion of media coverage about identity theft and other high-tech dangers promises to force vendors to merge convenience with security in their products, and high-tech consumerdom might very well have reached the point where security has actually become a part of convenience, but to date most products let you set up your wireless network most easily, and with the greatest speed, without security of any kind in place.

Even so, you can easily detect a trend toward security. Install a new router/AP device today, and you'll likely encounter a wizard that steps you through the process of configuring your WLAN with

encryption and authentication security in place. Windows XP Service Pack 2, set for release roughly the same time as this book, offers a WLAN creation wizard that forces you through the security setup without an option to avoid it.

This chapter outlines Wired Equivalent Privacy (WEP), the most common and basic method of WLAN security and authentication. Chapter 7 features WEP's probable successor, Wi-Fi Protected Access (WPA). Chapter 8 offers a number of tips and tricks for helping you create and define a more highly secured wireless network.

What Is WEP?

WEP stands for *Wired Equivalent Privacy*, and that says it all. The entire purpose of WEP is to provide the degree of security, or at least privacy, available on a wired LAN. Unfortunately, it's difficult to know exactly what that means, and even more difficult to understand how it's possible. As we've mentioned more than once, to access a wired LAN you need a wire, while radio waves are simply out there, ripe for the plucking. So how can WEP provide the same level of privacy, given the immediate shortcomings of wireless security?

WEP operates on the medium access control (MAC) layer of the 801.11 protocol. The MAC layer operates, in effect, as the communications manager in a wireless network, determining the whereabouts of access points and enacting the protocols to ensure the success of data exchange over the radio waves. Without the MAC layer, your data wouldn't go anywhere on the WLAN.

The MAC layer handles the following stages on the WLAN:

- **Stage 1: Scanning.** The MAC layer begins its job by assisting wireless equipment in the search for access points. In passive scanning, all WLAN adapters scan individual channels for the best available signal, waiting to receive access point information. Access points regularly broadcast their coordinates to the network for adapters to pick up. These AP broadcasts, called ***beacons***, include details about the network's SSID (service set identifier), broadcast channels, and the data transfer rates it can handle. In active scanning, the WLAN adapter probes for APs by sending out a signal (a broadcast of its own, if you will), to which all APs in range respond by sending information to that WLAN. While active scanning might seem a better idea from a security perspective than AP broadcasts, the combined probe and response create considerable overhead on the network, hence the preference for passive scanning. Note that the scanning stage has nothing to do with WEP per se, except of course that without a successful scan no further communication (encrypted or not) can occur.
- **Stage 2: Authentication.** In network communication terminology, to ***authenticate*** means to prove your identity to be accepted for access. Here WEP does come into play, and this is the stage in which the initial problems with Wi-Fi security occur. The 802.11 standard includes two authentication systems. Open System authentication, the more basic of the two, sees the WLAN adapter request authentication from the access point, with the AP responding with permission or denial. Without a specific reason to deny (as configured on the AP itself), authentication takes place. In the second system, Shared Key authentication, the same process takes place, with the adapter sending the authentication to the AP

and ultimately receiving a signal granting or denying permission to access, but in between is the crucial step of correctly answering a security challenge. The encryption technology (WEP for our purposes here) sends an encrypted challenge message tied to a specific key. To pass the challenge, the adapter uses its matching key to decrypt the message and sends it back to the AP. The AP compares the two and, if they match, sends the approval signal. One problem here is that the AP doesn't actually know if the adapter has the correct key; it simply assumes this point because it receives the decrypted text. In other words, anyone who finds a way to decrypt the challenge message without having the WEP key can also gain access to the network.

- **Stage 3: Association.** After the AP has authenticated the WLAN adapter, a few more details need clearing up before data transfer can take place. The two devices must ascertain that they know the shared SSID and channel, the data rate(s) over which the transfers will occur, and any other configuration details for the AP. Once the two devices have established this association, they can get to work. With WEP enabled, the adapter will encrypt all data transfers before sending them, and the AP will decrypt them upon receipt (and vice versa). Both devices use the common key for encryption and decryption.

WEP kicks in, as you can see, in the second and third stages, providing an encryption method with an encryption key. You authenticate using WEP, and you associate with WEP. More specifically, WEP uses an RC4 stream cipher, a standard from the security organization RSA Security, to encrypt the contents of all transmissions sent over the network. The sending and receiving devices share a secret key, which WEP abbreviates further with a randomly generated initialization vector. In other words, the secret key gets a random number attached to it that the AP in turn decodes to determine if the received data matches the original, only after which does the AP decrypt the transmission using the shared secret key.

At its most basic, WEP uses a 40-bit secret key, although it is also capable of employing a 64-bit key. To offer even better WEP security, however, equipment vendors such as D-Link and Linksys offer proprietary WEP encryption that increases the key to 128-bit or even higher. To get the maximum benefit of this stronger but proprietary key, all devices on the network need to be able to share it, which means, of course, stocking up on that vendor's products (precisely because the enhanced WEP technology is different for each vendor). That's not a bad thing if you're setting up a WLAN from scratch, or getting rid of older equipment to take advantage of today's 802.11g technology, but it's obviously an issue if you're adding to existing WEP-enabled WLANs. If you stick with standard WEP, you can buy any Wi-Fi product with the full reassurance that encryption will function among all your products, but WEP isn't as good at the various enhanced versions of WEP at security. So it's up to you: proprietary but stronger—and more expensive because of the need to buy from one vendor—or standard but weaker.

One thing to keep in mind is that WEP covers only the wireless transmission itself (the 802.11 portion); if the transmission moves beyond the WLAN onto a wired Ethernet LAN (or any other wired LAN), WEP no longer functions. In effect, it loses its authority to provide security at that point. Don't count on WEP to handle your full encryption needs in a combined infrastructure network.

But surely WEP is reliable for daily wireless transactions, right? Well, yes and no. WEP was the first encryption technology available for Wi-Fi, and it remains the standard. However, its benefits can be summed up in one telling phrase: it's better than nothing. Without question, a WEP-enabled

WLAN stands a much better chance of resisting intruders than a non-WEP network with open key authentication. But it has its flaws, and these have conspired to render it next to useless as a technology for protecting truly sensitive data from falling into unwanted hands.

The primary problem with WEP lies in its inability to exchange keys on the fly. Unlike future encryption and authentication technologies, in which devices will be able to constantly change keys automatically, basic WEP requires the manual configuration of keys on the WLAN adapters. The results are predictable. On large networks, administrators don't have the time to reconfigure everyone's adapter manually, so they tend to stick with the same keys for an extended period of time. On small networks (home and small office), nobody knows about changing keys in the first place, so these keys never change, either. Anyone with a Wi-Fi monitoring tool (of which several exist) can simply keep trying until they retrieve the keys, eventually hacking into the network. Another problem exists in WEP with the 24-bit limitation on initialization vectors, because even though the AP generates them randomly, before long it must reuse keys. This, too, allows for hacking possibilities.

Finally, as with all networks, any time you add to the basic technology, you create an overhead that can erode performance. WEP is no different. In the early days of 802.11b networking, enabling WEP caused two major problems. It made connection difficult, and once you did connect, you often wished you hadn't. The process of authenticating and encrypting caused the wireless LAN to slow to a crawl, often to the degree that requests to the Internet from a notebook PC ended up timing out, because of the time it took to get the request through the AP. Today's WEP implementations work considerably better, but you will still typically notice a speed difference — sometimes significant — between a WLAN with WEP enabled and a WLAN that operates without encryption. Safety first, the dictum goes, but most of us care more about speed, especially when it comes to networks.

Access Point and Adapter Settings

The rest of this chapter covers WEP configuration settings for access points and WLAN adapters. You should always consider enabling WEP only after you know that your WLAN works properly. If you don't, you can easily run into the classic computer problem of not knowing which component isn't working properly. True, you'll have a few minutes of an unsecured WLAN on your hands, but unless someone's sitting outside your door waiting to receive a signal, you won't likely be in much danger of intrusion until you can get WEP up and running.

Tip

In networking, perhaps more than any other aspect of computing, setting up one thing at a time pays dividends. Because establishing a network compounds the number of elements that can go wrong (a single computer on its own can cause enough trouble, let alone 30 of them strung together), if you step through the process bit by bit, ensuring the validity of each step as you go, you can more easily troubleshoot your configuration. This rule of thumb certainly holds true for establishing security systems of any kind, and wireless security in particular. Make sure it works, and only then make it secure.

As with everything else to do with wireless networking, you should configure the access point before bothering with the WLAN adapters on the networked PCs. You don't actually need to do it in this order, especially if you have only one or two clients to connect, but you'll have to adjust the AP at some point, so it makes sense to do so right away. This demonstration will operate in that order: AP first, network clients afterwards.

To begin, take a look at Figure 6-1. This figure shows the D-Link DI-624 router's configuration screen in its factory state, with an SSID of "default," the channel set to 6, and the authentication configured as open system. In the process of configuring security for your WLAN, you'll alter only the WEP-related settings, even though you could change several others, including the SSID and the channel, to make the WLAN even more secure.

In addition, look at Figure 6-2. This figure shows the D-Link utility for the company's DWL-G650 CardBus WLAN adapter. Like all utilities included with wireless adapters, you can access this one from any Window 9x or Windows 2000 PC, but in Windows XP it's available only when you deselect the option "Use Windows to configure my wireless network settings" on the Wireless Network Properties dialog box. Microsoft has built 802.11x support directly into Windows XP, in part to eliminate the need for proprietary utilities, but in many cases, especially when configuring WEP or WPA security (Chapter 7 covers WPA), you'll quickly discover that the proprietary utilities work more easily and often better than those built into Windows XP.

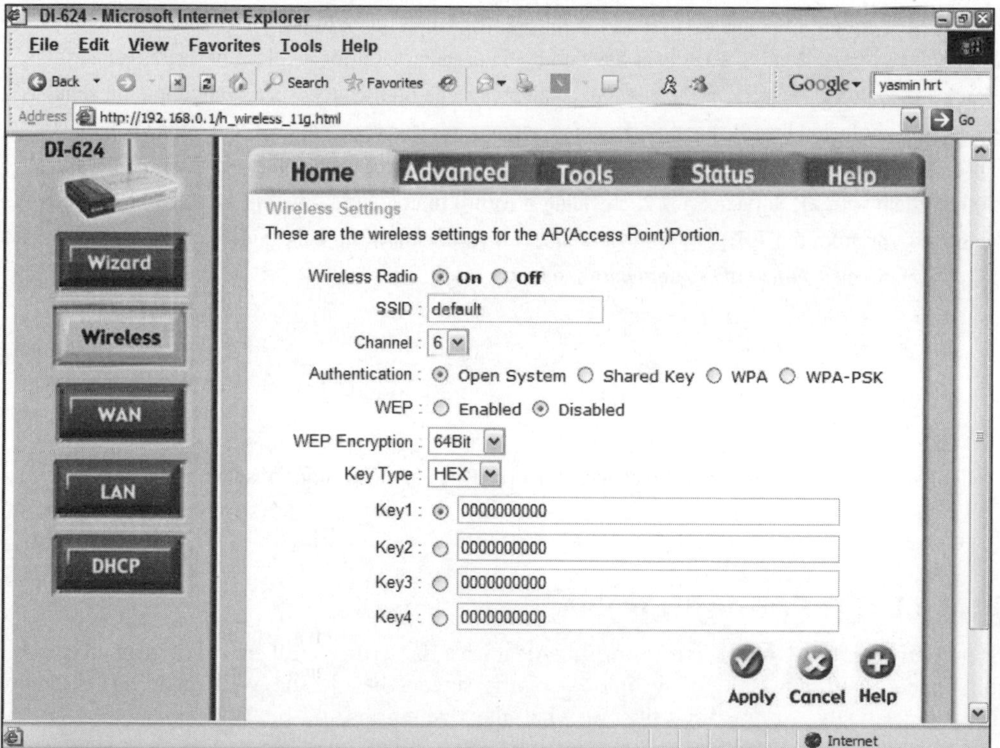

Figure 6-1: The default AP configuration.

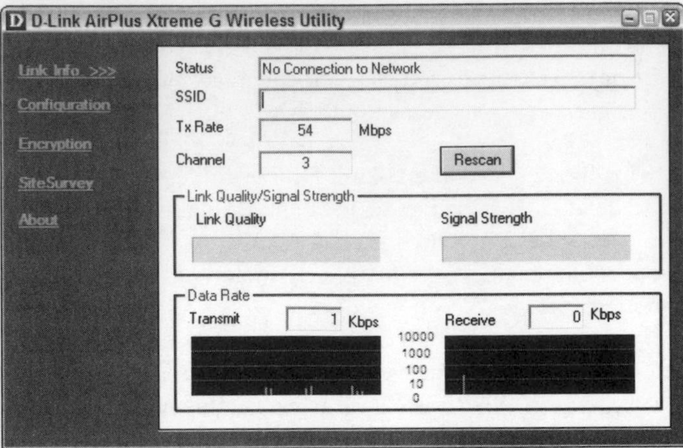

Figure 6-2: The default WLAN client configuration.

Caution

When you use the configuration utilities built into Windows XP, pay attention to which version of the utilities you have on your system. Windows XP itself has one configuration menu for wireless networks, while XP Service Pack 1 provides a changed utility, one that eliminates some of the necessary configuring but simultaneously causes confusion by automating encryption settings in ways you might not find intuitive because your AP provides those settings anyway. As if that's not enough, Microsoft has changed the configuration screens once again with XP Service Pack 2, providing a wizard to configure a wireless network, but once again distancing you from the AP's own configuration. Not surprisingly, the built-in configuration screens work fine with Microsoft's own wireless hardware products.

Cross-Ref

Chapter 8 deals with reconfiguring additional elements of the AP as part of its series of security tips and tricks.

Enabling WEP Encryption

The first step in providing WEP security, for this AP at least, is to turn WEP encryption on. To do so, click the Enabled radio button in the middle of the screen, beside the WEP heading. To keep the WEP key relatively simple, but still somewhat effective, choose 64-bit WEP encryption and a hexadecimal key type (note that the DI-624 does not support 40-bit encryption, only 64-bit and 128-bit). For the sake of demonstration, although certainly not something you'd do if you hope to have any true degree of security, use the key 0123456789. The ten digits are required for a 64-bit hexadecimal, but you don't have to remember that fact. If you type too many or two few digits, the D-Link utility displays an error message telling you the legal length of the key. Once you have the key you want, click Apply. The results appear in Figure 6-3.

With the access point now the way you want it, the next step is to configure the client PCs so they can connect to the AP. Figure 6-4 shows the D-Link utility on the laptop, set to match the configuration on the AP. Note that WEP encryption and open authentication are both selected, with the network key typed into the first key field, and the key set to 64 bits and hexadecimal format. Every single detail between the two devices must match, or they will not be able to communicate. If you discover later that you cannot connect an adapter to your AP, open the configuration menu in each and study them carefully to ensure that they match precisely. Otherwise, you won't have the network you want.

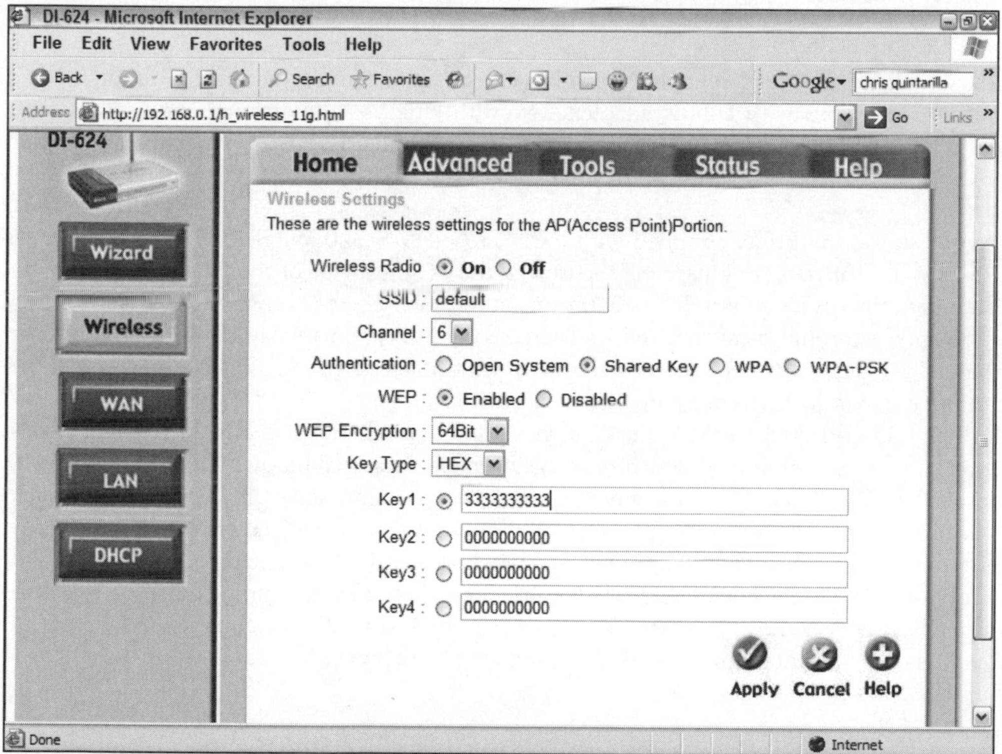

Figure 6-3: The access point configured for WEP encryption.

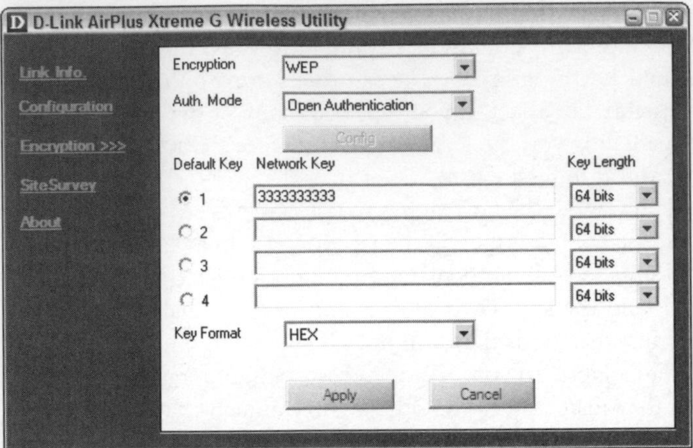

Figure 6-4: Matching the encryption details between laptop and access point.

Of course, not all networks contain PCs with identically matching equipment. You might very well have two notebooks with D-Link adapters, two with Linksys adapters, and another two with Microsoft adapters. Fortunately, 802.11b and 802.11g are standards, so theoretically any adapter you buy should work with any access point you buy, as long as both share at least one of the 802.11 protocols.

Figure 6-5 shows the utility supplied with the Microsoft MN-720 Wireless Notebook Adapter. After installing the software and inserting the card in the PC Card slot of the laptop, a connection wizard automatically runs. On Windows XP, the operating system takes over from the wizard, allowing you to connect through it instead, but in any case the utility remains available, even if, unlike other vendors' utilities, you check the Wireless Network Connection Properties box instructing the connection to use Windows to configure the networks.

With this option selected, clicking the Configure button yields the standard Wireless Network Connection Properties dialog box, which once again differs among Windows XP, XP SP1, and XP SP2. For this demonstration, therefore, only the proprietary configuration utility will be used, which appears in Figure 6-6. This figure shows the SSID of the AP to which the network card has already connected, and also the checkbox for configuring wireless security. Note that, out of the box, this product supports WEP only, not WPA. That's because the pictured PC is running on Service Pack 1, which, like all earlier Windows XP versions, requires you to download a patch to use WPA security. This limitation obviously does not affect this chapter, which deals with WEP anyway, so we will proceed with the adapter as installed.

Cross-Ref

Chapter 7 covers WPA and includes the procedure for downloading and installing the Windows XP Support Patch for Wi-Fi Protected Access.

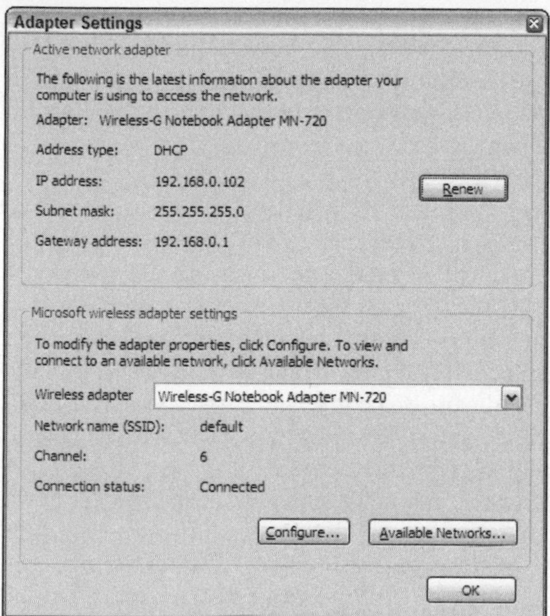

Figure 6-5: Using the built-in utility for configuring your Microsoft WLAN adapter.

Figure 6-6: Providing WEP encryption settings for the Microsoft WLAN adapter.

Configuring the Microsoft adapter for WEP encryption is very similar to configuring the D-Link adapter. Click the Use Wireless Security checkbox, select Standard (64-bit WEP) from the Security Strength drop-down menu, and type the security key in the two remaining fields. The confirmation is necessary because Microsoft's utility treats the keys like passwords, displaying bullets instead of alphanumeric symbols when you type, so confirming gives you reassurance that you've typed the right characters.

The primary difference between the two utilities lies in the number of keys you can include. The D-Link utility accepts four WEP keys, matching the D-Link access point, while the Microsoft utility lets you type only one. As a result, if you change the WEP key regularly, as you should in order to gain the best possible security, on the Microsoft utility you must type the new key from scratch, while on the D-Link you need only select the next one on the list. You could argue — as Microsoft probably does — that storing four possible keys in the utility allows would-be intruders to steal the information more readily, but this argument applies primarily to people who have access to the notebook itself. Still, there's certainly nothing wrong with retyping the security key each time you change it — it merely becomes tedious if you have a network of more than a few PCs.

Once you have applied your settings through the adapter's utility, all that remains is to test to see that your secure network functions. Check the status screens for the AP and all your adapters to make sure they state that WEP encryption is in place. Next, use My Network Places to ensure that you can still connect to the same network resources, including printers and shared folders. Finally, open a Web browser and navigate around the Internet to make sure that the shared Internet connection remains in place.

Configuring Authentication

Now that you have WEP encryption in place, a few more clicks will give you additional security in the form of Shared Key authentication. On the utility for the access point, select the Shared Key option and click Apply (depending on the interface of your particular AP). Next, on your WLAN adapter's configuration screen, enable Shared Key authentication as well. On some utilities, this option is easy to locate. Oddly enough, however, on Microsoft's it is not. In fact, to configure the adapter to use Shared Key authentication, you must open the Wireless Network Connection Properties dialog box, click the Configure tab, and choose Shared from the Network Authentication drop-down menu. Figure 6-7 shows this menu in the process of being configured.

Once again, don't consider the network setup complete until you've tested the connections. Ensure that you can print across the network and that you can upload and download files to the appropriate shared locations. And again, test the Internet sharing. If you can't get onto the Internet, undo the authentication and try again until you can do so. Otherwise, the entire purpose of the infrastructure network might well be lost.

Tip

When testing your Internet connection across the network, don't start dismantling and rebuilding your configuration until you've ascertained that the Internet connection itself works properly. Leave the wirelessly connected PC and sit at one connected to the AP/router via standard Ethernet cable, and access the Internet from there. If it works, then you know the problem resides on the Wi-Fi connection; if not, then wait until your ISP comes back online before attempting the wireless configuration again.

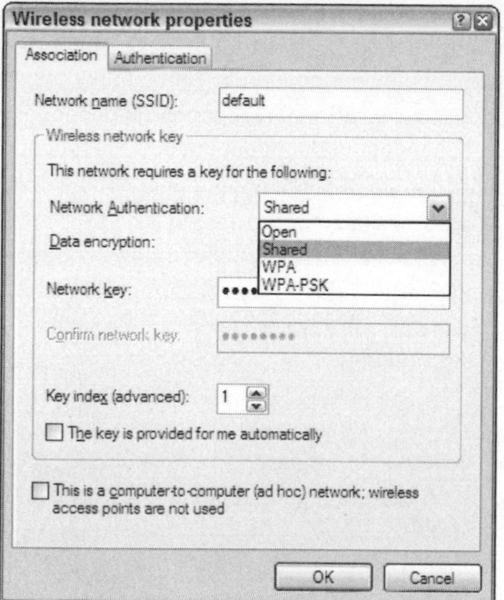

Figure 6-7: The Association tab on the Wireless Network Properties dialog box.

Upping the Ante to 128-bit Encryption

Once you have 64-bit WEP encryption in place and functioning, you have a much more secure LAN than you did before configuring your access point and wireless adapters to use WEP. But as noted earlier in this chapter, 64-bit WEP, while certainly stronger than the older standard 40-bit WEP, is still much more prone to intrusion than even higher degrees of security. To provide an even better guard against unwanted access, configure your WLAN for 128-bit security.

Once again, you perform this configuration in two locations: on the AP, and on each WLAN adapter. This time, however, the length of the security key changes, the primary reason for the security enhancement. A longer key means less chance of breaking the code of that key, and thus less chance of intruders finding a way to include the key in their own adapter configurations to use your network. The key lengths are as follows:

- 64-bit ASCII — 5 characters
- 64-bit hexadecimal — 10 characters
- 128-bit ASCII — 13 characters
- 128-bit hexadecimal — 26 characters

As you can see, the hexadecimal key type doubles the key length over the ASCII key type for both security strengths. But moving from 64-bit to 128-bit with either type more than doubles the length in each case, and changing your configuration from 64-bit ASCII to 128-bit hexadecimal more than quintuples the length of the key. The result: an exponential decrease in the probability of cracking

your key, and almost no chance of simply guessing it. As you probably expect, intruders have come up with numerous tools to do the cracking for them, so saying a 128-bit hexadecimal key network gives you true security is inaccurate. Keep in mind, however, that one of the primary goals is to prevent casual access to your network, or even casual and beyond, so by all means choose the strongest possible security you have available.

As with passwords, you should make the key as difficult as possible to guess. Practically, this means you need to write it down so that you can type it into appropriate configuration fields on each WLAN adapter, unless you develop a mnemonic system that will let you recall it. Even here, though, remember to store it somewhere you can find it because even the best mnemonic system breaks down unexpectedly at precisely the wrong time. Murphy's Law and all that.

Figure 6-8 shows the D-Link access point utility with a 26-character key. Again, this example is hardly one you'd want to try because it's too easy to guess. But to get your network running in the first place, it certainly doesn't hurt to use something memorable and then change it once you know precisely how to ensure connectivity.

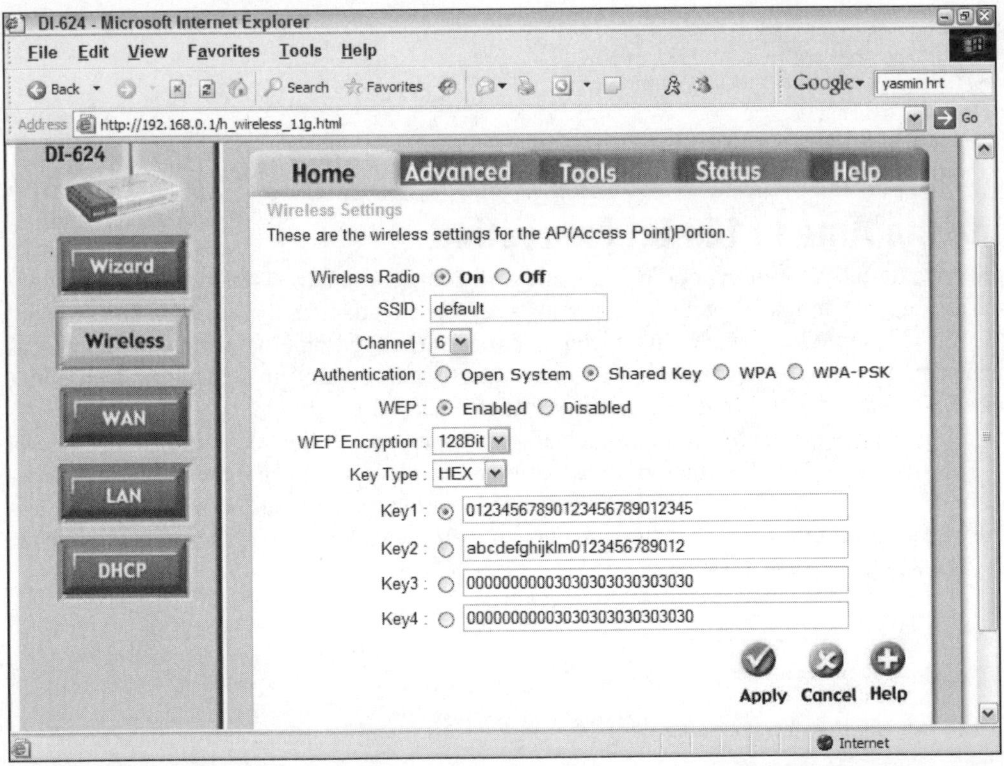

Figure 6-8: Multiple 128-bit key strings.

As with 64-bit WEP (or 40-bit, if you have that available), once the new encryption strength is in place on the AP, you need to configure all WLAN adapters to use it as well. Load your adapter's utility, make the changes by selecting 128-bit security and typing the new key in the appropriate field(s). If you use Windows XP, you might be better off at this stage using the built-in networking utilities, primarily because Windows XP simply connects more effectively when you do. Starting with Service Pack 1, you don't even need to specify if you're using 64-bit, 128-bit, ASCII, or hexadecimal. The Windows XP dialog boxes are designed to accept only keys of the required length—5, 10, 13, and 26 characters—and when you click OK, the operating system adjusts itself to use the appropriate encryption. Figure 6-9 shows the Service Pack 1 Windows XP configuration tool.

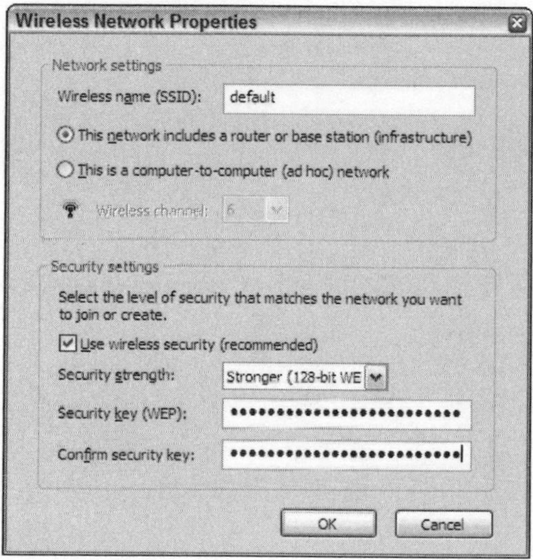

Figure 6-9: SP1's encryption settings dialog box.

Summary

You now have an encrypted WLAN operating, with a decreased opportunity for hackers to find their way in. In fact, with Wired Equivalent Privacy in place, you could go no further with your encryption and security plans and have a decent chance of nobody ever breaking into your network. At the very least, WEP stops casual intruders from accessing your network resources, and if you use some of the proprietary WEP technology available from numerous vendors you have a good chance of denying access entirely. So you've done well: you've at least got a lock in place.

In the next chapter, you'll learn how to take that security one step further by configuring your network for WPA encryption instead of WEP encryption, and while WPA remains significantly less than ideal in the security world, it does guard your system better than WEP.

Chapter 7

Configuring WPA

If you've just gone through the process of setting up your WLAN to use Wired Equivalent Privacy (WEP) security, the subject of Chapter 6, you might want to skip ahead to Chapter 8 to learn a number of tips and tricks to make your infrastructure network even more secure. Why? Because this chapter discusses another wireless security technology, Wi-Fi Protected Access (WPA), and takes you through the steps necessary to set it up. Obviously, that's not a problem — you can never have too many security options — but WPA replaces rather than enhances WEP. Configuring your WLAN for WPA means dismantling everything you did in Chapter 6, and you might want to spend a short while simply glorying in your newly encrypted setup.

WPA represents a stepping stone between the limited security capabilities of WEP and the projected "real" security of the upcoming IEEE protocol called 802.11i, also known (adding to the confusion) as *WPA 2*. This chapter takes you through the basics of the underlying technologies of both security systems, albeit with a focus on WPA. For now, you should know that WPA exists, and works reasonably well, while 802.11i remains a technology around the corner. In other words, it's not yet a solution, although you can expect it to appear, in force, in products in late 2004 or early 2005. In the meantime, WPA has captured the interest of security-minded IT professionals and even some home and small office users, primarily because their existing equipment already includes it (as is the case of almost any 802.11g-based device) or — and this is extremely important — they can upgrade the firmware of their existing equipment to get it. By contrast, when 802.11i hits the market, you will almost certainly need to purchase new APs and WLAN adapters to take advantage of it.

Practically speaking, this means WEP and WPA will continue to secure WLANs for quite some time to come because homes, small offices, and even some larger companies won't immediately spring for new equipment. As with all security expenditures, the return on investment is nearly impossible to prove because security acts as a preventative, and the only way to believe in the effectiveness of preventatives is to be convinced that whatever they were preventing would have happened in the first place. Obviously, you can't predict anything of the kind, so justifying the cost becomes difficult.

In the meantime, then, you have WEP and WPA. This chapter examines how to configure your WLAN for WPA, giving it today's best security possible.

Note

The WPA initials apply to two elements in PC-based computing today: Wi-Fi Protected Access and Windows Product Activation. Both deal with security, but the second definition deals primarily with securing Microsoft's coffers. In this chapter, WPA refers to the wireless security protocol, which, unlike the other WPA, we hope doesn't go away.

WPA and 802.11i

If Wi-Fi Protected Access provides a stepping stone to the more secure 802.11i (WPA 2), what sort of stepping stone is it? The answer to this question begins with the answer to another question: How is WPA different from WEP?

As discussed briefly in Chapter 6, the primary disadvantage with WEP lies with its fixed security keys. Once they are set, WEP administrators can change them, but in many typical WEP installations the keys simply don't get changed, and the protocol, with its lack of built-in ability to cycle through keys on a periodic basis, doesn't help things. As a result of this problem, WEP security is breachable and breakable, to the degree that home networks can end up sharing Internet connections and other resources (such as files) with intruders, and company networks can become seriously compromised. WEP is unquestionably better than nothing, but for networks with a lot to lose, better than nothing hardly fills the bill.

The 802.11i protocol addresses these and other security issues in depth, where WPA addressed them only to a degree. WPA begins by improving WEP's implementation of the RSA Security RC4 encryption technology, specifically the size of the initialization vector, which resides in the first bytes of data and begins the process of recognizing the key shared by the sending and receiving devices. If you recall from Chapter 6, WEP uses a 24-bit initialization vector early in the process of a network transmission; in WPA, this vector increases to 48 bits. As with all encryption technologies, increasing the size even a small amount increases the difficulty of cracking the encryption almost exponentially, so a doubling from 24 bits to 48 bits renders the initialization vector far, far harder to crack. Right from the start of the data transmission process, therefore, WPA shows its enhanced strength.

Among WPA's most prominent additions, Temporal Key Integrity Protocol (TKIP) provides the greatest security for individual data packets, the small "chunks" of data into which networking protocols divide your messages before sending. TKIP mixes keys on a packet-by-packet basis, changes these keys automatically and regularly, and verifies the security configuration with each change. These key changes are crucial to the security capabilities of WPA and 802.11i both, and make up for the inability of earlier 802.11 implementations (including 11a, 11b, and 11g) to change the encryption key for some transmission types. WPA mandates rekeying the case of all transmissions, with TKIP providing the frame by frame rekeying, and WPA itself providing the mechanism by which the AP communicates the changed keys to the adapters. In addition, TKIP provides a means of checking

the integrity of the message, a technology known as *Message Integrity Checking (MIC)* (but often referred to as *Michael*), that blocks intruders from adding small bits of data to a packet to calculate the encryption key (which is a problem with WEP). TKIP is therefore a part of WPA's overall key management feature, and the two together eliminate the problem of static encryption keys that renders WEP so vulnerable.

Authentication, an especially weak component of WEP, also undergoes a significant upgrade with WPA. First of all, you can no longer configure your WLAN to operate without authentication encryption, as you can with WEP. In addition, WPA authentication is based on the Extensible Authentication Protocol (EAP), a secured extension to the Internet's long-lived Point-to-Point Protocol (PPP), and a core element of 802.11i as well. EAP handles digital certificates, secure IDs, and other authentication elements in the security world, and does its job in part by preventing connection to the WLAN by rogue APs and adapters. Furthermore, WPA supports the technology known as ***preshared key authentication***, an option in WPA equipment configuration abbreviated to WPA-PSK. In this configuration, the AP and the adapters share a predetermined key, with the sharing itself password-protected. When the AP determines that the passwords match, the adapter can gain access to the network. This system simplifies the user-specific credentials required in WPA itself, and eliminates the need, in smaller networks, for a special server to handle authentication requests. Even so, PSK technology is more readily breached than straight WPA, so use it only for the sake of ease of use. Put another way, it's better than WEP, but not as good as WPA on its own.

Despite these changes, however, TKIP operates perfectly well with existing wireless devices; as long as you add WPA capabilities to your APs and WLAN adapters, you don't need to run out and buy new equipment. Such is not the case with 802.11i, which as we write this looks as if it will require new hardware to incorporate its significantly stronger security features. If you want high security, you're going to have to pay for it.

802.11i extends the improvements in WPA even further. Perhaps the most important single addition is the addition of the Advanced Encryption Standard (AES), a block cipher technology already available with some implementations of WPA, but not mandatory because it often requires new hardware to perform effectively. A U.S. government standard authorized by the National Institute of Standards and Technology (NIST), AES enables security among WLAN nodes operating in both ad hoc and infrastructure mode. AES encryption can use key sizes up to 256-bits, possible today with even some proprietary modifications of WEP but, when combined with WPA's other improvements, an even greater improvement to what we have now.

AES encryption is simply one part of 802.11i's Robust Security Network, which of course abbreviates to RSN (nobody in the computer world actually spells any term out, as you'll see in the next sentence). Combining 802.11 itself, along with EAP and AES, RSN provides a method of dynamic authentication and encryption designed to eliminate both the security problems and the performance downgrades currently experienced with both WEP and WPA. RSN replaces TKIP's constantly rotating encryption keys with the more secure AES implementation, and requires a Remote Authentication Dial-In User Service (RADIUS) server to provide full authentication. For this reason, 802.11i will be found primarily in larger businesses and organizations, with home and small office APs providing, quite probably, a less comprehensive version of RADIUS.

Figure 7-1 shows a typical diagram of the data flow for a full 802.11i implementation.

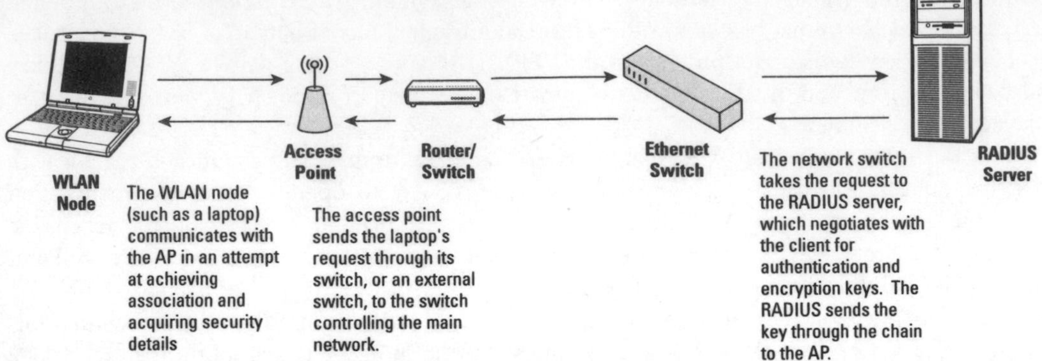

WLAN Node
The WLAN node (such as a laptop) communicates with the AP in an attempt at achieving association and acquiring security details
Access Point
Router/ Switch
The access point sends the laptop's request through its switch, or an external switch, to the switch controlling the main network.
Ethernet Switch
The network switch takes the request to the RADIUS server, which negotiates with the client for authentication and encryption keys. The RADIUS sends the key through the chain to the AP.
RADIUS Server

Figure 7-1: The Robust Secure Network in operation.

In this process, the WLAN user (from a laptop, say) performs some network activity. The laptop's WLAN adapter sends a request for association and security to the AP. The AP forwards the request through the switch to the RADIUS server, which performs the authentication, thereby allowing the switch and the laptop to create the necessary encryption key for that session. The switch encrypts the key with AES and sends it back through the access point to the laptop, and the WLAN adapter, configured for 802.11i, now encrypts all signals for this session with this key. As the laptop makes new requests, a new authentication and key creation process begins, and this same process, with different encryption results, occurs with each client on the network.

Establishing WPA on Your WLAN

To get WPA up and running on your wireless LAN, your first step is to make sure you have WPA capabilities on your WLAN hardware. Otherwise, there's no point. You can check by examining the configuration dialog boxes for each access point and wireless adapter on your network, looking for drop-down menus or setup screens that display the option for WPA and/or WPA-PSK.

WPA on the Access Point

As with your WEP-enabled network, configure your access point first, so that you can simply configure all the network clients afterwards with the AP up and running. Figure 7-2 shows the relevant configuration screen on the D-Link DI-624 configuration screens.

Note that the D-Link supports both the normal and the shared key modes of WPA. Most APs manufactured in the past year or so offer support for both, and as long as your WLAN adapters support these modes, you can use whichever you prefer. Well, not exactly. To use WPA rather than WPA-PSK, you need a RADIUS server, so unless you have one of these devices, you have no real choice but to choose the PSK version. For the sake of this book and its intended audience, we stick with WPA-PSK for the demonstrations, but where discussions of RADIUS-based WPA seem applicable, we continue to refer to that technology as well.

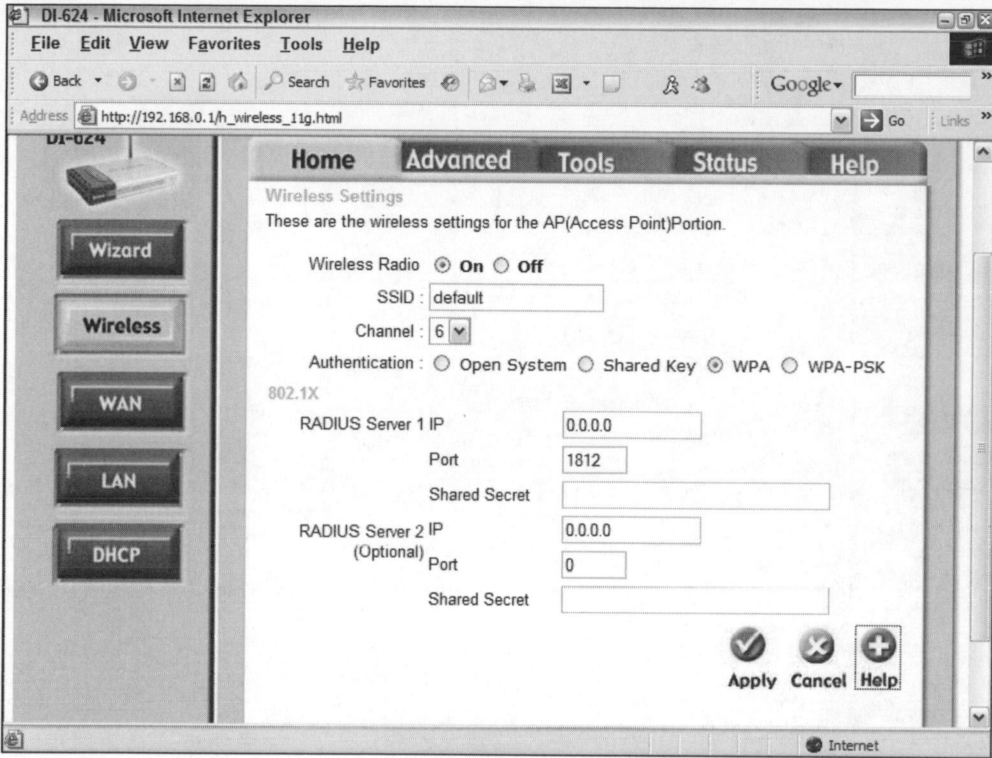

Figure 7-2: Setting the D-Link access point to WPA mode.

To see the difference, look at Figure 7-3 in conjunction with Figure 7-2. Figure 7-2 shows an areas for 802.11 configuration, in which you must specify the IP address, the port, and the shared secret key of at least one, and possibly two, RADIUS servers. Without a RADIUS server operating, you obviously can't do so. Figure 7-3, by contrast, shows the WPA-SPK option in place. Here, you have only two fields below the Authentication line that you can complete: Passphrase and Confirm Passphrase. Here, as you probably expect by the format, you simply type the passphrase (also called the Shared Secret) under which you want WPA-SPK to operate. As you'll see in a minute, you must enter the same passphrase in the configuration dialog boxes of each node on the network to allow WPA security—and, indeed, to allow any form of wireless data transfer, because once WPA-SPK has been established on the AP, no WLAN adapter can connect without conforming to the AP's security requirements.

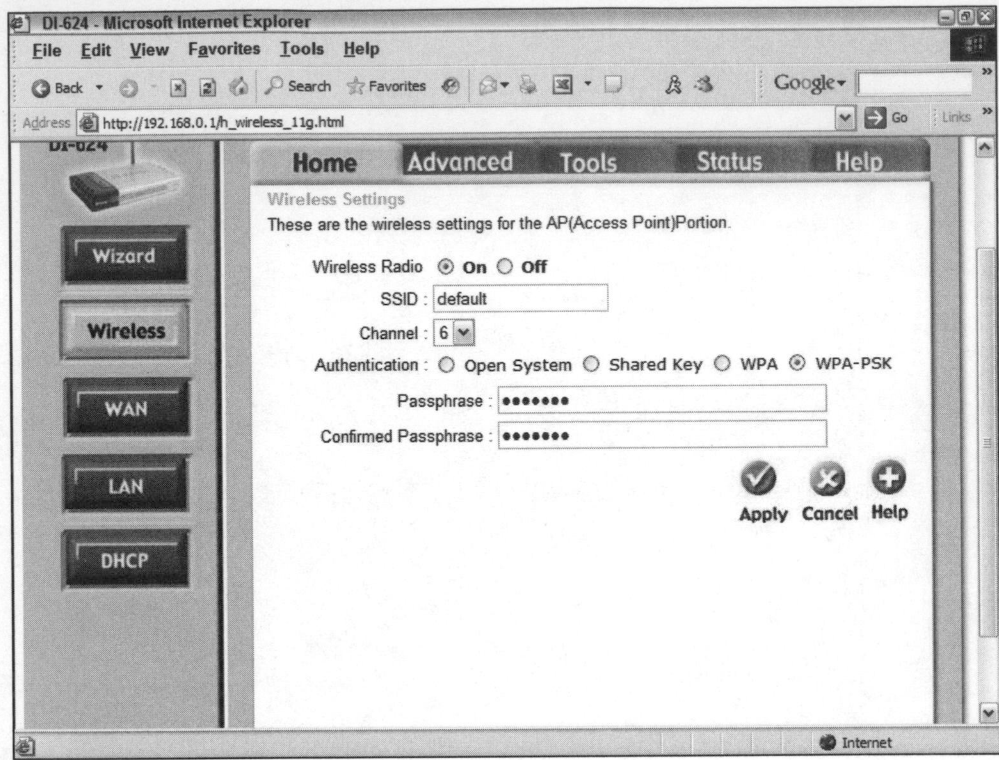

Figure 7-3: Setting the AP to WPA-PSK mode.

As with every other password or passphrase you have on your computer system, make this one as secure as possible to make intrusion as difficult as possible. In fact, because the WLAN adapters happily store the passwords for you, provide a password that's almost impossible to memorize, precisely because you have to type it only once on each machine. Yes, you'll want to change the password periodically, but WPA-SPK does tend to be harder to crack than WEP, so as long as you perform a periodic passphrase update, say once a month for a home network and once a week for a small office network, you should be reasonably safe. Of course, you can change the passphrase daily for even greater effect, as long as you remember to change it on each network client PC as well. In this way, the WPA-SPK passphrase resembles the Encryption Key in WEP, the effectiveness of which increases dramatically the more often you change it. The passphrase must contain between 8 and 63 characters.

Note

Some wireless access points, particularly the more expensive devices oriented toward the business market, can in fact run WEP and WPA simultaneously. For such devices, you can configure each network client to signal the AP using whichever of the two encryption methods you wish. If you want to force all clients to use WPA, and your network is domain-based rather than workgroup-based, you can create a Windows XP group policy to switch to WPA and simultaneously disable the WEP group policy. This book does not cover group policies; for more on this network administration feature, see *Windows Server 2003 Bible*, from Wiley.

WPA on the WLAN Adapters

If you had a WEP-encrypted network functioning up until now, your various nodes no longer have access to the network as soon as you configure the AP to use WPA security. Once again, WPA replaces WEP, it does not enhance it. As far as your client PCs go, they are effectively shut out of the network because the security system no longer recognizes them as legitimate members of that network. They cannot be authenticated, so they cannot participate, even though they could, as sharers of a WEP key, only a minute ago.

At this stage, you need to move to each would-be network client and enable WPA-PSK, set the passphrase, and test the connections once again.

WPA for Windows XP

Windows XP ships with support for 802.11b built directly into the operating system. With that support, it also includes — naturally enough — built-in support for WEP as well. It does not include WPA support, however, because the initial release of Windows XP predates the existence of WPA by several months. Windows XP Service Pack 2 adds WPA support, but if you have the original Windows XP, or even an incompletely updated Windows XP Service Pack 1, you can add WPA through the process of a simple download.

To get the download, point your browser to the Microsoft site (`www.microsoft.com`) and do a search for WPA. In a few seconds you'll be presented with the titles of a number of articles related to WPA. Click the link "Download Windows XP Support Patch for Wireless Protected Access" and examine the information. The only element of this page that truly matters is the Download link; click it and choose Run to launch it (or click Save if you want to save it to your drive and launch later).

If you are not already running Service Pack 1, a dialog box will tell you that you need to install it in order to install the WPA patch. Go to `www.microsoft.com/windows` and click the Windows Update link, choosing Windows XP Service Pack 1 as your only download. Before doing so, make sure you have something to do for the next hour or so, as Service Pack 1 downloads and installs itself. After that, download the WPA patch anew, or open it from the hard drive location to which you saved it earlier.

You can find everything you need to establish client-level WPA-PSK on the Wireless Network Properties dialog box found in Windows XP with the Wi-Fi Protected Access patch installed. Figure 7-4 shows this dialog box with both options selected. The first is the Network Authentication option, the first drop-down menu, here shown with the WPA-SPK choice selected. The other three options in this dialog box are Open, Shared, and WPA, the first two of which are WEP options, as discussed in Chapter 6. The other, WPA, depends, like its access point configuration counterpart, on the existence of a RADIUS server, and has no function on an AP network without such a server.

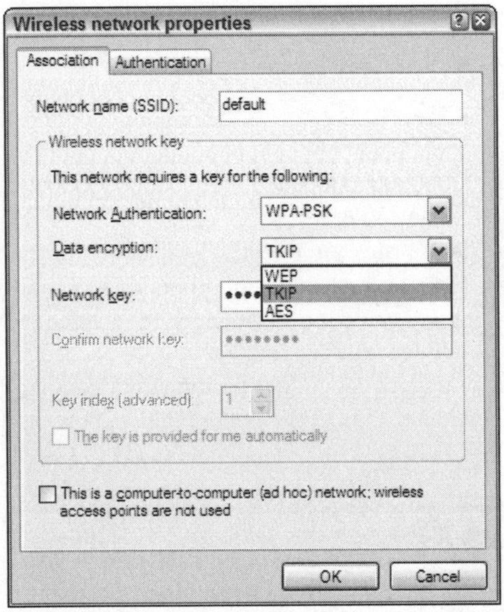

Figure 7-4: WPA options on the WLAN adapter.

The second drop-down menu, Data Encryption, offers three choices: WEP, TKIP, and AES. Unfortunately, Windows gives no clue which one you should use, via neither embedded help (instructions on the dialog box) nor context help. Nor, for that matter, in the Help and Support Center; here, a search on WPA reveals absolutely no hits whatsoever, not even for the aforementioned Windows Product Activation. Clearly, as of this writing the Help system has not caught up with the addition of WPA, but by the time you read this, with Service Pack 2 officially released, that deficiency will almost certainly be addressed.

In fact, the lack of official Help for WPA networking displays just how recently this security feature has emerged. The D-Link DI-624 access point configuration system offers its own Help pages, and while they range from the somewhat useful to the completely worthless, they, too, offer nothing on the WPA options, even though the radio buttons for WPA and WPA-PSK settings feature prominently on the Wireless screens. Again, this lack will probably disappear over the next few months, and the products you buy will probably include the necessary details in the Help system, as embedded help, and in the manuals. As we write this chapter, none of the three recently produced access points offer any assistance.

In other words, you're left to your own devices, and you can choose either to engage in a process of trial and error (always frustrating with networking products) or know enough about WPA in advance to know which setting to choose. Having read through the beginning parts of this chapter, you'll automatically know that of the three Data Encryption methods offered on the Wireless Network Properties dialog box, TKIP gets you where you want to go. WEP won't work because WPA replaces WEP entirely, and AES, while possible on WPA equipment, remains a technology primarily for the future, when the full 802.11i spec appears in the new range of wireless products.

With the correct network authentication and data encryption settings in place on the access point, all that remains is to type the passphrase, identical to that established on the access point. In the Windows XP Wireless Network Properties dialog box, you don't need to specify what kind of key you're typing because, as with the various WEP keys, the combination of authentication and encryption choices, when combined with the key length, tells Windows XP what the key represents. It would help, however, if the dialog box changed, on selecting WPA-PSK, to reflect the terminology of WPA, with Network Key relabeled either Passphrase or Shared Secret. This way, nobody would get confused wondering precisely what to type in the Network Key field. Still, the trick is simply to type the passphrase, click OK, and then wait while Windows XP reconfigures itself to recognize the newly defined network and connect to it with the enhanced security in place.

As with WEP configuration, you need not use the Wireless Network Properties dialog box supplied by Windows XP. Instead, you can uncheck the box labeled "Use Windows to configure my wireless network settings," under the Wireless Networks tab of the Wireless Network Connection Properties dialog box, and open the configuration screens supplied with your WLAN adapter. You have little reason to do so, however, because Windows XP really does know itself best, so save the device-specific configuration menus for other operating systems and make use of those in your operating system when setting up your enhanced security. Obviously, this statement does *not* necessarily hold true if your vendor has included proprietary technology in the wireless WLAN adapters, especially if you're using the adapter in conjunction with an AP that shares this proprietary technology. Given the trend of vendors to include non-standard speed and even encryption technologies on their wireless products, you should check to ensure you're making the best use of your product before working with the default Windows XP configuration boxes.

Enabling 802.11x Authentication

When you configure your WLAN adapters via the Windows XP dialog boxes, with the Wireless Networks tab set to allow Windows to perform wireless configuration automatically, as soon as you choose either of the WPA settings, WPA or WPA-PSK, Windows enables IEEE 802.1x authentication for your adapter as well. Figure 7-5 shows the setting in place, as indicated by the grayed-out checkbox instructing Windows to enable this technology.

IEEE 802.11x authentication goes hand in hand with wireless networks, particularly those configured to use WPA or its eventual successor, 802.11i. In Windows XP Service Pack 1 and later, as well as in the Windows 2003 Server operating system, you can enable 802.1x authentication only on infrastructure networks that require a network key for access. In other words, you can use 802.1x authentication for WEP as well as WPA-encrypted networks, and Microsoft encourages you to enable it for both, but when you put WPA in place, Windows does the job for you.

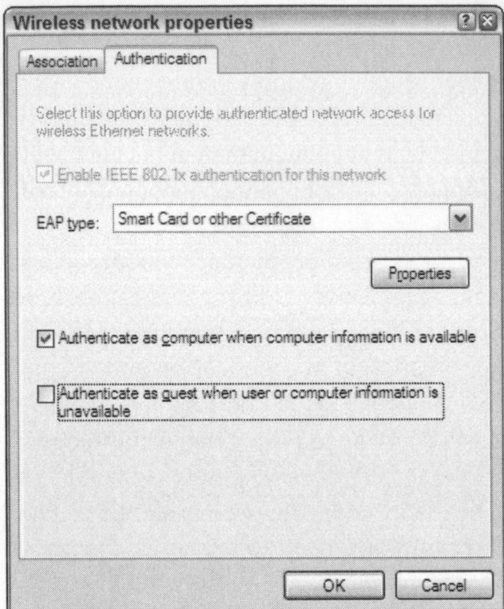

Figure 7-5: The network with 802.1x authentication established.

To use this authentication method, Windows needs to know the Extensible Authentication Protocol (EAP) type you wish to use. The default, and the one you should stick with until you know your AP or server can handle anything else, is Smart Card or Other Certificate. As mentioned, there's no need to change this; as long as your network connects successfully, the authentication is in place (it's part of Microsoft's attempt to automate all wireless configurations). However, you have several choices besides this default, both an entirely different EAP type and numerous options accessed via the Properties button with the Smart Card option selected.

Figure 7-6 displays the result of clicking that Properties button. Here you can see numerous possible locations from which your WLAN adapter can acquire the certificate information necessary to continue. If you have a specific server that stores certificates you can use (as on a larger business network), check Connect to these Servers and fill in the server details (as supplied by your network administrator). The list of Trusted Root Certification Authorities in the large pane in the middle of the dialog box provides numerous certificate types that you can instruct Windows to use, but again you would find these in place in a business or organizational network, never a home or even small office network. If you know the certificate you are to request, check the appropriate box; otherwise, leave the defaults in place. The Validate Server Certificate checkbox lets you instruct your PC to guarantee that the certificate used for these purposes remains valid, by checking its credentials.

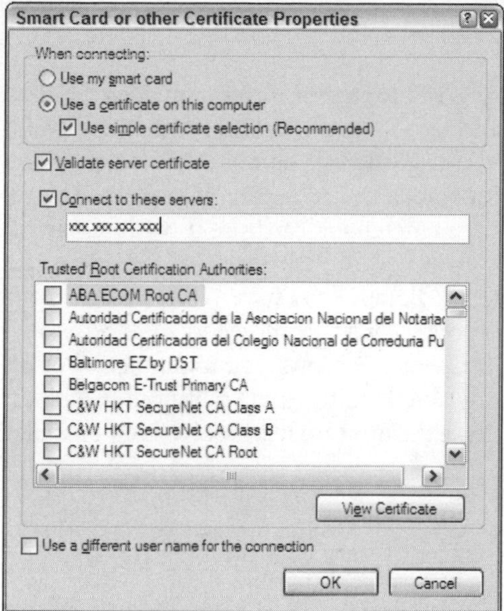

Figure 7-6: The Smart Card or Other Certificates dialog box.

Returning to the Authentication tab, you can click the EAP Type drop-down menu and select the alternative EAP type, PEAP. Protected EAP (PEAP) extends the EAP protocol to enable highly secure transactions in a manner similar to a virtual private network, by creating a secure tunnel in which the packets can move. Specifically, EAP provides a flexible alternative to EAP-TLS (Transport Layer Security), improving on EAP-TLS itself by removing the requirements to install and manage certificates on the clients. Essentially, PEAP begins by authenticating the connection, by using digital certificate technology, and then creates the encrypted tunnel along with encryption keys for the data. The data is not only encrypted, but also checked for integrity, as it moves through the connections.

Again, on a home or small office network you will have little reason to consider PEAP. But its prominence on the Wireless Network Properties dialog box points to the increased concern by Microsoft and, as should now be apparent, by all wireless networking vendors and technologists, for WLAN transmission security. You will see services in the near future to provide increased security for even small WLANs, through a certificate lease or rental kind of configuration, just as security services for standard LANs are now available from third parties. This is all good news, of course, for anyone with even a small home network, because while you could argue that the data you transfer over your personal WLAN is of less overall importance the data that travels through a corporate WLAN, in fact this assumption is only partly valid. True, your personal data affects fewer people, but you have far fewer means of recovering from data or resource theft, and you don't have anything approaching limited liability in matters surrounding your own life. The point is, of course, that securing your WLAN should become a top priority for you, no matter how insignificant it may seem, and WPA, with its extremely friendly WPA-PSK subset, lets you do precisely that.

Summary

At this point in the short history of wireless networking, Wi-Fi Protected Access provides the best security you can get for your WLAN. To implement it, however, both your access point and *all* your wireless network adapters must support it, and if you're working with one or more older adapters (as many home and small business users are), you'll need to upgrade before putting it in place. There's no point having WPA enabled on the access point if even one notebook can't use it because having even one unsecured component on a wireless network gives you a weak link that intruders can exploit. The upgrade might very well be worthwhile, however, because you have WPA in place on all your devices; you can come as close to resting easily as is possible with Wi-Fi security concerns.

But there's more to security than either WPA or WEP. Chapter 8 shows you a number of other options for stopping intrusions, ranging from the extremely simple to the more advanced. Combine these with your preferred encryption technology, and you have the most hacker-proof WLAN possible.

Chapter 8

Security Tips and Tricks

It's never enough. You get your ad hoc wireless network up and running, and you think you've got it made. Then you get an infrastructure network up and running, and you think you've got it *really* made. But then you start reading about all the ways in which intruders can access your WLAN, and suddenly things don't look quite so rosy. Despite everything you've accomplished — and believe me, getting a wireless network going is nothing to sneeze at — you realize your network contains several vulnerabilities. Among other things, you realize you can see straight into the Shared Documents folder of not only the PCs on your own LAN, but those of the people who live next door as well. So you start thinking that if you can see them, they can probably see you, and that's simply not what you want your neighbors to be able to do. Add to this the newfound stress over those people who drive around locating open wireless networks, and you start considering the possibility of shutting your WLAN down completely.

Well, don't. Although wireless networks offer more than their share of security concerns, you have a wide range of options at your disposal which, either individually or in conjunction with one or more other options, can render your WLAN increasingly difficult to crack. This chapter offers a variety of tips for improving your network's security, and in the process provides a look at configuration menus and dialog boxes that will likely spur you into investigating security measures even further. Best of all, you can use these tips as a springboard for developing security checklists and troubleshooting guidelines, and as a basis for coming up with your own tips.

Quick and Easy Security

It takes very little time to improve your WLAN's security even a small amount. You don't have to know anything about WEP, WPA, or anything else of even that technical a nature. Just change a few of the default settings for the WLAN equipment, toss in a few Windows tricks and a few more simple everyday tips for all types of computers, and you've filled in the most obviously open holes.

Change Your Admin Password

Your first step in security *anything* on computers is to change the default password that lets you into the administrative utility. Whether you're working with an access point or a router/AP combination, the admin utility has a default password that you can change within that utility. Locate it and make the change so that an intruder into a networked PC can't access the utility. As with all other passwords, make it difficult to figure out, writing it down for your own access if it's too difficult for you to remember yourself.

Stop Broadcasting Your SSID

When you broadcast your SSID, you make it easier for legitimate users of your WLAN to connect to your network because the WLAN adapters can "see" the access point and connect automatically. Unfortunately, you also make it easier for everyone else in the area to connect as well because broadcasting an SSID is very much like broadcasting a radio show: it's available to anyone who tunes to that frequency. Of course, radio stations want as many listeners as possible, and the last thing they try to do is keep people away. If you want a wide-open neighborhood network, by all means operate the same way. But most of the time, of course, you don't. You want your WLAN available only to a restricted group of users, and for that reason you should stop the open broadcast.

Interestingly, access point vendors tend not to see the SSID broadcast issue as particularly significant. APs typically default to having SSID broadcast enabled as part of the factory setup, and in some cases, disabling this feature takes some digging. In the case of the Microsoft Wireless Base Station, the option to disable SSID broadcasts conveniently resides on the main page of the Wireless configuration screens (see Figure 8-1), available simply by clicking Wireless from the main menu on the left, although strangely enough WLAN security configurations occupy another screen entirely. By comparison, with the D-Link DI-624 you need to drill down to the Performance screen on the Advanced tab. Figure 8-2 shows this screen, with the option for SSID Broadcast disabled.

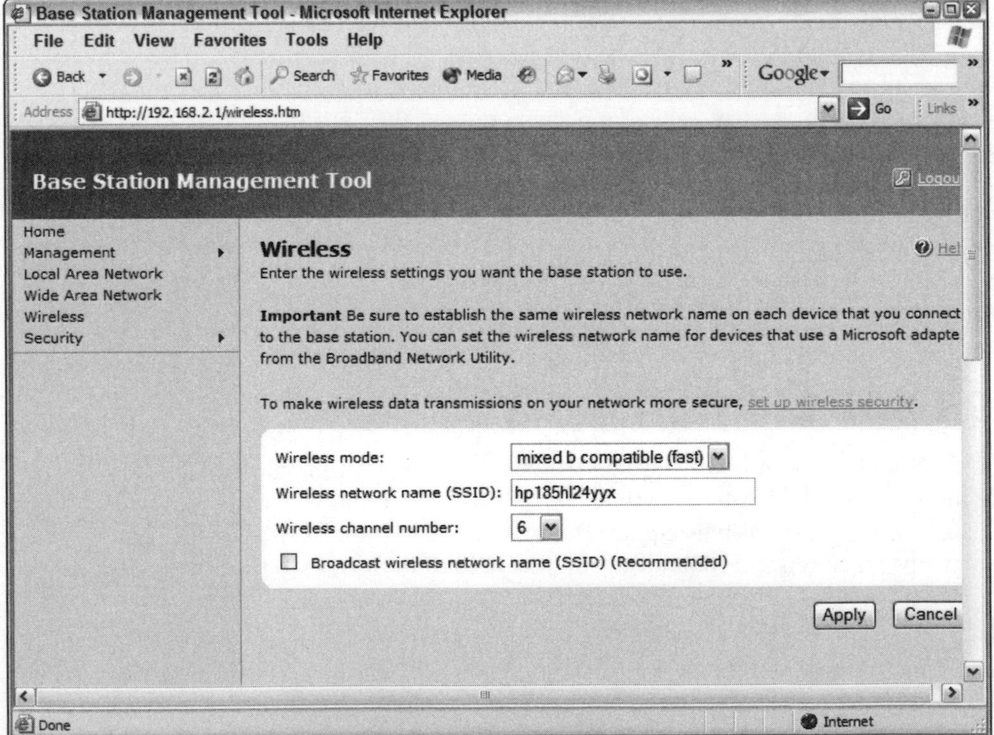

Figure 8-1: Disabling SSID broadcast on the Microsoft MN-700 Base Station.

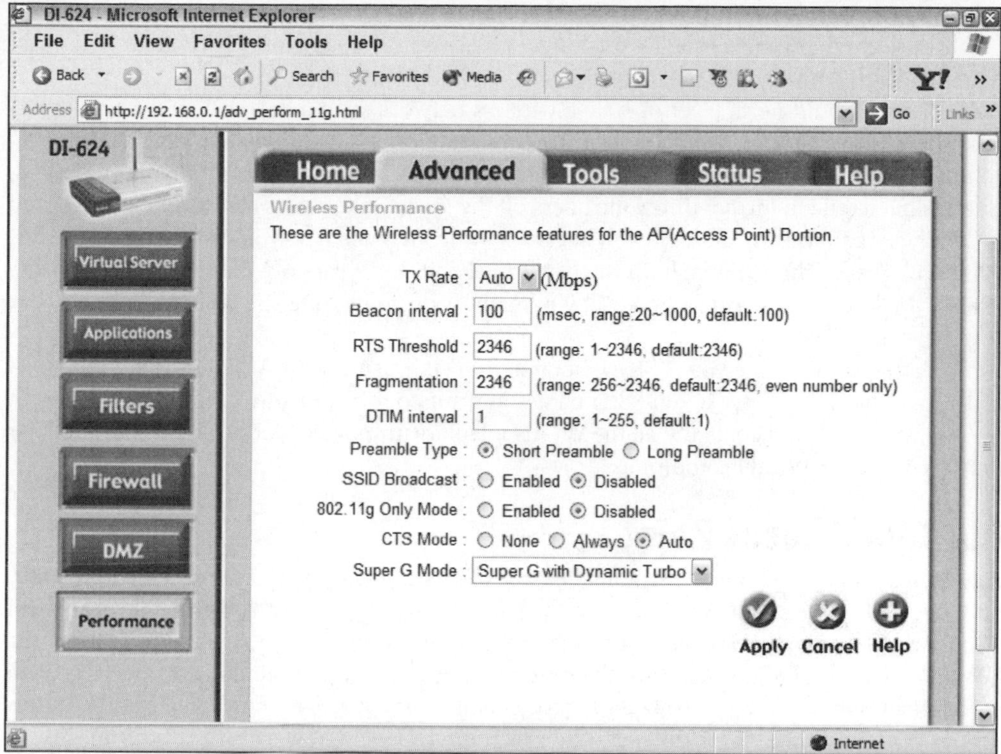

Figure 8-2: Disabling SSID broadcast on the D-Link DI-624 router.

What's the effect of disabling the SSID broadcast? Simply this: You need to know the SSID of the network before you can connect to it. The principle is similar to the classic interface design principle that recognition is easier than recall. Menus and icons work better than command lines for many users because on the former you simply see the choices and select from among them, while command lines force you to remember what you need to type, and if you've never used a particular command before, you won't be able to use it now either. A broadcast SSID is analogous to the menu/icon interface, with the user presented with the name of the SSID, while refusing to broadcast SSIDs forces the network user to manually type it into the configuration dialog boxes for each client PC. If the user doesn't know it, the PC cannot connect.

As you might suspect, even this doesn't do the trick, unless you change something else: the SSID itself. Which brings us to the next tip.

Change Your SSID

If you've already stopped broadcasting your SSID, you might very well ask why it matters if you change it. Because, quite simply, most SSIDs are known whether or not they're broadcast. Access points ship with factory settings in place, and one of these factory settings is the default name of the SSID. Typical defaults include "wireless" and, in fact, "default" itself, and anyone with even a small

degree of background in setting up APs, let alone trying to steal their signals, knows these defaults very well. All would-be intruders need do is configure their WLAN adapters with a default SSID, and chances are they'll find an AP for the connection.

As a result, you should never, ever operate a wireless network with a default SSID. After configuring your AP not to broadcast its SSID, open the configuration screens again and change the SSID to something an intruder will find hard to guess. As with a password, use a combination of letters, symbols, and characters, to further throw intruders off the scent. Take a pet's name, for example, and add some characters to it, so your dog Ralph becomes *ra5lp3h*. Make it so you can remember it, but no one else will guess. The SSID ra5lp3h might mean: Ralph is 5 years old and he's my third dog. Who'd know? In a business setting, of course, you might want something less personally based, but the idea is the same.

Not only should you change your SSID as soon as you start using your AP, you should change it periodically as well. Create a set of ten SSID names and rotate them, or just keep coming up with new ones. Yes, you have to reconfigure all the WLAN adapters in your network's clients, but that's far better than having your WLAN compromised.

Unplug Your Access Point

Okay, maybe this tip comes close to offending because of its sheer simplicity, but it's absolutely valid: when nobody needs to use your WLAN, turn it off by unplugging it (most router/AP devices don't have power switches). For a home network, this is obviously easy to arrange by shutting down the router/AP and, for that matter, your PCs if the house will be empty or before the last person goes to bed, but for small businesses it can be equally easy. Unless an employee is working late and requires access to the WLAN, unplug it for the night — in fact, teach people how to plug it back in, just in case they do come back to the office later. No question, cable and DSL providers emphasize the always-on capabilities of their Internet services, but there's no reason that you have to adhere to it.

In the case of multiple access points or WLAN extenders, in office buildings, don't hesitate to power one or more of them down, even if you don't unplug the main router/AP/switch combinations themselves. If you have an access point in the foyer, for example, for use primarily for guests or sales personnel to use in that area, unplug it after hours as a matter of course.

If you do power down an AP, be sure to give it a few minutes to restart when you plug it back in. The AP needs to acquire an IP address from the broadband modem, and to transmit addresses via DHCP to all the network clients.

Watch Where You Place Your APs

Like unplugging your APs, this security issue is based on common sense, not on configuration screens. APs have specific ranges beyond which the signal will not reach at all, or will reach only weakly. In an office building, place the APs as far away as possible from where you might get intruders attempting to access it. For the most part, this means placing the APs as far from the street in front of the building as you can, unless of course you're concerned (as you should be) with intruders driving around the back of the building and connecting from there. In that case, set the APs in the middle of the building if at all possible. Obviously, your primary responsibility lies with ensuring that legitimate users can access the AP, but usually you have quite a bit of flexibility in this regard inside the building, especially a single-story building where beaming signals through floors and ceilings doesn't present an issue.

Watch Your Wireless Log

In all likelihood, your AP or router/AP tracks wireless connectivity and lets you view the results in a log file. Typically, the log screen shows time of day of each connection and the IP address from which it occurred, as well as, importantly, the MAC address of that device. In a multi-PC environment, you can use the log to determine the extent and the duration of the WLAN connections, and you can use this information to see if any unauthorized access occurred, when it occurred, and from which computer it occurred. Although it is certainly not a detailed report, the log can provide a quick and easy way to see if access occurred at an unexpected time of day (such as the middle of the night) or from a MAC address you don't recognize, and you can take steps accordingly to block this access.

Figure 8-3 shows the Status screen of the D-Link DI-624, while Figure 8-4 shows the similar screen on the Microsoft MN-700. In the former case, you can specify which types of activity you want logged, and you can tell the AP to send the log information to an e-mail address of your choice. Unfortunately, this utility on the DI-624 isn't sophisticated enough to enable you to set a schedule for sending the log data, nor an option for SMTP servers that require username/password authentication. Still, the feature can certainly be useful. The Microsoft log doesn't offer an e-mail option at all, though, so even the primitive feature of the DI-624 gets at least some points here.

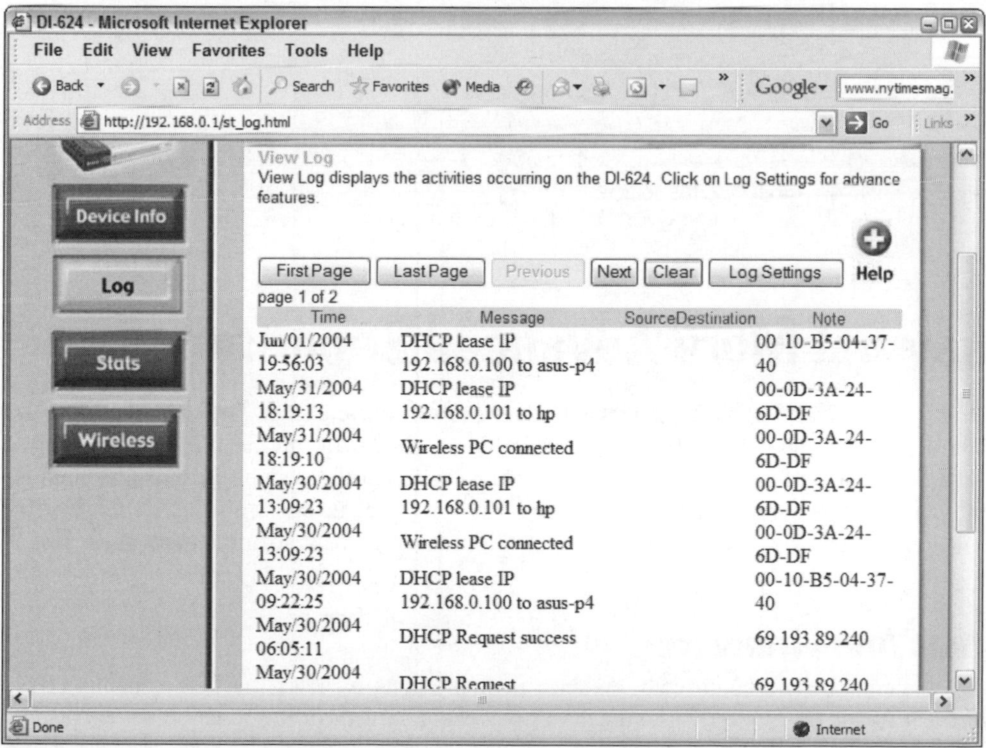

Figure 8-3: The D-Link wireless status screen.

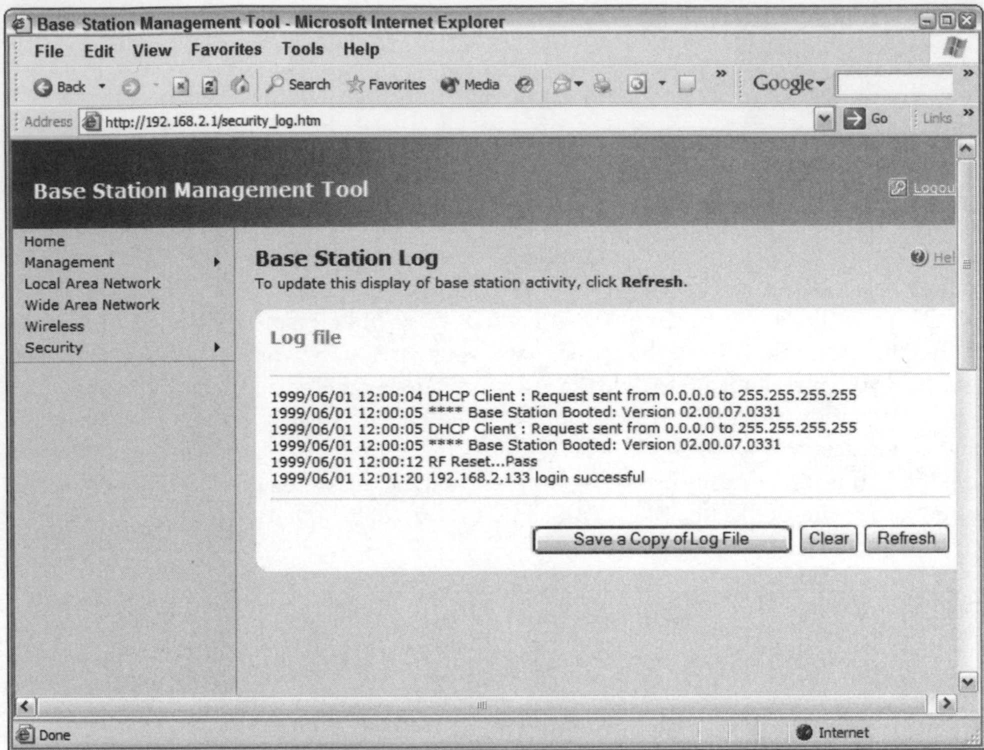

Figure 8-4: The Microsoft wireless status screen.

Somewhat More Advanced Security

The security tips presented so far in this chapter are relatively simple steps you can take to secure your network without digging too deeply into your AP's management interface. If you're willing to work a little harder at configuring your AP, however, this section outlines some advanced techniques you might want to implement. You could certainly argue that there's no such thing as too much security. You'll need to decide for yourself, though, if the time investment to implement these tips is worth it to you.

Upgrade Your Firmware

Access point manufacturers continually enhance their products by releasing new versions of the *firmware*, the software built directly into the device that enables the device to function with all its features. Firmware updates typically fix bugs in the existing software, but they also can add features and improve performance in specific areas. Often after a firmware update, you'll notice additional configuration items or even entire configuration screens, but usually the changes are relatively minor.

In some cases, you can even lose features, as shown in Figure 8-5. Here, the D-Link DI-624 firmware page states that only versions 2.25 and 2.28 are compatible with the Xbox Live gaming system; downloading and installing the latest version on this page, 2.42, would render the game console inoperable for live play.

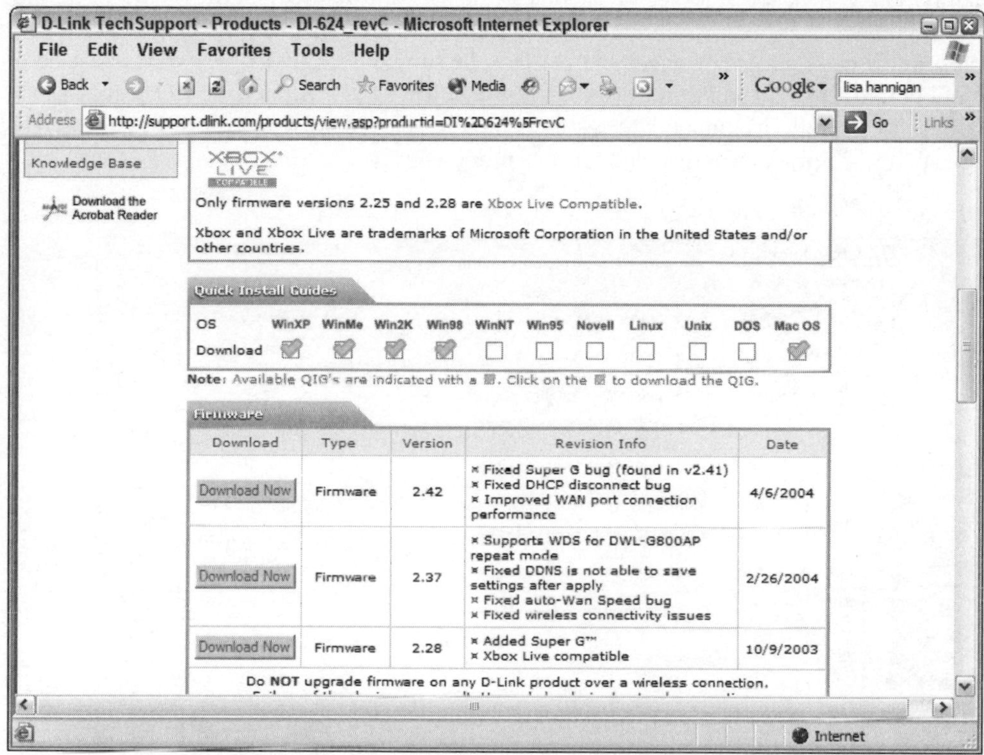

Figure 8-5: Updates can be downgrades, rendering certain features inaccessible.

The importance of upgrading firmware lies primarily in the enhancement and repair of security features. Frequently, no such enhancements exist, mostly because the manufacturers focus considerable attention on getting those features correct from the beginning, even at the expense of other less important items. Visit the firmware upgrade page regularly, however, to determine if a security fix has become available, and if so, download and install it immediately, even if you do lose the ability to play Halo online.

Don't Allow Remote Management

The ability to manage a network remotely provides the convenience of not having to physically move to a PC experiencing problems. Unfortunately, the legitimate administrators aren't the only ones who find remote management convenient; so do all the intruders out there looking for a way to break into

unsecured networks. An intruder need only fire up a Web browser, type in the IP address of the router or AP, and open the configuration utility after that. Figure 8-6 shows the small but important Remote Management configuration items for the D-Link DI-624. By default, D-Link disables this feature, but some manufacturers set the default to Enabled, especially on older routers. Note the asterisk in the IP Address field; if you enable the feature with this setting in place, any computer on the Internet can remotely manage the router/AP as long as the user knows the IP address and the admin password. Not good.

If you absolutely need remote management in place, be sure to change the password to the configuration utility frequently. In addition, if you're logging in from a PC with a fixed IP address, specify that address as the only legitimate address for remote management. But unless you absolutely need this capability, simply leave it disabled for maximum security.

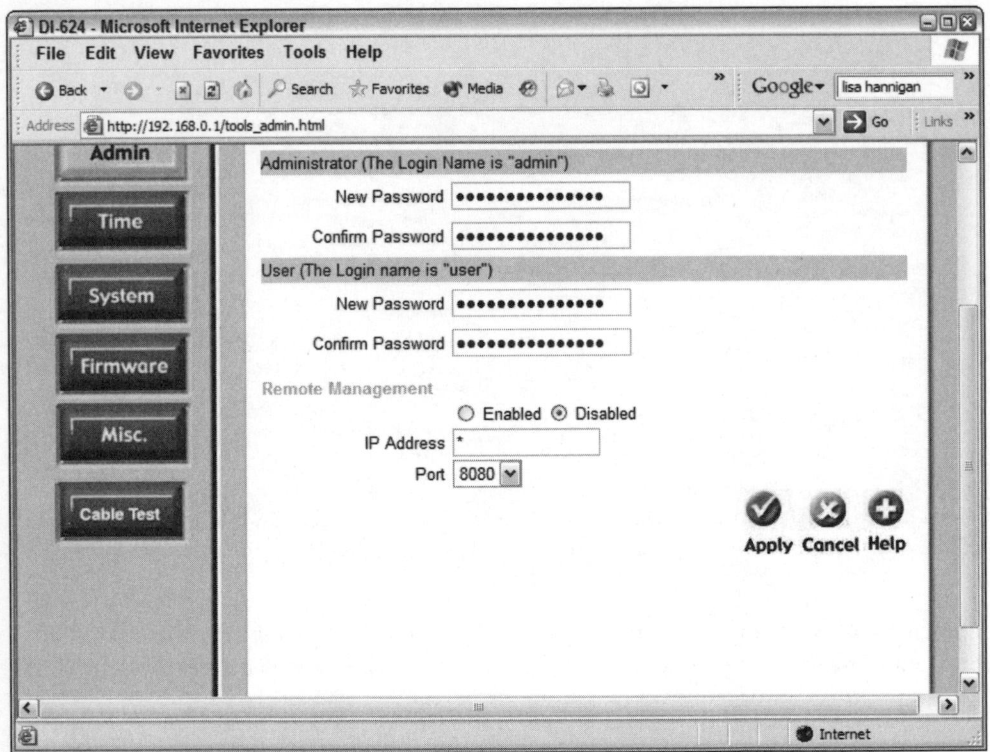

Figure 8-6: Configuring the AP to disallow remote access.

Use Static IP Addresses

DHCP brings something approaching magic to your network. Instead of opening the configuration dialog boxes of each network PC, you set them to acquire network addresses (IP numbers) automatically, and the DHCP server takes care of the rest. In the case of an infrastructure WLAN working in conjunction with a cable/DSL router and a broadband modem, you actually have three DHCP servers in place: your router, your access point, and your Internet service provider's server. The broadband router acquires an IP from the Internet service provider's DHCP server, and in turn acts as a DHCP server for the AP. Once the AP has acquired its IP from the router, it then turns around and provides DHCP service for the WLAN adapters.

At each stage along the line, anyone accessing the DHCP server can also access the network. This isn't much of a problem in the case of either the broadband modem or the cable/DSL router because both require that the would-be user connect the PC via Ethernet cable, an obvious physical difficulty if the user isn't actually in the building or the switch room. Anyone who knows the SSID name of your wireless LAN, however, can gain access without any physical connection because the AP happily provides an IP address to that user's machine via its DHCP technology.

To get around this vulnerability, stop your AP from assigning IP numbers dynamically (automatically). All of today's APs offer this option, typically available from the DHCP settings screen. Figure 8-7 shows the configuration screen for the D-Link DI-624 that allows this to occur. Static IPs work by tying each IP address to the MAC address of the network adapter. An abbreviation for Media Access Control address, the MAC address is also known as the physical address, and refers to the unique identifier of each adapter — or, practically speaking, each PC. Your DHCP configuration screen reports the MAC address of each adapter it has located, but you can determine the MAC address yourself by opening a Command box in Windows XP or 2000 and typing **ipconfig /all**. The extensive amount of information presented as a result of this command includes a variety of addressing information, with the MAC address at the bottom, labeled as Physical Address. In the D-Link screen shown in Figure 8-7, the AP labels the DHCP Client with a combination of the host name (the name you initially gave the computer) plus the MAC address.

The MAC address is significant in the configuration of static DHCP. To assign a specific address to a specific PC, you need to enter the MAC Address of that PC into the appropriate fields on the configuration screen. In effect, you conjoin the IP address with the MAC address, whereas in a dynamic IP situation the DHCP server performs the joining at the time of connection, assigning whatever IP address comes next to that particular MAC address. When configured for static IP, the AP reserves each IP number for a particular MAC address, allowing no other adapter but that one to acquire that IP address.

Even after typing the MAC addresses and assigning them an IP number, you're still not finished. You now have to sit at each network PC, open the TCP/IP configuration dialog boxes, and type the specific IP number assigned to that PC. Figure 8-8 shows the Internet Protocol Properties dialog box for the same PC as that was assigned in Figure 8-7, this time with the IP address, subnet mask, and DNS servers entered manually. In the typical dynamic DHCP setup, these fields would remain empty, and the DHCP server would provide them to the PC.

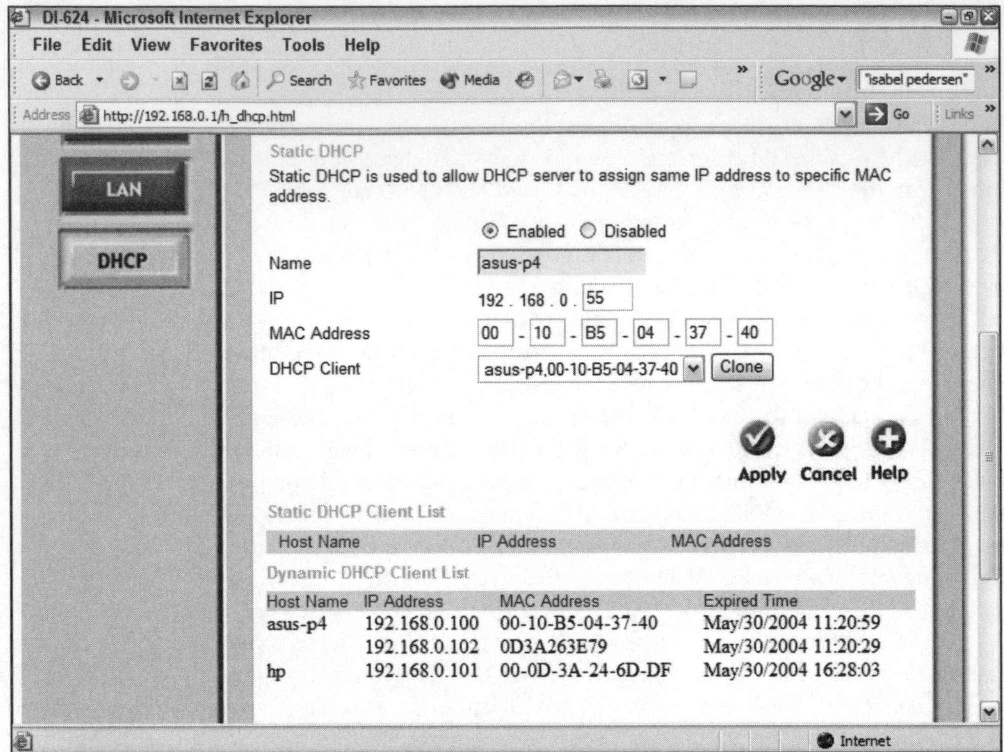

Figure 8-7: Configuring the AP for static IP addresses.

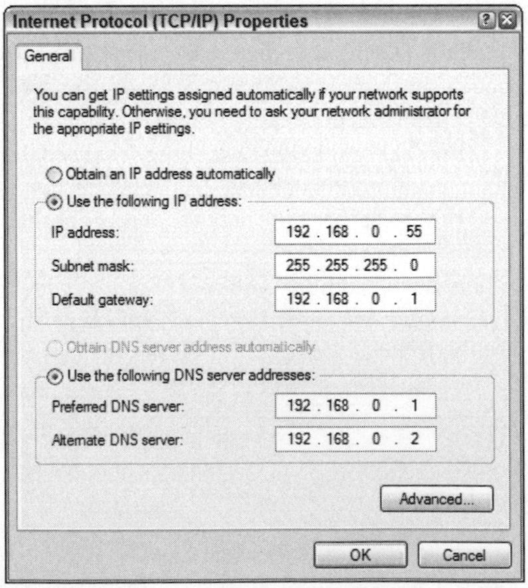

Internet Protocol (TCP/IP) Properties
General
You can get IP settings assigned automatically if your network supports this capability. Otherwise, you need to ask your network administrator for the appropriate IP settings.
Obtain an IP address automatically
Use the following IP address:
IP address: 192 . 168 . 0 . 55
Subnet mask: 255 . 255 . 255 . 0
Default gateway: 192 . 168 . 0 . 1
Obtain DNS server address automatically
Use the following DNS server addresses:
Preferred DNS server: 192 . 168 . 0 . 1
Alternate DNS server: 192 . 168 . 0 . 2
Advanced...
OK Cancel

Figure 8-8: Manual configuration of TCP/IP Properties.

Use MAC Filtering

Not only can you use the MAC addresses in static IP range restrictions, you can further increase the security on your WLAN by enabling MAC filtering on the access point. All recent APs offer this option, typically available in a menu item or screen section labeled Filters (additional filters are discussed in the following sections). Common to any network configuration, MAC filters let you specify which WLAN cards will be granted access to the wireless network, and which will not. That is, you can either allow or deny access to each MAC number.

Typically, the default configuration allows all IP addresses to gain access, and enabling the MAC filtering option lets you specify which machines can do so. You have the choice of either ***allowing*** only specific machines to have access, or of ***denying*** access to specific machines. Obviously, the Allow method gives you stricter control, but the Deny method can be extremely useful if you want widespread access but you want to shut out a particular group of machines, permitting access to everything else. It's a bit like crowd control for international soccer matches: stadiums and arenas allow access to everybody except specific people or groups. Come to think of it, and to bludgeon the analogy into oblivion, these venues use both kinds of control. They allow only those with tickets, but they deny a smaller group within that larger group.

Restrict the Range of IP Numbers

As a means of making static IP numbers even more effective, configure your AP to allow only a limited range of IP addresses. This way, you control precisely how many clients can acquire an IP address, thereby lowering the chances even further of the intruder not only guessing the legal range of IP numbers, but being able to use one. As soon as you power down one of the client PCs (or unplug the network cable), that PC's IP number becomes available, so this system has its vulnerabilities as well, but obviously with this option in place the intruder has more work to do.

Restricting the IP range works extremely well with dynamic IP addressing as well. While not as secure as a WLAN in which each adapter has a fixed IP, a small range of dynamic IPs does make discovering the valid range at least somewhat more difficult. Provide a range that will allow as many users to access the WLAN as necessary at any given time, and you've provided a useful security service. Figure 8-9 shows an AP configuration screen set to dynamic IP distribution, but with only a small range of IP numbers.

In fact, depending on how your users access the WLAN, you might need a smaller IP range than you first think. Unless all users access the WLAN at the same time, you can restrict the range of dynamic IPs to a number smaller than the total number of users, because as soon as one user disconnects, either by powering down the PC or removing the WLAN adapter, that IP number becomes available for use. In the case of static IP addresses, here too you can reuse IP numbers. As users leave their workstations for an extended period of time, you can disable that PC's connection (in the Network Connections window) and have another PC use that static IP. This method takes reliable management skills because if you have two PCs configured with the same IP address, you'll get a network error, but it's certainly possible. In a small office, for example if you have four PCs, only two of which need to access the network at a time, you can configure your AP for a two-number dynamic IP range, or you can configure it to use only two fixed IP numbers. Either way, you significantly lower the chance of intrusion.

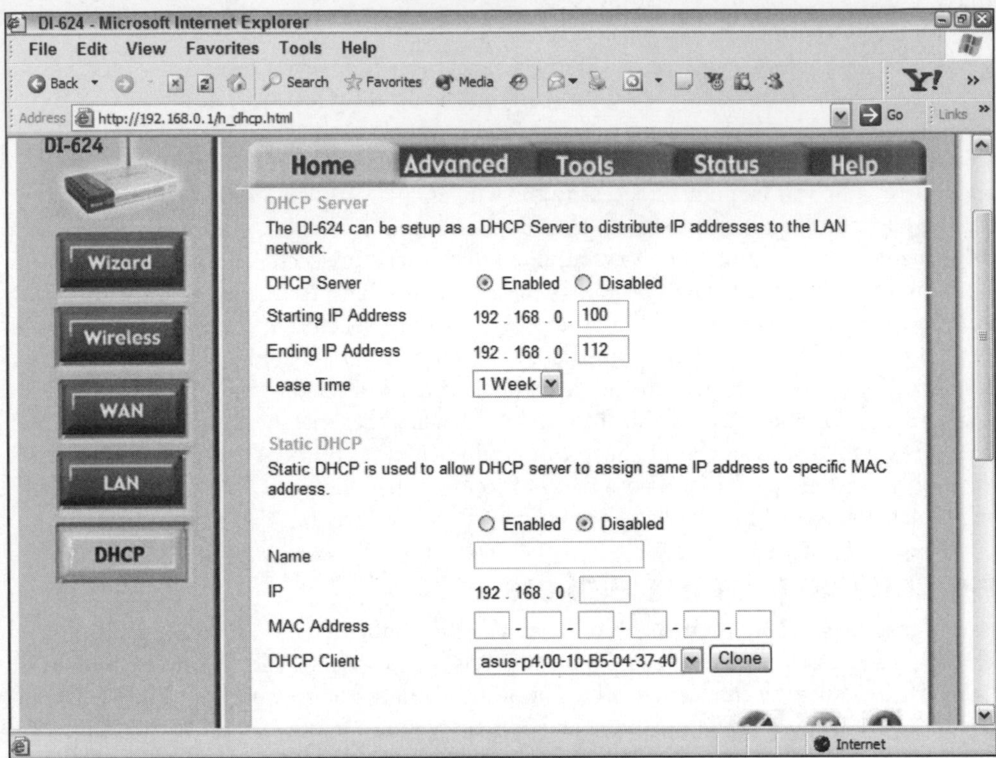

Figure 8-9: Restricting the IP range to 13 addresses.

Change the Names of Additional Access Points

When you add additional access points to your system, each one adds the same vulnerabilities as the original. You can complete every security configuration possible on the original access point, but the minute you add another, you open up the possibility of people easily connecting to it, and through it, to the primary access point. It's a bit like pinning a note to your front door to remind yourself of the hiding place for the door key and the access code for the burglar alarm system.

For this tip, we use the Microsoft MN-700 Base Station as the example. As Figure 8-10 shows, you can change the base station to access point mode, in which the device no longer acts as a router and no longer connects directly to the cable or DSL modem. Instead, it becomes simply another network device on you wired LAN, but unlike the other PCs on the network, this device provides wireless service. If you already have an existing LAN, adding this device in access point mode gives you an infrastructure LAN, but if an AP is already in place, as is the case if you connect the MN-700 to an existing MN-700 or another AP/router, the new AP provides a second wireless LAN, complete with all the possible security issues of any other AP with its factory settings established.

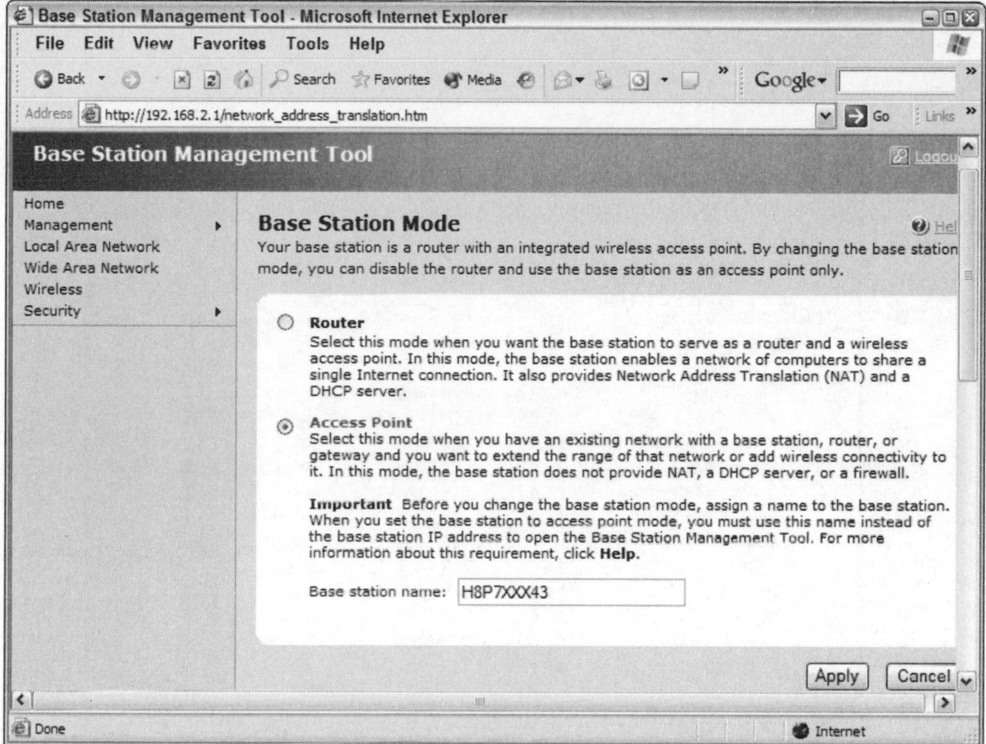

Figure 8-10: Setting the router to access point–only mode.

From a security standpoint, you provide the first round of security by giving the new AP a new name. Any name will do, but once again, try to make it something an intruder won't easily guess. This particular product uses MN-700 as its default name, and obviously anyone seriously interested in breaking into your WLAN will know the industry defaults. Give it a new, unique name, to shut the door as much as possible.

Use Virtual Servers

All routers manufactured today have a virtual server feature, one that gives you control over precisely which network services the router/AP will allow network users to access. Usually this feature defaults to disabled, so you needn't worry about configuring it unless you have a specific reason to do so. But once you enable the virtual servers for any purpose, monitor the feature closely to ensure that you don't open your network to unwanted access.

Figure 8-11 shows the virtual server feature available on the D-Link DI-624. In each case, you can configure and edit the local, private IP number dedicated to that specific network service, and you can schedule the times during which that service is accessible. Scheduling, in fact, works very well as a deterrent for intrusion; as with anything else related to networks, don't have something turned on if nobody needs to use it at that time.

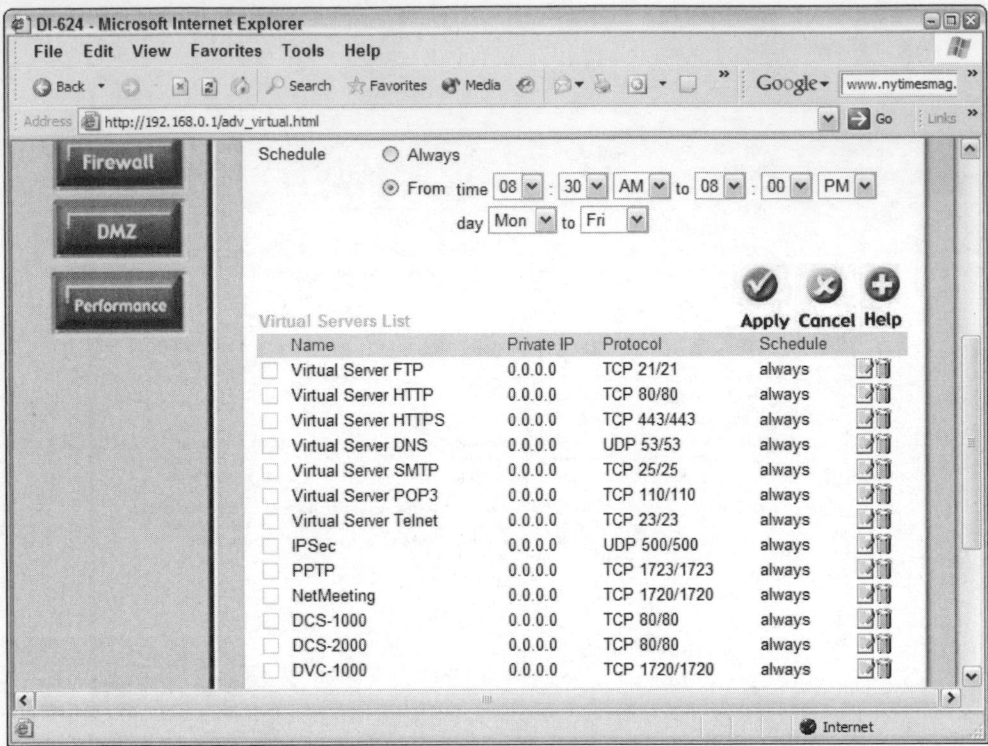

Figure 8-11: Configuring the virtual server feature.

As Figure 8-11 shows, the DI-624 configuration screen offers several typical server functions:

- FTP — File Transfer Protocol (old-style but fast data transfer)
- HTTP — HyperText Transfer Protocol (that is, the Web)
- HTTPS — Secure Web services (using encryption)
- DNS — Domain Name System (conversion of user-friendly addresses into IP numbers)
- SMTP — Simple Mail Transfer Protocol (standard for sending e-mail)
- POP3 — Post Office Protocol version 3 (standard for receiving e-mail)
- Telnet — Accessing Windows NT/2000/XP machines via a command line
- IPSec — IP Security — security mechanism used on Virtual Private Networks
- NetMeeting — Allows remote users to use NetMeeting with one another through the local network
- Other D-Link products such as Internet cameras

Without enabling these items, your router will not admit traffic for these protocols. If you want to run an intranet Web server from behind your local network, for example, you need to enable it, although you can help your security issue by specifying a different port than the standard for that protocol. For example, configuring the router/AP to use port 8080 for Internet access, instead of the standard port 80, or to use port 26 for SMTP service, instead of the standard port 25, can significantly reduce the danger of intrusion (although you should change these ports regularly as well).

Note that these changes affect all network activities, not only those involving WLAN users. But their importance for security is such that even when setting up a WLAN, they become significant. When you configure a server at the router level, you need to configure all network clients, including those connected through your AP, to access the correct port.

Honeypots and Fake Access Points

One of the most interesting ways to protect your resources from wireless intrusion is to do the unexpected and ***invite*** the intruders inside. Still relatively new in the world of security, ***honeypots*** have acquired a kind of cult following, as well as a practical usefulness, precisely because what they do seems both obvious and strange. In effect, a honeypot litters the airwaves with simulated access points, inviting intruders to take advantage of the network but, in simple cases at least, offering them nowhere to go. Instead of trying to hide your real AP by engaging all the other security mechanisms mentioned in this chapter, you put it out in the open with a crowd of other APs, hiding the real one simply by giving the intruder too much to do. They might never know which is the real AP.

A true honeypot, in fact, has a purpose different from simply disguising the real AP. Administrators design them to monitor and study what hackers do and how to defeat their attempts at unauthorized access. In fact, at least one group of researchers has banded together for the sake of creating honeypot-like environments to catch intruders and learn their methods. The Honeynet Project (project.honeynet.org) has a four-phase process in the works to develop ever more sophisticated ways of luring intruders in and studying their behavior, and has even developed a bootable CD-ROM that automatically establishes a Honeynet gateway for your network. Called the Honeywall, the CD-ROM creates a system that hackers can target as they wish, while the system monitors and records their actions.

For the purposes of this book, however, and indeed for most users, the honeypot has value for its ability to deceive intruders rather than capture them. In all likelihood, you simply want people to stay away from your valuable resources — your files, your Internet access, and so on — and you have less concern for who attempts to gain access and with what tools and methods. Let's proceed with that assumption.

While an organizational-level honeypot requires multiple computer and multiple access points, you can create a small virtual honeypot using several different tools. And what exactly is a virtual honeypot? A real honeypot requires real computers running real operating systems and holding real and frequently changed data — in other words, it's a front, designed to draw the intruder inside and keep him occupied by making him think it's the real thing. By contrast, a virtual honeypot offers numerous false fronts to the intruder, with the goal of simply having him lose interest in trying to locate the real resource. In the Linux world, one of the better known honeypot utilities is Black Alchemy's Fake AP (`www.blackalchemy.to`), which automatically generates several thousand simulated access points in an attempt to confuse would-be intruders. For Windows users, a program such as Honeyd-WIN32 (`www.securityprofiling.com/honeyd/honeyd.shtml`) creates fake APs while simultaneously simulating multiple operating systems.

Despite the usefulness of honeypots, however, keep in mind one interesting and important point: legalities. Luring a hacker into a honeypot could be interpreted as entrapment, and you could be liable. To date, the matter remains untested in court, but you can rest assured that someone, somewhere, will make the claim someday. And as you've come to know with other computer matters, it's almost impossible to predict which way the electronic wind will blow.

To get an idea of how virtual honeypots work, this chapter examines KF Sensor, which bills itself as a honeypot-based Intrusion Detection System (IDS). It functions by simulating the ports that make Windows PCs vulnerable to attacks. KF Sensor simulates system services on the application layer of the OSI Network Model, which means, in effect, that it will look like any other server on the network, making simulated use of Windows security technologies. The idea, indeed, is to run KF Sensor on a separate PC entirely, alongside other servers, but you can run it on user machines instead, obviously a more realistic situation on a small network.

KF Sensor lets your target PC operate in two modes: Sim Banner and Sim Standard Server. Sim Banner offers a basic server emulation, sending a small piece of data that lets the visitor (KF Sensor's term for any intruder, including Trojan horses and viruses) think it's a legitimate server. Sim Standard Server provides a much more sophisticated emulation, enabling you to configure your server as a fake FTP, HTTP, POP3, SMTP, SQL, Terminal server, and more. You can also minimize the number of connections and log file size in an effort to fend off Denial of Service (DOS) attacks, intrusions that make a huge number of near-simultaneous requests to a server in order to overwhelm it and thus bring it down. Figure 8-12 shows the DOS Attack Settings dialog box.

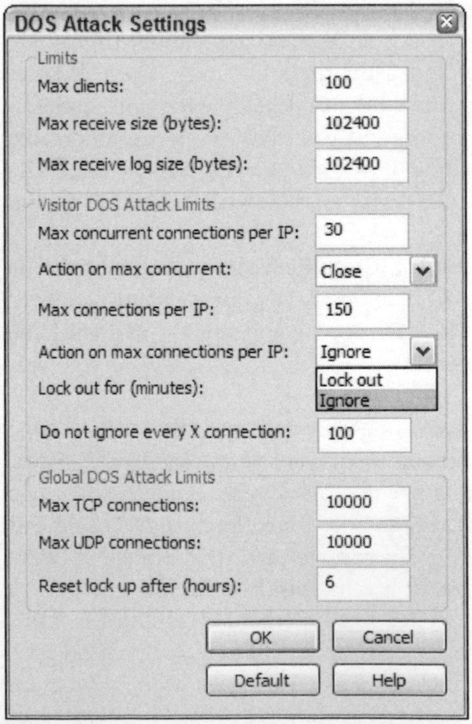

Figure 8-12: You can specify DOS settings in KF Sensor.

After installing KF Sensor and rebooting Windows, the Setup Wizard opens automatically. Your first choice is to decide which components to add, with each component offering a different potential target. These range from NetBIOS through Trojans, Universal Plug and Play, and a variety of standard services, and unless you have a reason to exclude specific services — for example, if you're attempting to trap intruders attempting one or two attack types — leave the default. The next stage of the wizard asks you if you want to install the program as a system service; in Windows NT, 2000, or XP, a system service runs on launch, continuing to run no matter which user logs in. For the most part, only systems administrators want to experiment with luring attackers, so don't install as a systems service unless you plan to use this particular computer as a central target.

With KF Sensor installed, you can set to work luring and monitoring intrusions. Figure 8-13 shows the Edit Sim Servers dialog box, one of several Edit dialog boxes offered in the KF Sensor interface. This figure shows the default configuration of the servers simulated when installing KF Sensor, with a variety of Banner Servers not visible above the list. This list offers typical settings for these servers, but as Figure 8-14 shows, you can edit any of them to specify your own configuration.

Edit Sim Servers

Sim Servers

Sim Server Name	Type	Port	Description
Time Protocol UNIX	Sim Banner	37	
FTP Guild	Sim Std Server - FTP	21	File Transfer Protocol Server
HTTP Proxy	Sim Std Server - HTTP	8080	HTTP
IIS	Sim Std Server - HTTP	80	IIS Sim
kfSubSeven Chat	Sim Std Server - External Co...	2774	
kfSubSeven Matrix	Sim Std Server - External Co...	7215	
kfSubSeven Server	Sim Std Server - External Co...	27374	
NBT Datagram Service	Sim Std Server - NBT Datagr...	138	
NBT Name Service	Sim Std Server - NBT Name ...	137	
NBT Session Service	Sim Std Server - NBT Sessio...	139	
NBT SMB	Sim Std Server - NBT SMB	445	
POP3	Sim Std Server - POP	110	Post Office Protocol
SMTP	Sim Std Server - SMTP	25	Microsoft SMPT Server
SOCKS	Sim Std Server - SOCKS	1080	SOCKS 4/4A/5
SQL Server	Sim Std Server - SQL Server	1433	
SQL UDP Server	Sim Std Server - SQL UDP S...	1434	
Telnet	Sim Std Server - Telnet	23	Basic Telnet Server
Terminal Server	Sim Std Server - Terminal Se...	3389	MS Terminal Server
VNC	Sim Std Server - VNC	5900	Virtual Network Computing S...

Add... Edit... Delete OK Cancel Help

Figure 8-13: The list of Sim Servers in KF Sensor.

To make KF Sensor as flexible as possible for any implementation, you can build scenarios with differing simulated servers in each. The default scenario, shown in Figure 8-15, includes a wide range of possible intrusions, and functions as a kind of Swiss Army knife for catching intrusions. However, you can edit any of these settings to tailor each component to the port number and protocol expected from that particular intrusion, and to establish the severity of the intrusion type and the action you want KF Sensor to perform on intrusion.

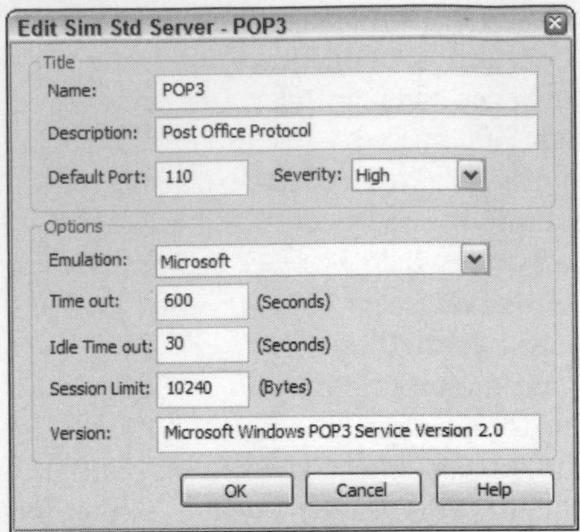

Figure 8-14: Configuring a simulated POP3 Server in KF Sensor.

Edit Scenario

Name: Main Scenario   Domain Name: randall.com

Listen

Name	Active	Protocol	Port	Sensor Bind	Severity	Action	Sim Server
GateCrasher, Tr...	True	TCP	6969		Medium	ReadAndClose	
GateCrasher, Tr...	True	TCP	6970		Medium	ReadAndClose	
kfSubSeven Matrix	True	TCP	7215		High	SimStdServer	kfSubSeven Ma...
Unknown	True	TCP	7394		Medium	ReadAndClose	
HTTP Proxy	True	TCP	8080		Medium	SimStdServer	HTTP Proxy
Hack Office Arm...	True	TCP	8879		Medium	ReadAndClose	
Syphillis, Trojan	True	TCP	10085		Medium	Close	
Kuang 2, Trojan	True	TCP	17300		Medium	ReadAndClose	
Millennium, Trojan	True	TCP	20000		Medium	Close	
Lovegate worm	True	TCP	20168		High	ReadAndClose	
GirlFriend, Trojan	True	TCP	21544		Medium	ReadAndClose	
Donald Dick	True	TCP	23476		Medium	Close	
kfSubSeven Server	True	TCP	27374		High	SimStdServer	kfSubSeven Ser...
The Unexplained...	True	TCP	29891		Medium	ReadAndClose	
Eleet, Trojans	True	TCP	31337		Medium	ReadAndClose	
Bugbear	True	TCP	36794		Medium	ReadAndClose	
Unknown	True	TCP	41170		Medium	ReadAndClose	
SubSeven2.1 Tr...	True	TCP	54283		High	SimBanner	SubSeven2.1 T...
Back Orifice 200...	True	TCP	54320		Medium	ReadAndClose	
NetRaider, Trojan	True	TCP	57341		Medium	ReadAndClose	
mIRC Trojan	True	TCP	60609		Medium	ReadAndClose	

Change All... | Active | Add... | Edit... | Delete

Proxy Rules... | Rules... | OK | Cancel | Help

Figure 8-15: Editing a KF Sensor scenario.

The range of possibilities is almost limitless, and to understand them all you need a studied awareness of what these intrusions do. Some of the listed items represent Trojans and other malicious programs, but others, such as PC Anywhere, refer to perfectly legitimate programs designed to access your PC, but which can be used by would-be intruders. Indeed, one of the more fascinating results of studying a program such as KF Sensor is the amount you can learn about the sheer possibility of intrusion, and the extent to which intruders will go to break into your system.

Summary

This chapter wraps up the security section of the book. You've learned how to implement the two most common wireless security protocols, and you've learned that WPA offers much better protection than WEP. This chapter has outlined a range of additional security tips, from the simple expedient of unplugging unused access points to setting up phantom networks to confuse intruders. We can't stress enough the importance of securing your network, which is why we're devoting so much time to it so early in the book.

You can, of course, become obsessed with security. The degree to which you implement security measures should depend entirely on how important your data is, and how likely it is that anyone will want either to steal that data or otherwise use your wireless network for their own uninvited activities. Generally speaking, what you want is a network that uses encryption (either WEP or WPA), that excludes certain users from certain resources, and that does not broadcast its SSID. But you also need to be able to remember your settings for your own convenience, so don't make things so complex that you can't access your network yourself. No matter what you do, change the security settings fairly frequently, and record everything you've done in the way of security so that you can locate the details if you need them.

Now that your network is set up and as secure as you can make it, it's time to build on it. The chapters in the next part of this book show you how to expand your existing network to encompass your entire home or office building, or even out into your neighborhood.

Part III

Expanding Your Wireless Network

Chapter 9

Wireless Through Walls and Ceilings

If you've ever set up a wireless network, you know that there is a great mismatch between what a manufacturer claims the range of its router or access point is, and the ability to connect to that device from different points in a home or office. The range you can achieve is greatly affected by the environment. Your 802.11 devices may claim anywhere from 150 to 300 feet of range, but where you place your access points, residential gateways, and the computers you want to connect can have a major impact on the quality of your network. Walls, ceilings, sources of RF noise like microwave ovens, 2.4 GHz wireless phones, other wireless networks, and other interferences lower throughput and diminish the range of your WLAN.

Consider these two facts. Every wall between your client and its network access device diminishes the range of the connection by about 100 feet (this varies according to construction details). Furthermore, if you connect up to a wireless device through a 1-foot wall at a 0-degree angle, the wall behaves like it is a 1-foot wall. But if you try to connect to an access point in your basement using a computer in your bedroom, and there is an 85-degree angle, that wall will appear to your computer to be 11.47 feet thick ($\cos \alpha = 1/x$). If there are multiple WLANs in the same space using the same channels, then wherever they overlap there is interference and signal loss.

All is not hopeless, however. Regardless of your situation there are techniques you can apply to improve your wireless coverage. You can compensate for loss of range by adding more access points, by using repeaters, by altering the channels of different WLANs so that they don't overlap, and by better placement of the devices you have. This chapter examines these factors with a special view on the impact of physical interference to see how to minimize problems and get the best return on your technology dollar.

Where to Place the First Access Point

The best place to put your first access point is in a central location away from walls and any other electronic gear. If possible, a location several feet off the ground is best. You may simply want to try experimenting with placement until you find some sweet spots in your location. If you took an organized approach to creating your WLAN, you may have started with a connection diagram that placed the location of your access points, routers, and clients on a map. This map doesn't have to be drawn to architectural scale, but it's best if it is approximately representative. You can draw this map on a sheet

of paper, or if you want to be a hit at cocktail parties you can use the back of your napkin. However, we recommend that you create this map inside a drawing program. It can be a simple drawing program using common shapes for the identities of your network components, or truly representative icons from a networking library that Visio might offer you. The advantage of an electronic file is that you can move the objects around as you learn more about your devices and their capabilities.

You may have some ideas as to where to place your access points (something that we will discuss more fully in the next section), but to really know what's going on you need to *measure* your network connection and throughput. A really good measurement would include signal strength and throughput, but for a small environment it is probably adequate to simply measure signal strength. Chances are that your signal strength will vary during the course of a day, so you should check the strength at different locations at three or four different times during the day. Good times are times of maximum network usage such as the morning e-mail check, and the end-of-day last minute desperation hour before 5 p.m., as well as times of low network usage such as late night. Atmospherics do make a difference, and 802.11 essentially is a radio technology, so nighttime reception is often much improved over daytime reception.

Location, Location, Location

There are really two logical places to put your first access point:

- In the center of your office or house to get the maximum possible range
- In a location where you want the best wireless connection possible; say a den, study, or bedroom where you want to work wirelessly often

Each location for your first access point has both advantages and disadvantages. Given the amount of material written on Wi-Fi, it's rather amazing how little has been said about location selection. The first consideration for location is that you have to have your access point attached to a network connection. If you have no wired LAN to connect to, you have to locate your first access point so that it connects to your broadband connection, or to a hub that you've connected to that router. If you have a wireless router and that is your outside network connection, then you are limited to the length of your direct connection to the outside wire.

It's best to choose a location as high off the floor as possible, and with the clearest location, or for smaller rooms, on a desktop. Don't put the access point on the floor. Remember that placement of your access point is a little like placing a radio: don't put the access point on top of your TV, near a stereo, anything with a power supply (a computer), or with a strong magnet (speakers, for example) or any other RF source.

This is a good point in the process to determine the impact of changing antennas and other tweaks you might want to use. All of Chapter 12 is devoted to antennas, but suffice it to say here that the use and placement of an antenna can be just as significant as the placement of the access point itself in determining performance. Don't forget to move the antennas around to different positions to measure the effect. It's a little like positioning antennas on a TV; direction does matter.

You can also improve access points, repeaters, and other wireless devices by adding a better antenna to them than the one that they come with. This is one important reason to purchase an access point that lets you swap out its antenna. Most 802.11a devices have fixed antennas, but most of the new 802.11b and 802.11g devices let you add a different antenna.

Discovery and Measurement

There are a number of ways to measure your signal strength. The one way that is the most accurate is to take your wireless laptop and move it around your location to see how the signal strength varies. Most wireless NIC cards come with a utility that displays signal strength, and for those that don't you can open your network connection to view the signal strength.

To view your wireless network signal strength in Windows XP, do the following:

1. Locate the wireless icon in your system tray as shown in Figure 9-1 and right-click it. Alternatively, right-click Network Neighborhood and select Properties to view the Network Connections dialog box. Then find the Wireless Network connection icon there to right-click on.

Figure 9-1: The Wireless Network icon in the system tray provides direct access to your connection status dialog box.

2. Select the Status command from the context menu. The Wireless Network Connection Status dialog box appears with the signal strength indicated in a five-bar display, as shown in Figure 9-2.

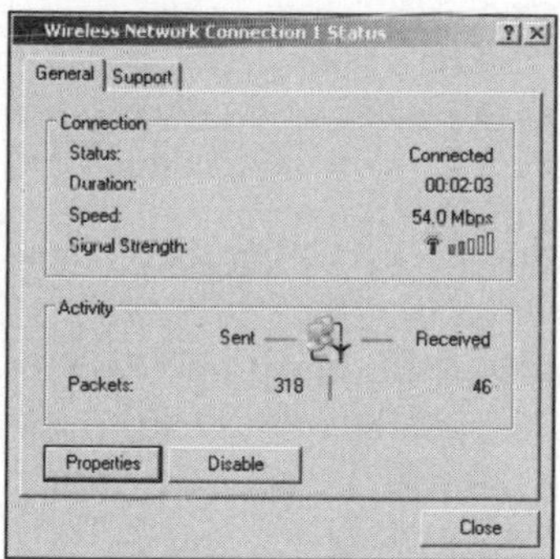

Figure 9-2: The Wireless Network Connection Status dialog box.

3. With this dialog box open, transfer a file from another computer on the network to your wireless client and measure the time it takes to transfer. Perform a transfer of a file large enough so that you can adequately measure time. A folder of a few MP3 song files is ideal.

4. Check the Packets Sent and Packets Received both before and after the file transfer. The ratio of the Packets Sent (or Received) / time is your ***average*** throughput during the time of the transfer. To be thorough you should really perform this test at different times of the day when there are different network activities taking place.

The advantage of using the built-in system applet is that it is measuring your throughput with a device that you actually are going to use for the connection. This is what we call in the industry ***reality programming***; you don't get voted off the island for a measurement that isn't based on a real connection. However, given that different NIC cards and connections of different protocols give different results, don't get too carried away with a complete set of measurements based on your single laptop unless that is the only one that you will be connecting up. Try to use other people's notebooks to test your theories of location.

Going around your home or office with a laptop taking measurements is a bit cumbersome, however, and not really what you need for a first pass. The easiest way to gauge connectivity is to walk around with a small Wi-Fi detector that measures the signal. There are a few of these on the market, and they aren't particularly expensive. The Kensington Wi-Fi Finder is a $30 device that shows the signal strength of a b or g network up to 200 feet from their source. The claim is that this device filters out interfering signals from other wireless devices not using the 802.11 protocol. We've used this device and it works well in home environments. You'll be surprised as you map connectivity in your home how the signal varies across different floors and in different rooms. It is very hard to anticipate the first time you measure your signal strength which rooms will be live and which will be dead. But after your first go round it become easier to predict performance. Once your ad hoc measurements are complete, move your access point to different locations and see if you get better connectivity where you need to have it.

As an alternative to the Kensington Wi-Fi detector you might want to consider looking at the SmartID WFS-1 Detector. The SmartID also detects both 802.11b and 802.11g, and costs about the same as the Kensington model. They seem to perform about the same indoors, but SmartID's model has a better range outdoors (500 feet is claimed), and has an internal directional antenna that helps detect the location of the source. The disadvantage of a directional antenna is that your readings will vary depending upon how you orient the device. Still, this detector has four red LEDs for signal strength and one green one for battery level.

Finally, many people recommend the use of NetStumbler (`www.netstumbler.com`) to perform wireless network quality studies. NetStumbler is freeware, and you can download version .0.4.0 from `www.stumbler.net`. What NetStumbler offers you is a lot more detail about what particular wireless networks you are receiving, their SSIDs, whether they are using encryption, their channel numbers, and other factors. For a single access point, the other methods suffice, but for the discussion about adding additional access points and having multiple WLANs, NetStumbler is invaluable. Be sure to read the README file that's posted with the software because it contains notes about specific models and brands. Not every model or brand works with this software. Marius Milner, the author of NetStumbler, also offers a program called MiniStumbler (on the same site) that is meant for Windows CE devices, which is a pretty nifty application for a hand-held wireless PDA to have.

We'll be returning to NetStumbler later in the chapter, but there are several features that are of particular value in measuring the performance of a single access point. One cool feature is that you can turn on a sound feature so that you can hear NetStumbler's signal strength tones, similar to a

Geiger counter. This feature is very useful when you're configuring an antenna or creating a long directional link between devices. You can also measure signal strength over time in the form of a histogram (see Figure 9-3). You can even use this software with a GPS device if you are configuring a network over a larger distance. What NetStumbler can't do is detect closed or passive wireless networks. NetStumbler is an active network scanner and as such it sends out requests and waits for the requests to be answered. Closed networks don't respond to probes of this type, so if you are trying to detect that kind of WLAN, use either Kismet or KisMac for passive monitoring.

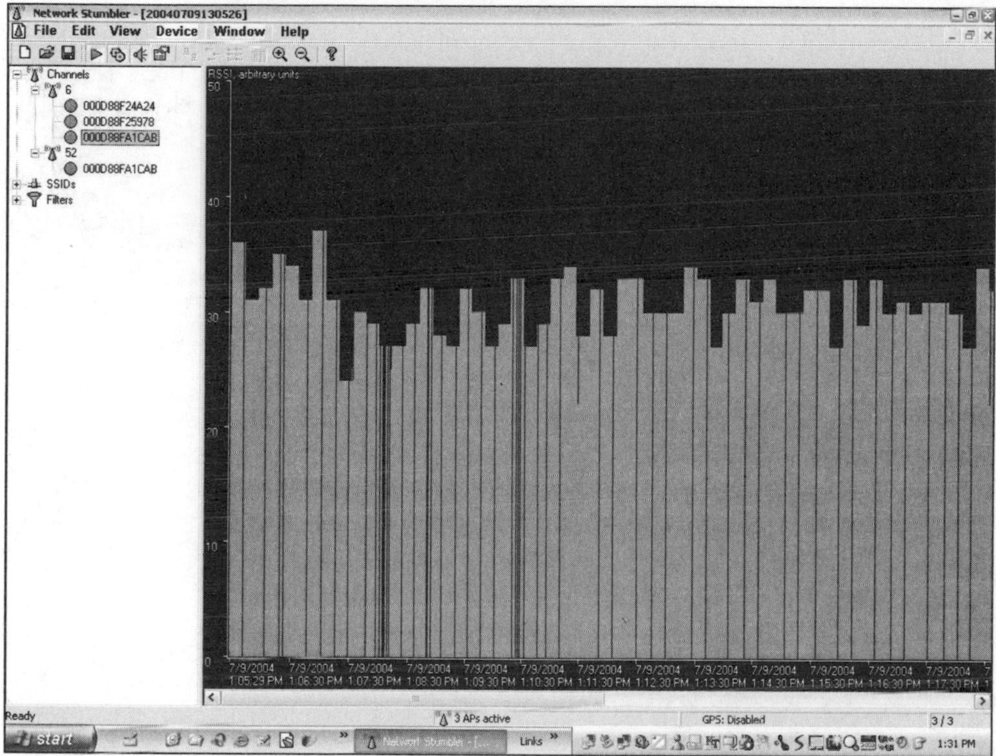

Figure 9-3: NetStumbler is useful in detecting multiple networks, and displaying their characteristics. Here is the signal over time window.

There's other scanner software out there to consider, although none has the popularity of NetStumbler. For Macintosh OS X you'll find MacStumbler (`www.macstumbler.com`) and iStumbler (`homepage.mac.com/alfwatt/istumbler`). None of these "stumblers" is related to NetStumbler and its light version MiniStumbler.

None of these products actually tests your connection automatically for throughput. You can initiate a transfer, but there are tools available for you to use to test a wireless connection. One recommended free tool is called QCheck, which you can find on Ixia's Web site (`www.ixiacom.com/products/qcheck/index.php`). The product was originally developed by NetIQ, and is now

offered as an inducement to consider Ixia's other products. Qcheck has a number of valuable features, including:

- Response time analysis
- Throughput measurement
- Streaming testing
- Traceroute tests

In a multi-access point wireless network, this portfolio of tests can not only tell you the condition of your connect, it can tell you how you connected and test for both data streaming (long data transmission communication) and response times (short burst communications). Qcheck is wrapped in an easy-to-understand interface, as shown in Figure 9-4.

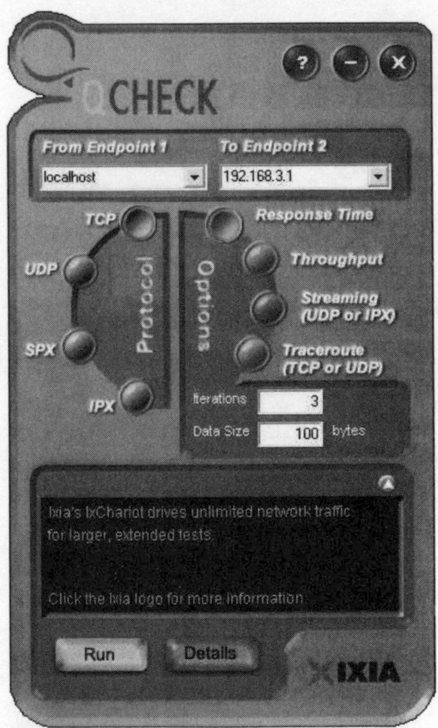

Figure 9-4: Use the freeware tool Qcheck to evaluate your wireless (and wired) connections replacing several tools such as PING and TRACEROUTE.

When you install Qcheck on your source system, it installs a small agent software called an *endpoint*. The endpoint is capable of responding to Qcheck's tests, and both systems being tested require an endpoint. Although Qcheck runs on Windows 2000, NT, or XP, you will find an endpoint for almost any operating system you could want to test on Ixia's Web site. You'll need to download the endpoint(s) you need and install that on your target machine. Qcheck's software creates a testing console for other systems on your network on a system it calls localhost.

There isn't much to know about using Qcheck. For testing wireless connections, you want to test the TCP/IP protocol and use the largest data sample you can. Qcheck can go to 1MB (1,000K) so you will want to use that size. Also, you don't need to have Qcheck installed on either of the two systems being tested, you need to specify only what the two endpoints of the test are. Test when the network is quiet (no users) because Qcheck will saturate the network. Run a few tests to get an average number, and test different endpoints through the same access point to get an idea of overall network performance. You'll find that tests through an access point are most often symmetrical. When the data has finished transferring through the access point it takes about the same time to have the data returned. Qcheck is a great reality test for the claims that many wireless hardware vendors make. It's a shame that more people don't put these vendors' feet into the fire by testing with this utility.

Signal Loss

Signal loss is a major problem for WLANs. Signal loss occurs because the radio signal interacts with solid material and is transformed from electromagnetic radiation into heat, or because of other interference such as other radio waves canceling your Wi-Fi signal out. The causes of signal loss are numerous and include:

- Physical obstructions, such as walls and ceilings
- Interference from other radio frequency devices including microwave ovens and phones, and competing wireless networks
- Signal reflection and interference from metallic surfaces, mirrors, metal coated insulation, metallic paints, and even nails and studs in the walls
- Dense construction material such as concrete

Each of these factors lowers the signal strength, and the amount of degradation is also dependent on the frequency of the wireless signal. Thus an 802.11b access point will have a lower loss through material than an 802.11g will for the same signal strength because 802.11g is higher energy and has a more powerful interaction with material or other radio waves.

How Many Access Points Do You Need?

The short answer to this question is that you need enough access points to handle both the number of clients that will wirelessly connect to your network as well as provide the range necessary to remove any dead spots in your location. There is a benefit of having a second (or third) access point in your network, as it provides fault tolerance. Should one of your access points fail, you still have another one to connect to.

You might think that the more access points you have the better, but that is not the case. Every additional access point interferes to some degree with the other nearby access points. This requires that you plan to use different channels for each access point that overlaps with another. You'll often see network designers draw wireless overlap diagrams for their site maps which look similar to Venn diagrams. Figure 9-5 shows an example of a multi-access point site.

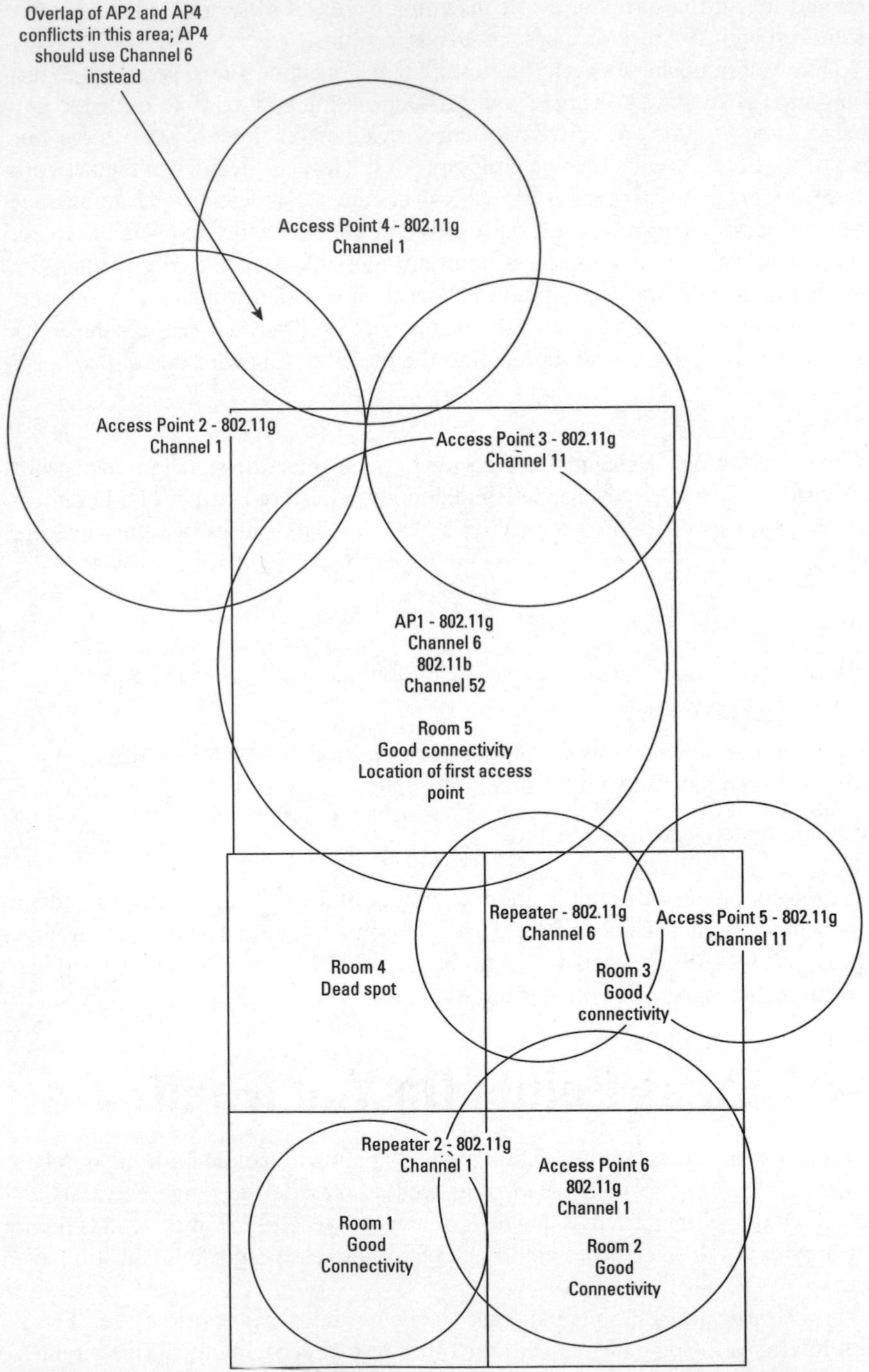

Figure 9-5: An overlap diagram is an important figure to develop for your site and prevents device contention.

The more important consideration is throughput. If you have an access point that is based on the 11 Mbps 802.11b standard you have the ability to provide on average about 7 Mbps of throughput. That translates to connections for about 50 intermittent users, 25 knowledge workers (office suite users), and perhaps 15 power users. For a 54 Mbps 802.11g standard device, you can probably figure on about 35 Mbps throughput on average, which would translate to about 250 intermittent users, 125 knowledge workers, and up to 75 power users. It's not uncommon for 802.11b access points to only provide 4 Mbps and to get 11 to 15 Mbps out of a g device, so it pays to be realistic in your assessments. Based on these types of calculations you can determine your requirements. However, keep in mind that planning for average use will most certainly get you in trouble at peak times. It's more realistic to build a wireless LAN that has anywhere from 50 percent to 65 percent of its bandwidth in reserve.

Many, if not most, of the newest access points, wireless NIC cards, and other devices are dual-band (ab, bg, or ag), while the higher performing devices are often tri-band (abg). In performing your throughput calculations, it is best to use the lowest possible throughput protocol in your calculations. You shouldn't assume that devices will connect up with the fastest protocol unless you have control over the selection and use of different devices in your network. An assumption of this type means that you don't have to figure additional overhead into you calculations to keep bandwidth in reserve. It's a very conservative approach, but provides the margin necessary to absorb not only peaks in your usage but the inevitable growth of the number of wireless devices you'll be forced to connect over time.

These throughput figures make it clear why companies with large number of workers are forced to add additional access points to their network. If you are setting up a network for a convention, you would want both redundancy and significant capacity for your network. If the range of coverage is the issue, then you should consider other means of improving your access point(s) range such as repeaters to keep the complexity of your WLAN to a minimum.

If you have a particular vendor's product line in mind, you may find that its Web site has a network configuration tool for building wireless networks. D-Links Configurator (see Figure 9-6) will lead you through an analysis of the number of clients, distance you must connect up to, types of content being transferred, and quality and type of NIC cards, and from that analysis suggest the number and placement of devices necessary to implement that network. All of these choices are multiple choice questions, and there are two decision trees, one for Home & Small Offices and the other for Small to Medium Businesses. The resulting suggestions are a good starting point for considering what devices you need.

There is one other reason to add additional access points to your network, and it's an important one. If you have more than one access point, you can subnet your network and provide access to the Internet or network services while limiting which parts of the network can be accessed. If you're setting up a hotspot that is managed from your company LAN, this is one option to consider. Subnetting is beyond the scope of this book, but there are numerous Internet tutorials and books on the subject.

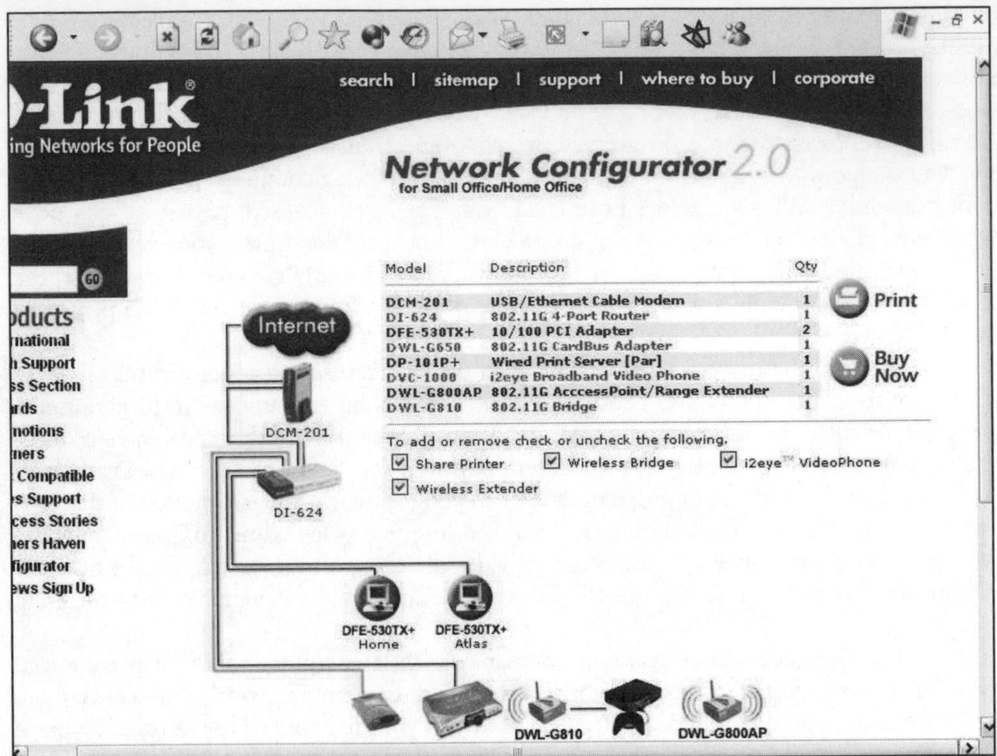

Figure 9-6: The D-Link Configurator is one tool that suggests the kinds and number of devices necessary to support a wireless network.

Adding the Access Points to the Network

Once you've assessed your need for additional access points, the next question is where they should be placed. The two considerations are improving range and improving throughput. You can improve your range by locating additional access points in dead spots in your location, places where signal strength is negligible. To improve throughput you'll want to have access points overlap, but keep in mind that there will be contention among wireless signals. If a laptop can detect two or more different signals, it will connect to the strongest access point to get the fastest throughput.

Note

When you have multiple access points on a network, you want to be able to recognize them. You can PING an access point's IP address, but access points aren't given a NetBIOS or hostname. If your access point is assigned a DHCP address, that address will be listed in your DHCP service. However, some vendors allow their devices to have a name label, and that name appears in the manufacturer's management software. If your hardware allows you to give it a name label, by all means do so. It's a useful feature.

When the signals are of approximately the same strength, the receiving device (your laptop, for example) can become confused and have connection difficulties. Your NIC card is trying to lock onto the strongest signal, but the maximum signal is not coming constantly from the same device. With differences over 20db, most cards will lock on the strongest signal consistently.

Another thing to keep in mind is that bandwidth is not dispersed equally among competing devices. All things being equal (the same computer, the same wireless NIC card, and the same bandwidth demand) a computer that is closer to the access point and has a stronger signal will be able to demand and get more throughput than a system that is further away. Unless you buy a wireless network adapter meant for the corporate or enterprise market, you are unlikely to be able to specify which access point you would prefer your system connects to. Some of the higher-end cards do offer this feature. With some of the Cisco NICs, for example, you can specify your desired access point with a list of four prioritized MAC addresses. But few, if any, devices for the home, SOHO, and SMB market have this feature.

In some of the small network products, you can do MAC filtering at the access point. You can specify which clients can connect to an access point by adding their identities to a list. This isn't a dynamic feature, but at least it gives you some control over the number of connections and bandwidth usage.

You can't just do a throughput calculation and determine the number of access points required, although that is a useful thing to do for a first pass. Where you place the access points is going to affect how many access points you might need. If you are locating access points in different rooms, floors, or buildings, their physical location will limit the amount of overlap and therefore the coverage you can provide for each part of your location. You might need five access points based on your throughput calculation; however, if you have to cover six floors of a building and two of the floors have almost all of your clients, you might find yourself putting three access points on those two floors and an additional four access points, one each on the remaining floors.

Your life is easier when you are building a multi-zone wireless network that doesn't require a roaming feature. ***Roaming*** is the ability to move from access point to access point without having to log on again. Without roaming, you can use almost anyone's access points in combination; however if you want roaming you need to make sure that the product you are buying supports that feature. This is one reason for not mixing devices from different vendors. You'll find this feature on higher quality "enterprise" or corporate access points such as those from Cisco and Proxim. For other vendor's products, check carefully if they support this feature and that their roaming is actually reliably implemented.

Just as roaming can be an elusive feature in wireless access points for the home and small business market, you'll also find that buying multiple access points to perform network load balancing is also problematic. With load balancing, network requests are dynamically routed to the access point that has the least traffic. While error checking is part of the 802.11 protocol, load balancing is not. Don't expect devices from different vendors to perform load balancing for you, and be wary about expecting this feature from lower cost devices. Load balancing is not an easy feature to implement in wireless technology because throughput is a direct function of signal strength, and most wireless NIC cards don't know the difference between a Cisco and a Crisco access point (a fried Cisco), or Proxim and an Approxim. So it takes some system smarts at the access point to figure out how to balance connections from different systems so that the throughput is balanced out.

Solutions to the problem of roaming and load balancing are therefore proprietary solutions. Most load balancing routines use MAC address filtering to perform load balancing. Furthermore, because only channels 1, 6, and 11 don't overlap for 2.4 GHz Wi-Fi access points, if you are using any more than three access points, you will have contention. Each access point in a network must have the same SSID value, that of your network, or they don't connect up. For three access points, you might assign channels 1, 6, and 11 to each. Once you get beyond three access points, you want to use your network map to start placing different channels next to each other. Location's impact on the overlap of access points is therefore important to determine.

Access points are relatively inexpensive network devices. They aren't much more expensive than Ethernet hubs or switches, so there's a tendency to put more access points in a wireless LAN than is probably necessary. We're not big fans of this approach, however, because each access point needs to be managed and each access point represents another possible path for intruders to use to enter your network. Therefore, we recommend that you "right size" the number of access points and use other methods to improve your WLAN range when throughput is not the issue.

Siemens and Ashoka, among others, have wireless routers and access points that connect to your network via your power line using the HomePlug system. The devices available are 802.11b devices, and realistically HomePlug can't give you the kind of throughput that 802.11g and future 802.11 standards will. However, for a difficult-to-reach location, this can provide an easy-to-set-up wireless connection.

Compensating for Signal Loss

As a wireless signal propagates through the air, its strength is diminished as a function of distance. To calculate the free space loss formula you can go to sites such as `www.swisswireless.org/wlan_calc_en.html` or `www.zytrax.com/tech/wireless/calc.htm` and figure out the range of a device. While that range might be of interest in an outdoor application or in a large conference hall where you have direct line-of-sight throughout the device's range, those formulas aren't useful for indoor purposes. You've measured signal strengths and done an RF site survey (if you took our advice) simply because it is so difficult to accurately predict the factors that diminish your signals.

Signal Strength and Attenuation

When a wireless signal is forced to propagate through denser material, it suffers a greater loss of signal, called attenuation, as it passes through the material. The strength of a signal as measured in milliwatts is attenuated by a certain amount as it is output from the transmission medium. Attenuation is measured in decibels (dB), the same unit as sound strength, and is the logarithm of the power input to the medium divided by the output power over a specified distance. Thus if you input 300 milliwatts into a wall and the output is 150 milliwatts, you have attenuated the signal by +3dB. A repeater that doubled the power would have an attenuation of –3dB. An omnidirectional antenna with a 6dB rating therefore improves the performance of a signal by four times.

As a signal is attenuated and diminishes, you reach a point where the signal strength won't decode cleanly at the receiving end. That forces the two endpoints in the transmission to have to request and resend the part that doesn't error check correctly, which lowers the effective throughput of your connection. Thus not only do you lose range during attenuation, but you lose throughput. Below a certain point, the wireless connection drops out completely. When maximum attenuation is calculated, a formula called *EIRP* (*Equivalent Isotropically Radiated Power*) is used. For information on measuring the amount of acceptable loss using EIRP, go to `www.wi-fiplanet.com/tutorials/article.php/1431101`.

It is important to understand that attenuation isn't a linear function. The further away from the wireless source that you put a barrier, the more effect it has on dropping the signal strength. Thus, a single wall close to the source will have considerably less impact on the signal strength than the same wall would have a couple of rooms away. Of course, what the wall is made of is important, too. The following estimates of attenuation are offered for common building features:

- **Plasterboard:** 3dB
- **Office window:** 3dB
- **Concrete or cinder block walls:** 4dB
- **Glass wall in a metal frame:** 6dB
- **Metal door:** 6dB
- **Metal door in brick wall:** 12.4dB

The type of wireless protocol you are using affects the attenuation of a signal through the same media. The higher frequencies and larger ranges of the 802.11g devices you might use suffer more degradation of their signal than an 802.11b device.

Improving Connectivity

There are several methods for improving your signal strength that go beyond simply adding additional access points. Consider the following suggestions as practical methods to improve your range and better utilize your access points' native throughput. You encountered the first method earlier in the chapter when you measured and optimized the placement of your first wireless access point. If you can eliminate an extra wall, you can improve your connection for essentially no (or low) cost.

Improve the quality of your device's antennas. This includes not only adding or modifying the antenna on your access point but improving the quality of the antenna attached to your connected systems. Buy devices that let you substitute better antennas than the manufacturer provides, or ones that are known to have quality reception. This advice is relatively easy to follow for access points and NIC cards that go into desktop computers' PCI slots; those devices most often have screw-on antennas. About half of the wireless PC cards that go into laptops are closed cards with no possibility of altering their antenna.

The only practical thing you can do to improve your signal for those kinds of laptop connections without an external antenna is to try different orientations of your laptop to see if there is a preferred direction. Try turning your laptop in 45-degree increments. Also, try adjusting the plane of the laptop. This isn't really ideal, but we often do the same thing for AM/FM radios, so the technique does work more often than you think it would. We have a slight preference for notebook wireless cards with a replaceable antenna. However, given a choice between one card that has a replaceable antenna

and another card that doesn't but is from the same vendor and offers enhanced proprietary protocols, we opted for the matching vendors. Usually you are better off matching vendor products to one another. Buying an up-to-date wireless NIC card is often a good idea in any event because the industry has been pushing up the power of these adapters. Earlier NICs had strength levels of 30 mW (milliwatts) or less. You can now find cards on the market that have signal strengths of 100 to 200 mW. Consider the strength of the card as one of your criteria for its purchase, it's often the major difference between the lower end and the upper end cards in a vendor's wireless NIC line.

Here's a short checklist of things for you to consider in order to improve your connectivity:

- Eliminate as many walls and ceilings as you can. Each wall or ceiling can diminish your access point's range by anywhere from 3 to 100 feet depending upon construction and the angle of the transmission reception.
- If you have to transmit a signal through a wall or door, select the material that is most transparent to the signal, such as plaster walls over metal doors.
- Lessen the angle through an obstruction. A 1-foot-thick wall would appear 2 feet thick at a 45-degree angle; at an 85-degree angle that wall would be the equivalent of 11.5 feet thick.
- Keep your wireless devices away from sources of RF noise, and try to eliminate interference of 2.4 GHz networks with other 2.4 GHz devices. If possible, consider using 5 GHz wireless networks as a base.
- Do adjust and work with your devices' antennas and positions to maximize the signal.

We're big fans of wireless repeaters. There aren't a lot of these devices on the market yet, but they have started to appear. DLink sells a model for home networks that can be used as either an access point or a repeater, the D-Link DWL-900AP+ AirPlus Enhanced 2.4 GHz wireless access point. It's meant to mate with one of the other access ports in that series. We've used two of these devices as repeaters, one on a floor below and another on a floor above the D-Link access point that connects to our network. In repeater mode these units improve the signal level by about 50 percent. The range of the signal from the repeater isn't strengthened enough to dramatically improve the signal on one of the floors in a room that doesn't have line-of-sight access, but they work well in line-of-sight applications.

Summary

To add additional coverage to your wireless network and to improve throughput, fault tolerance, security, and the number of possible connections, you may find it necessary to add additional access points to your network or to add devices like repeaters that will amplify the signal of your access point.

In this chapter we covered some of the things you need to consider to successfully add these capabilities. As in all things, your addition should start with testing and planning. You need to know how well your network is performing with the first access point. This chapter offered some suggestions on how to test your wireless connections, as well as tips on placement.

Picking the right type and number of additional access points is a question of your required throughput. There are some considerations about connecting clients, available channels for access points, and management that need to be considered as you build your network. When selecting components such as access points and wireless NIC cards, you also need to consider features such as positioning, addition of antennas, and whether you need roaming and load balancing capabilities when making selections.

This chapter focused on adding capability to a single network. In the next chapter, we'll consider the possibilities that exist when your wireless devices connect to more than one network and some of the advantages and complexity that these types of networks offer you.

Chapter 10

Extending Your Wireless and Wired Networks

You can add additional wireless devices to your wireless network to enable you to cover more area, or to give you greater bandwidth over which to communicate. You can also extend your coverage by wirelessly connecting two or more LANs. Because very few people have completely wireless networks, nearly all networks start out as wired LANs to which wireless capabilities are added. Wireless networking can extend your network to places that are either difficult or impossible to run a wire to. Wireless links can serve as bridges between two LAN islands. Given the right antennas, you can create wireless network links up to 10 miles in distance with 802.11 technology. That makes wireless technology useful for bridges across a campus, a city, a county, or anywhere else where you need a long distance or temporary link.

Given these uses of wireless networking technology it is the natural next step to want to extend your network's range further. Perhaps you have a bedroom on another floor at the far end of your home or you want to extend your network out to your patio where you can work in the sunshine; or perhaps you have a network running in your shop or guest home that you want to connect to another network in your house. In this chapter you'll learn how you can create multi-zone networks in your home and small office.

Additional networks and zones mean additional possible points of entry for outsiders trying to gain unwanted access to your systems. That's true of any situation where you add complexity to a computer network. So we'll also take a look at what the security concerns are and how you can manage them. However, having multiple networks also means that you have additional tools to make things tougher for the bad guys, too. By applying techniques like protocol isolation (proxy servers), firewalls, software traps such as honey pots, and so on, you can make your primary data networks more secure.

Extending Your Wireless Network with Repeaters

Let's start with what is perhaps the simplest way to extend your wireless network's reach, by adding repeaters. A *repeater* is a device that amplifies the signal from a wireless network and operates in a combination of bridging and access point modes. A repeater takes a signal from an wireless access point or router and broadcasts it to wireless clients. We're particularly fond of repeaters because they are simple to install and to move around as you need to. A repeater does not connect to an Ethernet port, except for when you are configuring it, so these devices are entirely portable. A repeater can help you get your wireless signal to a remote bedroom, the basement, or your patio, and may allow a small network to use a single access point.

Repeaters take the same settings as the device they are repeating and they don't add much to the complexity of a wireless network. Strangely, most wireless books and articles don't spend a lot of time describing repeaters, probably because they are only recently appearing in consumer wireless devices. Normally you don't buy a repeater per se; you buy an access point that can be placed into repeater mode. The first generation of access points did not offer a repeater mode, but most of the current crop of access points do have this feature.

A repeater is also called a range extender and, depending upon the protocol and placement, can amplify the signal 50 percent or more. The theoretical specification for the range of the DWL-G800AP repeater is from 328 feet (100 meters) indoors up to 1,312 feet (400 meters) outdoors. You'll typically get less than that for any real application where there are interferences. Given the variance in environment and signal strengths, no vendor publishes range numbers that are actually meaningful to most people.

One recent review of the D-Link DWL-900AP (`www.80211-planet.com/reviews/AP/article.php/1492131`) found that the range of a signal was increased about 160 percent. The access point signal was lost at 55 feet from the router/access point without a repeater. With this particular repeater, the reviewer was able to get a signal strength of 72 percent at 140 feet. So this technology does work and is worth considering when you want to keep things simple.

The D-Link DWL-G800AP is an example of an access point/repeater. This particular repeater amplifies an 802.11g and 802.11b signal. This particular repeater is meant to mate up to D-Link's AirPlus Extreme G series of routers and access points, so it's a good idea to check for compatibility when you are purchasing repeaters. Remember that the use of access points as repeaters isn't really part of the 802.11 standard so, as is often the case, you should try to use the same manufacturer's equipment in your setup.

When you use it for this series, these repeaters enable you to use 128 WEP and Wi-Fi Protected Access (WPA) security. You configure this repeater through the browser-based utility shown in Figure 10-1.

When the DWL-G800AP is an access point, a repeater takes a different channel from the other adjoining access points, but when it's in repeater mode it needs to be set to the same channel. To be part of the same network it must use the same SSID settings.

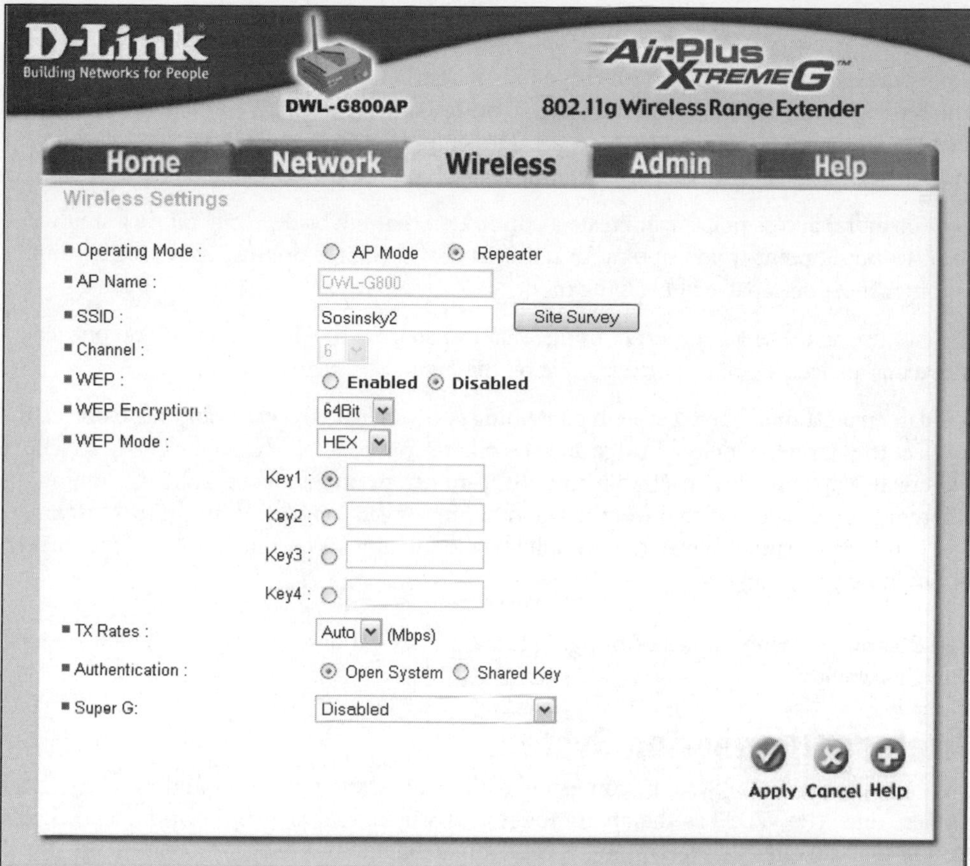

Figure 10-1: The management interface for a D-Link DWL-800AP access point/repeater.

Repeaters do lower throughput, which is one reason that they aren't heavily used on enterprise networks or when there is heavy wireless network traffic. You are asking the device to both amplify a signal as well as broadcast it, which doubles the number of frames that the device transmits. But for a home or a small office that isn't limited in wireless bandwidth, this is a good solution.

Wireless Bridging

Bridging is a connection you make between two LANs at the link layer, each node of which is identified by the device's MAC address. Any node on an IP network has a MAC address, and this is the way access points and network cards recognize each other.

You'll find that there are several different ways to create wireless links and bridges:

- Many wireless gateways come with the Wireless Distribution System (WDS) technology by which the gateway can serve the dual role of bridge and access point (provided that there is sufficient bandwidth available to do so). The simplest solutions are a wireless repeater and a wireless bridge with one access point on each side of a WDS connection.
- Two (or more) access points can create a connection that is a bridge-only mode for either point-to-point, point-to-multipoint, or redundant bridging. To do this, your access point or router must be capable of bridging mode.
- You can use an 802.11 to Ethernet bridge that can connect to a hub or switch on one side and act as an access point or bridge node on the other.
- You can create a dual homed system containing two wireless NIC cards and have one card connect to your network as a bridge and the other serve as an access point. Doing so lets you create a system where each different NIC card can be on a different subnet, running different protocols, or isolated from one another in some other way. With protocol isolation you have essentially created a firewall situation that makes it much harder for a hacker to penetrate your network.

Figure 10-2 shows some examples of bridging topologies. We'll describe these different options more fully in this chapter.

The Wireless Distribution System

Using the Wireless Distribution System, you can expand your wireless network and even create an entirely wireless one. The WDS has the ability to let access points serve as both bridge and access point, meaning that any area in overlapping access points would automatically connect up. You'll find that WDS is most commonly used in wireless networks where there are large open areas and where connecting devices by wiring would be complex and expensive. In WDS connections, all devices use the same channel, and you can enable WEP for this system.

An Ethernet switch with WDS maintains a list of systems it's connected to, and broadcasts that list to the other devices' ports. The purpose of the broadcast is to maintain a current list of your devices' MAC addresses, with a WDS link defined as a MAC address pair. When a device has data, to send it addresses the data with the destination, and following the WDS standard the switch is able to recognize the target of each packet and assign it a route to the correct port using the updated list of device MAC addresses. Any access point functions similarly to a port, tracking MAC addresses and routing packets to the best access point through any required paths. Unlike other bridging solutions that have a master and use a Spanning Tree Protocol algorithm, WDS does not always require a master device. However, without a master you have to pay special attention to configuring this system correctly, especially to avoid creating loops.

Here's the rub about WDS: it's a non-standard standard. Every vendor has its own version of WDS, and not all vendors' equipment works with other vendors' equipment. You have some chance of being able to use different vendors' equipment if the devices you want to use are using the same chipset and firmware levels. WDS requires at least two gateways, but depending on the vendor, you can use up to six gateways. The system most often sets up a master when WDS requires that a single device connect to three to five relay devices.

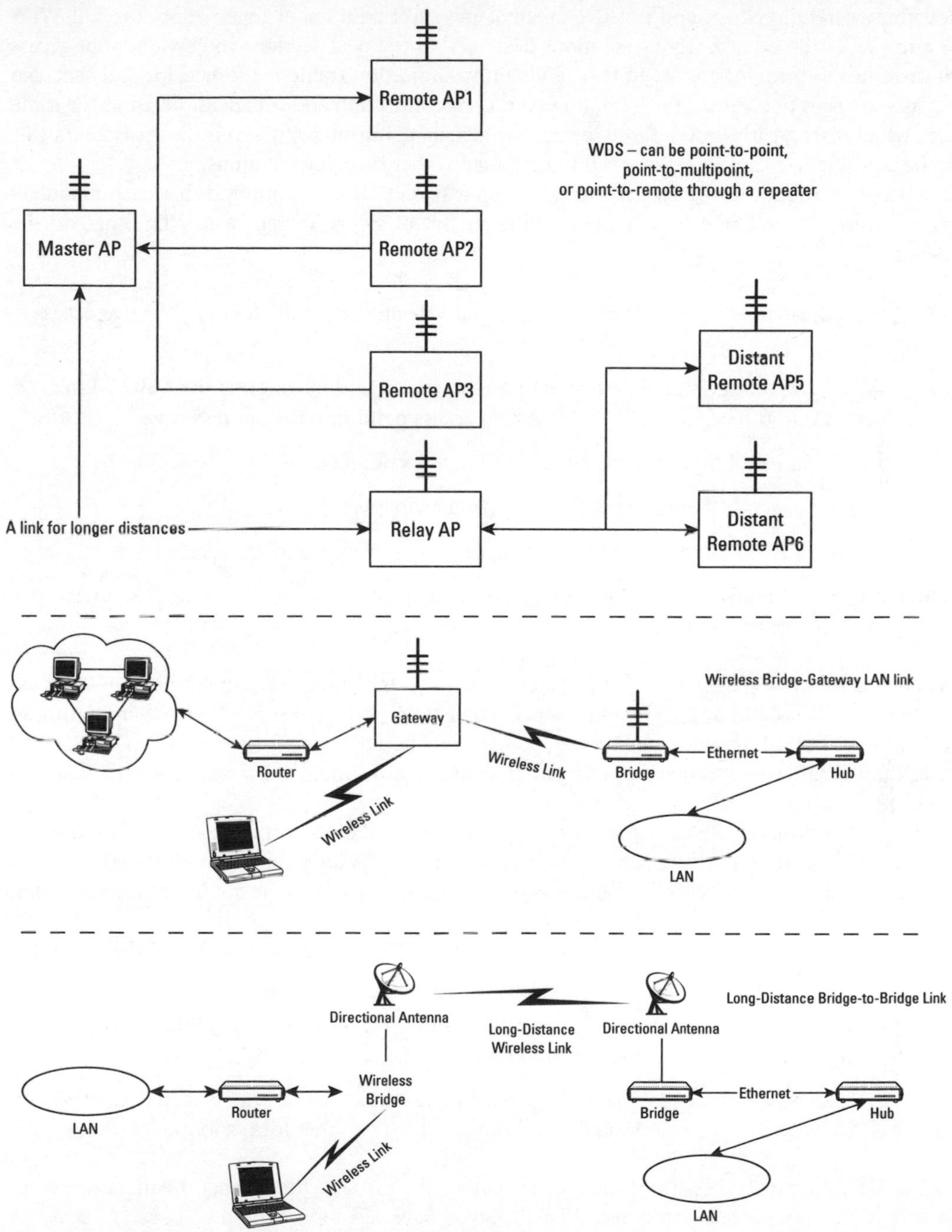

Figure 10-2: Examples of different types of wireless bridges.

You must carefully check and test the different pieces of equipment together to know if WDS works. In one of the other bridging solutions described in the next section, you switch your access point or router to bridging mode. In that mode only connection traffic is listened for and sent. No broadcasts are sent to clients. For WDS, however, both connection and broadcast occur at the same device, which can greatly lower throughput. For signals going through several access points this could be a problem, and if it is, you need to investigate other bridging solutions.

Here's a general outline of how you would set up a WDS link. Keep in mind that each manufacturer's management software may require a different set of steps. To set up a WDS link, do the following:

1. Open your wireless network management software and select the first of your two access points.
2. Enable WDS and point the first access point to the second by entering the MAC address (such as 00-50-32-10-12-76) of the second access point into the address box.
3. Set the channel of the first access point and note its number.
4. Go to the page for the second access point and enable WDS there.
5. Enter the MAC address of the first access point into the appropriate place.
6. Check the channel of the second access point, and if it isn't the same as the first access point, change it to match.

When you set up a WDS system for just a couple of access points, you can connect those access points to hubs. Your cable and DSL modems may come with ports that serve as an Ethernet hub, so look there first. For a LAN with more access points, you should use an Ethernet switch. When you need additional Ethernet locations for a large deployment, you should use a master switch that fans out to smaller switches.

It's relatively easy to create network loops with WDS where data is sent back and forth to the two access points along the same loop, and is duplicated endlessly. A loop can crash your network, and must be avoided. There are several different ways of creating loops, but here are three common ones:

- Two access points are connected together with a WDS link and also with an Ethernet link, forming a loop.
- Two access points are connected by two WDS links, one of which is an 802.11a link while the other is an 802.11b/g link, again forming a loop.
- Three access points are connected together by three links one of which is an 802.11b/g link while two of the others are 802.11a links, which together form a loop.

Figure 10-3 illustrates these three looping scenarios. The message here is that the more protocols you use, and the more access points and WDS links you have, the more careful you need to be about eliminating data loops.

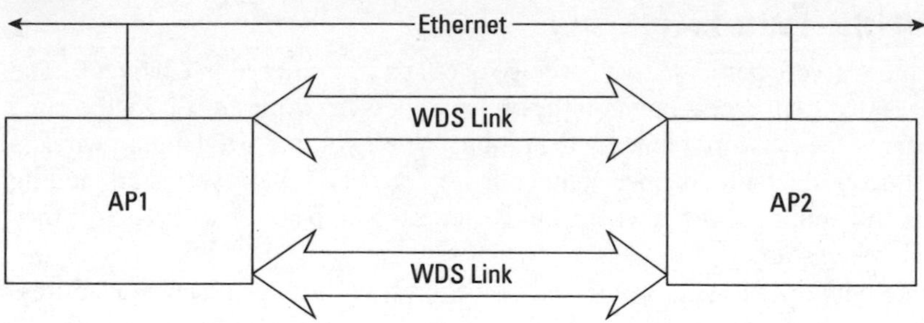

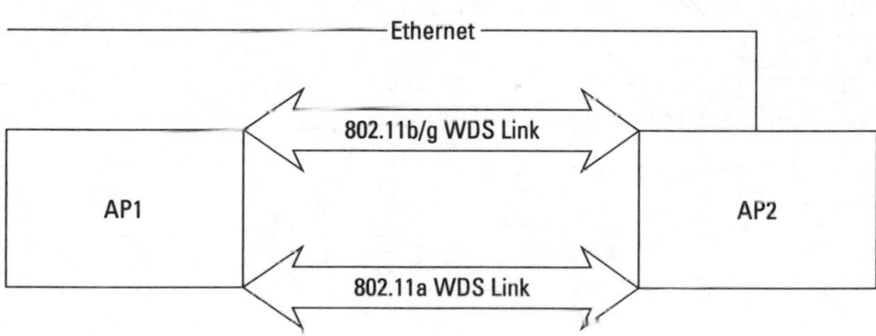

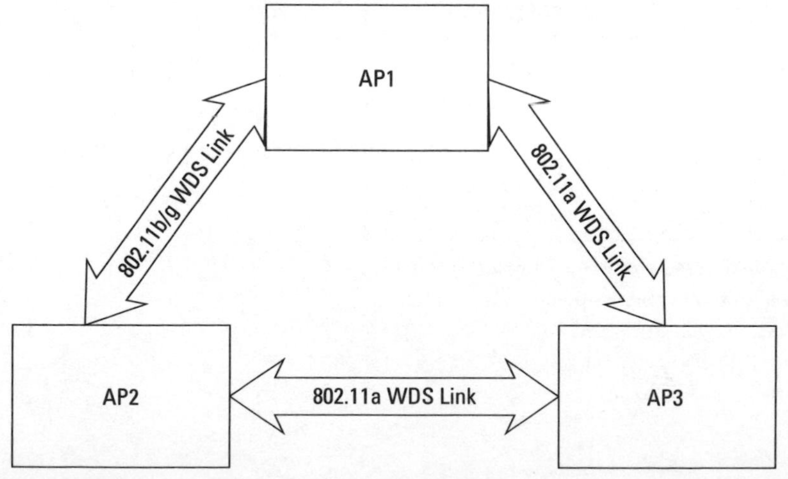

Figure 10-3: Multiple paths between two access points can lead to looping and bring your network down.

Wirelessly Bridging Two LANs

The simple act of adding more access points so that coverage overlaps was covered in Chapter 9. The essential point to consider is that each access point on the same wireless network must have the same SSID value. The SSID value is the network name by definition. When you are overlapping wireless access points, they must use different channels (either 1, 6, or 11). Once you start adding wireless bridges these facts still apply. However, when you use repeaters in place of access points they use the same channels for transmission.

If you have two separate networks in your home and office, each with its own separate address pools, and you wish to bridge them, you would normally connect two of the hubs or switches on each network with a wired connection. If a direct Ethernet connection isn't possible, you might try establishing a connection using the electrical wiring in your house or office. There are instances where even those kinds of connections aren't possible or desirable and it makes sense to bridge two networks with wireless devices. The essential connection sets up an access point on each LAN in a bridging mode and then connects the networks together. Figure 10-4 shows a D-Link access point being set for bridging mode.

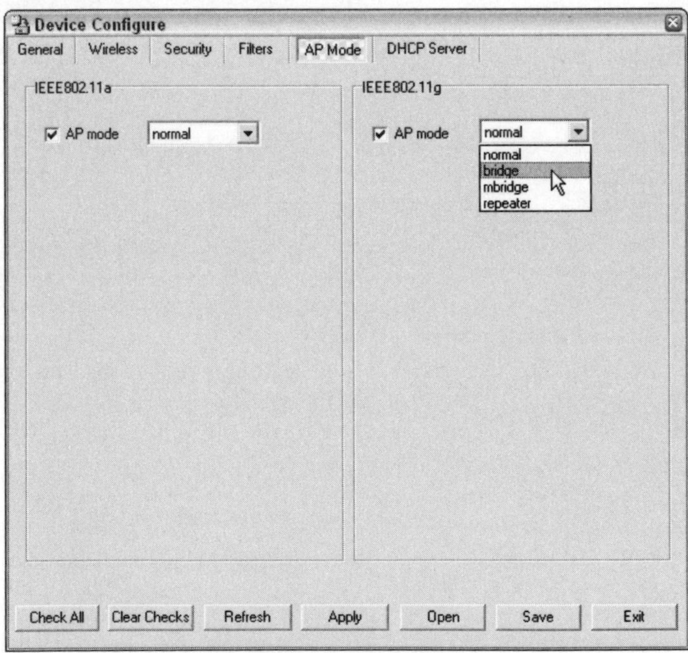

Figure 10-4: You need to set an access point to bridging mode to have it transmit and receive signals from other access points only, and not broadcast a signal that wireless clients can connect to.

Here are some scenarios in which a wireless bridging solution for two LANs makes sense:

- You need to find a way to inexpensively connect two separate LANs.
- You need the flexibility to connect to an inconvenient or a changing location.
- You want a secondary means of connecting two LANs for fault tolerance.
- You want to link a wireless LAN to a network with Internet access.

There are many more places where a wired connection makes sense even if it costs more. The arguments for a wired connection are faster throughput, better reliability, easier management, and better security. So before you create this kind of connection, you need to ask yourself if it is really necessary or desirable.

Adding an additional wireless network to a LAN that already has one isn't much different than adding the first one. You can add your wireless router or access point any place that you can connect to your network. With wireless technology that's really the rub, because the places you want to put a wireless signal are the places where you can't get your wires to go to. So the choices you have are extending your wireless network so that coverage of two or more wireless networks can overlap, or finding another way to get your wired LAN to a point where it can support a wireless connection.

Signal Loss

The essential issue in setting up a wireless bridge is one of distance and the resulting signal loss. Both are affected by the nature of your wireless devices and the path from one device through the other. You can greatly affect your connection by selecting the right kind of antenna and positioning your devices correctly (see Chapter 12 for more details). If you are connecting two sides of the same house together, an omnidirectional or semidirectional antenna might be enough to create a strong link. For a separate guest house on the property a more directional antenna might work, at one or better yet both wireless network nodes. Finally, for very long distances where you have direct line-of-sight, a high-gain antenna such as a can or waveguide, or a parabolic reflecting antenna would be the choice. These highly directed signals are very sensitive to anything in their path, even leaves of trees.

Whatever equipment you use, the goal is to calculate the strength of your direct signal. It should be more than 20dBm above your access point's sensitivity. Less than 20dBm results in signal losses that degrade the signal too much. You can calculate the power of the received signal with this general formula:

```
Received signal = Input power - total losses + total gain
```

where both Received signal and Input power are measured against a reference level such as dBm (1 milliwatt over a 600ohm impedance) and the total losses and total gain are in dB. Your measurements also need to consider any signal loss over wiring such as coaxial cabling or connectors on each side of the bridge. A consideration of signal loss over distance will give you some appreciation of the needed equipment. For example, the calculated signal loss over a one-mile connection is 104dB.

Note

You'll find a nice explanation of what a decibel and its various forms mean at `www.sizes.com/units/decibel.htm`.

Access Point Bridging Mode

Not all access points or routers enable you to configure them in a bridging mode, and those that do often aren't particularly good at bridging. It's something you need to check on when you purchase your equipment, particularly if you purchase the equipment for this particular purpose. You may also find that more recently released firmware will update your device to allow bridging. When in bridging mode, an access point provides only connection transmit/receive and doesn't broadcast a signal to wireless clients.

As with all wireless equipment, if you can connect a single manufacturer's equipment together you are probably less likely to experience problems, and more likely to get a satisfactory connection, as well as benefit from any proprietary improvements that the vendor has made to the 802.11 standards. You'll find that the more expensive access points are designed to allow bridging mode operation. Only a few of the access points manufactured for the home and small business market have this feature. The truth is that bridging longer distances isn't something that most consumers do, so the tendency is to provide range extension solutions, repeaters, and overlapping additional access points to extend coverage.

It's worth remembering that different manufacturers set their devices' default access point IP address to different networks. One device might have a default of 192.168.1.1; another might have 10.100.0.50. You need to access the device and change the IP address to either a fixed IP address or a dynamically acquired DHCP address. However you do this, you need to communicate with the device, which generally means connecting up a laptop (or another disconnected computer).

Assuming that your equipment supports it, here is a general approach to setting up a wireless bridge between two LANs:

1. Place both wireless devices where your management software can configure them.
2. Collect all the Ethernet MAC addresses of your endpoint devices. This should be available in your wireless network device management software.
3. Enter the MAC addresses for node 1 into the connection device's MAC address for device 2, and vice versa.
4. Set the SSIDs for both access points to the same value, and the connection to the same channel.
5. Set the device mode or operation mode to point-to-point or to wireless bridge (the name varies by manufacturer).
6. Test your bridge connection on a short distance to make sure that your settings work.

7. Take your remote bridging device and locate it so that it can connect up to your remote LAN. Try to keep the run of coaxial cable and other connections to a minimum. For a remote connection without power, but where you can run a CAT5 Ethernet cable, consider a PoE (Power over Ethernet) solution, discussed later in this chapter.
8. Carefully position the antenna(s) for best reception. This is something that you might want two people to do together, so that you can save time and effort. When you have the best position, fasten your antenna into a firm and unmovable position.
9. Storm-proof and weatherproof any outside antennas. CAT5 cabling should be enclosed to prevent weathering; all metallic parts should be grounded in case of lightning.

Note

Because signal degradation over coaxial cables is very high, the APs have to be located very near the antennas, most of the time outside in the open, so you need to put your APs in a weatherproof enclosing as well.

Bridge Topologies

Different manufacturers and authors label different wireless bridging topologies with different names: access point mode, workgroup bridge mode, point-to-point, redundant point-to-point, point-to-multipoint, and so forth. There are only a few principles that you need to keep in mind about these technologies. Figure 10-5 shows some of the multipoint bridge topologies.

In the first topology one access point is a root bridge and the other is a non-root bridge. A root bridge transmits the network topology along with authentication, while non-root bridges do not. A root bridge should be given the lowest bridge ID number. Root bridge topologies are helpful in preventing circular loops from forming. For large networks, you should place the root bridge in a central location to minimize the connection lengths. In a point-to-point connection when a root bridge can't be located, the non-route bridge assumes the duties of a root bridge.

If you are configuring a wireless network to reach several rooms or buildings, you'll want to look into a point-to-multipoint bridge connection, something found in enterprise equipment. In this connection a single root bridge's signal is received by two or more wireless bridges serving additional LANs. If the network you are connecting to is a large flat network, that is, one that only uses the addresses of a single class-C network of 255 addresses, then the recommendation is that you use a router to connect to that network. For an important connection, perhaps in a mission-critical system, you might want to use redundant wireless bridges. Here, two or more point-to-point connections are used to link the same networks. Redundant bridging devices use the Spanning Tree Protocol (STP) to monitor their wireless network links. STP analyzes traffic flow and reconfigures your paths when it detects problems. All of these topologies are for larger wireless installation and are expensive and difficult for the average person to implement.

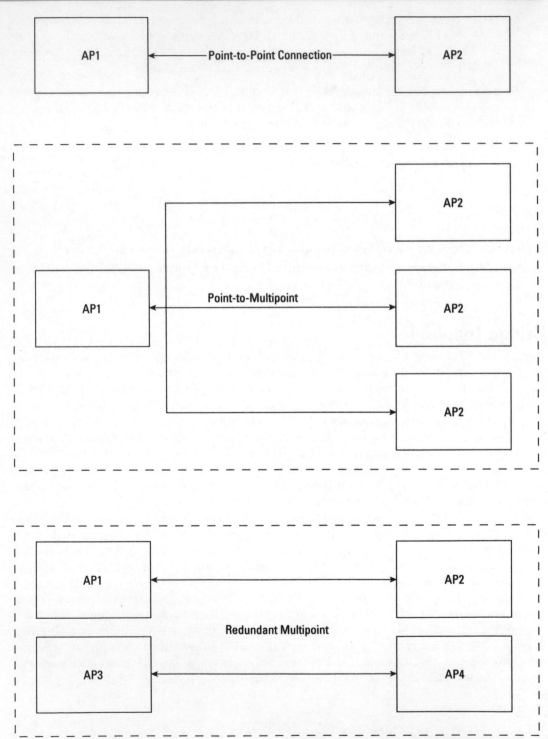

Figure 10-5: Three different bridging topologies, both point-to-point and point-to-multipoint.

Roaming and Throughput

With a single wireless access point, you can move about with a laptop and still be connected to the same network. The situation gets more complicated when there is more than one access point. As you move about you are doing what is called ***roaming*** and when you lose your connection you need to reestablish a new connection. As with bridging, roaming isn't always well implemented in access points for the consumer market. A standard called the *Inter Access Point Protocol (IAPP)* for wireless roaming for 802.11f was published by the IEEE task group, but it may be some time before you see this feature implemented. First we need to see 802.11f devices, and then there has to be a demonstrated demand for roaming in the consumer marketplace — something that might never happen. Most home and small business users don't have multiple domains and thus don't require roaming.

There's another situation where you would want to install multiple access points to increase throughput. Consider a small design company where large files are transferred by several workers. To better serve this group, multiple access points are installed to overlaps so that the different clients could connect to different access points and thus balance the load of traffic among them. Load balancing isn't a feature you'll find on consumer devices, and it's difficult to implement because consumer devices lock onto the strongest signal they find. A load balancing solution requires the software control to select the access point that has the largest bandwidth available instead.

Power over Ethernet

If all you want to do is provide a location where you can put a remote access point, your best bet is to plug the remote access point into a hub or switch nearby. If you have to set up an access point where there is no existing power but to which you can run an Ethernet line, you can accomplish this by employing what is called a *Power over Ethernet* or PoE solution. An access point on a roof would be an example of this application. PoE is an IEEE standard that is hoped will remove the need to have power lines near every wireless device. It uses unused wires in your Ethernet cabling to carry the DC current. The reason to use PoE is so that you can place an access point next to its antenna. The longer the connection between the two, the weaker both the transmission and reception will be. A run of more than 3 feet of coaxial cable is enough to fatally degrade an access point's performance.

What PoE does is to use a device called an *injector*, which supplies the power to the right CAT5 wires, and a tap or splitter that has a power outlet attached to it where your access point's power adapter plugs into. An Ethernet signal flows through both of these devices transparently. The technology further provides both passive and active injectors and taps. The difference is that an active device offers some short-circuit, overcurrent, and voltage regulation protection. You'll find that injectors use five to ten times the voltage of your access point to maintain a strong signal down the wire. An active tap will have a voltage regulator in it that will adjust the voltage down to 5V DC, which is what many access points use. With PoE technology, pay special attention to the connection from these devices to your wireless equipment. Some of the plugs are proprietary and incompatible with one another.

PoE not only can cut down on costs, but it can also lower your power bills and help you control your devices. Using the management software for PoE devices you can program when these devices are active. If you have these devices shut off when people are not around, after hours or at night you can lessen the chances of a security intrusion.

When possible, buy PoE kits from the same manufacturer as your access points. For example, D-Link has a PoE adapter, the DHP100 that retails for $95. You'll find a Web site devoted to PoE at: `www.poweroverethernet.com`.

Powerline Ethernet

Of course, the reason we call it a "remote access point" is that there is likely not going to be a hub or access point available, and it is difficult if not impossible to run Ethernet cabling to that location. One way of circumventing the problem is to add a HomePlug Powerline Ethernet bridge to each end of the connection you need to make.

Powerline plug adapters plug into your network's router or switch and also into a nearby standard electrical socket. The signal runs over your existing house power circuitry and communicates with a plug adapter on the remote end that is attached to your remote wireless access point. Powerline technology is a standard supported by the HomePlug Powerline Alliance (`www.homeplug.org`) which certifies compliance to this standard.

Linksys has the PLUSB10 adapter that uses USB networking over power lines. You need two of each of these devices to make a Powerline connection. Linksys also has a bridge for Powerline, the Linksys Instant PowerLine EtherFast 10/100 Bridge which can connect the Ethernet port on a router, cable, or DSL modem to a power line connection. Finally, you'll find that Netgear XE102 Powerline adapter is another choice. The technology is easy to install and often requires no drivers, but it is pricey and has a slow data transfer rate inappropriate for many applications such as video streaming.. Powerline can transfer data at about 14 Mbps, which is a little faster than 802.11b. This technology isn't really fast enough to exploit 802.11a, g, and other wireless standards fully and the parts tend to be expensive. However, there's no arguing with how convenient this solution is. For access to e-mail, simply browsing the Web, or streaming music to a remote location, Powerline would be sufficient.

Isolating Networks from Each Other

Network isolation provides a barrier that hackers must surmount to gain access to your data. The advantage of isolation is that penetration of one of your networks doesn't necessarily mean that other more sensitive areas have been compromised. Indeed, one of the favored approaches to managing hackers is to create ***honeypots***, systems that are specifically set up to be hacked and to identify the method of penetration, as discussed in Chapter 8. You can use many different methods to isolate your wireless networks from one another, including: addressing, filters, bringing down links, and using different challenge and response mechanisms.

Addressing

You may want to consider creating a separate set of IP addresses or a domain for your wireless LAN, and additional ones for each of your extra wireless LANs. This helps give you some measure of control over traffic flow because traffic must authenticate itself as it travels from domain to domain. There's also a performance benefit for additional domains. There are network devices that broadcast packets continually on an Ethernet network. One such device might be a cluster looking for each computer's "heartbeat." Another might be a management console that is sending out "discovery" packets, and there are many others. When you are in a situation where there is a lot of this traffic (typically very large deployments) you may find that these broadcast packets rob you of much of your wireless network's available bandwidth. By creating a domain for your wireless network and separating it from your wired LAN by a router or through a virtual LAN or VLAN network, you can remove this network overhead from your wireless traffic.

A common recommendation is that each wireless network be put on its own subnet. A subnet is a set of IP addresses in the same domain where the subnet mask is set up to restrict the available address range and pool size. You'll find a subnet tutorial at `www.ralphb.net/IPSubnet/` and at `www.learntosubnet.com/`. With subnetting, you can restrict which devices are allowed access by specifying a range.

For larger wireless networks, consultants often suggest that each of your wireless networks be a different domain that is a set of computers with different IP address ranges. For wireless networking, different domains means that each wireless domain has its own SSID. When you have an IP domain interface, you can add additional barriers for hackers. The first barrier is address complexity. It's not that easy to figure out private addresses on one NIC card when you are probing from a network using a different NIC. So install a firewall of some kind, or a proxy server. Many access points and routers offer this capability.

Creating multiple network domains in the classic sense means that you have different domain servers on each side of a link. Different domains have their own different security databases and network directories, which translate into different challenge and response mechanisms, and the requirement for different passwords. When you start to deal with this level of complexity you have to consider trust relationships, pass through authentications, single password logon software, and other systems that really aren't part of any home or small businesses' capabilities.

For home networks and small business networks where only a portion of the range of available IP addresses are being used, we strongly encourage you to use static IP addresses for devices and clients. Disabling DHCP means that a hacker can't just jump onto your network and get the network address (IP) provided for them, they have to know the address range. With static IP addresses, you can filter traffic based on the IP address at your firewall or proxy server.

You can also create what is called ***protocol isolation***. With wireless technology this translates to using one protocol for one side of the connection, such as 802.11b for the outsiders, and another, such as 802.11g, for insiders. This doesn't afford a lot of protection, but anyone without a g card won't get in to test things. More traditional network protocol isolation has one transport protocol like IP on one side of a firewall, and another like NetBEUI, AppleTalk, or IPX on the other. With IP networking as pervasive as it is, these days most people just run IP on both sides of the firewall. Still, you can use encryption and have different keys on each network, and that further complicates the task of someone trying to gain entry to you network.

A better form of isolation is attained using MAC filtering. That is, you enter the numbers of known MAC addresses for your network's wireless devices and only those devices with the right MAC addresses can gain entry to the network. MAC filtering or Media Control Access Filtering isn't foolproof. A skillful hacker can spoof a MAC address, but doing this adds to the complexity of the job required to break into your networks.

Some wireless devices let you name them so that they can be discovered using things like SNMP or ***Simple Network Management Protocol***. SNMP is the engine behind most of the software that "discovers" network devices. If you can disable SNMP, you should, and you should be careful to avoid names that people can guess for your wireless networks.

Limiting Signal Coverage

Whenever possible you should test to see that your signal isn't leaking out into areas where people outside of your control can access it. That's part of any wireless site survey. When you have multiple networks, this becomes even more critical. You can also limit access by disabling your device's SSID broadcasts so that only those people who know what the wireless network is named can access it. Try to right size your coverage area by having the signal essentially end at your building's outer wall. There are several ways to do this. Probably the easiest is to take a site survey to assess your signal strength and adjust the position of your wireless devices to bring the coverage out of any public areas. You can also purchase antennas that aim your wireless signal away from a wall or corner, both directional and highly directional antennas.

If it's possible, you can lower your security risks by turning off wireless access points when you don't use them. We mentioned PoE management software as one solution to programming times when devices shut down, but you can use automated switches, building control software, X10 devices, and other systems to perform this function.

We cover antennas in Chapter 12, but suffice it to say that if you need to connect two distant LANs wirelessly, you want to purchase a narrow beamwidth antenna such as a Yagi, or for very long distances perhaps a parabolic dish reflector antenna. With a highly directional antenna only devices close to the center of the beam will be able to pick up the signal. Positioning and antennas are certainly low cost, low hassle partial solutions to the security issue; and they should be part of your arsenal.

Securing Multiple Networks

Multiple networks introduce additional complexity and points of attack, but they also offer tools that you don't have with a single network. All of the things you do with your systems to protect them from the bad guys should still be done for one or more networks, including:

- Turn on encryption such as WEP and do not accept default settings such as usernames of "admin".
- Use virus software and ***update*** it regularly.
- Run scans with anti-spam software like Spam Sweeper, Ad-Aware, Spybot, or your choice.
- Update your software to the current versions and be particularly attentive to applying all OS patches.
- Run regular tested backups.
- Use a firewall, either software or hardware.
- Consider closing your broadband connection at night when not in use; a network without an Internet connection isn't particularly appealing to a war driver.
- Update the firmware of your wireless devices; many times improved security is one of the major features of this upgrade.
- Don't open unexpected e-mail attachments

Performing each of these steps takes time — but you won't regret doing them. On the day you have to restore systems or chase someone down for ID theft, you'll be patting yourself on the back for following the preceding guidelines.

For a larger set of connected networks, and for enterprise use, you may want to consider installing a VPN or Virtual Private Network. A VLAN forces wireless clients to authenticate themselves in order to tunnel through the VPN, and uses Layer 3 encryption to secure the communication. You'll find VLAN technology on some of the devices meant for the small office such as the SOHO TZW or the similar Netgear FVM318. For less expensive solutions you can purchase VPN software.

Summary

In this chapter, you saw how you could extend your wireless network by using repeaters or setting up a wireless distribution system. These techniques maintain a single network but widen the area of coverage. There are many instances where you need to connect up remote systems using wireless technology, for any number of reasons. Wireless access points and routers can create wireless links called bridges that enable you to create that connection.

There are many different kinds of bridges that you learned about in this chapter. Some are point-to-point and are the most commonly used ones in home and small office settings. There are also multipoint and redundant connection bridges. Because bridging is more of an enterprise feature, it is only just starting to be used in the small network market. You will have better luck when you standardize on a single vendor's equipment, or use equipment using the same manufacturer's chip set.

You also learned some techniques for isolating and securing wireless networks with one or more connected LANs. Much of what you learned about security for a simple single LAN/access point setup applies to multiple wirelessly connected networks. However, you have additional vulnerabilities with multiple connections and points of entry. You can help secure your multi-zone wireless network by paying attention to settings, isolating networks through addressing, filtering, virtual private networks, and so on.

In the next chapter, you will learn how to make wireless networking available to your neighbors, across alleys and across yards. This is a real honest-to-goodness network neighborhood. There are some good reasons to provide this kind of service, and things you have to know and be careful about so that your neighbors don't walk off with the farm.

Chapter 11

Setting Up a Neighborhood Network

Given half a chance, most people want to live in communities and connect with other people. Maybe it is the hunter-gatherer in us looking to partake in this week's wooly mammoth barbecue. Whatever it is, Wi-Fi offers you the ability to create communities by extending your network to your neighbors and your neighborhood—creating a real "network neighborhood." This chapter continues the discussion from the previous chapter where you learned about the technology of extending your wireless network, and is a nice introduction to Chapter 22, where you learn about creating hotspots. In fact, you can use a "hotspot in a box" solution to create a neighborhood network, but because a neighborhood network doesn't need to be tracked for usage or billed against there's no particular benefit to deploying a specific hotspot package. You'll find that using techniques you already know that you can accomplish setting up this system.

Why You'd Want to Share Your Signal

A neighborhood network should connect the places that people live, where they work, and places where they congregate. Creating a community-based wireless network makes sense when you give users tools and uses that are different from what they might use their computers for at home. For example, special content such as you would find in a local portal and the ability to interact with others in new ways are good reasons to consider this kind of network. If you want to see an example of a community-based Web portal, check out DigitalTexas (`www.digitaltexas.com/`). This site was built by ClearChannel Radio with DynaPortal software (`www.dynaportal.com/`). It's the local content that makes these sites particularly valuable.

Although some people think that Wi-Fi network access should be free and universally available, most people create wireless networks to serve or to establish a community in a contiguous area. A community could be your immediate neighbors, a condominium complex, your city block, or your

entire town. Your purpose in creating a network neighborhood for each of these different sets of users can be entirely different. Some reasons might be:

- For your neighbors, you might want to share your Internet connection or provide access to a file share, a networked photographic wide-format printer, or some other resource.
- For an RV park where vehicles come and go every day.
- For a city block, you might want to offer network access in an area where your neighbors aren't served by an ISP or broadband connection.
- For a condominium where you want to provide share network access to a central broadband connection or T1 line.
- To an entire town to expedite a whole range of community services.

Note

If you are setting up an open network, pay special attention to your ISP's rules and requirements. Most ISPs have language in their contracts that forbids sharing your network Internet connection with other people, something that they may refer to as "bandwidth theft." Most ISPs are not keen to have you eliminate potential new customers. Behind a firewall or proxy server, Network Address Translation (NAT) hides the identity of the systems connected to your network. Still, if you are going to exceed the allowable bandwidth (called a bandwidth cap) your ISP provides you, then you should be careful about the legalities involved. However, you may find that your ISP does have packages such as business accounts that will allow some network sharing. These types of accounts are similar to the "café" accounts used for public hotspots, and they typically charge a base amount plus additional fees for data throughput every month.

Gone are the days when people offered network access for things such as BBS or bulletin boards; for most collaborative applications there are Internet tools that serve a similar function and are easier to connect to and less fussy. You could provide an instant messaging application for community chat sessions, but most people opt to use AOL Instant Messenger (available as a free downloadable application from AOL) or Windows Messenger these days. Fewer use newsgroups and contribute to blogs. So unless you wish to share some special kind of groupware or collaboration tool such as Lotus Notes, the reason most people give for creating network neighborhoods is the connection itself or access to network resources.

Ask yourself what the impact would be on a community that had an open, widely available wireless network that anyone could access at any time. The universal availability of a community network would enable all sorts of behavior that are hard to accommodate today. For example:

- You could go to the park on a sunny day with your notebook and get some work done.
- You could enable computer access to people who live in locations that are inconvenient or expensive to wire up, such as a large, old school building with lots of rooms.

- You could put up smart information signs that tell commuters about traffic patterns or problems around town, or display information about lost dogs or children, and put those displays even in hard-to-reach locations.
- You could enable mobile data collection devices for police, postal workers, and others.
- You could set up webcams to monitor intersections or school grounds.

Different Kinds of Community Networks

Most of the discussion in this book centers on what is called ***infrastructure mode wireless networking***. In this mode, for example, an access point transmits and receives signals from wireless clients in much the same way that a network hub can accept Ethernet cables being plugged into its open ports. Infrastructure networks force users to authenticate themselves and impose other restrictions to limit who can connect to a network, as well as provide fast direction for packets bound to one system or another. Also, when a wireless device such as an access point fails, most infrastructure networks lose their coverage for that particular area.

Depending upon your purpose, there are different types of community networks to consider:

- An ad hoc network for fast client-based peer-to-peer networking
- A portal WLAN with authentication, management, and restrictions to specific content
- An extended WLAN with users who have managed domain accounts
- A hotspot or an open WLAN where anyone who can receive the signal can connect

All of these different types of networks can serve as network neighborhoods, and each is useful in specific types of situations. Let's take a look at when you might want to use each one.

Ad Hoc Wireless Networks

For situations where there are transitory communities that need to wirelessly network, such as a class or lab session, a convention hall, or some such thing, users can create a wireless network in the ad hoc mode using their network cards as nodes in a temporary network. Ad hoc networking, sometimes called peer-to-peer networking, shares the same wireless bandwidth and only requires that a user connect up to the open network, usually without any authentication. When one user streams a large multimedia file over an ad hoc network the impact is felt by all users, as the bandwidth is used up. Ad hoc networks aren't meant to be performance champions; they are meant to provide substantial ease of use to the users.

Peer-to-peer networks is what Windows for Workgroups offered in the early 1990s, and is made available to developers for Windows as a Microsoft SDK (software development kit). The peer-to-peer model was probably made famous to everyone by the now defunct music sharing software Napster. You can find numerous examples of peer-to-peer networking applications that you can use on your own ad hoc network including LANster, Grokster, Blubster, BearShare, a variety of applications that

run on a Gnutella network, and others. If you want to set up an ad hoc network that provides Internet access to users, you can set up a mode on nearly all access points called "ad hoc" and that will allow connections

You might use an ad hoc network when you have a group of family members come to your house to swap digital picture albums, or to create a picture album from everybody's photos for a commemorative CD-ROM for your grandparents' fiftieth wedding anniversary. With everyone connected, you might share your My Pictures folder, allowing each person in the group to access and edit that folder, adding their photos as required. If you had thousands of pictures, you might want to let everyone view the photos of interest and add them to the final photo folder. An ad hoc wireless network would work well for this situation.

To set up an ad hoc network, do the following:

1. Check that you are all using the same networking standard: 802.11a, b, or g.
2. Have your clients set their network adapters to the ad hoc mode and set the network SSID to the same value.
3. Set all client adapters to the same channel.
4. Disable WEP for easier connection.
5. Save these settings as a specific network connection in case you want to apply them sometime in the future.
6. Set up your network shares.
7. Make sure that everyone has their personal firewalls either turned off or set to allow certain kinds of file sharing.

Note

You may find that your access point or router has a setting called "ad hoc" mode. In that setting the access point behaves just as your computer would in an ad hoc network.

Once your settings are correct, joining an ad hoc network means just showing up; your wireless NIC should connect automatically. You'll find instances where establishing an ad hoc network doesn't work. Sometimes this problem is hardware related; ad hoc networking is part of the 802.11 standard but few manufacturers test their cards for compatibility. More often you will find that there is some problem with the IP address. We recommend that you use static IP addresses for small ad hoc networks, so you want to make sure that the correct address ranges are assigned and that there are no IP address duplicate pair (address conflicts). If you are using DHCP for an address provider, you should check to see that your DHCP service has actually given out a valid IP address.

Captive Portals and Hotspots

There are different configurations for setting up a wireless network that your neighbors can use in the infrastructure mode. Infrastructure mode means that users are going to connect wirelessly through an access point or router on your network, or through a repeater. If that access point is inside your network, you need to take appropriate precautions, so most neighborhood networks tend to place their wireless access devices outside of their firewall.

The key factor that separates one type of infrastructure method from another is the amount of management that you do for each user. A managed wireless neighborhood network would identify your users and manage their traffic in some way, but not necessarily through a formal account — perhaps by password only. Management might include reconnect time or bandwidth restrictions, and restrictions on what can be transferred. Most certainly management includes restrictions on what resources can be accessed from outside; something that would be true regardless of the type of network you establish.

If you are supplying a WLAN that authenticates users individually and manages them with the specific goal of providing an Internet connection, you are creating a "captive portal." In less complex Internet times, the word *portal* was meant to imply a window on the Internet, a place where you could look out and see the part of the universe that that window allowed. AOL was considered to be a portal; so too was MSN. Yahoo, on the other hand, quickly got differentiated to the class of "directory service," although it too would probably be considered a portal now. A portal implies controlled access to and restriction to specific content. The captive moniker is given to this class of access because you are restricted in what content you can see. Anyone that has logged onto Boingo at an airport has an understanding of what captive means; no matter what you do, you are directed back to the Boingo site. Similarly, when working at Kinko's, the national copy and print chain now owned by Federal Express, you may find yourself logged in to a restricted browser that permits you no access to the computer and a limited range of services. That's a captive portal as well.

It was all the rage three or four years ago to build software that allowed you to create specialized portals such as custom home pages in Netscape or consoles in Lotus Notes. So you're likely to find that your bank, telephone company, ISP (certainly), and many other intuitions have portals. Any site that lets you customize content in some way is trying to be your portal.

However, as technology marches on, simple access by itself isn't enough to bestow "full portalship" status on your WLAN. These days you would have to limit Internet or network resource access to content in some meaningful way to get that moniker. It's probably semantics to differentiate between a WLAN behaving as a portal or one that is classified as a hotspot, as both can be managed solutions. Suffice it to say that if you are providing access to content and restricting access, then you have probably created a wireless portal.

If you have an interest in creating a captive portal and want to start with a device designed for this type of thing you might want to investigate the $800 Reliawave Internet Plug and Play Server Gateway (`www.demarctech.com`) from Demarctech. This device authenticates users using a RADIUS database system (the same standard used in remote access servers) and redirects their browsers to a special proprietary Web page. Among its software functions are:

- NAT
- E-mail and browser redirection

- DHCP services
- Challenge and response password/ID account management.

These are features that you need to implement in any captive portal solution. The Reliawave is meant to service a large number of users and requires the use of a standalone RADIUS server.

As you wander about with your trusty mobile device through airports, in hotels, restaurants, and elsewhere, you will encounter commercial wireless ventures such as Wayport.com, Boingo, or T-Mobile. Each is a subscription-based service that lets you log onto the Internet with an account, and each is more properly described as a network of hotspots. Chapter 22 is entirely devoted to hotspots, so if that is your interest, you should take a look.

Extended Networks

An extended network is what you would have when you give domain privileges to your network neighbors. Doing so implies that you have created a user account for them, and possibly a machine account. Chances are that if you were diligent about creating this type of network, you would also have defined and put into place a set of policies. If this sounds like a lot of work to you, it does to us as well.

You would want to create an extended network in situations where the number of users isn't excessive and for which you want to manage some type of application that isn't going to be Web-based. A Web-based application really only requires an Internet connection for each user with identification provided through their browser. An example of this kind of application would be a messaging application such as Exchange or Domino, or a collaborative information application such as Microsoft Sharepoint or Lotus Notes where a user account is required to access the service. While it's true that you can get mail from Exchange or Domino through a Web-based client, an application accessed over a network is more secure and less troublesome. Mail is there for your clients even when the Internet connection is broken.

Truth be told, we're not big fans of allowing domain access to outside users. It really isn't necessary and it has a number of security risks associated with it that aren't worth taking. Managing a large number of accounts for a network neighborhood isn't really something you want to do unless there is some very specific value in it. The better way is to create a second network domain for your neighborhood and set up the trust relationship so that if the outside domain authenticates the user that authentication can be passed through to your network domain.

Chances are that if all of this talk about domains, authentication, and machine accounts has your head spinning, then you aren't likely to want to be managing an enterprise application that makes an extended network necessary. You should probably concentrate on creating some version of a hotspot or a captive portal. The software necessary to create and manage both of these types of "open" networks is out there to be purchased; and entire turnkey systems can be deployed.

Wireless Mesh Networks

A number of towns have created public wireless networks with wide geographical coverage. These mostly use the extended network model, or create large hotspots. The Center for Neighborhood Technology (http://wcn.cnt.org/) in the Chicago area illustrates the use of what is called a ***mesh network***. CNT has implemented wireless networks for the communities of Pilsen and Lawndale in Chicago, the suburban community of Elgin that is 40 miles northwest of Chicago, and in West Frankfurt, which is in southern Illinois. Similar projects have been done in the Seattle area by SeattleWireless and in rural settings.

The projects are meant to encourage business and cultural development in these areas, creating a community asset that different organizations can leverage. CNT uses community partners, schools, community centers and other organizations to develop this network.

What's particularly interesting about the CNT projects is that they use what CNT calls a "mesh" technology in place of a hub and spoke topology. In a home network you would connect all of your wireless devices to a single access point connection to the Internet and rely on connections to additional remote access points for the network's fan out. By contrast, the mesh model has a central access point, but instead of managing wireless links to additional access points (with all the complexity that that entails), this mesh network uses a set of repeaters to enlarge the coverage area of the WLAN.

In either case you could fortify the access point that provides the connection to your Internet backbone in a number of ways, but managing a set of repeaters provides some fault tolerance because the areas of coverage can be made to overlap. If a repeater fails, only the area it covers is lost and other areas contiguous with that area will find other paths back to the main access point. Figure 11-1 shows you the topology of the mesh network that CNT offers.

Notice in particular that the main access point is placed in front of two firewalls, one for servers and the other for users. This protects the network's essential core services on servers from intrusion and has one firewall authenticate the users for network management — which are the two most important features of a secure network neighborhood.

What we particularly like about this mesh network is that the reliance on repeaters to spread the signal not only simplifies network management and settings, but it also allows the network to grow and scale as the number of users grows. Not only do repeaters provide you with the necessary geographical coverage, but additional routers can be put in the same coverage area to provide both fault tolerance and greater bandwidth. This topology is similar in design to a cell phone network where a signal is repeated from one transmitter to another until the message is received on a node directly connected to the network.

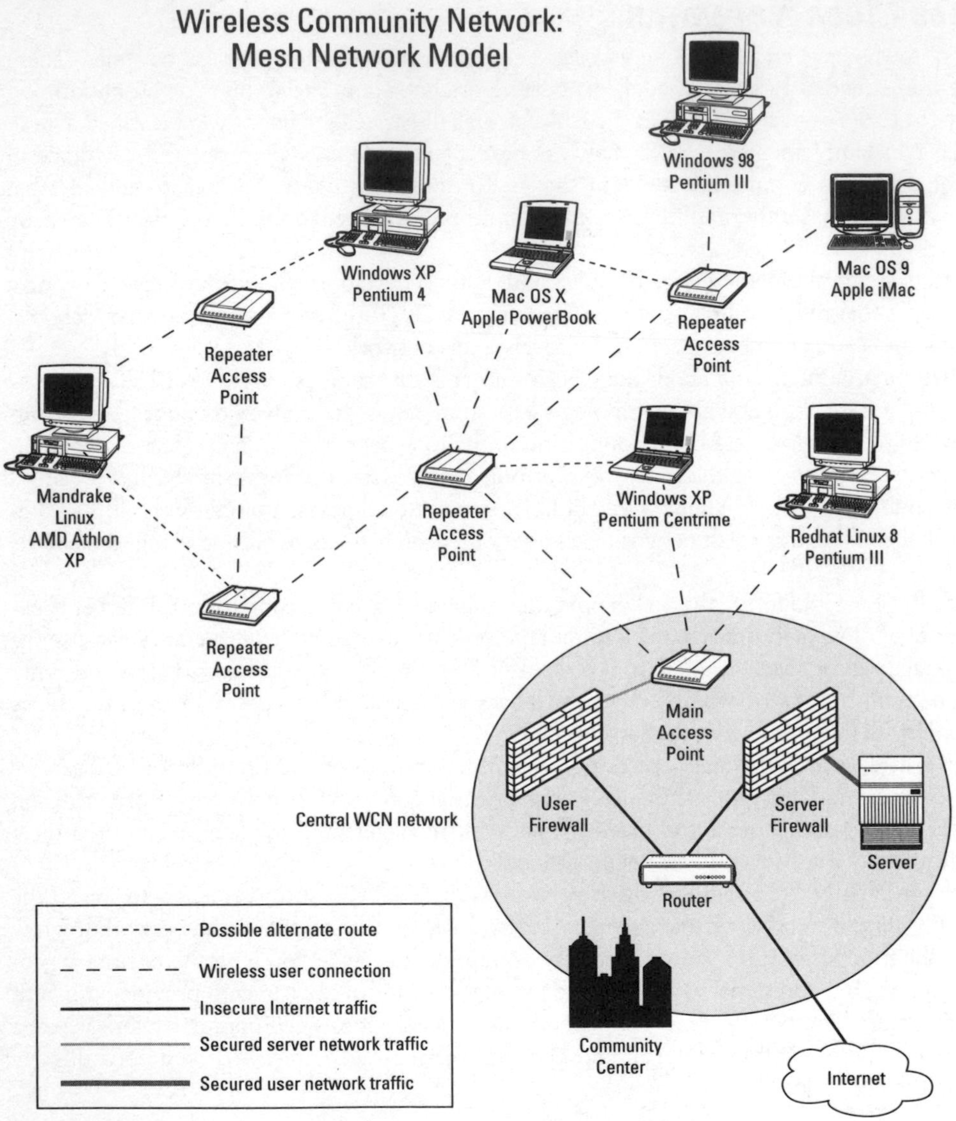

Figure 11-1: The mesh topology used to install a community network in the Chicago area relies on repeaters to scale out and up.

Adding Outdoor Access Points and Commercially Available Antennas

We cover antennas in some detail in Chapter 12, as well as discuss their use in multi-zone and extended wireless networks. The requirement of placing equipment outdoors imposes some important restrictions on the kinds of devices you can use. First and foremost, any access point, repeater, or antenna meant for outside use needs to be enclosed or made durable in some way. There are many antennas on the market today that fit this category because it is important that antennas be located in prominent locations. Directional antennas tend to do best in line-of-site situations, while an omnidirectional antenna will get better coverage if it doesn't have to travel through a wall to get to your neighbors' laptops. Many antennas therefore are set up for either roof mounting or mounting from a pole or high up on a wall. Yagi directional antennas are often pole mounted and use for outdoor links.

One consideration when you buy an antenna is to make sure that the antenna is properly grounded and isolated. Any metallic object high up can attract lightening, and attracting electrical signals is just what an antenna is designed to do. You may find that to properly locate a wireless signal you need to mount your devices on a tower, and that that tower doesn't exist. Therefore, you may also find yourself in the market for a radio tower, strange as that might seem to you. When locating your antenna, pay particular attention to that antenna's profile. Many antennas do better with either a horizontal or a vertical placement and that will affect how you mount them.

Many antennas connect to access points or repeaters using coaxial cable. The signal loss in coaxial cabling is high, and depending upon the wiring used the signal can degrade substantially over even as short a distance as three or four feet (a meter). That being the case, access points and repeaters may need to be placed in close proximity to the antenna that serves them. If that location is outside, then you also need to make sure that those transmitters are properly weatherproofed. An inconvenient location may not give you access to power lines, and therefore you might want to consider a device that has a Power over Ethernet or PoE connection, where your Ethernet cable provides the power. In instances where there is available power but to which you can't run a network line, your device should be able to work in a standalone mode that doesn't require a network connection.

Nearly all vendors that supply antennas, access points, and repeaters sell outdoor versions of these products. You also find that some manufacturers offer enclosures for their equipment that will make them weatherproof while not degrading the signal too much.

Equipment made for outdoor use is often made differently from devices designed for indoor use. Many outdoor Wi-Fi devices offer special internal firmware, different error checking, better client polling mechanisms, and other packet collision avoidance features. You may find that outdoor equipment comes with Orthogonal Frequency Division Modulation (OFDM) protocols to improve connections that don't have a true line-of-sight. So don't be surprised if outdoor equipment that you buy for establishing a network neighborhood costs significantly more than your indoor components. There is more going on under the hood than simply the hood itself.

Security on a Neighborhood Network

When you start providing networking services for your neighbors it's a little like inviting them into your house for a visit. You can let them and their children run around your house all hours of the day and night, pillaging and plundering as they go as if they are Peter Pan, or you can chaperone their visit making sure that they only go where you want and when you want. Any network that allows outside connections must install security features meant to limit the client if it hopes to maintain any security at all and protect its resources.

Sometimes it's not possible to be as secure as you might ideally like to be. If you and your family members are sitting around the dining room table with an ad hoc wireless network and their firewalls prevent file transfers, then most people will turn off their personal firewalls for the short time that they are doing that kind of work.

Any secure networking system must have a barrier to entry in the form of a firewall or authentication server. If you are setting up a network neighborhood and have a choice of devices, don't simply set up an access point and allow users to connect. Choose instead wireless devices that have the management features of a firewall. Those features include, but are not limited to the following:

- Authenticates users in some manner.
- Controls who gets a network address and for how long (DHCP).
- Limits the type of traffic that a user can communicate with; for example HTTP yes, AIM (AOL Instant Messenger) no.
- Controls time of access.
- Limits bandwidth so that the network isn't saturated and you can stop spamming and DOS (Denial of Service) attacks.
- Shields the identities of your internal LAN systems from outside view. That is, plays the role of a proxy server and offers NAT or Network Address Translation.

The two most important things you can do in terms of securing your LAN while providing wireless access are to make sure that your LAN is protected by a firewall and that your firewall is placed between your LAN and the publicly available access point, and that you use a mechanism such as a firewall (the same one or an additional one) to authenticate and manage users. A firewall can be as complicated as a specialized router/VPN setup, or as simple as a dual-homed computer serving as a router. It has been our experience that software firewalls are *not* enough protection. It's too easy to turn your firewall off (such as when you are installing some remote software package) and forget to turn it back on. A combination of hardware and software provides a stronger, more effective barrier to entry.

Summary

In this chapter we continued our discussion from the previous chapter on extending wireless networks to consider extending them to include other people outside your home or small network. You network neighborhood can be open and public or closed to only those neighbors you desire and private. There are different kinds of wireless networks that you can create. We considered simple peer-to-peer, ad hoc wireless networks, as well as networks based on extending your LAN. Many WLAN projects offered by organizations, including town and city governments, chambers of commerce, and others use a captive portal approach for wireless access. When you connect to a captive portal, what you can access is carefully controlled. Larger community WLANs can be more conveniently built using a mesh technology with distributed wireless repeaters extending the signal.

There are many reasons why you might want to undertake a project of this kind, and many different types of users that you can serve. We covered some of those uses and groups in this chapter. Whenever you create a network neighborhood, try to give your clients some value added by offering special content, tools, and uses that people wouldn't use their computers for at home.

A wireless network neighborhood is best when it is a managed solution. The chapter described ways of isolating network access by placing access points outside of network firewalls and by authenticating your users. Security is not to be overlooked and should be designed into your solution.

In the next chapter you'll learn about the different types of antennas that are used in wireless networks, and how to select among them for your particular needs.

Chapter 12

Selecting the Right Antenna

As you learned in Chapter 9, the strength of your wireless signal is a critical feature of your network. It's what separates the more expensive equipment from the less expensive equipment, requires the use of more powerful equipment and advanced protocols, contributes to your network's effective range, and determines what lengths you have to go to in order to get the network coverage you require. In this chapter we will look more closely at some of the equipment that you can use to improve the coverage of your network and maximize the potential of the devices that you have deployed — particularly antennas.

Not surprisingly the last thing people consider when purchasing a NIC card or access point is the antenna(s) that come with them. It's natural to assume that the vendor has supplied you with the best antenna, one that optimizes your device's performance. This is almost never true. The fact is that most devices sold into the home and small business market are sold as commodities and the vendors are always trying to shave off a dollar here and a dollar there. Antennas are one place people don't tend to notice the compromise.

You can greatly improve your range by correctly positioning the antenna, and by replacing the antenna that came with your device with one that provides the characteristics you need. Antennas come in different shapes and sizes and are generally either ***omnidirectional*** (radiating in all directions) or ***directional***. With a directional antenna, you can have your network signal jump from building to building on a campus hundreds of yards away, forming a link in an MLAN (a so-called *Metropolitan LAN*). For a ranch owner, a directional antenna can be used to control sprinklers and irrigation equipment a thousand yards or more away.

There are other means of improving your range, including adding repeaters and other devices. Repeaters extend your range by amplifying the signal. Other means for extending your wireless network provide strong point-to-point connections with amplification at both ends.

Antenna Principles

Antennas receive transmissions and focus their energy to improve the signal. An antenna to which power is applied also emits an energy transmission and has a profile characteristic of the particular design used in its construction. The efficiency of an antenna is called its ***gain***, with a rating in

decibels (dB) The gain is defined as the ratio of the output signal strength of an amplifier to the input strength of the signal, and it is more usually given in terms of the number of decibels that a hypothetical isotropic radiator (equal in all directions) would have, in units of dBi. An isotropic radiator is one that radiates signal equally in all directions. Most antennas are made from metallic material, from items as simple as a coffee can to antennas made of exotic rare earth metal alloys.

Antennas offer what is called ***reciprocal gain***—that is, amplification is for both transmission and reception. For two points in a connection, adding an antenna at either end will improve the signal for both devices.

For an antenna that radiates a signal isotropically (with the signal strength the same in all directions), the gain would be 1 or 0dB. Any antenna that has a gain of 2 or 3dB would double the signal strength. Each additional gain of 3dB doubles the signal strength again. To improve the quality of a transmitter, you would use a higher gain antenna. Be aware, though, that because you are using radio bands there is a legal limit to the strength of the signal you can create. For the United States the limit is 1000mW, in Japan it is 10mW/MHz, and for Europe it is 100mW (EIRP). EIRP stands for ***Equivalent Isotropic Radiate Power***. The gain of an antenna is often different depending upon whether it is sending or receiving, so just be sure that whatever the minimum gain is, you can create and maintain a stable communications link over your desired equipment.

You can measure the gain in a particular antenna by measuring the signal strength of a connection between two known antenna types. Carefully position each antenna on both ends so that the maximum signal strength is achieved. After waiting a while to test that the signal level is stable and doesn't fluctuate, replace one of the antennas with the one you wish to test. There are a number of ways to test signal strength, some of which were discussed in Chapter 9. Whatever method you use, your measurement of the difference in signal strength will give you your antenna's gain. For example, if you measure an original signal strength of 48dBi, and then replace a directional antenna with a Yagi antenna, your measurement jumps to 58dBi. You know you removed a 6dBi antenna, so the measured strength of your new antenna is 16dBi (58–42).

It's particularly important when selecting an antenna to have some idea of how the antenna behaves in a directional sense. A measure of an antenna's directional properties is the so-called ***Front to Back (F/B) ratio***. As you might expect the F/B ratio takes the measure of the strength of the beam at its center point and compares it to the amount of energy that is radiated along that line in the opposite direction. Omnidirectional antennas have F/B ratios approaching 1.0, and for highly directional Yagi antennas the ratio can be on the order of 5 or 6 to 1.

Some manufacturers publish their antenna's ***radiation pattern***—that is, the directions that a signal can cover and the amount of drop-off in signal strength. That's particularly valuable when selecting an antenna because it can help you optimize your placement of an antenna. When considering a radiation pattern be aware that you really need to see two profiles. The vertical slice of the radiation pattern, also called the ***elevation cut***, is generally very different from the horizontal slice of the radiation pattern, called the ***azimuth***. To really understand an antenna, you need to see this three-dimensional dispersion, but most of the time people tend to simply measure the transmissions in their WLANs when they do the site survey by considering just two-dimensional slices, one for each floor of a building. When you increase the power of a signal coming from an antenna, you narrow either the elevation plane or the azimuth plane coverage, or both. Furthermore, a radiated signal can be circular, or it can be primarily horizontal or vertical.

An antenna doesn't work alone. When considering an antenna, you must also consider the nature of the connection, that is, the interaction of both a sending and receiving antenna. The way the orientation of an antenna is measured is as a function of its ***polarization***. Antennas combine a magnetic field and an electric field that are perpendicular to each other. Some antennas are horizontally polarized, which means that the antenna is supposed to be positioned with its electric field placed parallel with the ground. A vertically polarized antenna, by contrast, should have its electric field positioned perpendicular to the ground. The important thing to remember is that both antennas in a connection need to be polarized in the same direction.

You'll also see the ***beamwidth*** of an antenna described. This term is expressed as an angle, and it measures the drop-off of a transmission in each of the two main axes. The angle measures the points in the transmission beam where the signal has dropped in half from the maximum signal found on the centerline. The narrower the beamwidth, the more powerful and longer range the antenna is. However, very narrow beamwidth antennas are also more difficult to adjust to create the best point-to-point link.

Antennas are also constructed so that they are tuned for a specific frequency, or they are tunable. An antenna designed for an 802.11b signal running at 900 MHz won't work well for a higher frequency 802.11b/g signal running at 2.4 GHz, although the reverse is commonly true. You'll see many antennas for the 802.11b/g market. When an antenna is matched to a specific radio device, it is described as having a low ***standing wave ratio*** or SWR. The SWR is a measure of the amount of energy that is emitted from the antenna versus the amount of energy that is reflected from the radio back to the antenna. You can measure the energy using a SWR meter or with a reflectometer. When there is a significant mismatch and a high SWR, you get poor reception. You can increase the power level to improve performance, but there is a point where you risk damaging your equipment. A better means is to tune the antenna by adjusting its length, the kind and size of its elements, or the reflection path length within the antenna. If this is possible, consult your antenna's manual or the manufacturer's Web site to see what they recommend.

Note

One very good general source of information on wireless antennas may be found at Paul Wade's site at `www.w1ghz.cx/antbook/preface.htm`. The site offers a compilation of his articles on the topic in PDF format.

When a radio signal propagates through space it bounces off of interfaces to create a secondary path to the receptor, a phenomenon known as ***multipathing***. A receptor locks on to the strongest signal, but at certain places in the path signals interfere with one another and create dead spots. You can see the effect of multipathing when you move a radio receiving a weak station around your house. At

some point when you encounter a dead spot, it only takes a few feet of movement to get the signal back. You observe the same effect listening to a radio in your car; rolling forward a car length is enough to get the signal to return. Multipathing also has the effect of interfering with a signal so that you can encounter a strong signal which is not decipherable. In that case too, moving the antenna's location or changing the antenna type can eliminate problem and clear up the reception.

Small movements of wireless transmitters and receivers can offer such an improvement in eliminating dead spots that if you have a dead spot in another room, try simply moving your devices and their antennas around a little. For example, if one bedroom is a dead spot and you have a repeater in another bedroom down a hall, move that repeater to a position where the signal can have direct line-of-sight down the hall to the other room.

When you deploy an antenna outdoors, the loss in the signal over distances is described by a standard function called the ***free space path loss equation***. It's predictable and varies as a square of the distance; see for example `www.softwright.com/faq/engineering/Free%20Space%20Field%20and%20Loss%20Calculations.html`. Indoors signal loss is much more complex and dependant upon the material that you're transmitting the signal through. Chapter 9 has a rough list of loss in dB for several materials, but here's one experiment that you can try that graphically illustrates loss of transmission. If you have an aquarium in your home, move your access point in back of it and measure the signal that is successfully transmitted through the tank. Water is an amazingly good signal absorber, so just the one obstruction is enough to dramatically reduce your signal.

Types of Antennas

For most indoor applications, you will choose one of three different types of antennas:

- An omnidirectional antenna
- A directional antenna
- A highly directional antenna

An ***omnidirectional antenna*** radiates transmissions out and receives transmissions in from all directions, although not equally in all directions. Most of the antennas in this category are thin rods or long flat sticks. The Hawking H-AI6SI shown in Figure 12-1 is a good example of an indoor omnidirectional antenna that offers from 2 to 6dBi of gain (4x). Meant for a 2.4 GHz b/g network, this vertically polarized antenna costs about $32. Hawking has a line of wireless antennas that can be added onto your devices, and this particular one comes with both an RP-SMA and an RPTPC connector.

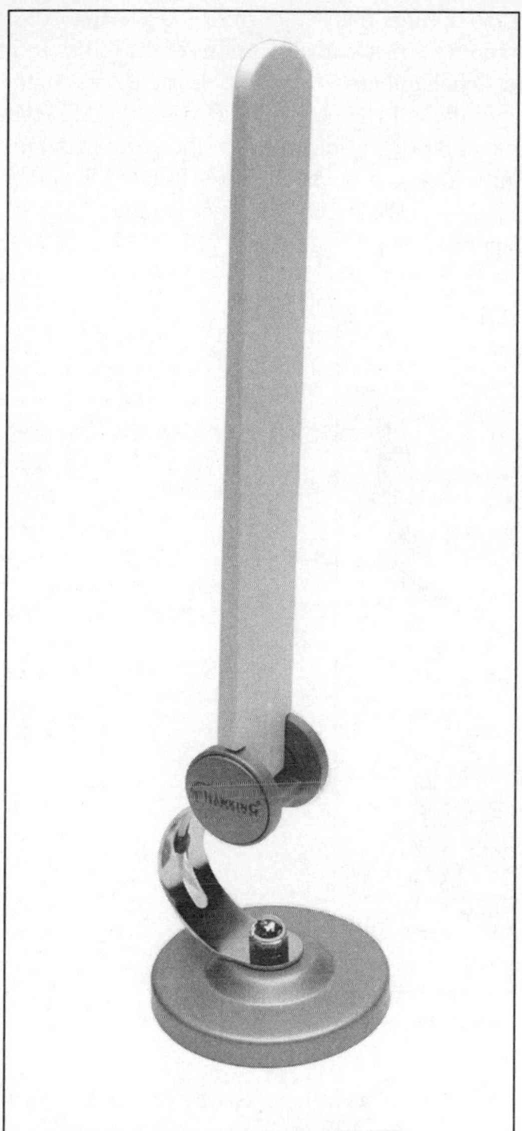

Figure 12-1: The Hawking H-AI6SI 6dBi omnidirectional indoor antenna.

A *directional antenna* is one that has a wide dispersion of more than 80 degrees and less than 120 degrees. They are often used for corner placement in a room to radiate to all portions of the room, and point in the direction of the main network path. Directional antennas use parabolic reflectors, right angle deflectors, and panel deflectors. Figure 12-2 shows the 2.4 GHz Hawking HAI6SDP/HAI6SDA directional desktop antenna, which has a 6dB gain and an 80-degree beamwidth (the angle between 50 percent drop-off of signal). This type of antenna uses a curved or parabolic surface to focus the beam and improve gain without focusing the beam too narrowly. A classic corner antenna is illustrated by the Hawking HAI15SC antenna, shown in Figure 12-3.

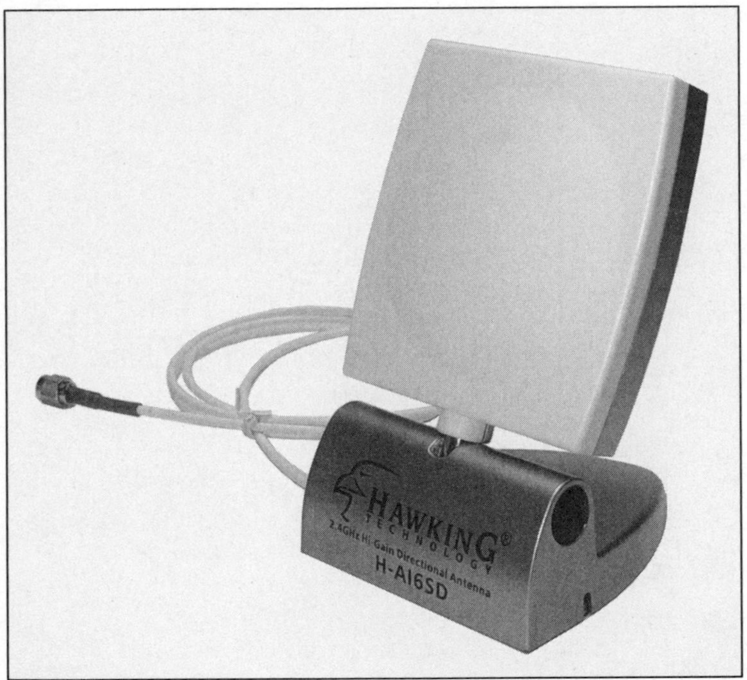

Figure 12-2: A directional desktop wireless antenna with a parabolic reflector.

A highly directional antenna has a dispersion of 80 degrees to as little as 28 degrees, and is used for point-to-point transmission. Highly directional antennas use a line of perpendicular elements, a can or cylindrical enclosure, or both. The classic example of a highly directional antenna is a Yagi antenna. Some Yagi antennas are built so that their signal propagates in a tube, while others are built with a set of perpendicular elements. Figure 12-4 shows a picture of the 800 MHz Maxrad BMOY Yagi externally mounted, an antenna that can provide up to 15dBi gain. What's particularly nice about Yagi antennas is that they can be adjusted to be vertical, horizontal, or a user-adjustable linear combination of the two.

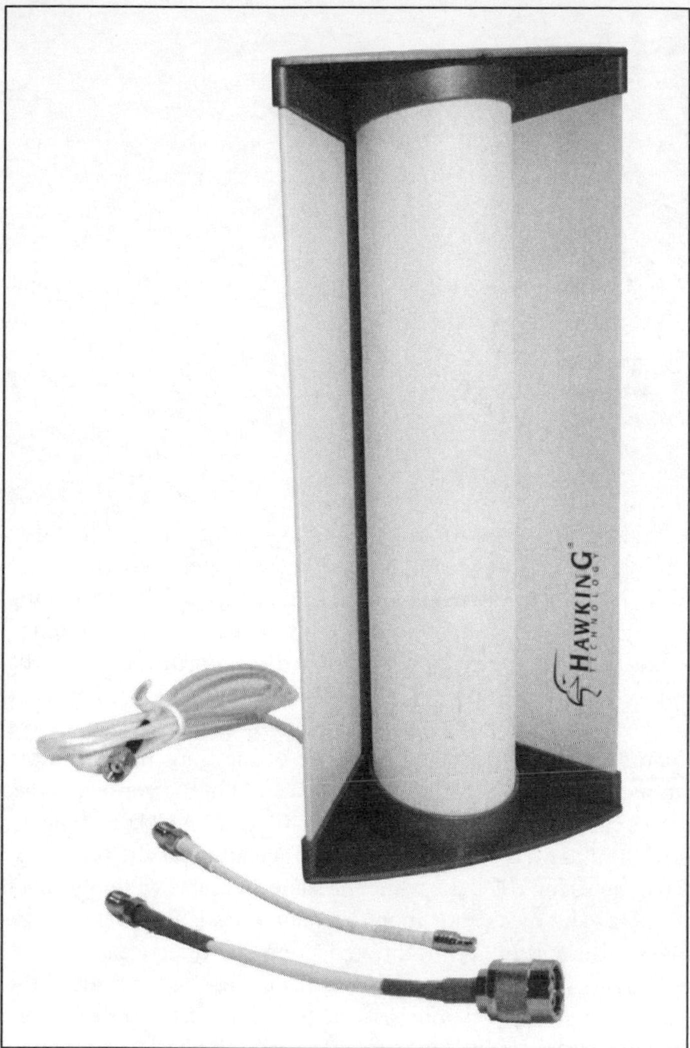

Figure 12-3: A corner wireless antenna with a parabolic reflector.

Figure 12-4: The Maxrad 800 MHz BMOY enclosed Yagi antenna.

You can also construct very highly focused antennas with a 10-mile range using a parabolic satellite dish like the Primestar dish antenna and a microwave emitter, as described later in this chapter.

As a general rule you should deploy an omnidirectional antenna in the center of the area being covered, with the antenna pointing up. For an antenna mounted at the top of a room, the antenna should be pointed down. Directional antennas are meant to be positioned toward the center of the area to be covered from a side position, or for point-to-point communications.

The dispersive angle and gain of an antenna is not only dependent upon the design of the antenna, but is also changed when you alter the frequency and power of the transmission. More power and higher frequencies result in narrower angles and more amplification in the vertical plane. For example, a directional antenna that is capable of dispersion of 28 degrees at 2.4 GHz will have a broader dispersion of around 70 degrees at 900 MHz You can purchase Yagi antennas that have dispersion angles anywhere from 25 to 80 degrees for 2.4 GHz, while the same antennas will only cover from around 70 to 80 degrees at 900 MHz. The nice thing about Yagi antennas is that they can be aimed in any direction, and their entire power output is concentrated along that direction.

Some access points enable you to adjust their power output, thus adjusting both the radius of the coverage size as well as the dispersion of any directional antenna attached to it. Examples of access points that have this feature are the D-Link DI-614+, the Linksys WRT55AG, the Buffalo Airstation WBR-G54, and many of the Cisco access points. You can see how changing the size of a cell would be useful in limiting your WLAN to just those locations you want your WLAN to serve. It's less well appreciated how different power levels can be used to narrow or widen the directional focus of your wireless communication.

Figure 12-5 shows the three different types of antennas in use in home and small office wireless networks.

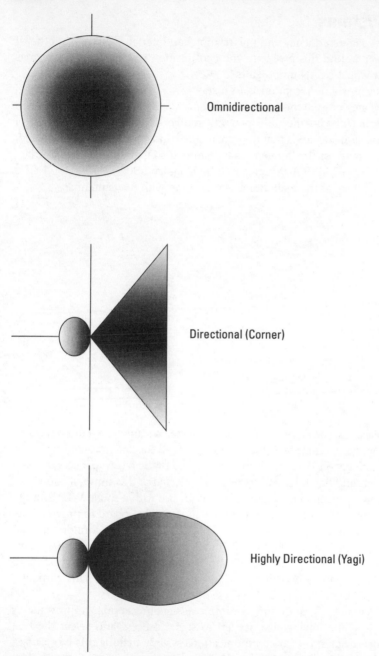

Omnidirectional

Directional (Corner)

Highly Directional (Yagi)

Figure 12-5: The angular dispersions of the three different types of antennas in common use in wireless LANs are shown.

Diversity Antenna Systems

Two antennas broadcasting at the same frequency and polarization can interfere with one another if they are in the same place. To get around this problem, you can position *sector* or *panel* antennas that enable you to partition your wireless LAN into sectors.

Another technique for improving signal reception is to install a set of diversity antennas, with each antenna in the same general area or even mounted on the same access point. This is the reason why some access points have two antennas — they are operating in diversity mode. The advantage of mounting the two antennas on the same device is that they are aligned and equivalently constructed, and with the same radiation pattern across the frequencies transmitted so that their signals overlap. Figure 12-6 shows the D-Link DWL-7000AP AirXpert Tri-Mode Dualband 802.11a/b/g 2.4/5 GHz wireless access point that one of us uses as the main home access point with dual antennas.

Figure 12-6: The 2-antenna access point like the D-Link DWL-7000AP is an example of a set of antennas used in diversity mode.

A diversity antenna system places two or more antennas in the same area and uses a radio receiver to monitor the signals. When a message is detected, the antenna polls all the antennas and takes the best and strongest signal for its connection. That same antenna is used to the return packets unless a problem is encountered, and then another antenna in the set is selected and communication proceeds using that connection. A diversity antenna system is meant for use with a single WLAN only.

You'll often find diversity antennas mounted on the ceiling or above ceiling board to provide line-of-sight coverage. Maxrad's 2.4 GHz bi-antenna system, the ISM UFO (Ultra Flat Onmidirectional) diversity antenna, is shown ceiling-mounted in Figure 12-7. Like many diversity antenna systems each mount contains one or more antennas in close proximity. Maxrad claims a power rating of 20 watts, with an isolation of 25dB between the two antennas, and a gain of 3dBi (2X). This particular antenna is often mated to the MACMAP Cisco AP 1200 access point.

A diversity antenna system has fault tolerance and can improve signal reception, improvements that do not come without a price. The intelligence needed to signal process and select the best antenna signal puts additional overhead into your communications system, making this type of system more expensive to implement (beyond the need for additional antennas). The overhead often also results in significant power dissipation, which can lower coverage area.

Figure 12-7: The Maxrad 2.4 GHz ISM UFO diversity antenna.

People install diversity antenna systems because unlike single antenna systems, when the link degrades you don't have to just accept the lowering of your transmission rate. With a diverse system you can change the link frequency rate to adjust for worsening channel conditions, thus improving directionality and improving your data transfer. Therefore, unlike single antenna systems that simply receive signals, a receiver participating in a dynamic diversity system requires link quality assessment circuitry. Link assessment also allows for the implementation of full diversity systems, which are the equivalent of "antenna multipathing," allowing multiple connections and data streams.

Criteria for Selecting an Antenna

Nearly any wireless device can be improved by adding a better antenna. So if you want to improve your signal transmission or reception, it is worth considering an antenna upgrade. Now that you know what different antennas exist, let's consider when you would want to select one type of antenna over another. Table 12-1 has some recommendations.

Table 12-1: Selecting the Right Antenna

If you want to do this	*Select this*
Cover a room	Select an omnidirectional antenna and put it in the center of the room.
Get an unobstructed line-of-sight in a room	Mount the antenna high off the ground or on the ceiling. If you use an omnidirectional antenna in this situation, be careful that you don't place the antenna in a position so that it's along a direction where the antenna has a low signal strength to the receiving antennas you hope to connect to.

Continued

Table 12-1: Selecting the Right Antenna *(continued)*

If you want to do this	*Select this*
Get a stronger signal throughout a room	Select a device with a diversity antenna system. Cover a room but not overlap out of the room. Select a corner or directional antenna and place it on a wall or corner.
Improve the reception in a room down the hall	Select a directional antenna such as a hemispherical reflector, a Yagi, a waveguide, or a can antenna.
Connect to a building across campus	Use a parabolic disk with an emitter.

Maximizing Reception

As you know from the discussion in Chapter 9, placement of your devices is of critical importance when it comes to maximizing your signal. If you followed our advice, you created a site survey to aid you in placing your devices to give you the best coverage. When you add a new antenna, or even when you are positioning the one that came with your device, it's a good idea to try different orientations for the antenna. You know that when you position an FM radio's antenna the signal quality can change. It is similarly true for wireless LANs.

You can get a sense for how well your wireless network is set up in a general way by using a Wi-Fi detector and noting the signal strength as you move around. The three or four lights on these devices will give you a feel for the signal strength, but not a quantitative result. Be careful when using these devices; although they claim to reject outside interference, often they don't. A better and more quantitative approach is to use your laptop and wireless NIC with a program such as NetStumbler to test signal strength, especially if that is the device you are going to use on your WLAN.

It's important to realize that you are measuring the effect of several variables when you test signal strength. One variable is the time of day and weather. There is some change in the signal strength at different times; for example, signal strength at night is typically stronger than the day. So it's a good idea to test at different times to find out what the best antenna angle and placement is. If you can enlist a compadre to either read the signal strength or position the antenna while you read the signal strength, this whole process will go a lot faster.

Omnidirectional antennas really have only two positions: vertical or horizontal. In the great majority of cases these antennas are best both positioned horizontally. The way an omnidirectional antenna is designed there is no benefit to moving the antenna around the perpendicular axis. To maximize reception for an omnidirectional antenna you need to pick the best position, usually higher up in a room and away from competing radio wave sources.

If you are using directional antennas, then chances are that line-of-sight is your best direction and there's little you can change about that. If you are trying to get a directional signal to work outside of its line-of-sight you have two choices: you can add a repeater or some other device between the two endpoints, or you can create a reflective surface from which the signal can be bounced.

Building Your Own Antenna

The truth is that do-it-yourself antennas are really enthusiast projects. Chances are that you can buy a suitable antenna for not much money, although many people like to build their own wireless antennas. It's not particularly difficult and can be a satisfying project. The designs of many wireless antennas may be found on the Internet. People get very inventive with this sort of thing. We've seen simple-to-build omnidirectional antennas built from wireless connectors and metal pins, from cut feed cables, to slotted waveguide antennas (see `www.trevormarshall.com/waveguides.htm`) of both an omnidirectional and unidirectional variety.

The coffee or Pringles potato chip can antennas are famous, and a good example of one may be seen on Andrew Clapp's site at `www.aeonic.com/~clapp/wireless` along with a long discussion of its design and theory. It is possible to build a can antenna with from 12 to 15dBi of gain that rivals the performance of commercial models, although not the fit and finish. You'll find many designs, from panel reflectors to omnidirectional models. Another popular project is modifying or creating dish antennas to enhance their performance.

Keep in mind that many wireless vendors' warranties do not cover the use of a substitute antenna in place of the one that they supply with their router, access point, or NIC. However, unless you are amplifying an antenna to power it, you likely won't run into problems. If you are creating a wired antenna, then you not only need to be careful about the grounding, but also not to exceed your local wireless power limits.

That being said, it is very easy to modify an existing antenna to dramatically change its properties. The simple addition of a parabolic or corner reflector to any standard omnidirectional antenna can turn that antenna into a highly directional one. The two antennae in Figure 12-8 are examples of ones you can modify. Reflectors work with any frequency and with any access point or wireless device.

On Michael Erkine's Web site `www.freeantennas.com`, you'll find a number of different models. The parabolic antenna for a 2.4 GHz may be seen at `www.freeantennas.com/projects/template2/index.html`. Similarly, Michael Erkine also offers a template for a corner reflector at `www.freeantennas.com/projects/Ez-10/`. Figure 12-8 shows the FreeAntennas Web page instructions for a corner reflector. It's rather amazing how simple these two designs are, but it is claimed that you can create links of up to a kilometer with two parabolic antenna equipped devices, and have a 10dBi gain out of the corner reflectors. You are not limited to the sizes of these templates, only their shapes, and you can shrink or enlarge these templates to suit your antennas. Changing the size of the reflector will alter their gain and F/B ratios, however.

What's really nice about the parabolic or corner add-ons is that they are dead easy to build, don't require changing any circuitry or settings in your access point, and don't void your warranty. In many instances you will find that the simple addition of reflectors creates devices that are almost as good as the commercial models you can buy.

One of the easiest antennas to build is the can type antenna, and there are many sites on the Internet describing them. A place to start is "802.11b Homebrew Antenna Shootout," found at `www.turnpoint.net/wireless/has.html#intro`. You can supplement this information with a book devoted to the subject, like ***Wi-Fi Toys*** by Mike Outmesguine (Wiley, 2004).

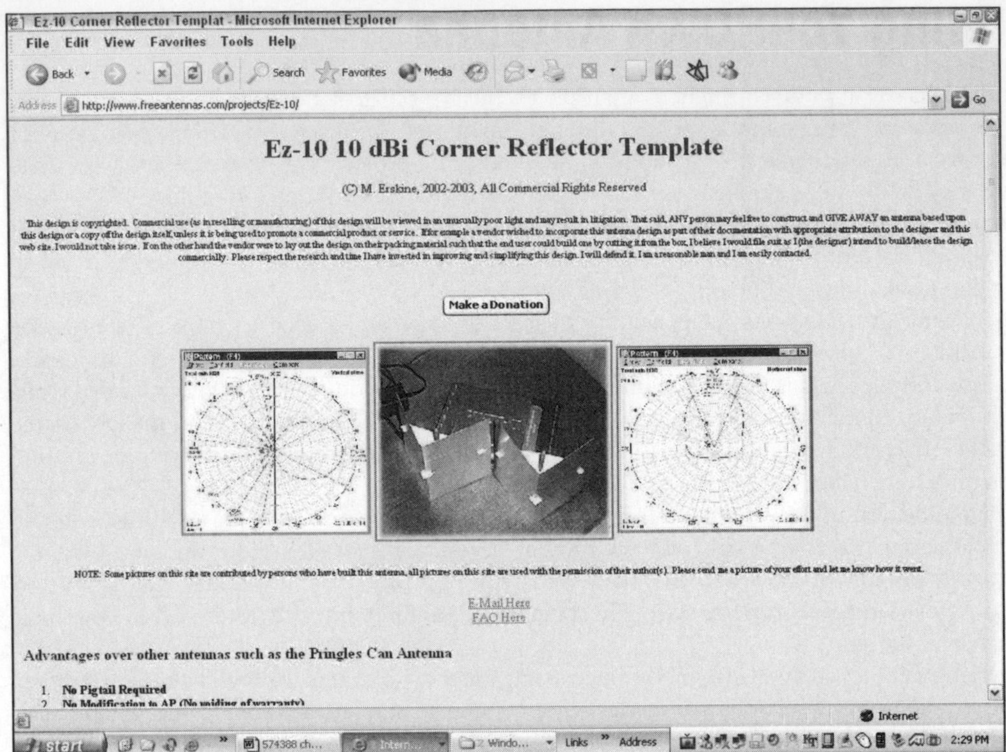

Figure 12-8: Shown here is the Corner reflector template at FreeAntennas.com. This site is a great place to look for designs for antennas that you can build yourself, or for additions to the antennas you already have.

The original "Pringles" can design was finicky and required precise construction. Newer versions of this type of antenna, also called ***microwave waveguide antennas***, use completely metallic cans and don't contain an internal set of elements like the Maxrad Yagi antenna shown earlier. When properly mounted, it is possible to obtain a gain of 16 to 18dB for an 802.11b signal. You can use this kind of antenna with not only b networks, but 802.11b+ and g networks. You'll find many examples of these home brews on eBay, but one we like is from Alan Rothberg; you can read his shtick at `http://home.carolina.rr.com/harothberg/CantennaFAQ.htm`. His cAntenna is shown in Figure 12-9.

For instructions on how to build your own can antenna, you can go to "How To Build A Tin Can Waveguide Antenna" at `www.turnpoint.net/wireless/cantennahowto.html` for an example.

Figure 12-9: The home-brewed cAntenna, a can-based directional antenna. Figure courtesy of www.EtherDesigns.com.

Strangely, many people turn dish antennas into very effective high-performance directional antennas. All that's required is a parabolic dish such as a Primestar antenna and a microwave cable or USB converter such as the D-Link DWL-122. Examples of this design are supposed to have a tested range of up to 10 miles when operated in the 2.4 GHz range and in clear line-of-sight. If you are interested in this kind of antenna, you can find instructions for its construction detailed in the articles:

- "Use a Surplus Primestar Dish as an IEEE 802.11 Wireless Networking Antenna" at `www.wwc.edu/~frohro/Airport/Primestar/Primestar.html`
- "Low Cost 802.11a Directional Antenna Using Obsolete Primestar Dish" at `www5.cs.cornell.edu/%7Eeckstrom/802.11a/primestar`

There really isn't a whole lot more to creating a Primestar waveguide 802.11 antenna than adding the can assembly to the dish. You can get a gain of about 22dB out of this arrangement, but in a very narrow beamwidth. So when they say line-of-sight, they are not kidding. There are reports that this type of design is dramatically reduced in performance by any obstruction, even leaves on a tree.

The directionality of this antenna means that you need to create a mount that will very accurately position the antenna, and will maintain that position. Changing the size of the can and the excitation antenna tunes it for different frequencies. Some designs are for 802.11b/g antennas, where the corresponding 5.0 GHz 802.11a version is sized 48 percent smaller (2.4/5.0 = 0.48).

Summary

In this chapter you learned how critical the selection and placement of a wireless antenna can be to your wireless network. To get the most out of the equipment you buy, pay careful attention to this factor and you can dramatically improve your system's performance and save money by having to buy less redundant equipment. All antennas break down into three categories: omnidirectional, directional, and highly directional. Chances are that the access point or router you bought can be improved through the addition of a better antenna. Also, whenever possible try to buy a wireless NIC card that enables you to substitute a better antenna.

You also saw how easy it is to make your own antenna, and how you can add reflectors and concentrators to the antennas you already possess to improve their signal strength where you need it.

In the next chapter we'll round out our discussion of extending your wireless network's range by considering how you can use local wireless protocols to connect up peripherals such as printers, video cameras, and other devices. Wireless protocols such as Bluetooth were specifically designed for this purpose.

Chapter 13

Wireless Peripherals

You probably don't tend to think about wireless networking when it comes to your keyboard, mouse, or printer, but you should. You can make your life easier by cutting the cords attached to your computer so that you can put everything where you really need to have it. In this chapter you are going to learn about three different but complementary wireless technologies that let you connect your computer to local peripheral devices: infrared or IrDA, Bluetooth, and wireless USB.

Chances are that you've been using infrared remotes for some time now. That's one form of IR technology. Several years ago vendors started adding an IrDA port to laptops (which is a slightly different protocol) so that you could use control devices to transfer information to and from a computer wirelessly. Infrared technology is line-of sight and restricted to a small distance, typically less than 25 feet. You can use IrDA with your computer to do a lot more that most people do with the IR technology at the moment. With IrDA you can control TVs, print to printers, and so forth.

The second technology is Bluetooth, and it's a little different than IrDA. Imagine having a 30-foot bubble around you and being able to wirelessly connect together any devices within that bubble. Bluetooth does that, and more. Because of the intelligence built into the Bluetooth technology, your PDA or laptop can tell a printer from a cell phone and can make the connections easily. Bluetooth also knows what the capabilities of the connected devices are, so that you can tell your printer to print and your cell desk phone to call out (and not the other way around). Bluetooth has been around for a few years, but it's only now catching people's attention because Bluetooth devices are becoming ubiquitous. Bluetooth is probably already in the newer equipment you've purchased recently. You can easily add the technology to most peripherals by purchasing a Bluetooth USB adapter and a Bluetooth hub.

The last of the three technologies is wireless USB. With wireless USB, you can connect any USB device to a hub connected to an access point and have that peripheral work across your desk or across your home. Some of the wireless USB devices have the wireless transceiver built into them and don't even require a hub at all. They are place and play in just the same way that your wireless laptop is.

The point of all of these technologies is that they can help you create your own personal LAN and make it easier for you to use and share your peripheral devices throughout a home or an office with much less fuss and bother. So get ready to cut those cords, and read on.

Desktop Wireless Connections

Each of the three technologies to be discussed in this chapter has a special niche that it can fill. In some cases their niches overlap, but for the most part they don't. Table 13-1 has some examples of when you might want to use each of them:

Table 13-1

To connect	*Use this*
Your computer to a cable box	An IrDA connection
An enabled device in a room	Turn on your Bluetooth devices
A printer in another room	Use wireless USB
To beam from one Palm PDA to another	Use the Palm's infrared port
To print from your laptop to an enabled printer	Use your laptop's Bluetooth networking

Figure 13-1 shows you the three different situations in which you might want to use each of these technologies. Let's briefly consider where you might have overlap between these different technologies. For line-of-sight applications where you are pointing one device at another, either IrDA or Bluetooth might work. If the two devices are in the same room but not directly in line-of-sight, then wireless USB or Bluetooth might work, assuming that the device you want to connect with has either of those capabilities. However, for long distances, wireless USB is your only choice.

You would deploy wireless USB when you have a USB device you want to deploy in a near or remote location. Because wireless USB is an 802.11 technology, all of the same advantages and disadvantages of 802.11 apply. Bluetooth gives you a local room-sized range, while IrDA is room sized but highly directional. All of these technologies can penetrate walls, but each suffers signal loss when it does so.

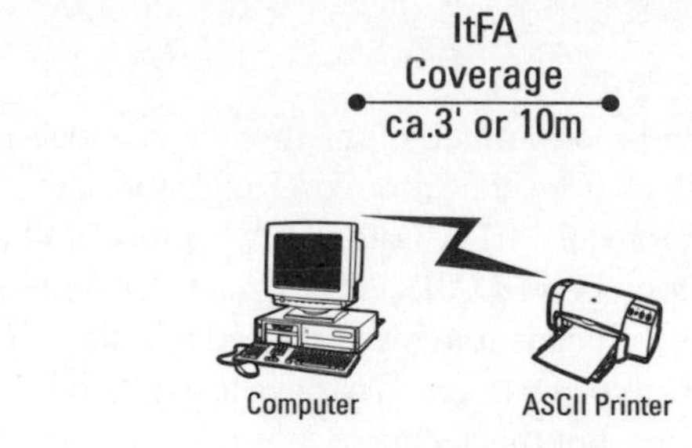

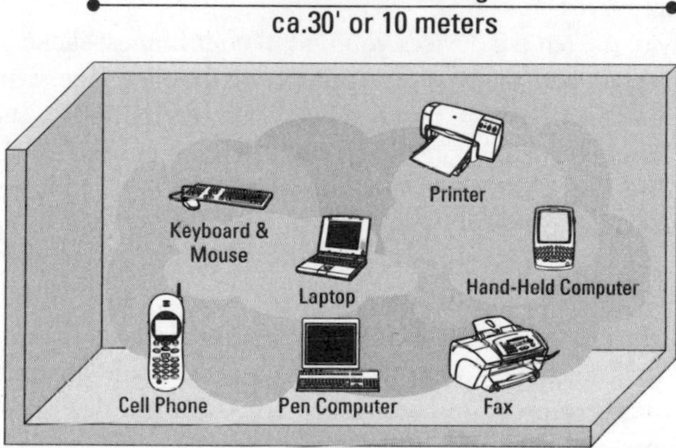

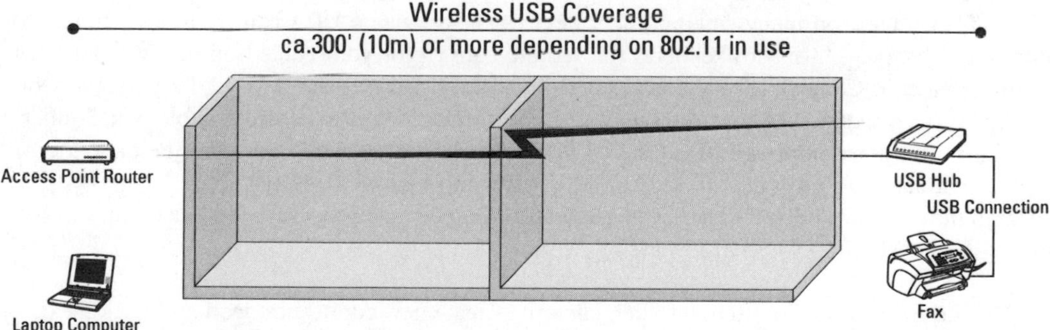

Figure 13-1: The three different wireless peripheral networking scenarios.

IrDA

We'll start out with both the simplest and most limited of the three technologies at hand. IrDA is a set of infrared communications specifications from the Infrared Data Association (www.irda.org) that includes the following three different protocols: IrDA-Data, IrDA-Control, and a new standard called Air. The protocol that is useful for computers is IrDA-Data because it transmits and receives signals at a data rate of from 9,600 bps to 4 Mbps, which is roughly the speed of a slow modem up to the speed of a slow 802.11b wireless link. There are plans to one day have a standard for IrDA-Air, which may eventually reach speeds of up to 16 Mbps, but this technology is never going to be really fast.

IrDA is best used for transmissions that send only limited data over the link. That is, you can send control signals to a cable box with it or print text to a printer; but IrDA probably isn't your best choice for printing large picture files.

You'll find IrDA in many of the remote devices you find in your homes: clickers for your TV or hi-fi, cameras, phones, and pagers, and many more applications besides. The vast majority of these devices are IrDA-Control devices, which are much slower than the IrDA-Data standard, so most of these devices connect to a computer serial port (when you use them on a computer at all). The IrDA technology that you find on laptops (those little windows on the front) and on PDAs such as the Palm typically uses the IrDA-Data protocol, which is the faster of the two. In either case, both of these technologies are point-to-point and short range. When "Palmists" say they are beaming, they aren't kidding. Your IrDA-Control transmission starts to become unworkable when the angle between the two devices is greater than 15 degrees or so, depending upon the distance.

When you want to use IrDA to control other devices, you need to add an emitter to your system and configure the device to accept program commands. IrDA-Control devices are made that plug into serial ports, parallel ports, and even USB ports.

Take a look at ACTiSYS's Web site (www.actisys.com/IrDAProd.html#WiFi), as they offer examples of each of these IrDA-Control devices.

IrDA is also used on many entertainment devices. TiVo uses an IrDA control to switch a TV or cable box's channels; in most likelihood the remote control for your cable box or TV is an IrDA-Control device. In Chapter 14, there is a description of the SnapStream Beyond TV personal video recorder, and a discussion of how to set up a serial port IrDA emitter to control a cable box. Similarly you might use the pass through IrDA parallel port adapter from ACTiSYS and their Palm, Windows CE and Symbian PDA print control software to control and manage a printer.

Here's how you would set up an IrDA connection between a laptop and another computer running Windows XP SP2:

1. In the Network Connection folder, click the Create new connection icon and click Next, which launches the New Connection Wizard.
2. Select Set up an advanced connection in the Network Connection Type step, and then click Next.
3. Select Connect directly to another computer, and then click Next.
4. Specify whether this computer is the Host or the Guest (will send or receive information), and then click Next.

5. Select Infrared Port from the Device for this connection, and then click Next, as shown in Figure 13-2. Note that you will see only the infrared port appear in the list if your computer detects that you have one and the proper driver is installed. If you have a port but it doesn't work, check the device's support in your computer's Device Manager.

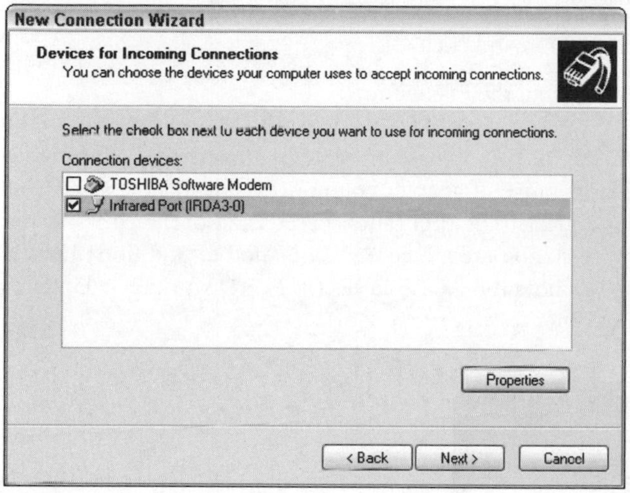

Figure 13-2: Selecting an infrared port to connect to.

6. In the User Permissions step, click the users' group checkbox that you wish to use this connection, and then click Next; and finally click Finish.

Infrared connections in Windows XP are one-way. When you've successfully created the connection you will see an icon that looks like the one in Figure 13-3. Some systems require that you reboot to activate the port.

Figure 13-3: An Infrared connection icon.

You don't see IrDA devices used much in computer networking because of the distance and placement requirements, but it can be used with enabled devices—some cell phones, for example. Typically the IR ports in computers have about a 3 foot or 1 meter optimum range.

To use an IR connection on your PC, you would do the following:

1. Create the connection, as explained previously.
2. Open the Network Connections folder from the Control Panel.
3. Double-click the IR connection that you want to use to network.
4. Check the connection information and click OK.
5. Select the Connect command from the File menu.

The only real advantage IrDA has is that it has an aggregate bandwidth four times that of Bluetooth. In addition to a fairly large range of adapter components, ACTiSYS has a Point of Sales (POS) business it supports. POS is a great IrDA application because all of the components that are used in a cash register or card swipe station are all close to one another and don't have large data transfer demands. Figure 13-4 shows how the ACTiSYS IR 100M IrDA printer adapter is used to connect a laptop or computer to a printer.

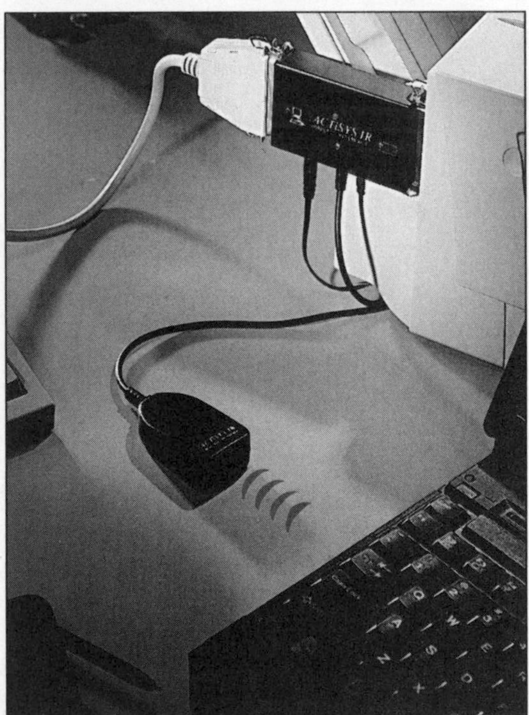

Figure 13-4: IrDA is well-suited for a point-of-sale application, connecting printers, card swipes, and modems to computers over a short distance.
© Copyright ACTiSYS Corp.

You can get some idea of the performance of IrDA-Control device by pointing your household remote control at the device it controls and seeing what kind of angle and distance it achieves. In most instances, an IrDA device has about a 30-degree and a 3 to 30 foot or 1 to 10 meter range of operation. You can deploy repeaters to extend an IrDA signal further. You would employ IrDA when a strongly directional control signal or data transfer is required.

The narrow beam and short distance of communication, say beaming Palm to Palm, offers some protection against anyone else being able to listen in on the communication. Occasionally you will find IrDA used in dial-up connections or voice links when the particular application is right for it. For example, you might find an IrDA system in a mobile phone base station.

IrDA has only minimal security mechanisms built into it, so security must be provided by the operating system or applications of the two devices involved in the link. Depending upon your thinking and the specific application this is either a benefit or a fault. IrDA doesn't have to do a lot of device discovery because it works only when its target device is in its beam path. Removing discovery from the picture and lowering the need for a number of security checks like a challenge and response system (ID/password) lowers the overhead in IrDA communications and makes the standard easier to implement; an IrDA packet goes a longer way.

Because IrDA has been around for a while, it holds a decided cost advantage over the other two technologies mentioned in this chapter: it has an almost 10 to 1 price advantage over Bluetooth and wireless USB. Depending upon volume, an IrDA device costs between $1 and $2 to acquire and install in a system by a manufacturer. Compare that with $20 for a Bluetooth device. Eventually Bluetooth devices may fall to under $5 a piece, but are unlikely to be as cheap because Bluetooth devices have more intelligent technology built into them. Some of this price differential is part of the penalty that Bluetooth pays for being a radio frequency broadcast system, and as such being highly regulated. IrDA is infrared technology and isn't regulated, although the more powerful versions of the specification will move from infrared to the more powerful laser diodes and LED transceivers. When the transition to these more powerful devices occurs, the potential danger users may face to their vision may bring on more government scrutiny than IrDA has today.

Now that you've seen a little about IrDA, let's turn our attention to a more capable and powerful technology — Bluetooth.

Bluetooth

First, let's address (so to speak) Bluetooth's funky name. Harold Bluetooth was the Danish king in the tenth century who united many of the tribes of Norway, Sweden, and Denmark, and early developers hoped that Bluetooth would unite the many tribes of wireless devices in a similar way.

Bluetooth the networking protocol seems like it's been under development for nearly as long, but is now found in enough cell phones, pagers, printers, and a few high-end keyboard bundles such as the Logitech diNovo Media Desktop (see Figure 13-5) that it finally may be useful. You will also find Bluetooth in products such as the Nokia Image Viewer and Media Master; a Toshiba microwave oven, electric dishwasher, and refrigerator freezer; garage door openers, baby monitors, you name it. The solution works well for mobile phones and PDAs, and is found in the late (lamentable) Sony Clie PEG-UX50, Palm Tungsten, Zire 72, as well as add-ons for these PDAs; GPS devices; bar code

scanners; tablet PCs; and many other products. The available mix is very eclectic, and contains some novel products. Vendors who add Bluetooth are looking to provide added value for wireless devices.

Figure 13-5: The highly-regarded Logitech diNovo is more than just a simple wireless keyboard/mouse combination as its designer looks imply. The diNovo functions as a multimedia control center, a separate keypad with an LCD display, and a Bluetooth media hub. You can build a small Bluetooth PLAN around this platform.

Many, if not most, of the Bluetooth devices transmit 1 milliwatt signals omnidirectionally, which limits the range of these devices to about 30 feet or 10 meters. Bluetooth microchip transceivers are either embedded into the Bluetooth device, or they come with dongles that most often connect up through a computer's USB port. The range of 30 feet is not an accident; Bluetooth is meant to cover a single office room only — however, a Bluetooth signal can penetrate the average office or home wall. By comparison you'll find that most cell phones have a signal of 3 watts or more. Bluetooth is meant to be a low power draw on devices that don't store a lot of power to begin with. A Bluetooth personal network or ***piconet***, as it is called, allows for up to 8 connected devices, with up to 255 devices connected in what is called "parked mode."

Let's look at the procedure for connecting to Bluetooth devices using a Toshiba Portege 3505 Tablet PC. Bluetooth is a valuable addition to a device like this because the tablet PC is meant to be a portable writing surface with no wires attached to it. The steps for connecting with Bluetooth on a 3505 are the following:

1. Turn on the wireless communication switch (a software utility).
2. Start the Bluetooth Manager, which turns on the Bluetooth circuitry in the laptop; an icon appears in the Status area of the toolbar indicating that the service is available. Most Bluetooth devices are powered off initially and require that you turn Bluetooth on.

3. Right-click the Bluetooth icon in the Status area and select the Auto Power On command if you wish to have the service start up automatically as a service when your system restarts.
4. Open the Bluetooth Service Center by selecting that command from the Bluetooth Toshiba Stack folder on the Program menu. Figure 13-6 shows the Bluetooth Service Center, which indicates which COM ports are assigned to the Bluetooth service.

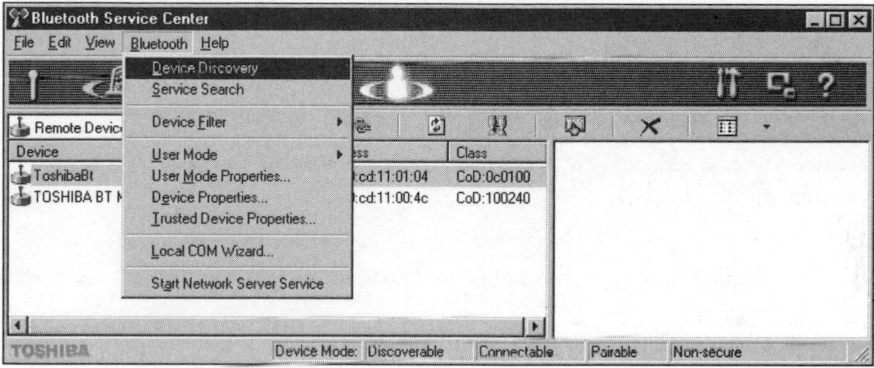

Figure 13-6: The Toshiba Bluetooth Service Center utility.

5. Initiate device discovery to determine what Bluetooth devices are in your immediate vicinity. Select the Device Discovery command from the Bluetooth menu of the Bluetooth Service Center.

   To connect to a Bluetooth device you need the following three pieces of information: the device name, the device address (which for Bluetooth takes the form 00.40.12.11.12.23), and the password or what Bluetooth calls a ***passkey***. Usually the passkey is set by the remote device.
6. Once you discover the device you want to connect to, click its name in the Device list and then click the Service Search icon.

This final step determines the services that the device you will connect to can provide. A multifunction printer might offer scanning, printing, copying, and faxing, while a simple printer has only a print function. It's also possible that the multifunction printer may make only printing and scanning available as a Bluetooth service. In many cases device discovery is automatic, particularly when it comes to simple devices and services.

You could, for example, use a Bluetooth modem to connect your laptop to the Internet. When you do device discovery and you click the Bluetooth Modem device you will see a set of services in the service portion of the Bluetooth Service Center as shown in Figure 13-7. To connect to the Internet you would click the Dial-up networking connection, then on the COM port you wanted to use, and then enter the Bluetooth passkey (PIN) into the Bluetooth Security dialog box. Your ISP settings should be part of your Dial-up Networking connection properties. When you are finished with your connection you would disconnect by clicking the broken link icon in the Bluetooth Service Center lower toolbar.

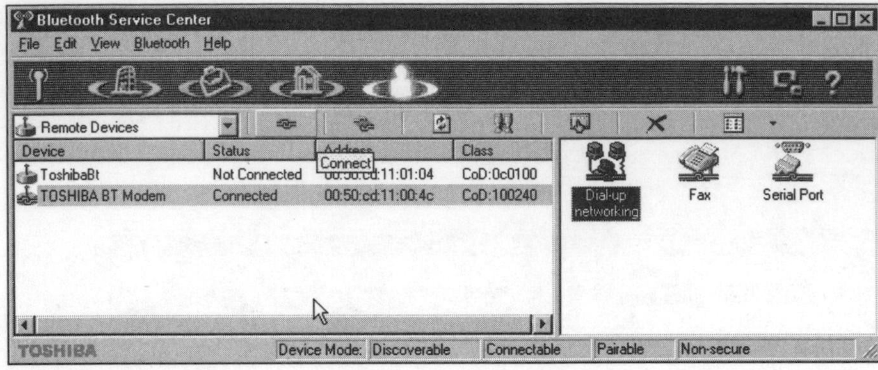

Figure 13-7: Connecting to the Internet with a Bluetooth Modem from the Bluetooth Service Center utility.

Among the other things that you might want to use Bluetooth for with the Toshiba Portege laptop are:

- Connecting with other computer on your network
- File sharing
- Setting up a NetMeeting session between two computers

You can add Bluetooth to any computer using a NIC card or to a laptop with a PC Card (PCMCIA) such as the 3COM Wireless Bluetooth PC Card. Bluetooth devices communicate with each other, automatically handshaking with one another just like modems do; that is, they configure themselves and provide a discovery service that locates and connects with other nearby Bluetooth devices. Supported devices can also communicate to a network wirelessly through Bluetooth access points or routers. Figure 13-8 shows a picture of the 3COM Bluetooth PC card.

Bluetooth is a wireless radio frequency technology operating at 2.45 GHz in both the United States and Europe—just about where 802.11g devices operate, a standard range for Industrial, Scientific, and Medical (ISM) devices. Therefore, Bluetooth is a standard that is regulated by governments worldwide. The actual range is about 2,400 to 2,483.5 MHz, spanning 79 1 MHz radio channels. In Japan that frequency is a little different for the 2.45 GHz signal with 23 1 MHz channels. The assigned bandwidth allows all Bluetooth devices in the same area to share a pipe that is up to 1 Mbps. Each Bluetooth transmitter/receiver has an address that was programmed into it by the manufacturer based on the type of device it is; and each Bluetooth packet uses about 20 percent of its transmission for its headers and protocol information.

Figure 13-8: The 3COM Wireless Bluetooth PC card with XJACK antenna (model 3CRWB6096B).

When you have multiple Bluetooth devices in the same cell, or coverage bubble, they don't interfere with one another because Bluetooth uses a spread spectrum frequency hopping technique to avoid interference. Cell phones employ the same technique, as do most other radio frequency data transfer devices. A Bluetooth connection picks one from 79 randomly chosen frequencies (23 in Japan) in its assigned range and then communicates over them changing between them at about 1,600 times a second or 625 microseconds each. Packets transmitted can span five time slices before they have to be broken down, up to 2,745 bits. That means that even if two devices should happen to send a signal on the same frequency at the same time, an error checking algorithm will catch the problem and get the devices to retransmit. The chances of collision are very small, and manageable.

Bluetooth supports both half duplex and full duplex operation. In half duplex, devices can send or receive, but not both at the same time, while in full duplex they can perform both actions. A phone is designed to be half duplex; you talk or you listen but you don't do both at the same time. At least, you are not supposed to. A conference phone is designed to be full duplex; people in the room can both talk and listen. The throughput of Bluetooth devices varies depending upon the mode your device supports. In a full duplex mode you can get a throughput of up to 64 Kbps each way. At that rate the human voice would be crystal clear, so a phone can break up that connection into a few connections each with its own conversation. That is, you can have Bluetooth phones that function as multi-line phones for small offices. In a half duplex mode as typified by a computer-to-printer connection, transmission is 721 Kbps in the data's primary direction when an optimized

connection is required and 57.6 Kbps in the direction of the sender (the so-called upstream device, paddle wise). A second half duplex mode, which calls for the same transmission speed in each direction exists, and that connection gives a maximum throughput of 432.6 Kbps in both directions. Don't forget that these are theoretical throughputs and your mileage may vary.

Another way to describe Bluetooth's data transfer modes is as either Synchronous Connection Oriented (SCO) or Asynchronous Connectionless Oriented. Bluetooth can support an SCO session where the master device communicates with up to three slave devices at a maximum rate of 64 Kbps. The master device provides a collision avoidance feature by managing the channels of connected devices in an SCO. In an ACL session, a single master connects to a single slave. An ACL session can either be a broadcast to all slaves or a point-to-point connection between master and slave. In an ACL connection the master initiates all communication data transfers.

Bluetooth's trade organization is found at Bluetooth.org, and they also maintain a consumer Web site at Bluetooth.com that will give you an idea about the number of products offering Bluetooth connectivity.

Wireless USB

USB has become one of the favored ways to hook up peripherals to PCs. We never cease to be amazed at some of the devices that you can put on a USB bus, everything from keyboards and mice to digital microscopes to scanners, printers, cameras, and more. Sometimes people get darn silly about USB, using it to recharge AA batteries, power a little fan or light for a laptop. If your PC is like ours, your USB bus is a busy place.

USB has gone through two major standard revisions, version 1.1 and version 2. Version 2 is almost always backward-compatible with version 1.1, and both standards are supported by all the current versions of Windows in the OS. The major difference between the two versions is the throughput; version 1.1 is slow at 12 Mbps, while version 2 runs at 480 Mbps. The original low-speed devices ran at 1.5 Mbps per channel. The upshot of all of this is that low speed USB devices are better supported for wireless connections than high speed devices can be. Most high speed devices need to be plugged directly into a port or a USB hub to work with wireless networking devices.

No doubt you've encountered wireless adapters or dongles that are used to connect a computer to a wireless keyboard and to a wireless mouse. A wireless dongle serves the same function for connected wireless devices as the USB host adapter serves for its connected devices. Most USB wireless connectors that are designed to meet the USB Human Interface Device (HID) standard have a 15-device connection limit. So there's also a 15-device limit to wireless USB host adapters and hubs. What the USB HID standard says is that any compatible wireless host adapter or hub must support plug and play, power management, persistent addressing, and be capable of being woken up from sleep. Part of the USB addressing scheme maintains both the serial numbers and port addresses of connected devices, the former being the default means of recognition.

In terms of what that means to you, when you plug in a USB device it should be recognized and automatically configured. If the operating system realizes that the device is unknown or that it doesn't have the proper driver to control the device, then the OS will either search for the driver or ask you to supply the driver file manually. USB is one of the best examples of Plug and Play (PnP) in action, and wireless USB extends this convenience to even more devices.

There are three different kinds of wireless connections to USB devices currently in use:

- Devices that turn a USB port into a wireless NIC
- USB devices that allow a direct connection between the peripheral (when it has a transceiver of its own) and the access point
- A wireless USB hub that you can plug other non-wireless USB devices into

In the first option, there are many examples of devices that can convert a USB port into a wireless NIC card. Most of these devices, like the Linksys WUSB12, have a form factor similar to a keychain USB flash drive and are 802.11b devices. More recently 802.11g USB adapters have begun to appear. Buffalo Technology's WLI-USB-G54 Airstation is a wireless USB 2.0 device that retails for anywhere from $30 to $70, while the Linksys WUSB54G is a nearly identical device. USB wireless G adapters offer fast throughput without any USB penalty. Not surprisingly, you'll also find that vendors offer combination wireless USB/32 MB flash storage drive adapters, like the SMC WUSB32 — EZ Connect for $65. If you need to add an IrDA capability to a computer, check out the USB 1.1 IrDA adapters s from CP Technologies, a $30 device.

There are several examples of wireless USB hubs on the market. Take for example the AnywhereUSB hub from Digi (`www.digi.com/products/usb/anywhereusb.jsp`). This hub lets you connect USB devices to either a LAN or a WLAN without a computer to manage the process. Digi calls this USB over IP technology, but somewhere on the network is a computer or server that has the necessary drivers to do the translation. The USB/5 (5 USB ports) has the same characteristics as any USB hub for PnP, and enables you to connect devices such as a bar code reader, a fingerprint scanner, or a portable display. Digi also sells a line of USB sensors called Watchport that can measure things like temperature, as well as a USB camera, and the Edgeport USB to serial converter devices. So with the AnywhereUSB system you can remotely place USB peripherals. Figure 13-9 shows a picture of the AnywhereUSB wireless hub.

Figure 13-9: The Digi AnywhereUSB wireless hub.

Other examples of wireless USB hubs include one from a company called Silex. They offer a single port wireless USB 2.0 hub for a high speed printer, scanner, or storage device connection, model SX-3700WB. Pricom's SX-5000U2 can serve as a four port USB hub and print server, and when you attach another USB hub to one of the SX-5000U2's ports you can fan out (from one port to many) up to nine USB 2.0 devices. These two devices connect using the 802.11b standard.

The SX-5000U2 is more than just a simple wireless USB hub. It comes with software to convert a multifunction printer and a scanner into a shared network resource. There's support for HP JetAdmin and Web JetAdmin management software, printer status notification, as well as automated e-mail printing. To set up printers and other devices on the SX-5000U2 you would create the configuration on your computer and then copy the settings to a USB pen drive (supplied with the product). You then take the pen drive to the location of the wireless USB hub/server, insert it, and configuration is complete. Security features of the 5000U2 include IP filtering, and it will also support IPv6 addressing.

There are efforts underway to develop Wireless USB (WUSB) for high speed transfers up to the current 480 Mbps USB limit using ultra-wideband (UWB) and multiband technologies, and longer range plans suggest it might be possible to reach 1 Gbps. WUSB is a hub and spoke network with the host initiating data traffic to client devices, directing traffic, and time slicing the bandwidth among what is called its *cluster*. Each cluster of WUSB has a 127-device limit and two or more clusters can use the same radio cell (reception area for a signal). This high speed is possible for a relatively low powered bus because the typical device connection is meant to be less than 30 feet or 10 meters. That will make a WUSB bubble about the same size as Bluetooth's. An article on the emerging WUSB standard may be found at `www.intel.com/update/contents/wi02041.htm`.

Summary

In this chapter you learned about three very different technologies for wirelessly connecting to nearby peripheral devices. The very heavily deployed standard IrDA is an infrared point-to-point directional connection I/O technology. You would use IrDA in situations where the two connection nodes are very close together. Inexpensive and highly reliable IrDA has important applications that neither Bluetooth nor wireless USB can duplicate.

The second technology is Bluetooth, which enables devices to broadcast over about a 30-foot radius and discover other Bluetooth devices. Once a connection is negotiated you can command the two devices to transfer data or control signals. Bluetooth is used in all manner of appliances, information devices, and consumer products, and is just starting to come into wide use. With Bluetooth a session has a master and from one to three slaves that are connected. Bluetooth can operate in both duplex and half duplex modes with different transmission rates and connection requirements.

USB and its extension, wireless USB, connects a specific I/O port to a Wi-Fi access point or router allowing you to connect remote printers, scanners, cameras, and other USB devices to your computers without having a wire running to those devices. Therefore, USB is an interconnect standard that has been used to provide networking services. USB can have up to 127 devices per channel, and some wireless USB hubs can connect to up to nine other USB devices.

Both wireless USB and Bluetooth are notable in that they can help you create small, highly configurable personal networks. Each of these technologies is meant to be highly consumer friendly, with plug and play features such as automatic addressing and configuration.

In the next chapter you are going to see how to use wireless technology in your home to create an entertainment network. With 802.11 technologies you can stream audio and video throughout a home without undertaking expensive wiring retrofits. You'll learn about the first generation of wireless home entertainment devices, personal video recorders, networked Internet radio devices, and more. For most people who are interested in wireless technologies there are probably no other areas in which completing an installation project can be so satisfying.

Part IV

Wireless Home Solutions

Chapter 14

Setting Up an Entertainment Network

Although the application of wireless networking to the creation of highly configurable entertainment networks is in its infancy, many of the pieces you need to create such a network are starting to be introduced. Some of these devices are conventional adaptations of components you already have in a sound system, such as the 900 MHz Sony Wireless Speaker system. The wireless station of this system broadcasts an audio source from a receiver or TV to a couple of wireless speakers (or headphones). Other devices, such as the SMC EZ-Streaming Universal Wireless Multimedia Receiver (SMCWMR-AG), are relatively new types of low-cost file servers specially configured for streaming media files over a wireless connection. The typical streaming multimedia device is limited in the file formats it can work with, and that is one of the reasons for selecting one device over another. In this chapter, we look at the wireless devices that you can use to stitch your home entertainment network together, and what capabilities those devices offer.

Wireless technology makes great sense in home entertainment networks because of the relatively low cost involved in adding wireless capability to devices, and because of the convenience they give you. When you factor in the speed of some of the more recent 802.11 protocols, even streaming large video files is workable. With wireless technology you have a much greater degree of freedom in placing the components where you want them. Most people do not live in homes or work in buildings that have special audio/video (AV) wall jacks, nor do most homes have CAT5 Ethernet pulled through the walls. Although you can retrofit buildings to accommodate new networks, it is both costly and troublesome. The flexibility that wireless links provide also allows you to manage your entertainment WLAN from different locations and with different devices and software, shifting to better technology as time goes by.

Digital media transmission also allows you to remove physical barriers to entertainment access, as well. Through the use of network shares and servers, you can access digital libraries of audio and digital video files from anywhere you have wireless coverage, resulting in entertainment and information on demand. A wireless MP3 jukebox (when they finally become available as a standard feature) would allow you to choose the music you want to listen to at any time by downloading just those tracks from your audio library before you head out the door to the gym or to work. (At the moment, we are limited to add-on wireless playback devices such as Belkin's TuneCast Mobile FM transmitter, which turns your iPod into an FM radio station.) With a Personal Video Recorder, or

PVR, you can record just the programs you want and view them later (time shifting), and eliminate commercials, which greatly improves the quality of what you watch. Devices such as TiVo (which, after all, is a special-purpose Linux box) as well as specially configured computer systems you'll learn about later can be part of your entertainment network, and they can dramatically improve the TV viewing experience. Networking computers has always made sense because it lets you share precious resources; and with an entertainment network you get the same value.

So many different approaches exist to creating a home entertainment network that it's impossible to delineate them in a stepwise fashion. You'll find that some people add entertainment devices to networks with a wireless connection, others add a computer such as a PCTV or Windows Media Center edition to their entertainment system, while still others find that they have a network provided for them by their cable operator. There's no right approach, but there are differences in the requirements for the use of wireless networking to tie all these different approaches together. It is "early days" for these technologies with lots of new products coming to market every month, so it's also impossible to know which product types will become consumer and industry favorites. Still, there are sensible principles you can apply that are described in this chapter. We'll discuss what adherence to standards, doing what you can to minimize cross-vendor incompatibilities, and other choices can do to help.

Digital Convergence in the Wireless Era

Digital convergence generally means the integration of consumer electronic devices with intelligent information management devices. When you combine digital media with the ability to manipulate audio, video, text, and binary data of all types, you can create new types of applications, new types of devices all networked together. It's an area that you as a consumer should not take lightly because this technology will become a pervasive component of your everyday life.

An entertainment network should offer you the following capabilities:

- Simple connectivity for your devices (strive for device interoperability)
- A software framework built on standard methods for device discovery, configuration, and management (such as SNMP, the Simple Network Management Protocol)
- Standard media formats and transport or streaming protocols
- A standard way of managing your media within your framework
- A digital rights mechanism that protects intellectual copyrights so that everything is nice and legal

That's a tall order to fill (particularly on the software side), but the industry can achieve it in time. You should do all you can to strive for maintaining these characteristics in any home entertainment network that you choose to build; these are the elements you should look for when you purchase and install new components that will be part of your entertainment network.

The consumer electronics market dwarfs the computer market in scale. At the Comdex and Consumer Electronics Show in Las Vegas, that difference is very obvious. Consumer applications of computer technology have been a bright spot over the past three or four years in the computer industry, and computer vendors have been rushing to position themselves for what they see as an essential emerging new industry based around a home network (see Figure 14-1). The new products being introduced seek to take advantage of developments like HDTV, surround sound, digital cameras, the Personal Video Recorder (PVR), the Digital Versatile Disk (DVD) and other new storage devices, and home automation by integrating those technologies into their products. For example:

- Microsoft offers the Windows Media Center edition operating system for the home market and both Microsoft and Intel have connected home initiatives.
- Gateway has a best-selling plasma monitor to complement one of the better Media Center PCs (the Gateway Media Center FMC-901X) on the market, which is a natural extension of the company's pioneering efforts from its Destination PCTV series.
- Apple dominates the MP3 jukebox market with its iPod series.
- Epson offers the Livingstation HDTV projection TV, which comes with a dye sublimation printer and smart media support built in allowing you to print high-definition images on demand.
- Any number of companies including HP, Sony, Netgear, D-Link, SMC, and others sell wireless streaming media hubs or receivers.

The list of computer-related products coming from the traditional consumer electronics market is also actively growing, as evidenced by the fact that

- Comcast can offer you both high-speed broadband Internet access as well as on-demand video services (see Figure 14-2).
- LG Electronics is offering a networked/Internet refrigerator (something that Motorola demo'ed as a concept in 1999).
- Westinghouse has a line of connected home appliances that use the Windows CE .NET operating system. Its line includes a microwave oven, coffee maker, and bread maker, along with a home hub with a CD/FM/clock and Internet access and the iCEBOX kitchen PC with an LCD screen and wireless keyboard.
- Omnifi's DMP2 (`www.omnifimedia.com/products/omnifi_products.jsp`) car audio/video player synchronizes content with either a USB or 802.11g connection with your home media servers so that you can play it in your car.
- Motorola's Home Theater System DCP501 (see `http://broadband.motorola.com/consumers/products/dcp501/`) provides a digital cable receiver, DVD/CD/MP3 player, 100 watts × 5-channel amplifier, and an AM/FM stereo receiver in one package.

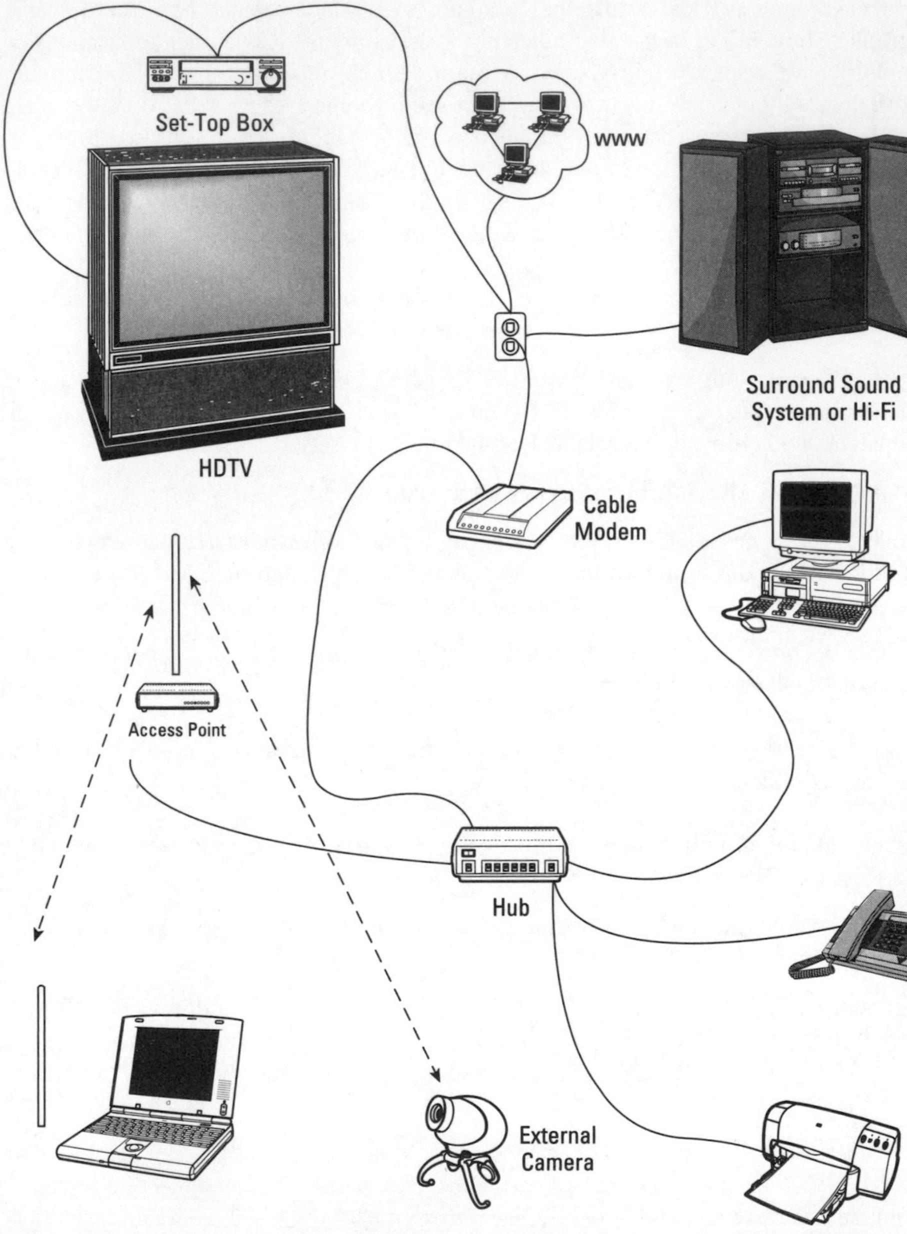

Set-Top Box

WWW

HDTV

Surround Sound
System or Hi-Fi

Cable
Modem

Access Point

Hub

External
Camera

Figure 14-1: Wireless technology can help create a home entertainment network with many different types of devices.

Figure 14-2: Comcast's on-demand video service lets you view programs at a time of your choosing with VCR-like controls. The set-top box plays the role of a computer and uses video stored on remote servers.

The Different Viewpoints

The problem with digital convergence and with the marketplace in general at the moment is there are few industry standards in place, and what standards do exist are in a flux. This goes beyond the simple things that come to mind such as file formats and media types to the entire philosophy of how to wirelessly network your entertainment system. Ask different vendors to describe their ideal entertainment network and you have a situation similar to the parable of the blind men describing an elephant. Each different vendor views digital convergence with a unique perspective, and sees it for something different. Thus:

- To a PC vendor, the central control is exercised by a multimedia PC as part of a network operating system.
- To a cable provider, the focus is on the set-top box, a centralized computer system, and very fast signal transmission.
- To an AV house or to a custom hi-fi system integrator, convergence is when they program a remote control (RC) with some intelligence such as the original standard setter, the programmable Philips Pronto remote, more recent entries like the Home TheaterMaster MX-300 (a superior hard button remote), to the new embedded software solution from Universal Electronics called Nevo (`www.mynevo.com/home.htm`), shown in Figure 14-3.
- To the audiophile, the focus is a surround sound receiver, and to the movie buff it's an HDTV-based home theater.

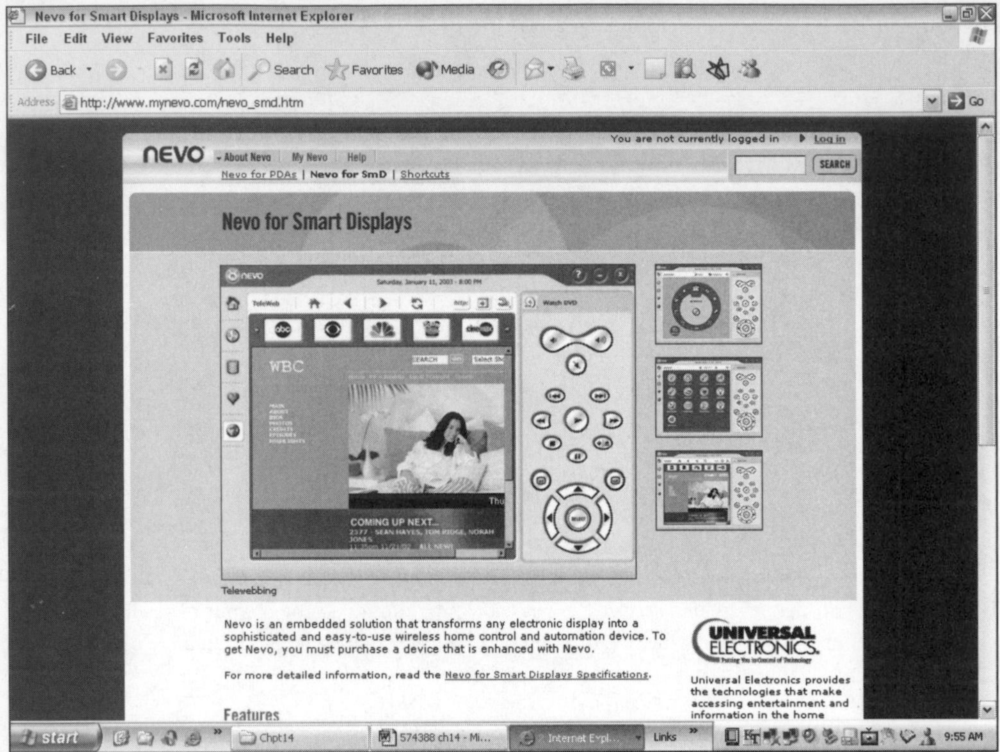

Figure 14-3: Nevo is a new embedded software system that allows developers to create sophisticated and easy-to-use control devices.

These different viewpoints have direct consequences for you, as each industry tries to tie together the different devices used in a home entertainment network using different types of network connections. A PC might use Ethernet or the 802.11x family of wireless radio frequency networks; a cable company's transmission is over a coaxial line or is a downlink from a satellite feed; an HDTV might connect to a video source using a DVI cable; a video camera uses FireWire; handheld remotes use infrared or radio frequencies; and stereo and surround sound setups make direct high-quality component connections between devices using component video and audio cables. What a mess.

From your viewpoint, however, none of this should really matter much. It simply makes sense to use the best current technology that you can find to get the job done and hope that over time the industry will create better interoperating products.

There's a strong incentive for vendors to do just that. Any wireless vendor with a product that conflicts with other wireless devices is just asking for trouble. If you wander about your house using a 900 MHz Sennheiser R85s wireless headphone, your primary consideration is the connected range. A frequency of 2.4 GHz on a wireless headphone might be better for hi-fi sound, but not if it conflicts with an 802.11x wireless network or your microwave oven — something the Amphony 2000 headphones apparently did. You can live with the momentary loss of your headphones, but you undoubtedly will be sending a component back if it never works. Wi-Fi products that don't interoperate well will also get replaced.

The Digital Living Network Alliance

To make home products interoperate, a number of computer and electronics vendors have assembled a working group that hopes to drive standards and test interoperability. Originally called the Digital Home Working Group (DHWG), it is now called the Digital Living Network Alliance (DLNA) (`www.dlna.org/about`). The goal of the alliance is to define what a digital home should include, and how to make products compatible with one another. Although wireless networking is only a part of it, some studies have been published by the alliance detailing wireless usage. The number of home entertainment network connected devices is predicted to double every year through 2007. The study shows the 35 connections in 2003 on average per network rising to 183 in 2007.

The DLNA sees the overall market as focused on three converging areas of technology:

- Consumer Electronics (CE)
- Mobile
- Computers and Computer Networks

An Overview of Wireless Digital Devices

The DLNA has tried to classify the major product types of a convergent entertainment network. Its developed categories are instructional. The first classification is Digital Home Server (DHS) devices. DHS devices create content, provide storage and access capabilities, and allow copyright protection while maintaining a standard digital home interoperability model (which is to be developed). DHS devices are characterized by component and user service management capabilities in a rich user/network interface, the built-in intelligence to respond to events, and media management.

Some DHS devices include:

- Advanced set-top boxes
- Personal Video Recorders
- PCs
- Stereo and home theaters with hard disk drives
- Broadcast tuners
- Video and imaging capture devices, such as cameras and camcorders
- Multimedia mobile phones

The second device category is Digital Home Rendering (DHR) devices. DHR components play content and render or display content. DHR devices include:

- TV monitors
- Stereo and home theaters
- Printers

- PDAs
- Multimedia mobile phones
- Wireless monitors
- Game consoles

The first step in building a wireless home entertainment network is to determine the places where wireless technology makes sense and can offer value. The most logical possibilities are the following:

- At your incoming broadband connection (most typically cable or DSL) with a wireless router. You might choose to select this location if you want to have an entirely wireless network, or if your incoming broadband connection is in a place that isn't easily wired to your main network.

  Examples of products in this category are the D-Link DI-624, Linksys Wireless-G WRT56G, and the Netgear WGT624. These products cost around $125 and give you the functionality of a router, a hub, and some firewall capabilities. You'll find a review of some 802.11g models at `www.pcmag.com/article2/0,1759,1574346,00.asp`. That review chose the Linksys Wireless-G WRT54GS router as its editors' choice.

  It's even possible to find wireless cable modems such as the Motorola SURFboard Wireless Cable Modem Gateway SBG1000 (see Figure 14-4), although many ISPs require their own modems be used and managed remotely.

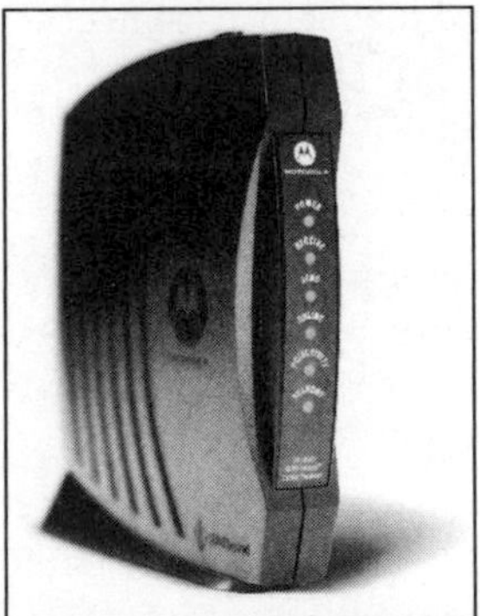

Figure 14-4: Motorola has been an early innovator in the area of wireless home networking devices. Its SURFboard Wireless Cable Modem Gateway SBG1000 unifies a number of functions needed to access and secure Internet traffic and digital content transmission.

- At an Ethernet hub with an access point. This location provides support for mobile devices in a location where a wired network can be connected to your entertainment network.

- At a pair of Ethernet hubs with two access points in a bridging configuration. A bridge would serve as a wire replacement for the connection of your entertainment network and your computer network.
- At important central control devices such as a digital media receiver or home theater TV. This location provides wireless support for mobile devices at the center of your entertainment network.

Note

A number of wireless products for the home that were discussed in this chapter were evaluated as part of a *PC Magazine* project wiring the homes of Bruce and Marge Brown. The article "Home Networking from the Ground Up," by Stephanie Change, appeared in the April 6, 2004 issue of *PC Magazine*. You can find it online at `www.pcmag.com/article2/0,1759,1545750,00.asp?kc=646`.

TVs and Set-Top Boxes

Many modern TVs, especially ones that are HDTV or HDTV-ready, are intended as stand-alone systems. They come with a set of connections that any receiver might be proud of. Some can be set up to be a surround sound system on their own with a set of built-in speakers that create the front sound stage. The idea is that you add a subwoofer to get the bass response. Because many HDTV manufacturers create integrated displays, the obvious next step might be to add networking capabilities. At the moment, most people create a surround sound theater system by connecting an HDTV to their surround sound receiver, thus defeating the purpose of the internal speakers and amplification provided by their TVs. Today's home entertainment networks have a lot of redundant parts, so let's hope future choices will be more modular.

The current choices for cabling on HDTVs are optical connections (best quality) and RCA connections. Video can be S Video, component video, DVI, or on some sets FireWire (IEEE 1394). Component video gives reasonably good video display, FireWire is better, and there seems to be growing consensus that DVI will be the emerging high-end standard. If you choose to use a computer as your tuner, most of these connections are offered by a good tuner card and/or a breakout box (like the one that comes with ATI's All-in-Wonder boards, discussed later in the chapter). To date there are no TVs that are networkable because manufacturers have chosen to put that capability in set-top boxes, receivers, DVD players, and other components. Faster wireless networks may mean that a high-quality video signal can be transmitted, which might lead to networked TVs.

A cable modem is one of the places on the network where you can have control capabilities built in and where you might be able to wirelessly control an entertainment network. A cable modem is not a set-top box or cable channel selector. The cable modem's function is to provide digital services such as Internet access. Most cable companies will let you substitute your own cable modem, although some will not. It's best to check with your provider if you decide to install your own.

A cable service may offer a variety of set-top boxes, both analog and digital. There is a growing trend to push consumers to digital services as soon as the infrastructure allows. Comcast, for example, will stop showing many movie channels on its analog cable packages, so analog services' days are probably numbered. Although a small handful of wireless cable boxes are available, no cable company I know of offers them. If you want to incorporate a device like the Motorola SURFboard(r) Wireless Cable Modem Gateway SBG1000 shown earlier into your entertainment network, you will need to do so yourself.

The world of set-top boxes offers a unique opportunity to computer vendors, and everyone from Microsoft (with the Windows CE operating system), to Linux, to Sun with Java wants to penetrate this market. Set-top boxes are computers, and whether they include an embedded real-time operating system, Linux, Windows CE, or something else, it's clearly a great place to embed intelligent functionality to run a home entertainment network. The next generation of set-top boxes will be computers with storage capabilities. Depending on the components you have in your system, most entertainment networks connect a set-top box either directly to the TV, as a pass through in a home theater arrangement through a surround sound receiver, or as a pass through from a PVR (such as ReplayTV, TiVo, or a computer with those capabilities). The digital Motorola High Definition Cable Receiver DCT5100 (see Figure 14-5) that is attached to the author's HDTV is a good example of a next-generation set-top box that comes with three USB connections, a smart card interface, and an Ethernet port.

The set-top box arena is one of the most actively contested device categories in the entire entertainment networking area, and with good reason. Whoever controls the set-top market can control the content and capabilities of your system. You should pay particular attention to advances in set-top boxes; there's a lot at stake in this arena.

Figure 14-5: The Motorola High Definition Cable Receiver DCT5100 is one of the first all-digital set-top boxes designed to function as a bridging device on an entertainment network, providing not only A/V but also high-speed data services. It is meant to mate with the Motorola DCP501 integrated receiver.

Choosing Standards

You can choose many equipment types as a starting place when you want to wirelessly integrate components into a home entertainment network. Although a device like a wireless surround sound receiver with a built-in cable modem and firewall is a good starting place, if you were actually able to find one, chances are you wouldn't want it. First, any highly integrated device like that locks you into a specific blend of technologies in any area that is still in flux. More importantly, budgets and your evolving needs will probably limit what you can buy, but thankfully not necessarily what you can accomplish over time. When you are done you still should be able to manage and access music, photos, and movies on your network. So how do you make good choices?

Faced with choices, you should do what smart people and companies have always done: adopt standards. Home entertainment networks are often on the bleeding edge of technology, but you don't have to be. It's much smarter to be a little behind the curve on technology. Buying the second or third iteration of a device type once it matures can save you a lot of cost and grief. That buying philosophy would mean that you selected VHS instead of Betamax, DVDs instead of laser disks, and for wireless networking, 802.11g instead of 802.11b. You don't always choose the best technology, but often you will end up with something that is more useful. The old adage is true: you always can tell who the pioneers were — they are the ones with arrows in their backs.

There has been much discussion about the merits of one 802.11x protocol versus another in this book. The experience for streaming large media files seems to be that 802.11b is adequate for streaming music and small photos, but it is not fast enough for moving large video files around conveniently. The current preference for any system with video capabilities is 802.11g. You should also be wary of any wireless device that claims backward compatibility with an earlier protocol, and test that claim. An access point that is supposedly compatible with 802.11b/g may really be worthwhile only as a 802.11g network and have lackluster performance and range with an earlier 802.11b device.

Integrating new technology to create a hybrid network containing personal computers and consumer electronics is hard enough; if you can limit your compatibility issues you can save yourself time and trouble. Adopt one vendor's product line based on a review or testing and try to stick with its products. We would like to believe that products from the same vendor should be known and tested to play well together. Another advantage is that any vendor's products, such as D-Link's AirPremier AG Tri-Mode Dualband 802.11a/b/g or any other product that offers you "EXTREME-G", "MEGA-A", or "ULTIMA-G" (fictional standards) are proprietary and are going to give you something like the speed they advertise only when they are connected to other products from that vendor. Vendors use proprietary techniques to go beyond current standards, techniques that aren't going to work with other vendors' products (most likely). So if you are extending the range of this particular access point, you would need to purchase the DWL-G650 wireless repeater because without that unit you can't get above the normal limit of 54 Mbps in your extended range. The same applies to any NIC (network interface card) that you install in your laptop or desktop (which for this particular series would be D-Link's DWL-AG650 or DWL-AG530). We chose these specific products just for the sake of illustration; other good choices are available.

Wireless Digital Audio

One of the first wireless projects that people undertake is sharing their music library throughout the house. It's a good first project because many devices are available and because the demands that the task places on a wireless network are small. Music file sizes are relatively small, which means that even 802.11b devices will work well for this purpose. An MP3 song that is about 3 minutes long will run about 3MB when recorded at a 128-Kbps bit rate. A library of MP3 files of 30GB will contain something like 10,000 songs, or approximately 800 records. That's a fair-sized collection in anyone's book. An audio library is a compelling reason to go to the trouble of creating a wireless connection from your LAN to your receiver or TV. So it's no surprise that among the first wireless devices for home entertainment networks is a group of wireless receivers. The following sections take a look at some of the options you have when assembling an audio system.

Assembling a Wireless Audio System

You have some good choices when you are trying to assemble a wireless audio system. Most people create a music library first, and then look to exploit its existence. Thus a PC may serve as the MP3 repository. One of the obvious choices is to have your PC serve as your entertainment hub. Any PC with a wireless NIC gives you both a wireless network connection and lets you output audio directly from a sound card to a stereo receiver. Most receivers will accept digital output from an advanced sound card such as Creative's Audigy 2 series or the revolution 7.1 surround sound board from M audio. Outputs from these boards are either through minijacks (like typical small headphones) or through a standard RCA digital connection.

One of the author's first entertainment network was based around a Gateway Destination PCTV that was in service for about four years. The advantage of a PCTV is that it can directly attach to your entertainment components, serve as a tuner, a PVR, and you can use the computer to control just about any controllable device. With a PCTV, you can manage storage, input and output configuration, and multiple devices. PCs are often open architecture, so as a PCTV gets older you can upgrade components. My Destination went through three versions of the Windows operating system, three video cards, two tuners, and two sound boards before it was retired. The PCTVs of the present come with ever-improving audio standards. For example, the new Intel BTX motherboards have advanced sound capabilities as part of their motherboard. The modern version of this concept is the Windows Media Center PC.

You don't need a screaming PC to serve your entertainment network's needs. The truth is that even an old PC will serve well as an audio server. Mostly what you need in a multimedia PC serving up audio files is reasonable I/O to disk and the ability to support higher-end audio and video cards. These are very modest requirements. Computers with no AGP ports are at a disadvantage, but you can still purchase an ATI All-in-Wonder PCI card and have one of the newer Audigy boards work in a PC that is running an operating system as old as Windows 98. So your old PC might make a good choice as an audio file server and wireless connection point, and provide even longer service. Since your PCTV usually needs to be directly connected to your TV and cable, it's generally centrally located. A PCTV interface with a wireless access point makes wireless connections to other devices easy to create.

Networked audio receivers are certainly an intriguing possibility for starting to build a wireless home entertainment network. They can store and play audio files, give you Internet radio access, and perform other useful audio functions. There aren't many on the market yet, and the ones that are come with wired Ethernet connections. The HP Wireless Digital Media Receiver ew500 (see Figure 14-6) is one of the first examples of this type of device, and is meant for mass market at a price point of around $300. An example of a higher-end networked receiver is the Onkyo TXNR900 7.1 Digital Audio Receiver, shown in Figure 14-7. The TXNR900 comes with a built-in Linux system to manage the network connection. Included in this receiver is Internet radio with 30 assignable presets. This model requires a separate tuner for AM and FM reception. Although you can add wireless capability to this receiver, you will probably see more choices appearing on the market that are wireless devices straight out of the box.

Figure 14-6: The HP Wireless Digital Media Receiver ew500 can stream audio and video images wired or wirelessly over your network.

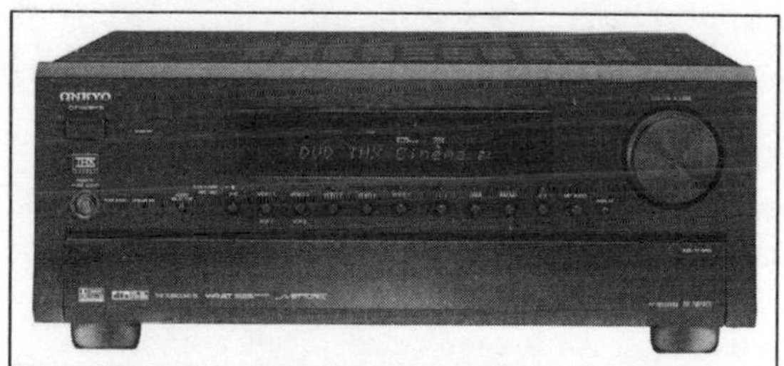

Figure 14-7: The Onkyo TXNR900 7.1 Digital Receiver is a higher-end audiophile receiver with a networked computer on board. This model comes with wired Ethernet, and eschews traditional AM/FM for an Internet radio setup.

Both a PCTV and a wireless receiver are typically the kinds of devices that you would use as a central hub in an entertainment network. In the years to come you'll see more and more wireless entertainment devices, such as wireless speakers, that make both of these components easier to connect

wirelessly. However, you don't need to make the investment in technology that a computer or receiver requires to wirelessly share your music. There are now some simpler ways to do so.

Wireless Audio Devices

Two basic kinds of specialized wireless audio devices have appeared: music servers that store the music locally and output the processed audio signal to a set of speakers or to a receiver; and streaming audio servers that access files stored elsewhere on your network. Music servers are usually wired Ethernet because they are supplying larger quantities of data to the network, whereas streaming audio servers are often wireless devices.

Marantz is one company that sells an audio server in the high-end category. Its DH9300 model comes with an Ethernet connection, which means that you can easily add a wireless capability to it. By contrast, Yamaha's MusicCAST Digital Audio Music Server (see Figure 14-8), which at $2200 (list) is a little pricey for a model with an 80GB hard drive, already has a wireless function. The MusicCAST is an 802.11b wireless server and can be purchased with a set of clients that can connect wirelessly to the MusicCAST receiver. When you set up the MusicCAST, you can purchase $600 MCX-A10 clients and a set of $120-a-pair MCX-SP19 speakers. The audio client is a complete stereo system that can display the MusicCAST's content on its LCD screen, connect to and run speakers, accept other audio input, and connect to a network.

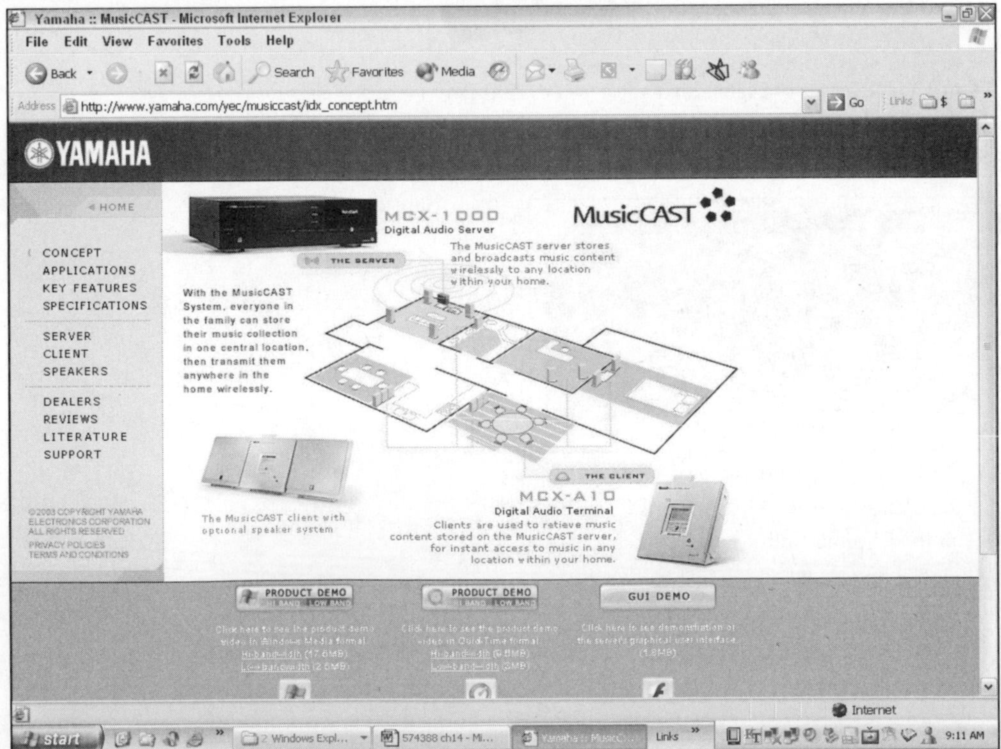

Figure 14-8: Yamaha's MusicCAST Digital Audio Music Server is an 802.11b audio server.

The sound and build quality of both manufacturers' units are as good as you might expect, but for the price and, considering the restricted capabilities of these hi-fi computer wannabees, we would argue for buying or building and then deploying a multimedia PC. Units like the Marantz and Yamaha do look nice and offer an easy way of getting hi-fi sound on your network, but they are really for people who have a high-end hi-fi system and want to have this component match the décor of the other components in the rack.

Any personal computer with a decent audio card can serve as an audio server. A variety of software can be used to serve up audio, including MusicMatch Jukebox, QuickTime, RealOne, WinAmp, Windows Media Player, iTunes, and others. This category of software was last reviewed by *PC Magazine* in March 2003 and can be found online at `www.pcmag.com/category2/0,1738,2378,00.asp`. Take a careful look at the new versions of these products before deciding on any recorder/player software, but they are all capable. All of these software players scan your storage devices and build a library of music for you. Additional features provide extras such as sound leveling, balance controls, special indexing and searching, Internet radio access, streaming audio from online sources, and so on. The main thing being added to this class of software at the moment is access to music libraries that let you download music. Media Player 10 will apparently create a marketplace for these different services.

For large entertainment networks with lots of clients (not typically a home entertainment system) you need a higher-end solution: audio servers with streaming server software. The three most widely deployed choices, in order of their deployment, are RealNetworks and its Helix Server, Microsoft's Windows Media Technologies, and Apple's QuickTime server. All are good products (see `www.pcmag.com/category2/0,1738,2378,00.asp` from October 2003), but RealNetworks' server software is the category leader. Microsoft's server software is capable and a much more economical choice. Web sites serving up audio files such as National Public Radio's sites will often offer two different audio types. For `www.npr.com` and associated sites, those two formats are Real and Windows Media. These streaming server technologies also create streaming video feeds. You'll often see QuickTime offered as a preferred video format on the Web. Luckily, few of us home users will require this level of complexity.

For home networks with modest throughput requirements you can purchase audio servers that are wireless streaming media products. As a class they can be had for as little as $100 up to $250, with the more expensive providing video and faster wireless networking. You have many models to choose from in this category. Early streaming receivers were notoriously finicky to set up and had build problems, but the category seems to be improving. There are a few standouts. Models worth considering include the Netgear MP101 (see Figure 14-9), Creative SoundBlaster Wireless Music, Hauppauge MediaMVP, Slim Devices Squeezebox, the Prismiq MediaPlayer, the D-Link DSM-320, and others. The critical features that you are looking for in this product category is ease of use and installation of the receiver, reliability, and output connections. All of these devices input to your TV and offer an on-screen GUI for simplified music access, and the quality of that software is very valuable when you have a lot of files to manage. Software should be able to search, sort, and find without relying on a PC software player.

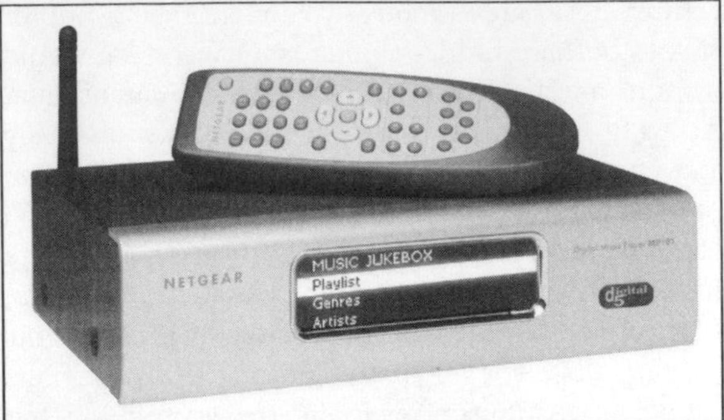

Figure 14-9: The Netgear MP101 is representative of the class of audio MP3 servers. Most look very similar to access points and should be differentiated by their on-screen display and quality of the wireless connection.

Note

A collection of streaming media servers were reviewed in the July 1, 2003 issue of *PC Magazine*. The article called "Diskless Media Hubs" can be found online at `www.pcmag.com/article2/0,1759,1137417,00.asp`. This area of technology has seen a lot of new entrants since this article was written, so it's best to use these reviews as a starting place for any serious purchase.

Audio Files and Formats

Approximately 200 different sound formats are in use (see `www.pcmag.com/category2/0,1738,2378,00.asp`), but only a handful have wide usage, most notably MP3 files. MP3 is officially called MPEG-2 Layer-3 (`www.iis.fhg.de/amm/techinf/layer3/index.html`), and it can store both video and audio information. It's a compressed format, and can record music at different levels of compression. At 128 Kbps it is claimed that there is little or no noticeable loss of quality; this compression results in sound that is similar (but not the same) as CD quality. You lose quality when you record an analog resource, such as ripping an LP album, but if the sampling frequency is greater than the one used for encoding, no sound quality is lost. Audiophiles with better ears than ours claim that MP3 does remove sound quality. Based on how analog records sound by comparison, we'd have to agree. An MP4 sound format is on the horizon, as is the application of digital rights restrictions, so it remains to be seen how popular the MP3 format will remain over time. All audio software players play MP3 files, as do all of the audio devices mentioned in this chapter.

MP3 is not the only format people use. The venerable WAV file format is Windows' native audio file format, and is supported by almost all players. WAV files are uncompressed and larger than MP3 files and they take longer to stream wirelessly across a network, but since they don't need to be uncompressed they are easily decoded and played. Other native formats are AIFF on the Macintosh and the AU format on Sun Solaris.

One up-and-coming format is Ogg Vorbis, an open source compressed audio (and video) format (`www.vorbis.com/`) that is favored in the Linux community. Ogg is the name given to the Xiph.org's container for audio, video, and metadata. Vorbis is an audio compression scheme that can be used in Ogg, along with others such as FLAC (`flac.sourceforge.net`) and Speex (`www.speex.org`). You don't see Ogg on many Windows devices yet, but the format is very high quality and is getting very favorable trade press from the audiophile crowd. Ogg has Real Networks as an investor, and the format is used in a number of popular computer games such as *Unreal Tournament 2003*, *Harry Potter and the Chamber of Secrets*, *Alchemy*, *Serious Sam: the Second Encounter*, *Candy Cruncher* and others.

Ogg will be increasingly supported over time. One highly regarded MP3 player that can use Ogg is the Rio Karma. Because many receivers may use Linux as an operating system to avoid expensive OS licensing costs, Ogg should gain further support. Ogg is meant to replace other formats like MP3. If MP3 licensing issues arise due to Frauhofer's patent for MP3 being pursued, or if the new digital rights management features added to MP3 get too onerous for many users, then the Ogg format will be a serious competitor to MP3. However, keep in mind that you can't just simply convert MP3 to Ogg without losing sound quality. Both are lossy compression formats, and each works by throwing away a different part of the audio spectrum. At the moment Winamp, foobar2000, CDex, and Goldwave support Ogg on Windows; Whamb on OS X; and XMMS and Zinf (formerly FreeAmp) on Linux/Unix.

The current streaming standards are Windows Media Technologies' Window Media Audio / Active Streaming Format (ASF) from Microsoft; MP3, used by a variety of streaming products, many with proprietary implementations (such as Liquid Audio); RealSystems' RealAudio format; and Apple's QuickTime. When you stream audio you wrap an audio file in a streaming format with an encoder, and decode it at the receiving end. Good streaming systems provide dynamic buffering to compensate for fluctuations in throughput of the streamed bit rate.

Playing Audio Files Across the Network

It is illustrative to consider the standards supported by some of the representative digital audio products at the moment:

- **Apple iPod:** AAC (16 to 320 Kbps), MP3 (32 to 320 Kbps), MP3 VBR, Audible, AIFF, and WAV
- **Rio Karma:** FLAC, WMA, Ogg Vorbis, MP3, and WAV
- **Yamaha MusicCAST server:** MP3 and linear PCM (native CD music format)
- **SMC WMR-AG EZ-Stream Universal Wireless Multimedia Receiver:** MP3
- **D-Link DSM-320 MediaLounge wireless media player:** MP3, WAV, and WMA
- **Slim Devices Squeezebox:** MP3, WMA, AAC, Apple Lossless, Ogg Vorbis, FLAC or uncompressed audio (WAV and AIFF)
- **Windows Media Player 10:** MP3, ASF, WMA, MIDI, AIF, AU, SND, WAV, CDA, and QT content.

- **RealOne Player:** ASF, AU, MP3, AIFF, RA, WAV, and WMA
- **Apple QuickTime:** AIFF, AU, FLC, MIDI, M4A/B/P (iTunes format), QT, and WAV

MP3 is a standard pretty much across the board, particularly for a streaming standard. No other format except WAV files makes sense on Windows-based devices. The advantage of WAV files is that that format is lossless and you can at a later date convert WAV to other emerging formats. With MP3 an 802.11b wireless device is sufficient; when you are streaming WAV files you should opt for a faster standard such as the 802.11g DSM-320 server. For a dedicated PC music server that isn't streaming wirelessly, you can use any format that your player supports, and all of them support a very wide array of formats (with the exception of the native formats of their competitors' players).

Once you have decided on your music format and have a music folder or library in place, the next step to creating a wireless music library is to create a network share that can be accessed from your streaming wireless receiver or PCTV setup. To share the folder in Windows, do the following:

1. Right-click the folder and select Sharing and Security to display the Sharing tab of the folder's Properties dialog box (see Figure 14-10). If you are using XP Home, you may need to turn sharing on for your system if you haven't done so already. XP Home sets up some default shared folders.

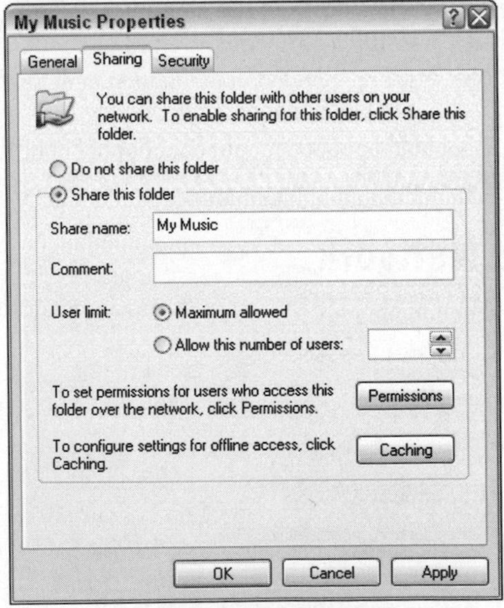

Figure 14-10: Sharing a music folder.

2. Click the Share this folder radio button, and enter a share name in the Share name text box. Your share can be named whatever you wish and does not have to have the same name as the folder in your file system. You could name the share "Audio Library," for example.
3. For large numbers of users you may want to limit the number of concurrent connections; however, for most home entertainment networks leave the Maximum allowed radio button as is. (The caching option is not useful for a wireless streaming server without local storage.)
4. Click Permissions and add the users or groups who can access your share in the Permissions dialog box. Set the kinds of permissions you will allow, primarily whether you will allow read only or read/edit (change).
5. Click OK and close your share.

If you are in another operating system such as Macintosh or Linux, the procedure will be similar. When you purchase a streaming audio server, make sure that that particular model will support your operating system.

Whatever playback device you use, you will need to connect it to your new music library share. For XP Professional, you use the Add a Network Place Wizard in Network Neighborhood, for example. Once you've accessed the share, you can open your media player (Windows Media Player, MusicMatch, RealOne, or some other) and index your music. Each player has the capability to scan disks or folders that you specify and add the audio content it finds to a list it maintains. Any information stored in the Properties sheet of each sound file is also indexed, allowing you to sort by song, artist, by album, by gender, and so forth.

For a streaming device the setup procedure will vary depending on the device's setup and capabilities. Here's an outline of how the SMC WMR-AG EZ-Stream Universal Wireless Multimedia Receiver (shown in Figure 14-11) sets up to stream audio files:

1. Insert the CD-ROM that comes with the product into your computer and install the management software on your system.
2. Specify which folders will be shared by the receiver.
3. Plug in the wireless streaming receiver and plug the receiver into your TV and/or audio system.
4. Use the on-screen wizard to set up DHCP or a static IP address on your network. (Note: this server can be used in a wired Ethernet configuration.)
5. Make your selections, set up a play list, and then begin playing audio files.

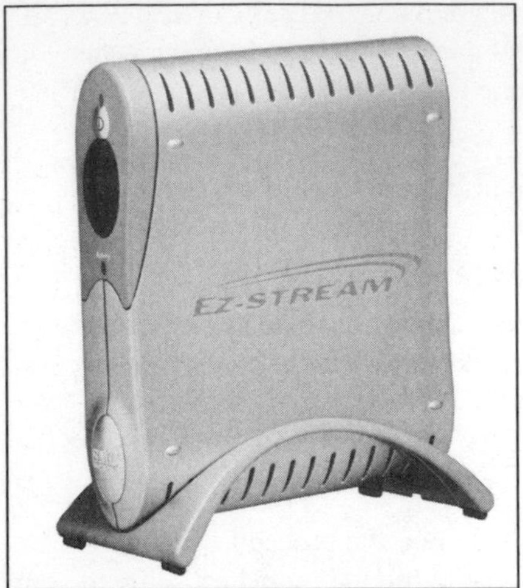

Figure 14-11: The SMC WMR-AG EZ-Stream receiver streams audio and video files using an 80211g connection.

Wireless Digital Video Transfer

As nice as streaming digital audio is on a home entertainment network, seeing your digital photos and videos on your TV is nicer still. Computer technology adds considerable value to the display of pictures and video content, and high-quality pictures really come alive on a good monitor. Most people think in terms of watching TV or storing recorded shows on their home network, but any digital image can be transferred and displayed with the power of computer software applied to the enterprise.

Digital Image Transfers

Most digital images stored on home computers tend to originate from digital cameras, and are thus stored as JPEGs. Other sources, such as scanners, might store TIFFs to disk. The process of transferring images from these sources to your computer is rarely done wirelessly, although that could change in the future. Most of the digital image capture devices are wired devices, usually with USB or FireWire connections; whereas older devices tended to use SCSI (as do high-end devices). There have been some introductions of wireless technology applied to source transfer, although most wireless devices produced to date have tended to use Bluetooth instead of Wi-Fi.

An example of one digital camera that does offer Wi-Fi capabilities is the Nikon D2H camera. By adding its WT-1A add-on adapter or the WT-1 for Europe and Asia you create an 802.11b connection between this camera and your computer. The D2H can transfer pictures through an infrastructure or ad hoc connection to a computer, with image transmission using FTP software. The WT-1 connects to the D2H by attaching to the tripod thread and draws power from the camera. It also connects to the camera's USB port. The D2H is a professional digital camera, meant for someone who takes a lot of pictures. The attraction of a Wi-Fi connection to a PC is obvious: it removes file size and storage limitations for an extended shoot.

Although wireless source image transfers are uncommon, displaying stored pictures over a wireless connection is not. All of the streaming media servers that will play audio could in principle display pictures from your computer on your TV, but many of the early models offered music support only. Newer devices include the ability to display photos in a slide show, as the D-Link DSM-320 shown in Figure 14-12 does. You'll also find devices such as the GoVideo D2730, LiteOn LVD-2010, and the Gateway Connected DVD Player, which are combo DVD player and streaming media players. All these players support JPEG, TIFF, or BMP; the LiteOn, DSM-320, and the HP ew5000 receiver also support PNG. Rarely you will find support for other formats such as JPEG 2000 on the DSM-320.

Figure 14-12: The D-Link DSM-320 is one media receiver that will stream photos to your TV and give you a remote-controlled slide show.

Depending on resolution and format, most picture file sizes are similar to audio file sizes. This is especially true of compressed formats such as JPEG. Therefore any of the 802.11b wireless receivers should work equally well for displaying pictures in a slide show. However, the actual ability of these devices to display pictures varies considerably. Some of the wireless media receivers' software gives you valuable features for controlling a slide show, letting you vary the time displayed, stepping forward and backward through images, and offering remote control of the display through their included remotes and so on.

Personal Video Recorders

Personal Video Recorders (PVRs, also called Digital Video Recorders or DVRs) have been available for a few years as an outgrowth of the video capture and TV tuner component market. ATI, Hauppauge, and others have sold TV tuner boards based on chip sets from manufacturers such as Philips, and mated those tuners with graphics boards. The Gateway Destination PCTV series that

appeared in the late 1990s offered TV display on a large screen CRT monitor, as well as a rudimentary record function. Early models of the Destination shipped with Windows 98 (first edition) and with STB Video Rage II boards. Later models moved to the ATI All-In-Wonder (AIW) integrated tuner/graphics cards.

PROPRIETARY SOLUTIONS: TIVO AND REPLAYTV

The best known PVR on the market today is the TiVo (`www.tivo.com`) player, now in its second series, and shown in Figure 14-13. Companies such as Philips, Sony, and Toshiba license the technology and create PVRs with TiVo branding. The first model TiVo shipped in March 1999, the same month that competitor ReplayTV shipped its first model. SonicBlue's ReplayTV 4000 is another good PVR implementation that differs from TiVo in that it can share recorded programs, as well as provide a commercial skipping feature — features that SonicBlue was forced to defend against litigation from the entertainment industry.

TiVo has the form factor of a set-top box, but is really a Linux computer in disguise. Once people realized that TiVo was a computer, enthusiasts began to open the box and modify it, something the company didn't actively discourage, although it voided the warranty. The early models offered 20- and 30GB drives, with an hour of video equaling about 1GB of storage (depending on the quality of the video you choose). Among the things you can do with your TiVo is to add larger hard drives (up to two), and even add a networking function. TiVo was meant to be a closed solution, not to be networked, and definitely not to be shared, but even in Series 1 workarounds were developed. A Google search on "TiVo hacks" or "TiVo add-ons" will give you some idea of how large this enthusiast community is and what it is doing.

With TiVo you buy a subscription to the TiVo guide service in addition to purchasing the equipment. We believe that the TiVo interface, shown in Figure 14-13, is one of the very best programs ever created on a computer for non-technical users (we have the religion, pass the clicker!). However, the death of TiVo has been regularly predicted by analysts (`www.pcmag.com/article2/0,1759,1550785,00.asp`). Although no competitor has yet captured TiVo's ability to predict desirable content, manage subscription lists (what they call season passes), and present a coherently organized system of finding content, TiVo has not been able to enter the set-top box market. Cable companies are not willing to pay TiVo's subscription rates and have gone a different route for programmed TV features like on-demand services.

Both current models of ReplayTV and TiVo are networkable and can be made into wireless devices. Although in theory you can use 802.11b, it is recommended that you use 802.11g devices for better performance. One site known for selling TiVo upgrades is PTVupgrade.com. It sells its TurboNet network cards for Series 1 with 802.11b capability; g is not supported. This upgrade lets you add telnet, FTP, and TiVo Web browsing to this product. The DVRchive Server and Client tools software has been written that can convert the TiVo video storage format to other formats that you can play on your laptop. Another well-known TiVo site is 9th Tee Enterprises (`www.9thtee.com`) and it sells a wireless Ethernet adapter called the AirNet for Series 1.

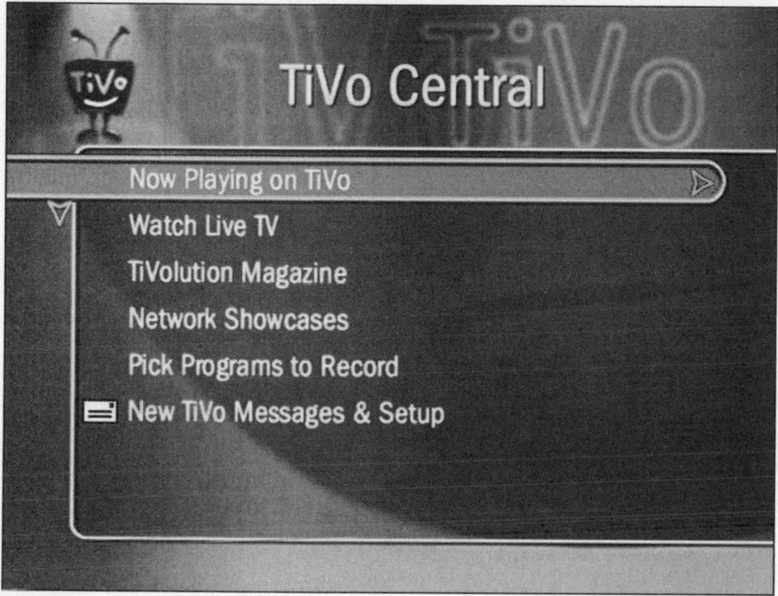

Figure 14-13: TiVo is a remarkably easy-to-use PVR appliance that can only be connected to your entertainment network with some work, as shown by its simple interface.

With Series 2, TiVo added USB to the system and offers the Home Media Option (HMO; `www.tivo-direct.com/tivo-home-media-option1.html`). It is on board new systems, but the software also has been downloaded to earlier Series 2 models. You'd expect it to be straightforward to wirelessly network a TiVo so that it can download program updates from the Internet instead of calling through its internal modem. It is not. First you need version 4.0 of the OS, and TiVo is very sensitive to the wireless adapter you use. ExtremeTech.com has an article on the subject of hooking up a wireless connection (`www.extremetech.com/article2/0,1558,1397309,00.asp`). The more important problem with TiVo's networking implementation is that its wireless file sharing is meant to go between TiVo boxes only; TiVo stores video in its proprietary file format. So if you want to play TiVo files on your laptop, or stream them through another device, you will need to use third-party software to access the files and do the conversion.

To wirelessly network a ReplayTV 5500 series is much easier than TiVo because that system already has Ethernet. First you configure a bridge to connect to your wireless access point or wireless router. You may need to use a crossover cable to do so. Then you connect the ReplayTV to the bridge. If you have more than one ReplayTV, each one will require a bridge of its own. ReplayTV's documentation contains additional details.

COMPUTER-BASED PVRS

If you want to record TV to files that you can move about your network wirelessly, and you don't need the program guide capabilities of the aforementioned appliances, you are better off creating your own computer-based PVR. Microsoft's Media Center 2004 (`www.microsoft.com/windowsxp/mediacenter/default.asp`) has this capability if you want a canned solution. You can purchase computers with this OS from a large number of Microsoft's OEM partners, in desktop, laptop, and even tablet format.

It's just as easy to add a tuner/graphics card in a PC and use software to record to standard video formats. The integrated solution is to buy a single board with both tuner and graphics on the same card, with the best-selling vendor in this area being the ATI Radeon-based All-in-Wonder (AIW) cards. Recent AIW cards come with FM radio, and ATI still sells a PCI version of this card.

Hauppauge also sells quality products with either a tuner only or a combination TV/tuner (and sometimes FM radio) combination. Similar products exist for nVidia-based graphics boards, and they work equally as well. When you use a graphics board/tuner combination, you are essentially installing a TV inside your computer. When you use the tuner for channel control you enable a number of nice features that aren't normally found on TVs, such as channel surfing — the software draws a thumbnail of the TV channels and updates them sequentially. Better yet, because it is PC-based, you can add exactly the wireless capability you need; and these vendors write video in standard file formats such as MP2 so you can play them over a network.

Note

Although ATI All-in-Wonder boards come with DVD-playing software, the boards don't let you record DVDs to disk. A chip on the board is set to prevent you from doing that. All DVD recordable solutions are software-based at the moment, and in the U.S. they are under legal attack from the entertainment industry.

PCTVs that you build yourself require program guides for scheduled recording, and the best of these are Web-based. When you install a Hauppauge WinTV Radio, that product sets up to use TitanTV (`www.titantv.com`), which is shown in Figure 14-14. This is a free service (ads sponsor the service), and you can sign up for TitanTV whether or not you have a tuner that you can control scheduled recordings with. TitanTV has information about programs, sorts and finds, and is a good solution. ATI's AIW uses Gemstar Guide Plus (`www.gemstartvguide.com/`) from the same company that owns *TV Guide*. Neither of these setups is as easy to work with, intuitive, or as sophisticated as TiVo or ReplayTV, but both are solid implementations.

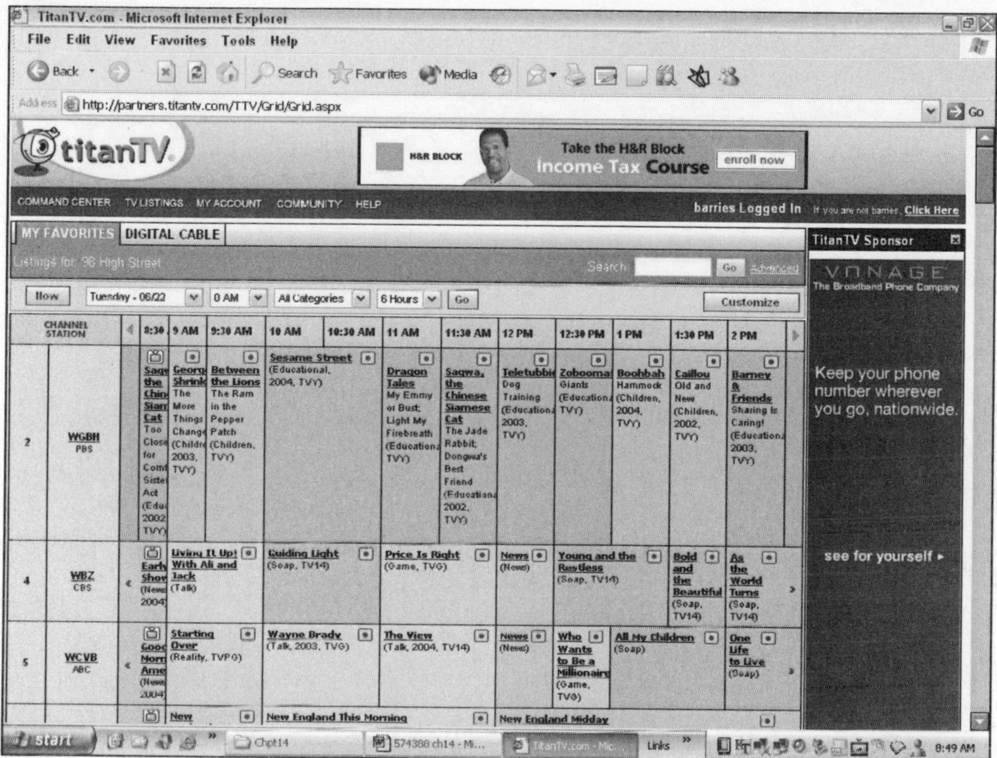

Figure 14-14: The TitanTV Web program guide lets you control a tuner in your computer to schedule recordings

Probably the best software for a PC-based PVR (and our current choice) is SnapStream's BeyondTV! (`www.snapstream.com`). Previously called SnapStream Personal Video Station, BeyondTV! (see Figure 14-15) has the ease of use of a TiVo, a very similar interface, and the ability to control cable boxes in the same manner as a TiVo. Its native program guide in the desktop player isn't as good as TiVo's, but SnapStream offers a program guide in its Web interface that lets you set subscriptions, and that implementation is quite good indeed. What makes SnapStream particularly good is that it writes standard MP2 video files, lets you set many video qualities, and has a number of convenience features that no other PVR has, such as program padding (it can add minutes to the beginning and end of recordings), commercial delineation in the video buffer display, and more. MP2 files not only play in the SnapStream player, but will play in almost any multimedia player such as Windows Media Player. All you have to do is share the folder containing your recorded programs located in your profile and any system that can view your share, like the aforementioned SMC wireless media receiver, has network access to that program. That makes streaming video to your entertainment network about as easy as it is going to get.

You'll find a nice article on homemade DVRs called "Building a Wireless Home Media Network Server" at `www.extremetech.com/article2/0,3973,1276366,00.asp`.

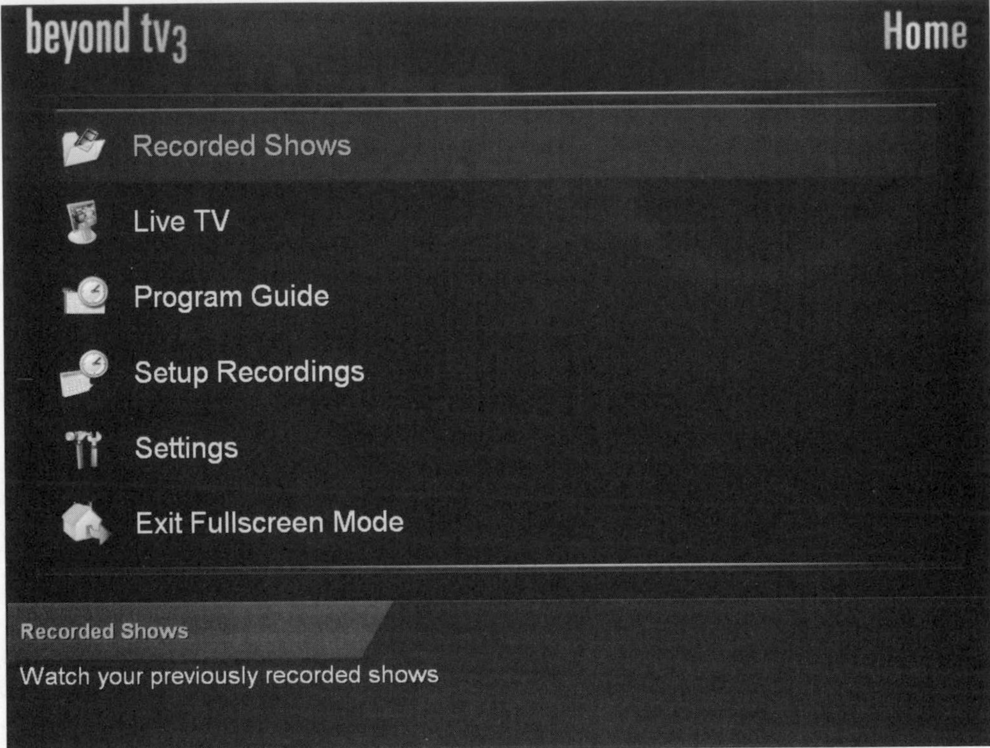

Figure 14-15: SnapStream's BeyondTV! is a particularly good software solution on which to base a PCTV-based PVR networked solution.

Video Files and Formats

Fewer digital video file formats are in use than audio formats, which makes it easier to pick a standard file format to use and stream with it. With the exception of proprietary formats like the ones TiVo uses, most video programs opt for standards to ensure interoperability with playback devices. Digital video on Windows uses the AVI file format, which replaced the older Video for Windows (VFW) format. AVI files are played using DirectShow and are stored with either DV Encoder Type 1 or 2. You need an appropriate CODEC to compress and decompress AVI files. CODECs can be software that you add to your system, an operating system component, part of a chip or hardware solution, or some combination. The CODECs you have installed are listed in the Sounds and Multimedia control panel on the Hardware tab. Windows doesn't come with a DVD CODEC, but when you install a DVD player you get a CODEC that Windows Media Player can make use of. Administrators can also download CODECs from the Microsoft Web site. Among common CODECs are MPEG, Indeo, and Cinepak (for telecommunications).

The first industry-standard video format was MPEG-1, the result of the Moving Picture Experts Group. MPEG-1 is CD-quality video and isn't used by streaming receivers. MPEG-2 (.MPG files) is the video file format used by DVDs and is what is most commonly written by non-proprietary PVR recorders. You can have 720 × 480 resolution with a high picture quality. To record MPEG-2 onto a CD, you can convert the format to SVCD (SuperVideo CD) with only about 20 minutes worth of video content. SVCD is a video CD standard that is meant to be a lower-cost replacement for DVD. The Windows streaming video format is WMF, or Windows Media Format, and it replaces ASF making use of an MPEG-4 encoding scheme. Both Real Video and QuickTime are also streaming video formats. Streaming video formats work by downloading a piece of the video to start playback and fetching more of the file as the buffer is used up.

Let's look at the video file formats supported by common programs and devices:

- **ATI All-in-Wonder:** MPEG-2.
- **SnapStream BeyondTV!:** MPEG-2, Windows Media (.WMV files).
- **D-Link DSM-320:** MPEG-1, -2, and -4, Xvid, QuickTime, and AVI.
- **Windows Media Player:** WF and ASF (Windows Media Files), WMV (Windows Media A/V), the native AVI file format, and MPEG, MPG, MPE, M1V, MP2 and MPV2 formats. You can support additional formats if you add a CODEC for its support.
- **RealOne Player:** MPEG, AVI, WMV, and QT.
- **QuickTime Player:** QuickTime Movie (MOV), MPEG-1, -2 and -4, AVI, DV Stream, and others. QuickTime has probably the most extensive file format support in the industry (see `www.apple.com/quicktime/products/qt/specifications.html` for a complete list).

Few recorders record AVI, opting instead for MPEG or the WMV format. The advantage of the Windows Media format is that its files are smaller than MPEG-2 and of similar quality, and you can stream WMV files over a home network or the Internet. However, WMV requires more computer resources, and for those systems like BeyondTV! that offer time shifting, WMV doesn't allow it, whereas MPEG-2 does. MPEG-2 is the portable solution because you can record it to a DVD and play it in another computer using player software. However, if you intend to view your recorded video on a DVD player you need to use a third party application to burn your recorded content. Products that work with MPEG-2 content are Roxio Easy Media Creator 7 for the PC or Toast Titanium 6 for the Macintosh (`www.roxio.com`), U-Lead's DVD MovieFactory Studio Suite Deluxe (`www.ulead.com/dmf/runme.htm`), TMPEnc dvd Author (`www.pegasys-inc.com/`), and many more.

Integrating Game Consoles into a Wireless Network

Game consoles are for many people what the word "entertainment" in home entertainment networks means. There's a good reason that people want to add high-speed wireless networking to their game consoles. You can create a multiplayer gaming environment when you use a wireless bridge, which allows for more exciting action in game play. You also can move the controller where you need it.

The three main consoles in use today are the Sony PlayStation 2, the Microsoft Xbox, and the Nintendo GameCube. Of the three, only the Microsoft Xbox has made it easy for you to connect your console with built-in networking with an integrated Ethernet controller. To use the Xbox as a wireless device, you need to purchase the $100 Xbox Wireless Adapter MN-740 from Microsoft (www.microsoft.com/hardware/broadbandnetworking/productdetails.aspx?pid=015). This is an 802.11g device that bridges to your Ethernet network, and it is reported that the MN-740 also is easily installed on a PS/2. You'll also find that the wireless adapter is set up to download software updates when they become available. Xbox lets you connect 16 consoles together.

To add the wireless adapter to Xbox, do the following:

1. Go to the Dashboard and select Update to download the latest software.
2. Attach the wireless adapter to your Xbox.
3. Insert your Xbox Live setup CD and configure your account.

The Xbox Wireless Adapter from Microsoft seems particularly easy to install and use by those who have commented on it.

Other vendors also sell wireless bridges for the PS/2 and GameCube game consoles, including LinkSys, D-Link, and SMC. Most of the early devices used the 802.11b.

Here's how you install a wireless network bridge on a PS/2:

1. With the power supply disconnected, remove the expansion cover at the back.
2. Remove the connection cover to reveal the connector for the network adapter.
3. Insert the network adapter and gently tighten the screens.
4. Plug your Ethernet cable into the connector that is under the Network connector label.

You can find complete instructions from Sony at www.us.playstation.com/hardware/SCPH-10281/install.html#config.

There aren't as many reasons to network a GameCube, with very few games that support online multiplayer action. The installation of a networking function in the GameCube is given on the Nintendo Web site at www.nintendo.com/online/bba_setup.jsp.

A good starting place for reading about wireless game console networking is the article by Dave Salvator called "Unwire Your Game Console" at www.extremetech.com/article2/0,1558,1336064,00.asp.

Summary

A home entertainment network isn't normally something you go to a store to buy. Most people start with some component like a hi-fi and then add a TV to it, perhaps adding a home computer next. It doesn't take long before you have numerous devices, some of which may be networked and others of which may not. The desire to view content created on one device on another device is the reason that people try to build home networks. Wireless networking is nearly perfect for sewing together diverse components and solving problems with location and accessibility that are difficult to solve with wired connections.

In this chapter you learned about some of the early wireless devices on the market, some strategies for constructing a home entertainment network, and the kinds of projects that people undertake. You also learned about some of the technical issues that argue for the selection of one device or technology over another one.

A wireless network is part of what could be a strategy of automating other aspects of your home environment. Did you ever want your coffee made for you in the morning automatically? Perhaps not, but who wouldn't want to save money heating and cooling their house, have better home security, get their lawn sprinkler system to come on at the right times and for the right amounts, and have lights turn on where and when they want them? That's all part of our next chapter on making a home smart; and wireless networking technology can play a role there too, as you will see.

Chapter 15

Making Your Home Think

The home of the future probably goes as far back as caveman Smith envying caveman Jones's cave and trying to better him. From Le Corbusier's homes to the Bauhaus school of architecture in the early twentieth century, people want smart homes. But homes that can "think," well, that is something that only the information age could offer.

Most people equate thinking homes with home automation. The 1964 New York World's Fair displayed a "Home of the Future." The Norge Kitchen in the Festival of Gas ground up plastic dishes and cutlery; and washed, dried, and then molded new ones from the pellets. In GE Progressland we were told that nuclear fusion was going to supply limitless energy. DuPont had Mylar stage curtains, Nylon carpets, and Corfam fabrics. This was the "Wonderful World of Chemistry" folks, as the DuPont actors "The Happy Plastic Family." There was the city of the future, GM's Futurama (no gridlock!), the Bell Telephone Picturephone, and the relatively new color television studio at RCA. It was the '60s, Ben, and the word was "Plastics!"

In one pavilion IBM tried to explain mainframe computers based on core memory with theater puppets. It was an era when knowledgeable computer scientists thought that the world might only need a dozen mainframe computers. Go figure.

Had futurists known that computers could be miniaturized with microprocessors, made inexpensive, or that radio frequency devices could replace wires, then they might have predicted that you could control devices in your home. But that was then and this is now. We live in a highly distributed mobile world where wires are an encumbrance.

Home automation is an area where wireless networking can and probably will make a difference. Although it's still in its infancy, we'll look at the current state of the home automation market, the kinds of wireless devices you can buy, and most importantly, the software you can use to control everything. In the next chapter we'll concentrate on older automation technologies such as X10, and how you can use them with your wireless network. For the house that thinks, then Bill, "Software!" is the word.

An Overview of Wireless Home Automation

Home automation means different things to different people, as shown in Figure 15-1. To some people, home automation means pressing a remote button and getting your lights to dim just before you head for the popcorn, or turning off your lights with two claps to the Clapper. To others, automation controls the security system, allows voice activation of a lock, sets the thermostats, or controls a

hi-fi system. Most people tend to take home automation one piece at a time. The most common projects people undertake are automation for the following:

- Lighting fixtures
- Climate control systems
- Phone systems
- Security systems
- Home theaters
- Water sprinklers

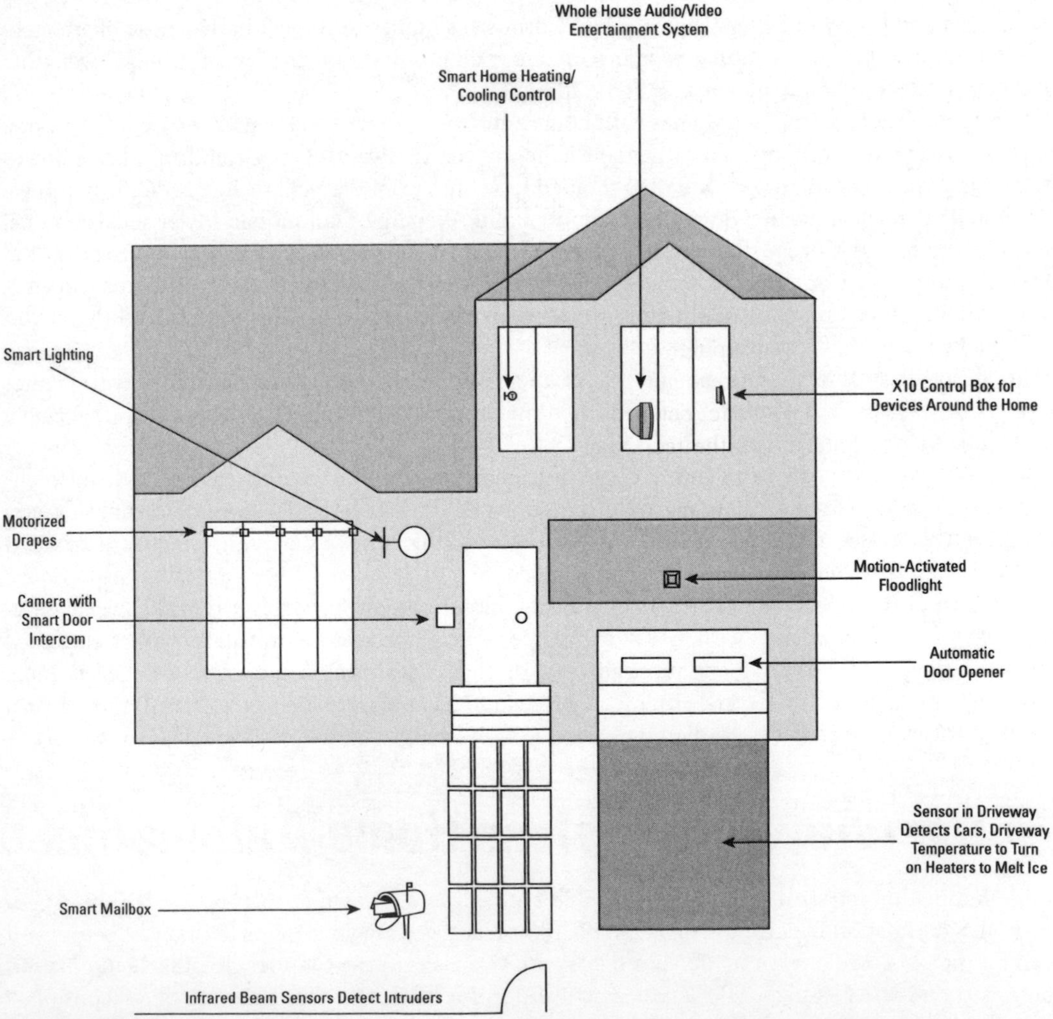

Figure 15-1: Wireless computer networking can be used in home automation projects.

With computers and networks, you can not only turn devices on and off, but you can program logic into your devices so that they are really smart. Given the right place to start, you can tie all of these projects together with control software, improving your house's capabilities over time.

Note

MIT's architecture department has, as one of its research aims, development of smart homes. The MIT Home of the Future Consortium at `http://architecture.mit.edu/house_n/` **provides some great resources for reading more on this topic. One page,** `http://architecture.mit.edu/house_n/web/resources/links/otherhousesofthefuture.html`**, has a history of some past attempts to create smart houses.**

Here's an example of how sophisticated automation works in real life, and how you might apply wireless technology to a problem. Fresh water is a precious resource, and will be even more so in the future. Because much of the water used to irrigate lawns or farms is wasted either by being applied at the wrong time or in the wrong amount, anything that you could do that would make watering more intelligent offers significant savings. This is especially true in desert climates and in many third-world countries.

A system currently in use downloads rainfall data from a weather satellite. Using calculations for your location that take into account factors such as wind speed, humidity, day of the year, and other things, a computer can signal to a sprinkler system when to turn on and for how long. If this sounds like science fiction, it isn't. Golf courses, farmers, and other businesses are currently using satellite downloads to a computer, along with wireless communication to irrigation devices that water fields and lawns. You can get an idea of the current technology by going to two of the vendors' sites at `www.automata-inc.com` and `www.rainbird.com/landscape/products/central/espsite_satellite.htm`. As the technology is getting cheaper, it is being applied to individual homes and home developments.

Perhaps the ultimate smart home is Bill Gates's $97 million home on Lake Washington near Seattle, which took seven years to build. Gates built his house as a test bed for home computer automation. When you visit the Gates's house, you put on a pin that lets sensors around the house track your position. A computer stores information on your likes and dislikes in a profile you've created. As you move about the home, each room's temperature is lowered or raised according to your preferences or to the combined preference of all the people in the room you are in. The computer can play music that you like, set light levels, and can locate you when someone needs to talk with you. The automation changes display panels on the walls, knows what TV shows you have watched, remembers details from your past visits, and learns about you. There's not a lot of information published on the details of the Gates's home automation system, but you can bet that Microsoft's Connected Home initiative has some of the fruits of this project.

Note

You'll find a very nice jump page that lists leading publications, message boards, FAQs, blogs on projects people have done in the area, home automation integrators, and more at both Google (`directory.google.com/Top/Computers/Home_Automation/Vendors`) and at Directory.net (`www.directory.net/Home/Home_Improvement/Automation/`).

The following resources should be useful to you in researching home automation projects:

- **Electronic House** (`www.electronichouse.com`). This is a magazine for the home automation industry.
- **HomeAutomation.org** (`www.homeautomation.org`). This is a directory listing of industry resources.
- **Connected Home Magazine** (`www.connectedhomemag.com`). This site contains project articles, discussion forums, and product listings.
- **Computer Electronics Association** (`www.ce.org`). The CEA is the group that runs the largest consumer electronics trade show and offers news, trends, and forecasts.
- **Smarthome.com** (`www.smarthome.com`). This is a print and online catalog described more fully in the material that follows. Also recommended is ***Automation Tips & Tricks*** (`www.smarthome.com/9354.html`), a book from the Smarhome.com crew.
- **HomeControls.com** (`www.homecontrols.com/cgi-bin/main/co_disp/displ/pgrfnbr/2/sesent/00`). This is an online product catalog.
- **SmartHomeUSA.com** (`www.smarthomeusa.com`). This is an online catalog company specializing in home automation. This catalog lists 161 products in the wireless category.

You can get a sense for where the market for home automation is at the moment by examining the popular catalogs of companies specializing in home automation products. There aren't many catalogs that offer a complete line, but the three good ones are Smarthome.com, HomeControls.com, and SmartHomeUSA.com. Even RadioShack (`www.radioshack.com`) offers products in this area, although not that many. HomeControls doesn't offer software, nor does RadioShack, which carries a line of control devices, but you'll find several in the Smarthome catalog. A good place to start is to see what hardware integrates with the software being offered. Along with the software package Premise from Premise Systems (described later in the chapter), there is the Indigo Home Automation Software for the Macintosh (`www.perceptiveautomation.com/indigo/`) and Control Assistant Plus 5.0. Indigo runs on Mac OS X and controls devices using the X10 protocol. Indigo's programming lets you set numerous commands and use program logic. The Home Control Assistant is meant to work with Smarthome's PowerLinc system of devices and can be used to integrate weather stations and thermostats, and import DXF file floor plans. The product pages describe what devices these packages can control; most rely on X10 devices.

A Plan of Action

Most people get into home automation on a by-project basis. They want their lights to go on and off programmatically while they are away on vacation or visiting the folks, or they see it as a potential savings on their electric bill. Adding wireless technology is their way of bridging this beginning project to the projects that come next. It isn't until later, when their automation is a hodgepodge of technologies, that it occurs to enthusiasts that they should be integrating the whole shooting works.

The problem with home automation technology is that you must integrate widely disparate types of devices, blending today's technology with yesterday's technology. While you wait for the technology to mature and coalesce around emerging standards such as TCP/IP as the wire protocol, some form of secure 802.11x standard that probably hasn't appeared yet, device IDs that may or may not be IPv6 or a radio frequency ID tag (described later), and other less predictable technologies, you need to work in a system that is flexible and can accommodate the types of device technologies you can find today. So here is my recommendation for a plan of action that will allow you do the projects today that you want to do today with an eye on the future.

In order of tasks, do the following:

1. Draw a diagram of your home with the available outlet types (wired, Ethernet, cable connection, and so on) and locations shown.
2. Make a list of the projects you want to do and prioritize that list.
3. Select a software package that will run on your computer system.
4. Start your first project by buying the component you need and the means necessary to connect that component to your computer network. For a close-in wireless connection you will need an access point, and for components farther away you may need a router or a repeater. Connect your components.
5. For designs that involve islands of automation components that are geographically far apart or in different sections of the house that aren't easily connected, consider buying one of the distribution panels available in this market and connecting to that panel using a wireless connection. You may need to find adapters that will convert your networked components from the I/O that they are capable of to what you need to connect to the panel. For a USB device such as a TiVo 2, for example, you will need a USB-to-wireless Ethernet connector, and sources are available for those devices. The manufacturers of distribution panels are a good source of information on how to connect devices into their panels.
6. Program your automation in your software.
7. Test your system and document your work.

Diagramming Your Home

Creating a diagram of your home prior to starting a home automation project offers multiple benefits: doing so gives you an idea of the number of specific devices you need, where they have to be placed, and which projects are going to be physically easier than other ones. Additionally, if you diagram your home you can show that diagram to anyone you contract out part of the project to, or to people with expertise that you talk with so they can better help you with your planning. The diagram doesn't have to be an architectural blueprint, drawn to scale. Distances are important, but more important are the relationships of one device or place to another.

That being the case, it is not surprising that depending on the software you choose, you will likely find that a design module is a significant part of the package. Most of these system approaches to home automation begin with you drawing your home layout in a specialized CAD, or computer aided design program. Actually the approach is usually simpler than most programs and more like drawing in a program such as Visio. Good ones come with a library of shapes that you drag and drop, and some offer specialized tools such as budget creation or access to online manufacturers. Oftentimes the software isn't any more expensive than any other common productivity app. This is a very good reason to take a software-first approach to any home automation project.

When you diagram your home, think in terms of the projects you are interested in. Place the devices you want to control on the diagram starting with the one you are most interested in first. Think in terms of a central location from which you will control your devices, and possibly run your connections from. If you intend to create wireless connections, try to integrate the wireless control of devices into any existing computer network that you have. You should also chart the different types of wiring that you need to accommodate as well as how your wireless devices will interact with one another, and what parts of your home each wireless device covers.

Choosing Your First Project

Some projects are easier than others to bring to successful conclusion. It seems that most people start their home automation projects by controlling the lighting and climate controls in their house. Both are excellent projects because they offer you the possibility to save money on your utilities as well as improve safety features. More complex projects, such as security systems, are best tackled later when you have some experience and know what you want.

Control Software and Systems

Let's assume you are not as rich as Croesus but you still want to automate your house and add conveniences. (Let's further assume that those around you don't mind that you treat your house like a toy.) Chances are that you aren't going to put in an entire system all at once, and that even if you wanted to, more components will become available over time that you'll need to integrate into your automation.

To our way of thinking, then, the best place that you can make your first investment is in the control software or integration system that will serve as your automation framework. We like to think of this as an operating system for a home. Since you want programmable logic and flexibility, you want a control device that has those features. A few remote controls (like the Philips Pronto) are smart enough to program complex macros and routines on. However, our particular preference is to start with a computer-based software solution because that will offer you the most flexibility to accommodate change.

The most important features for any software purchase in the home automation area are

- Ease of use and programmability
- The ability to control all of the device types you wish to automate, including X10 and PC networking
- A modular construction that will allow growth and flexibility over time
- A Web browser control interface
- The ability to manage zones, users, and scenes such as "morning," "nighttime," "vacation," and so on
- Integration with the remote control devices of interest

When you choose the software, make sure that you are comfortable with the programming involved, and that the program interfaces with modules that can control devices that use the important current home networking standards such as X10, Ethernet, 802.11, Z-Wave (described later in this chapter), and other standards.

Because you are trying to build for the future, you want the vendor you're buying from to have some stability so that your software and systems have the longevity to survive. No standard file formats exist for home automation programs that would let you output your programming in the same way that you can output your design work in the DXF format from a program such as AutoCAD and have it work in another CAD program.

If the software you purchase is part of a system like the Premise package that you'll see in a moment, then you can assume that Premise will work with all the automation products you may want to use in your home. If you use a software package from a vendor that isn't providing an integrated hardware/software system, you are going to have to rely on the industry to develop standards that you can use. Most vendors will give you a trial of their software, which may prove useful in your evaluations.

In either case you may find that the software has as one of its main components an integrated design and specification module. If that is the case, you can start your automation planning directly using the software you adopt.

Let's take a look at some of the software products you can buy today, starting with those that the average computer user might want to consider. Premise 2.0 (`www.premisesystems.com/products/`) from Premise Home Control Software was acquired by Latronix and has some significant backers such as Motorola. Its software (see Figure 15-2) comes in two versions, a Personal Edition ($200) and a Dealer Edition ($979), with the main difference being the amount of connectivity you have. Premise software runs on Windows 2000 SP2 or higher, and the Premise Home Control Browser needs either Internet Explorer on a client (800 × 600 screen resolution), Windows CE 3.0 or later for Web pads, or a Pocket PC 2002 or later.

With Premise, you can do the following things:

- Distribute audio through a house over an IP network, selecting what you want with the Premise Browser

- Set up a user-friendly interface using a selection of visual themes and custom sounds, and fit your interface to different screen sizes
- Connect to and control devices from thousands of devices (see `www.premisesystems.com/products/supporteddevices.html`) controlling your audio system, your climate controls, cameras, and other things

Premise is automatically updated (even remotely), and can be extended by developers using the .NET programming language, making use of remote server capabilities and client access.

A number of modules exist to support Premise, including a SerialPort to 802.11b Wireless Ethernet Server. With Premise you can build a screen with your desired functionality and download the control to a mobile device or to a remote control like the Philips Pronto. You can also control your house from a PC.

What's nice about Premise is that it is loaded with wizards and has a relatively easy-to-use IDE (Integrated Development Environment). If you can wrap your head around programming in Visual Basic, Premise should seem easy.

Similarly, Indigo and Control Assistant Plus (see Figure 15-3) are aimed at the enthusiast market. Control Assistant Plus is particularly easy to use and inexpensive. Control Assistant has a set of wizards that walk you through programming your entire house.

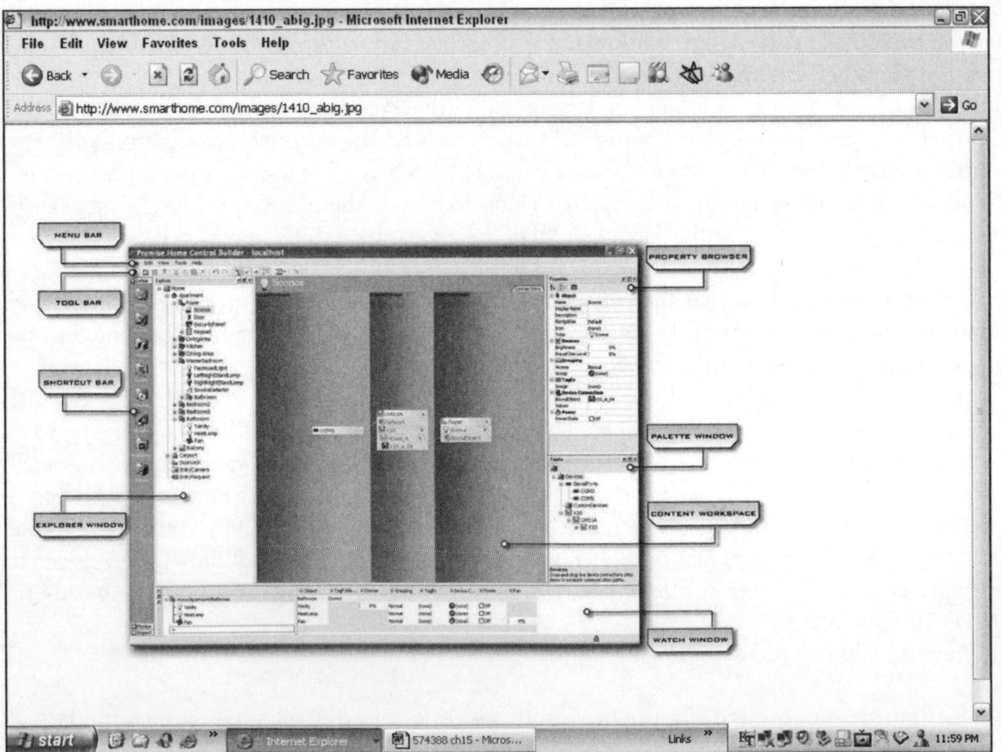

Figure 15-2: Premise is a complete development environment for home automation aimed at the home automation enthusiast and at integrators.

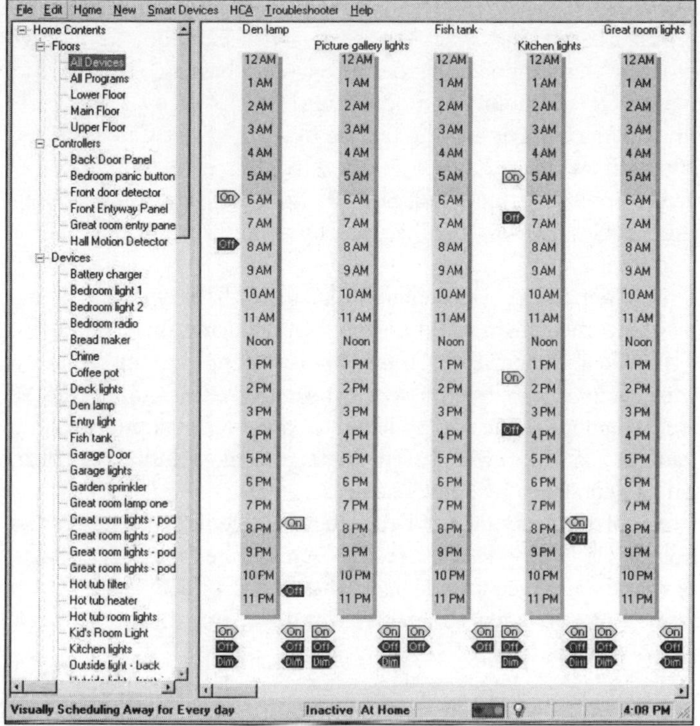

Figure 15-3: Home Control Assistant offers a straightforward graphical, wizard-based approach for home automation that is meant for the average knowledgeable computer user.

Simplicity isn't the rule for many other systems used to create smart buildings or homes for the integrator community. Integrators working on smart homes have had to choose from expensive systems from vendors such as AMX (`www.amx.com`) and Crestron Electronics (`www.crestron.com/`) in order to create the type of advanced system automation that Premise mostly allows. Both AMX and Crestron are powerful programs and have been used to build many stable systems for large projects and expensive home setups.

Note

You'll find a very nice listing of complete home automation systems on the Home-Automation.org Web site at `http://home-automation.org/Complete_Systems/`. It covers the entire range of products from novice to advanced and from proprietary to open. To view the software list by operating system, go to `http://home-automation.org/Software/`.

Another approach to the problem of smart home control leverages the Internet services offered by a company called Xanboo (`www.xanboo.com/aboutus/press.htm`). With Xanboo, developers create a program in their technology using the Xanboo SDK to create a Web-based command and control that clients can use. Xanboo claims its technology is modular and that its Web services platform is mission critical. You can also buy a line of devices from Xanboo that includes CCTV cameras, wireless sensors, controls, thermostats, and switches. Xanboo uses a 418 MHz wireless transceiver technology that can bridge to a variety of protocols including 802.11, X10, UPNP, CEBus, RS485, PLC, and Lonworks. A USB card, the Xanboo gateway, can be used for systems requiring DSL or cable modem access.

The average enthusiast wouldn't use Xanboo; it's too demanding. However, service providers, broadband operators, and other large companies might build device support using this technology. You'll find Xanboo technology in the Shell HomeGenie Home Management System, where a Motorola wireless gateway bridges your cable modem to your wireless Xanboo CCD Color or B&W MultiCam cameras through a Xanboo 4-Camera Sequential Switcher as one of their options (`www.shellhomegenie.com/`). The advantage of a browser-based management solution is clear. Anywhere you can pop a browser you can control your home's devices.

Another Windows-based automation software and device technology that gets mentioned in the trade press is from HomeSeer Technologies (formerly Keware Technologies). The HomeSeer system can work with both X10 and Z-Wave (see the next section) devices, and with products using Lutron RadioRA or Lightolier controllers. HomeSeer software is a Web-based product that allows: scheduling, scripting, conditionals, and e-mail notification.

Device Control

The vast majority of control software is made to work with the X10 protocol. We'll describe X10 in much more detail in the next section; suffice it to say here that X10 is a wiring protocol that is meant to run over power lines. There are no X10 wireless devices that work directly with an 802.11x network today, and few devices that can provide the translation from X10 to 802.11x wireless technology. What we have at the moment are mostly X10 on/off switches, and conversion devices to talk to those switches. The wireless technologies that exist for the home automation market have been developed by the home automation industry vendors. They are proprietary solutions, meant to work with only a specific chipset over a very particular set of frequencies and supported by limited numbers of software products. At the moment this isn't a particularly large area of consumer interest.

We've mentioned the Z-Wave protocol, which is supported in a couple of programs mentioned in the previous section. Z-Wave is a narrow bandwidth (9.6 Kbps) wireless protocol and wireless chip technology from Zen-sys (`www.zen-sys.com/`). Z-Wave is a bi-directional read and control system, and is meant to successfully compete with X10. You can't use Z-Wave for transferring files or rich media because of its narrow bandwidth, but you can use it to wirelessly control systems at a fraction of the price and power that broadband wireless transmission allows.

Z-Wave is unique because it offers a technology that is distributed and redundant. Any Z-Wave-enabled device that receives a message also broadcasts it. Therefore any device that fails is only one break in a web of redundant signal paths. Because Z-Wave is a narrowband technology, this system requires very little power to run and is both economical and can be miniaturized.

The Zen-sys product line offers a set of integrated transceiver chips. Other vendors use their Z-Wave chip technology and embed them in a variety of devices for both home and business. You'll find Z-Wave applications in appliances, lighting, HVAC, access systems, security, and automation. A number of software products support the Z-Wave technology, and when a manufacturer adds the Z-Wave device to its appliance, that makes that appliance networkable. A Z-Wave command is sent using the Z-Wave signal to each device in the network, thus ensuring full zone communication. Z-Wave uses error checking techniques to make sure that the signal is received. Sylvania sells a Z-Wave two-part connection kit with a controller and plug for $150.

802.11x Wireless Devices

The lack of 802.11x wireless sensors and control devices means that you are at the mercy of appliance and device manufacturers to add this capability to their devices. Alternative solutions such as wireless bridges that add the connection for an Ethernet-enabled device are too expensive to distribute throughout the house. For complete wireless automation you are forced (at the moment) to bridge to X10 or another home automation standard. So until these wireless controls appear on the market, anyone wanting to build home automation around their wireless network really has to kludge the current technology or wait for vendors to build it in.

Wireless devices based on computer networks' 802.11x technologies have not appeared in great numbers. Given the number of wireless laptops and home wireless networks it is reasonable to expect that there will be an explosion of such devices in the next few years. For any device that has Ethernet built in, you can control that device by attaching an Ethernet-to-wireless bridge, like the D-Link DWL-810+ (see Figure 15-4). This will solve the problem for any appliance that can take an IP address, but at $60 a shot for the bridge, this technology is still a little too expensive to be used on individual lighting features. When you buy into one of the current generation of control systems described in the previous section, you can often find an X10-to-802.11 adapter as an option in their system.

Figure 15-4: The D-Link DWL-810+ wireless-to-Ethernet bridge lets you add wireless capabilities to any device that has built-in Ethernet.

We are starting to see some of these adapting wireless devices appear on the market. Recently a couple of Wi-Fi/USB "keychain" adapters have appeared. They are of interest because USB offers more connectivity than a single PC Card slot, and keychain devices are likely to be more durable. You can plug in a USB device without having to use a program to remove the card slot contents, and they are plug and play. Simply plug it into the USB connection and it will detect an 802.11 signal. D-Link's DWL-122 (`www.dlink.com/products/?pid=175`) will support both Windows and Mac OS X and costs $40. Netgear's MA111 is a similar product. Both offer USB 1.1 support and 802.11b connectivity with a 300-foot range.

WLANs and Distribution Panels

A better use of current 802.11 technology is as a WLAN bridge between your software control system and a connection box for X10 controllers and other device types located in parts of your home where it isn't possible or convenient to run wires. HAI, QuickNetworks, SuperPro, and others sell distribution panels that accept 802.11b and distribute the signal to controlled components. These panels can be quite pricey — the QuickNetworks offering is $700, the HAI OmniPro II Automation Controller is $1,250, while the SuperPro Series distribution panel retails for $14,000 and is meant for larger scale applications. At the lower end for small- and medium-sized homes you can purchase the OmniLT Controller for $330 and the Omni II Controller for $750 (see Figure 15-5).

These panels support a veritable alphabet soup of protocols, including:

- UPnP
- HomeRF
- HomePNA
- PLC
- Echelon
- Lonworks
- CEBus
- Lone Wolf

The QuickNetworks distribution panel will accommodate the following:

- CAT3
- CAT5E
- CAT6
- RG-59
- RG-6 and other cabling

You'll also find that some panels support sound and video I/O as well with the ability to add additional cards to support multiple systems. More importantly, you can purchase software to control the devices attached to some of these distribution panels and controllers. For example, you can purchase HAI's Web-Link Software for $280 for the OmniPro Controller that will let you manage your devices with any Web browser. Meant to support homes of greater than 3,000 square feet, this software supports 64 Omnistat thermostats, 176 temperature sensors, and 99 users, with up to 1,500 lines of programming code. Figure 15-5 shows one of the less expensive models of the OmniPro series, something you might use for a larger home.

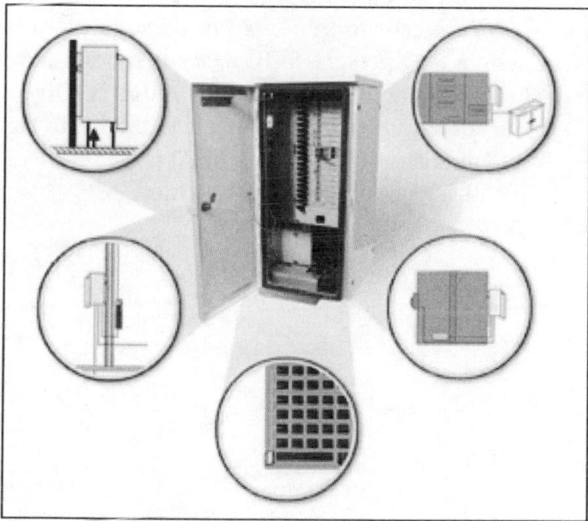

Figure 15-5: Distribution panels are good investments to make when you have to create a wireless connection to a set of wired devices in an area of your home that can't be connected by a wire.

Identification and Access

The ideal identification for any wireless device that you want to network to your computer is an IP address. Although some of the devices we've mentioned come with IP addresses, most do not, and perhaps never will. That's not for lack of trying mind you, because people are hard at work miniaturizing the components needed for IP access so they can be placed anywhere. One University of Massachusetts project reduced a Web server to the size of a matchstick head. Numerous companies are working at reducing the size of a TCP/IP stack for a world that is predicted by 2010 to have 95 percent of the devices connected to the Internet be things other than computers.

To be introduced successfully as a universal and mass-marketed device, ID components must be easy to manufacture and inexpensive. Put aside for the moment that IPv4 is pretty much tapped out as a method for assigning IP addresses and that the world needs to switch over to IPv6 in order to be able to make your light fixture a node on your network. Except for major appliances that need control, most of the things we want to have information about don't really need a control function as much as a simple identification scheme.

That's where the technology of Radio Frequency Identification tagging (see Figure 15-6) comes in. As Patrick Dixon of Global Change writes (`www.globalchange.com/rfids.htm`), there will be 10 billion of these tags produced in the next ten years and applied to everything from airport luggage to the family pet. Delta Airlines ran a test late in 2003 on 40,000 pieces of luggage tagged with RFID tags and was able to achieve an accuracy rating of 96.7 percent to 99.9 percent tracking luggage through its system. That compares to the current system's 80 percent to 85 percent success rate, leading one to predict that the technology could become standard in the airline industry. Dixon reports that Wal-Mart, Tesco, and the U.S. Pentagon are all requiring their suppliers to be able to tag their products with RFIDs in the future, while recent demonstrations of using RFID tagged devices in the Microsoft Connected Home project indicate that it's a technology worth watching.

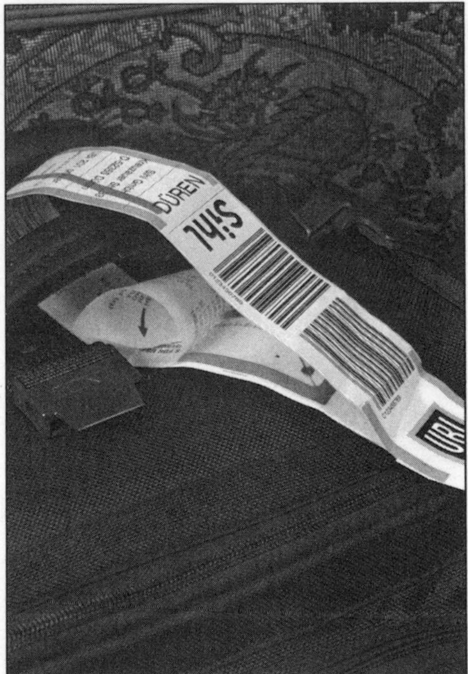

Figure 15-6: RFIDs will allow wireless identification of a vast number of devices in the next few years — in this case, an airport luggage tag.

An RFID is equivalent to a radio bar code. It is a small CPU that can communicate bi-directionally with short bursts of data over a distance of about 6 feet (2 meters) to a base station. Reportedly these tags could last as long as 100 years. RFIDs have been used in Swatch watches, ski passes, and the London Underground since 1997. An RFID currently costs around 25 cents to manufacture, but Dixon says that by 2005 they will cost around 5 cents, and perhaps less over time. In about 10 years he predicts that the industry will manufacture 20 to 40 billion tagged products ***each*** year. The technology exists to manufacture 10 billion RFID tags using a single room-sized processing plant.

With known identities RFIDs offer not only precise tracking, but traffic management, audit control, and almost innumerable applications. As Bill Machrone writes in the July 13, 2004 issue of ***PC Magazine*** (`www.pcmag.com/article2/0,1759,1613366,00.asp`), while the technology offers many different kinds of benefits it does pose serious potential privacy issues. Putting aside the curious stories that circulate about RFID'ing the eye of Hamilton on the $20 bill, RFIDs have a number of other issues such as security; they are apparently easy to compromise.

One technology under early development today is based on the U.S. Pentagon's plan to deploy "smart dust" sensors or "Motes." The DARPA project, started in 1999, is being worked on by more than 100 research groups around the world with a center for the research at University of California–Berkeley and at Intel. With open source Motes running the TinyOS operating system and the TinyDB database, the idea is to seed a battlefield with these sensors and have any movement of troops monitored. The system is designed to be a self-organizing smart network that filters information, only sending on events that are significant.

If smart dust sounds like science fiction, it is not. The Internet must have sounded like science fiction in the 1970s when DARPA funded a fault tolerant distributed network of computers that could withstand nuclear attack; or when the GPS satellites were opened up to commercial applications. So it's easy to believe that the sensors that will be created in the smart dust project will show up in medical applications (sensors in our bodies), in objects that need to be catalogued (books in a library), or items in the home (bottles of milk in the fridge). Sensors may be a more elegant solution to the problem of identifying objects, and more importantly controlling them; but they are probably a decade away from their widespread introduction.

Wireless Appliances

At the moment it feels to many of us as if the application of wireless control home automation is a solution waiting for a problem. Few of us care much about pressing a remote button and having our coffee automatically ground and brewed.

Important applications of home automation are on the horizon, however. Many futurists believe that the home of the future will be an energy source in a distributed power generation network. Perhaps there will be a solar solution, perhaps it will be wind power or river power (how quaint!), or some sort of recycler system like the atomic one Dr. Emmett Brown (Christopher Lloyd's character) used in the ***Back to the Future*** movies to jump through time. Most likely a home's future energy sources will be some combination of the aforementioned, intelligently managed by a home computer system on a network. Who knows? Home automation will play a role in sensing the condition of your home, managing climate, optimizing the performance of your appliances, and integrating various security and communication systems.

Several wireless 802.11 products are on the market today, so let's take a brief look at the categories that are best represented.

Wireless Home Security and Lighting

The largest categories of automated wireless home (or building) devices are probably security cameras and streaming media servers. You've seen streaming media servers in the previous chapter, so you know that this is a developing area of vendor and consumer interest. Security devices have long held out an interest to a variety of customers: banks, large residential buildings, prisons, ATM booths, and residential homes. This is a big market, and since you need cameras in locations that aren't easily wired, there are many examples of wireless cameras and mature software for use on the market today.

For example, D-Link sells Internet cameras (`www.dlink.com/products/category.asp?cid=60`) that provide Web-based access for remote security monitoring. The cameras come with bundled software that lets you record up to 16 of these cameras' output to a hard drive, and can be set up to allow for motion detection triggers. Some models pan and tilt, transmit input audio signals, and capture high-quality color and still images. You have a lot of choice when it comes to buying wireless cameras. Other companies selling this technology are Linksys and Veo's Wireless Observer series (`www.veo.com/Observer-Wireless/default.asp`; see Figure 15-7), among others.

You can buy whole wireless systems for home security, either from integrators or directly from the vendors themselves. There are many examples, of which Honeywell's Wireless Home Security and X10 Automation Kit ($99) is but one. The kit contains a control panel, PC software, some cables and sensors, a keychain remote control, transformer/powerline interface, telephone connection and jack splitter, and even a carbon monoxide sensor. Honeywell's system is low cost, but lets you add additional sensors, control panels, a remote voice dialer monitoring system, an X10 upgrade kit, and other things. All these kits are $20 to $70, and most are in the $50 range. Honeywell's product is aimed at the home do-it-yourselfer.

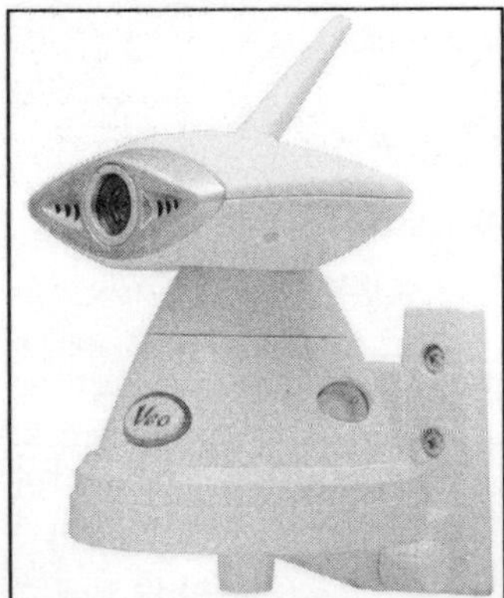

Figure 15-7: Many examples of wireless security cameras are available on the market, similar to the Veo Wireless Observer series shown here. Security home automation is the most mature of all the home automation technologies.

Another product in this category is the Shell HomeGenie Starter Kit - Internet Home Management System, a $600 product that is based on the Xanboo system. This product is a combination gateway, wireless camera, power switch, and contact sensor. You'll find wireless technology crops up in products that are meant for deployment outside a home—for example, weather detectors. Oregon Scientific sells a weather station product line that wirelessly connects to a display panel, but not to a PC.

Although there are security products that you can wirelessly connect up, almost no lighting and appliance control products exist that are wireless. The world of wired lighting and appliances is dominated by the X10 standard, and what remote control devices exist tend to be IR devices. For example, many software programs control lighting using a device such as the X10PC Pro Programmable Interface for Lighting and Appliance Control, a $40 grounded AC socket that connects your PC's serial port to the power outlet on the wall. Using this communications device over your power line, X10 switches throughout your house can be controlled. This particular product also comes with X10 management software.

The Kitchen of Tomorrow

Edward Driscoll, writing in Electronic House (`www.electronichouse.com/default.asp?nodeid=2023`), describes the kitchen of tomorrow as containing a "food network" to which large appliances are connected. Giving these appliances the ability to inventory and search their contents means that you would waste less food, be able to create automated food order and delivery systems, modify an oven's performance to optimize a certain recipe that you store in your computer, or make your refrigerator and freezer use less energy. Automated food and supply replenishment systems could save people a few hours a week and might result in some savings in cost because subscribers could be part of a larger group of purchasers.

Clearly the kitchen of tomorrow won't be melting plastic plates and cutlery to clean them anytime soon. Your kitchen, however, may turn out to be an important information node on your home network, one that offers numerous automation opportunities. In the Microsoft Connected Home initiative (see Figure 15-8) one of the areas under research is the smart kitchen. In Microsoft's version of the smart home, connected appliances can read bar codes and RFIDs to inventory and control items in their domain. Thus you would have microwaves that automatically set their own cooking cycles based on content (no popcorn button to push), refrigerators that do the shopping for you, a grocery list that gets updated for you to read on your mobile device (Windows CE, of course) at the store, and other amenities.

Summary

Home automation has been a reality for some time now, but it's been the domain of specialists in home automation. Protocols such as X10 and other proprietary systems are capable, but limited in their support, their programmability, and the ability of average people to afford them. Networking, and in particular wireless networking, promises to mate the power of personal computers and mass-marketed software with a new generation of control devices.

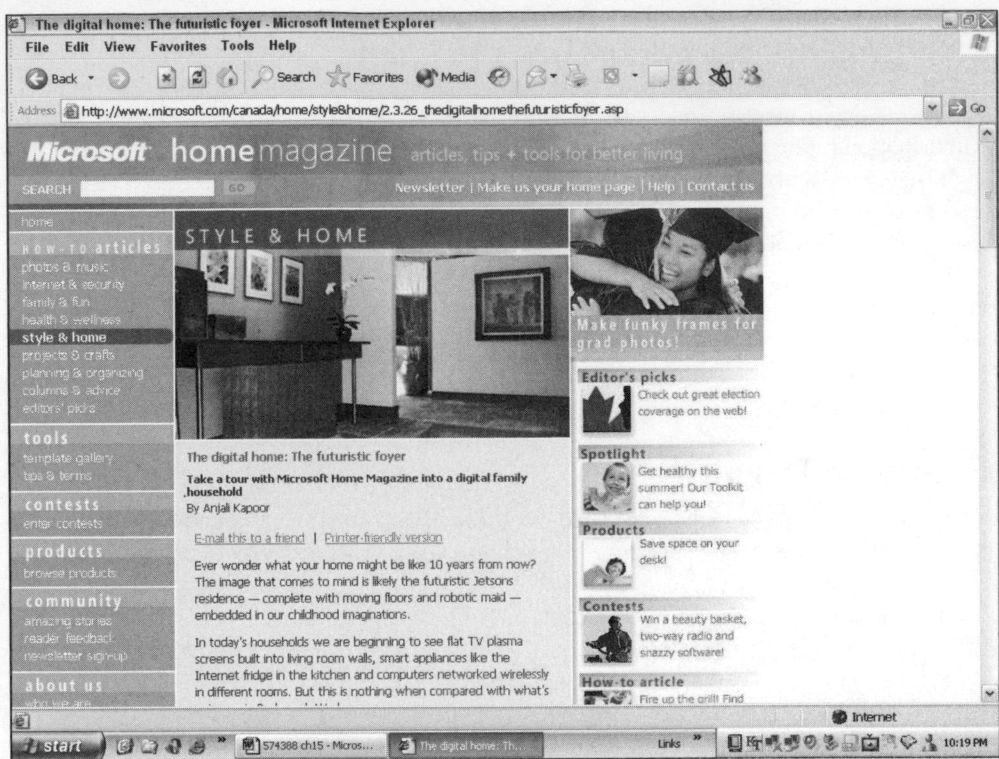

Figure 15-8: Microsoft's Connected Home initiative and its associated Web site offer a glimpse of one set of visions of near-future home automation technologies.

In this chapter we described how you might go about controlling devices in your home. You learned about the central role that software can play in your projects, and some of the capabilities they offer you. A smart home blends wireless technology with wired technologies and must be flexible enough to accommodate new devices.

In the next chapter you learn about the different types of remote controls that are on the market. Some of these remotes are souped-up versions of individual button remotes, most offer learning features, and some are fully programmable, allowing you to create completely designed touch-screen interfaces. Although many of these remote controls are meant for system integrators, many are now available for the average knowledgeable consumer. Real men and real women love their remotes, and in the next chapter you learn what features are desired and how to eliminate "clicker madness."

Chapter 16

Remote Controls and Other Devices

For many years, programmable universal remotes have been the province of high-fidelity enthusiasts. Complex, pricey, and difficult-to-program programmable remotes held little interest for most people. It was hard to reconcile a $200 price for an all-in-one when you could simply replace a remote control for any device for as little as $15, or purchase a limited code-based combination remote for under $30. The installation of home theater, the unbelievable proliferation and growing complexity of single-purpose remotes, and automated control systems such as X10 devices have changed a lot of people's minds about investing in a complete solution.

Today you can buy a decent universal programmable remote for as little as $50 that will control up to eight controllable devices with relatively easy macro programming. More complex remotes in the $100 to $150 price range offer features such as editable button labels, punch-through buttons (volume and channel controls that work for two or more of the same devices), Web setup, more programmability, better ergonomics, and numerous other features that you may find appealing. Still more expensive remotes are full-fledged PDAs in their own right. You'll find remotes in the $200 to $700 range that will let the user program them with a completely customized screen, customized buttons, and customized routines. Although these remotes are really meant for home theater system installers, the setup routines are simple enough that many enthusiasts find them valuable and terrific fun to use. A look at the higher end in this device category is an exercise in the best that the graphical user interface can offer.

In this chapter we take a short look at the development of the remote control from a historical perspective. You'll learn about a few of the significant historical remotes, what drives this market forward, and most importantly what makes one remote better than another. The determination of good, better, and best is certainly in the eye of the beholder. For the device owner or the person who programmed the remote, a little complexity is a small price to pay for a lot of control. However, with great power comes great responsibility, and those significant others, guests, and complete strangers who also have to use the remote control need to be accommodated.

So find a very comfortable couch, grab a bag of potato chips, and get your twitching finger ready. You are about to take control over your environment. Can life get any better than this?

Remotes Through the Years

The remote control is a child of the electronic age. Prior to the 1940s, remote controls existed only as prototypes in military applications. By some accounts they first appeared in German remote control motor boats in World War I.

What really fueled the commercialization of remote controls was the introduction of the television set. The Zenith Radio Corporation played a prominent role in the development of early remote controls. The first commercial TV remote that appeared may have been the single-button wired remote control called the Lazy Bone (how appropriate!) in 1950. Zenith followed up in 1955 with a wireless remote called the Flash-matic that shined light onto four photocells at each corner of the TV screen. Later in 1956 the Zenith Space Command used ultrasonic signals to six vacuum tube components in the TV, which made the Space Command very expensive, increasing the price of the TV by 30 percent. In the mid-1960s, the introduction of the transistor dramatically lowered the price of the Space Command so that more than nine million of them were sold. It wasn't until the early 1980s that infrared TV remotes replaced ultrasonic ones. Zenith also developed the first track ball remote control called the Z-Trak, to emulate a computer mouse.

TV was not the only market for remote controls. In 1954 the Alliance Manufacturing Co. released a radio controlled garage door opener called the Genie, a one-button remote, and the system was so well received that the company is now called Genie. These early controls were relatively simple; each remote had an ID code that set the frequency of the signal. You set the frequency in the receiver unit to match by setting a set of DIP switches on the circuit board, a system still in use today.

By the late 1980s, programmable remote controls started to appear, and the technology had largely switched over to infrared signals. With combination remotes, you could enter a device code ID and have one remote serve the function of several remotes. A significant milestone was reached in the late 1990s, when Marantz released the RC2000 remote for its higher-end audio receivers. The RC2000 was an important product because it not only offered a programmable remote, but it was a learning remote as well. You could program the RC2000 by taking other remotes and detecting the signal they emitted for each specific function. There were also limited screen editing features. The RC2000 was released to such rave reviews that Marantz sold a very significant number of these remotes as stand-alone units. The RC2000 influenced many products on the market today, and the RC series continues on at Marantz.

It became important for any higher-end audio/video component manufacturer to deliver a quality remote with expensive stereo receivers and TVs by the mid- to late-1990s. In 1998 Microsoft and Harman/Kardon developed a fully programmable remote called the Take Control (based on the Windows CE operating system), which sold for $349 and was unique when it was introduced. The Take Control, which appeared as several other brands and names (Madrigal IRIQ and the JBL TC1000) offered a superior ergonomic design as well as PC software for customization of the remote. Microsoft's software was especially good and its Setup Wizard got you going by setting up the main devices in an entertainment system using the large library of manufacturer IR codes. The learning feature allows the Take Control to control any IR remote control device, and is easy to use.

The year 1998 was a seminal one for programmable learning remotes, because it was also the year that the Philips Pronto TS 1000, shown in Figure 16-1, was released. Philips bought Marantz USA in

1980 from Marantz Japan and held the company until 2001 when it was again resold back, so they gained a lot of expertise in remote making. Philips' Pronto was a touch screen remote with fully programmable buttons. Its programming was more difficult than the Take Control, but also more powerful. The Pronto series continues on and its features are found in later models of the Marantz RC series such as the RC5200.

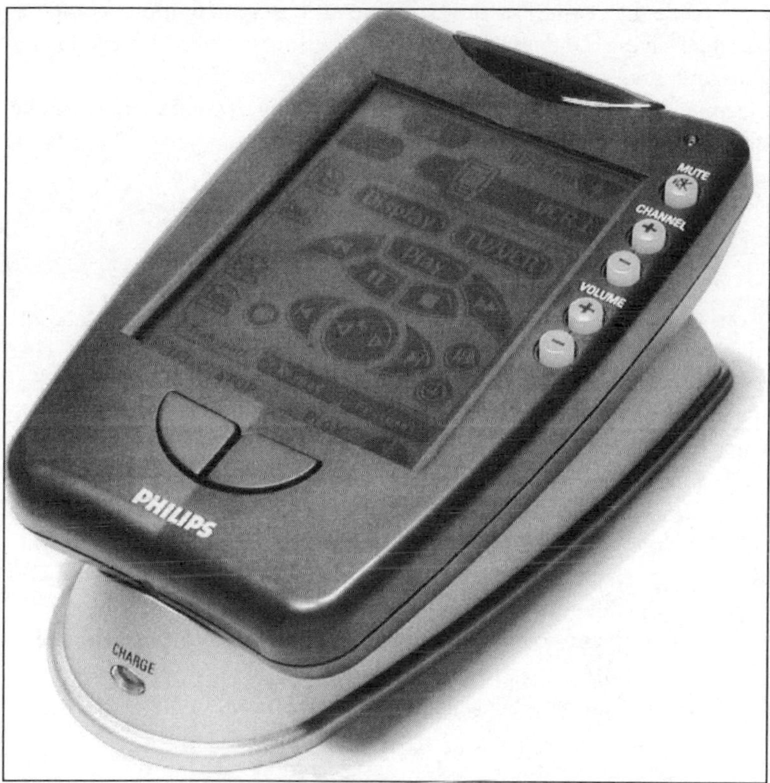

Figure 16-1: The Philips Pronto TC1000 was the first of a line of high-end remotes that set the standard for advanced home theater systems.

Note

Vintage entertainment equipment lives on at eBay. You can find all of the remotes described in this section being traded there. Software is still available for them, and although there are equally good modern components, these remotes hold their own against many others.

What's Important in a Remote

We've owned many remote controls throughout the years; the vast majority sit buried somewhere in a drawer. Although for years, we resisted purchasing a learning remote because of the price, we were one day struck down with a case of "clicker madness," replacing our current crop of remotes with a single Home Theater Master MX-700. Although you can hardly say that a programmable clicker can change one's life, it's definitely made life easier as our equipment has gotten more complex. Surrounded by Luddites as we are, it saves countless trips to turn things on and off. As Steve Jobs is reported to have said: "Save a second, save a life."

The single most important feature is usability: ***ease of use and programming***. A combination remote that isn't easy to use isn't worth having. The best remotes come in two flavors:

- Classic push button remotes
- Touch screen remotes

The argument for selecting one of these two types over the other is as follows. A classic push button remote already has all of the buttons on it that people familiar with remote controls expect. That makes it easier to match up buttons from one device's remote to the buttons on your universal remote. On the other hand, if you need a remote that will manage many systems, including a whole home, then a fully programmable touch screen–based remote is the way to go.

The second important feature is ***reliability***. No remote is going to survive constant abuse. Trust us; we know this for a fact. We've owned four of the MX-500 remotes (a particular favorite), three of which were destroyed by small people. The MX-500 is in fact a very ruggedly built remote. Unfortunately you can't know what the reliability of a remote is until you've had it a while, but you can read comments people have left for different remotes online (we'll get to that in a moment). Battery life and signal strength are also factors to consider. You can improve both through the use of better batteries, repeater systems, and so forth.

This is the essential list of automation features a quality remote should have:

- Access to a large library of device codes from which to assign a mode of your remote
- The ability to create macro buttons that perform two or more actions at once
- A punch-through feature that will let volume and channel controls work for multiple devices
- A strong learning capability, the ability to emulate ***any*** IR device's signals

On the list are some optional features:

- A manufacturer that's been around a while and offers a reasonable warranty
- A method for saving all of your device's programming

- Setup using a software program
- Firmware that can be upgraded
- A TV guide programming feature

Don't even think about purchasing a remote that doesn't have the essential features. Personally, we prefer to set up a remote by computer. Many remotes don't require that and can be programmed directly from the keys, as is the case with the MX-500. One step up the line, the MX-700, the programming moves to a software program (shown in Figure 16 2) that is not only faster and more convenient, but it also stores all settings. The MX-700 also comes with a second, dumbed-down remote that you can give to other users who aren't familiar with your custom settings. The MX-500 isn't particularly hard to set up (it takes an hour or two), but having had to do it three times for the same system is a little much. The MX-500 has a clone feature; it will beam its settings from one MX-500 to another, but you have to have two working remotes to make it work. So a system that saves settings, even if it's on the Web, is a good thing.

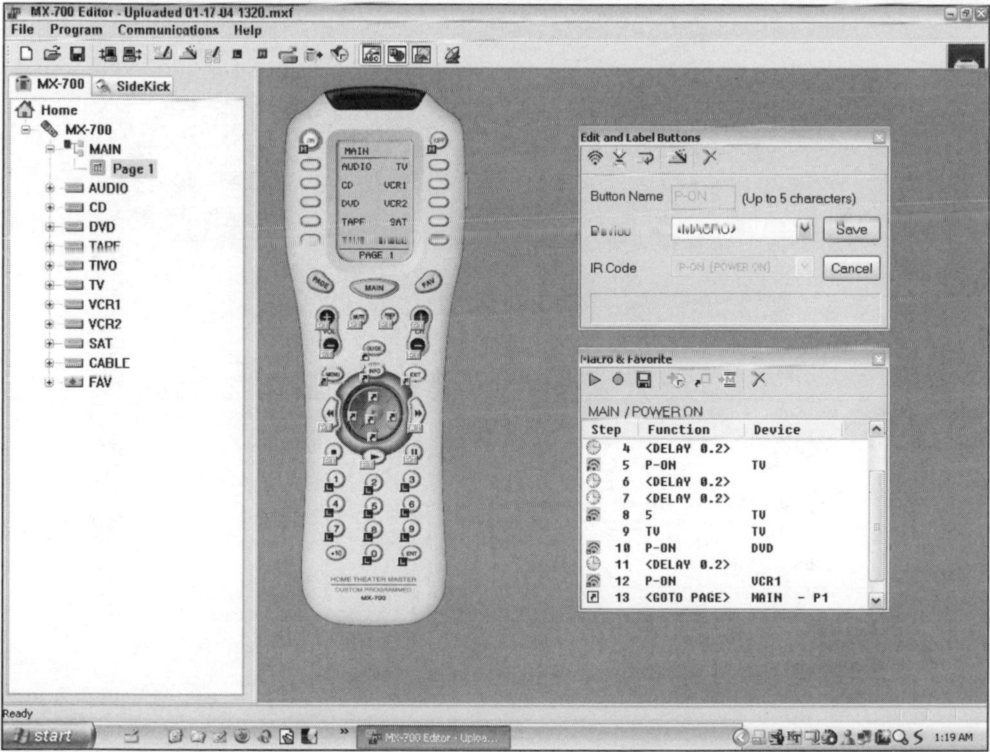

Figure 16-2: The MX-700's software setup program. The MX-700 is aimed at system installers who can set up a single system and then clone it.

If you want to read about remotes from an authoritative source, go to RemoteCentral.com, shown in Figure 16-3. This site gives you in-depth analyses of nearly every remote available for the home theater market, and a few of the remotes for the home automation market. A review is simply one person's opinion. What makes RemoteCentral.com special is its user forums. You can get a really good idea for how good a remote is by reading those reviews, learning about each remote's quirks, features, and reliability from actual users. We think that RemoteCentral.com is miles ahead of any other place we've seen talk about remote controls.

Of the remotes we've worked with and from the reviews that we've read, we recommend the following remotes to you: The Home Theater Master MX-500 and MX-700, the Kameleon 8 URC 9960 shown in Figure 16-4 (and its Radio Shack equivalent), the Intrigue Technologies Harmony H780 (formerly the SST-768), the Philips Pronto, and Marantz RC series.

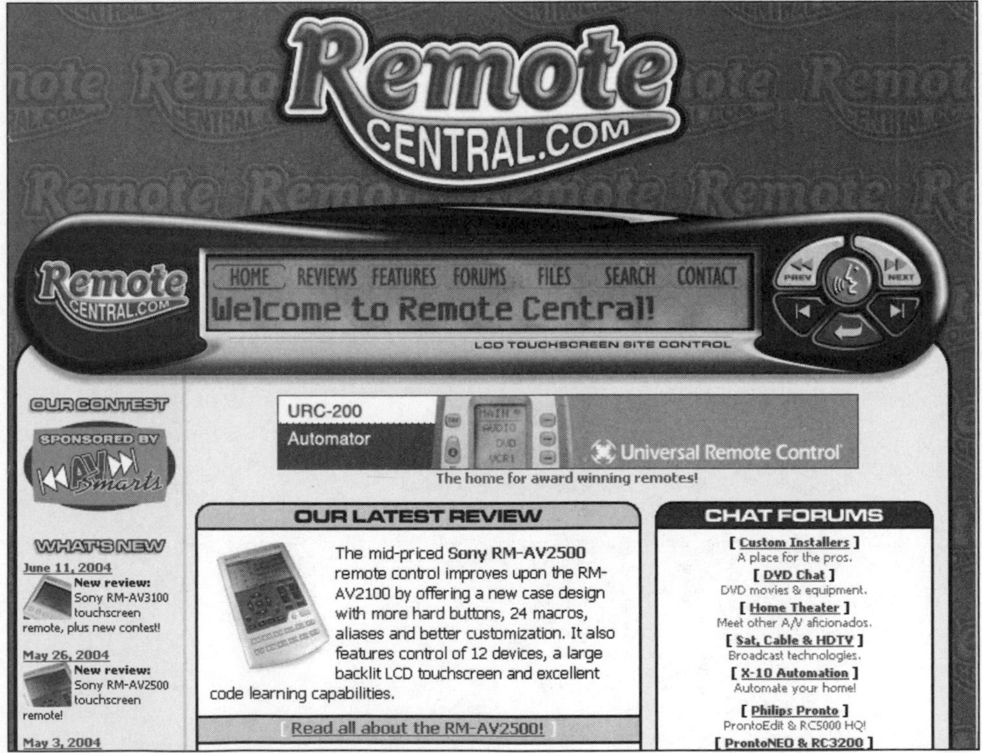

Figure 16-3: If you are interested in buying a remote and want to do some comparison shopping, RemoteCentral.com has the best set of reviews and forums in the industry. It surpasses what you can find even in the trade press.

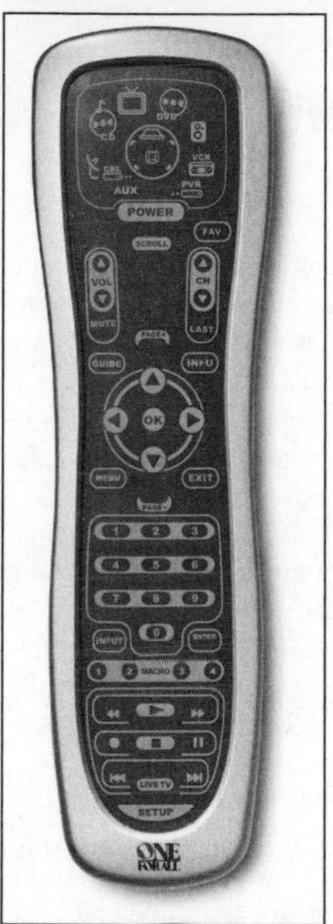

Figure 16-4: The Kameleon series of remote controls offers some very unique features. It is programmable through a browser interface and comes with its own TV guide service.

PDAs as Remote Control Devices

If looking at a Philips Pronto reminds you a little bit of looking at a PocketPC or Palm, you are not alone. Many people who are comfortable with their PDAs look for control software that they can put on the PDA. A market for software of this type exists and currently is being served mostly by shareware authors and very small publishers. The problem with using a Palm for a remote control device is that the audio/video components weren't really built into the product, the infrared signal isn't really that strong, and the only real port on the Palm was at the bottom end, facing the user. Still if that meant that someone had to write software that inverted the screen and added an IR booster for CIR, you could make a remote control out of a Palm. You can find solutions for around $30 for old Palm equipment. Newer models of Palm-style devices have fixed these issues by allowing add-in modules at the top, so undoubtedly this will get easier over time.

Note

The IrDA standard described in Chapter 13 is a high-speed, short-distance protocol. The infrared signal used in modern A/V equipment is the low-speed, longer distance CIR consumer format.

The PocketPC has fared better than the Palm, and more of this kind of software has been released for this platform. It's not too surprising then that we've begun to see remote controls from large computer vendors such as the Compaq iPAQ H3950 / UEI Nevo ($695). HP has put the Nevo software on a proprietary chip and loaded that on its iPAQ. That means that you can still use the H3950 for its information capabilities or to play games on (just like you can on the Palm and even on the $999 Philips ProntoPro), but you have a powerful remote control solution for your home based on the Nevo technology.

The UEI Nevo software, shown in Figure 16-5, is programmed directly on the PocketPC product, and starts you off with access to the UEI code database, which at 110,000 items long is probably the best in the industry. After programming Nevo, you end up with an interface containing a circle of icons that you can touch to enter any specific module. Nevo sets up with a Web interface at MyNevo.com, and there you can design individual screens and buttons, but you can't redesign the main screen. (This is similar in concept to its Home Theater Master series.) The site saves your settings so that can apply them to other Nevo devices.

The LCD touch screens of the Compaq iPAQ have always been exceptional, and that's true for this model as well. In our opinion, the introduction of the Compaq iPAQ and in particular the quality of the screen may have gone a long way toward saving the PocketPC platform when it was floundering. This iPAQ requires some basic knowledge of the PocketPC platform to set up, but once you have done so the actual control program is easy to use. The system lets you set up a system for eight individual users, which is unique for remotes. The ergonomics and fit of this iPAQ are excellent. Whether you want to invest in a remote as expensive as this one largely boils down to what you think of the Nevo software.

Figure 16-5: The UEI Nevo software's main interface.

Beaming Audio and Video from Room to Room

One of the issues people have is controlling their audio and video devices from a single remote in one room into another room. Unlike 802.11 and Bluetooth, which can penetrate walls, the remotes based on IR technology and CIR in particular have a range no better than about 50 feet, and most top off at around 25 feet. If you want to control your systems from a single remote and that remote isn't connected to a computer that can send signals to remote controllers, then you need to use a system that amplifies your infrared signal. Several are available that you can choose from.

Terk (`www.hometech.com/infrared/extenders.html`) has a line of infrared extenders that range from a simple $38 solution such as the LF-UNIV that adds a physical signal booster to any remote and transmits that signal to a base station up to 150 feet away, to the model LF-IRX that has two range extenders with a100-foot radius. Other models in the line include the LF-DISH extender for a Dish Network remote control extender, the LF-RCA RCA Satellite remote control extender, and others. Another infrared extender system is the Niles Remote Control Anywhere Kit, which retails for $199. This system lets you put up to six infrared wall-mounted sensors around your house that respond to your remote control. Signals are transmitted to a connection hub and then sent to a set of sensors that transmits the signal to your A/V equipment. Many systems of this type are on the market.

In Chapter 14 we discussed using 802.11 technology to stream audio and video around a house, as well as connect to devices such as surveillance cameras wirelessly. The advantage of 802.11 technology is that you can control it from a computer, and that it has a relatively long distance range compared to IR remote controls. We wanted to remind you of that discussion before we proceed to look at some of the systems that are available to send audio and video signals from a main TV to a remote TV in another room directly.

The best known products for direct wireless transmission of video and audio signals come from Terk: the Leapfrog WaveMaster 20 (see Figure 16-6) and the multi-room distribution system (`www.terk.com/multiroom/product/wavemaster.html`). The Leapfrog WaveMaster 20 comes with a transmitter and receiver, and up to three more receivers can be added. The stated range is about 100 feet. So with this system you can "beam" signals from TVs, VCRs, DVDs, CDs, cable boxes, satellite dishes, and of course your audio receiver. A newer model called the Leapfrog LF-30S is almost identical, but offers four different channels and claims a 150-foot range.

Terk's Leapfrog HomeNetwork system is a higher-end (and newer) wireless transmission system. It does the same thing that the WaveMaster does, but does it over phone lines. Both of these systems can be connected to a computer by a converter card. These two systems from Terk are really networking for the masses. The WaveMaster 20 is a 2.4 GHz 802.11g device with a directional antenna. The second system called the HomeNetwork is a phone network system. The "connector cards" to computers in both instances is an NIC.

Figure 16-6: The Leapfrog 2.4 GHz A/V sender system (WaveMaster 20) lets you easily connect one TV, audio, or video system to another wirelessly. That is, you can watch or listen to what is playing on the source in a remote location.

Terk's products are easy to use and set up, and they have all of the same characteristics as your computer wireless or phone networks without any configuration — and that's the rub. If you are running other 2.4 GHz devices (such as your computer network and even some phones) or a phone network, you will experience interference. But if not, you can get good results with these devices as long as you don't expect to get an HDTV signal on the receiving end. A nice feature of some of the models like the LS-30S is that you can use a remote to control a TV from the remote station.

Other products in this market include the RCA Lyra Wireless Transmitter, which at $99 sells for the same amount as the LS-30, and the Recoton JV2400 2.4 GHz Video Signal Sender. Of the bunch, the RCA Lyra seems to have the best reviews, but that system is meant for Internet radio and music only and so has an easier road to hoe. With a frequency of 900 MHz, this transmitter is probably using 802.11b technology.

If you have a need to beam multimedia content around a house and don't want to mess with computers, then these products will work for you.

Summary

In this chapter we took a tour of the wonderful world of remote controls, with a brief (and eclectic) first stop at the history of remote controls in the consumer industry. This chapter stressed in particular programmable universal remote controls. A remote control is a highly personal consumer electronic item — what works for one person may not work for another. You'll find that these devices range from $50 up to $1,000. Some very good remotes can be had for between $100 and $200.

A number of features are absolutely essential to have, and more are optional but nice. We stressed ease of use and setup along with a strong learning capability and macro creation features as the key features to look for. This product category is advancing quickly because the volume of devices of this type being sold is dramatically increasing. We are starting to see remotes that are very computer friendly, those that have Web-based setup routines, and at the higher end convergent devices based on PDAs and more advanced software that can control not only your stereo or home theater, but your home appliances as well.

These devices are infrared transmitters, but unlike IrDA they use the CIR protocol and are low power and have a larger radius. There are ways to extend the range of control devices. A computer-based entertainment system and wireless network isn't for everyone. Devices exist that will transmit audio and video signals wirelessly or over a phone line.

Part V

Wireless Mobility Solutions

Chapter 17

Cell Phones

We have seen the future of wireless, and the future belongs to your phone. Phones take pictures, phones connect to the Internet and get your e-mail, phones now come with keyboards and productivity suites — there are phones and more phones. Did I forget to mention that you can even hold a conversation on your phone? The cell phone is the single most successful wireless device, and in this age of digital convergence, your cell phone is asked to do more and more. Dick Tracy had his wrist watch, you have your phone. Tracy would be amazed.

This chapter overviews the technologies used in cell phones so that you can select a phone that best suits your needs. Many of the things you can do with cell phones are specific to your cellular network carrier, but we'll look at some of the more popular things people do to make their cell phones easier, more customized, and of course, more fun.

The cell phone has changed the way people interact with each other and has created a culture all its own. As phone networks get better, faster, and have nearly universal coverage, other wireless services are climbing on board. So please turn off your cell phone ringer while you read this chapter (so as not to disturb the audience) and let's have a look at the wonderful world of cell phones.

Cell Phone Networks

Even if your interest in wireless technology extends no further than your laptop, you can't ignore what's happening in the cell phone marketplace. The cell phone networks of the future will most likely be the mobile network of choice for any device that must maintain its connection during travel; and the cell phone of tomorrow may be the mobile PC of choice. The features that cell phone networks offer that make them attractive include large coverage areas, significant bandwidth, established service groups, and reasonable, although not worldwide, transmission protocol agreements.

Cell phone networking technology developed from the earlier radio telephone networks. Radio telephone networks used powerful, centrally located base stations and large antenna towers to provide around 25 channels per station; each station covered a small city with a 50-mile radius. The problem with this technology was that the number of channels limited the number of connected users. You'll find that a walkie-talkie works over a single channel (inconvenient on that crowded ski slope), a CB radio can use up to 40 channels, whereas a cell phone might have as many as a couple thousand channels to work with. Both CB radios and walkie-talkies use what is called a half duplex mode of operation. Both devices use the same single frequency, so that when one person is transmitting, the other is listening.

Cellular technology uses a very different system with very different results. On a cell network a system of distributed small transceivers called *cells* are placed in the coverage area. Because cells can overlap, you get many more channels than radio telephones could offer. Also, because your cell phone is much closer to the system transceiver, it can operate at powers as low as 0.5 watts, with smaller batteries, whereas radio telephones use as much as 4 watts and much more powerful batteries. The base station of a cellular network can also be much lower power than a radio telephone network, thus greatly diminishing the cost of the system.

Analog or Digital?

When you go into a cellular network store to purchase a cell phone you might be offered a choice between an analog and a digital phone and wonder what the difference is. Mostly the difference between analog phones and digital phones is how the network processes the signal. Over time cellular networks are being converted to digital technology, so this distinction will be significantly less important in the next year or two.

An analog cellular network assigns a frequency range to a service provider that can be sliced up into 832 different frequencies using what is called the Advanced Mobile Phone System (AMPS) protocol. To make communications in an analog phone system work, the send and receive signals in a duplex connection must be at least 45 kHz apart, each signal being 30 kHz wide in the 824 to 894 MHz range. When you connect to an analog cellular network, you use two frequencies to send and receive — a duplex channel mode. Of 832 possible frequencies, 42 channels are reserved as control channels, with 790 channels remaining. Thus the system can connect up to 395 users, or up to 56 channels and users per cell.

Digital phone networks offer features that can't be obtained from an analog network, including Internet access, e-mail, and more. In operation they aren't much different than analog networks, but they use the connection between your phone and the cellular network to compress the transmission signal in order to pass more data between the two devices. Thus many more digital phones can share a single cell in the network — up to ten times as many connections.

Your cell phone is a small personal computer in its own right. It has its own processor, memory, operating system, and a number of special processors that do digital-to-audio conversion and audio-to-digital conversion (DAC and ADC), as well as specialized Digital Signal Processors (DSP). That means that it's relatively easy to convert a computer with a little extra circuitry into a cell phone, and as you'll see a little later in the chapter, the first generation of smart phones is based on the operating systems of personal data assistants, or PDAs. That isn't a coincidence, as many of the PDA OSes were based on projects involving cell phone manufacturers and network providers.

When you buy a cell phone, the number one thing you want to get is a reliable, strong network connection to your native cellular network. However, for people who travel with their cell phones outside of their network area, it is also important to buy a phone that is capable of communicating with as many different types of cellular networks as possible. The way you connect to networks is called an *access technology*. You'll run across three common types: Frequency Division Multiple Access (FDMA), Code Division Multiple Access (CDMA), and Time Division Multiple Access (TDMA).

If you have to choose one of these access technologies, in the United States that would be CDMA. CDMA and TDMA can be and often are used over the same network. When you buy a phone that is dual mode or tri-mode, these are the transmission standards that they are talking about. It isn't important that you know all that much about these access technologies because you can't really choose which one is used in a connection. That intelligence is built into your phone. However, if you are traveling you want as many of these access methods as possible.

Unlike the United States, the rest of the world uses a cell phone standard called GSM, or Global System for Mobile communications. GSM uses a TDMA access technology, but one that is slightly different than TDMA in use in non-GSM networks. You'll find GSM in use in 900 MHz and 1800 MHz bands in Europe, and in the 1.9 GHz range in the U.S. where it is available, but not in the most popular networks. Among the digital cellular networks using GSM in the U.S. are PCS systems and IDN (Integrated Digital Network) systems used by Nextel with Motorola phones. The PCS, or Personal Communications System, is meant to differentiate that system from cellular phone networks, and offers additional digital services such as paging and e-mail.

Note

The GSM phones that you use in the United States use a different frequency than the ones used worldwide, and therefore can't be used when you are traveling. If you want to use a GSM phone in another country, either rent one when you get to your destination or buy a GSM phone from a vendor that specializes in this service. You may also need to pick up a SIM card, which is a prepaid phone card for cellular use.

The problem with traveling with a cellular phone across country is that you may need to use different bands or modes in different locations. A ***band*** is the frequency spread that the cellular network operates on. A dual band phone can operate at either 800 MHz or 1.9 GHz frequency bands. A ***mode*** is the type of transmission technology used, as we just described. A tri-mode phone might use AMPS for analog transmission, TDMA, and CDMA thus providing not only analog connections, but two types of digital connections. It's not uncommon to find dual band, tri-mode phones, and these phones provide the widest connection coverage you can get at the moment for cellular phone systems.

Making a Connection

Setting up a cell phone is similar to what you do when you set up a wireless network or network node. When you purchase a cell phone, your cell phone provider registers the identification code of the phone as set by the phone manufacturer (also called the Electronic Serial Number, or ESN) into its database and assigns that ID code to a Mobile Identification Number (MIN), which is most often your phone number. Essentially the ESN is the MAC address of the phone, and the MIN is equivalent to the device name. If you ever have to replace a cell phone, your provider may ask you to activate your phone by matching your ESN, which is fixed in each phone, to your MIN either through an automated system or by contacting its customer support line.

When you turn on your cell phone, it searches for available networks using its special control channel frequency, which is similar to the discovery process that a laptop goes through. Depending on the System Identification code (SID) of any network—a unique five-digit number assigned by the FCC—your phone finds it and knows whether it is in your service area (if the SID matches your provider), whether it's roaming outside of your area (if the SID doesn't match), or whether it's outside of any coverage area and thus cannot provide service.

An SID of a network other than your own may be a provider who has a reciprocating agreement with your provider and part of your network service. Otherwise, you are in an area where you are "roaming," and additional charges (often excessive) may apply. With many phones you will see a different colored flashing light, get an "R" icon on your screen, hear a different ring or dial tone, or some other feature that lets you know that you are roaming and out of your service plan area. The quality of your service provider's network is one of the most important features you should look for when purchasing a service plan. As we all find out, calls in a roaming area of a cellular network without a reciprocating agreement can be quite expensive. Different levels of service agreements may include areas of the country that other levels do not.

When you make a phone call, you create a registration request at the MTSO, and the system validates your phone and account, determines your current cell, and then assigns you a frequency pair that it knows isn't in use at the moment. The process is similar to a directory service search and authentication. You are connected and your conversation begins.

Cellular networks monitor your signal strength in your current cell and determine when its strength has dropped in one cell and is higher in another adjacent cell. Then over the control channel your phone is sent a switching signal to switch to a different set of frequencies in that second cell, essentially handing you off seamlessly to that cell. Of course, if there is no adjacent cell and you are in an area of no service, you've lost your cell, meaning you've been dropped, and your connection terminates.

The Rise of Smart Phones

You know you have a smart phone when it comes with a manual that describes how to use it, and you actually have to read that manual. Even rather inexpensive phones these days come with a raft of features that are meant to make them easier to use and more enjoyable. You can buy a very substantial cell phone for $80 or more, and often these phones are given away "free" as part of a service contract. Of course there are no free lunches — the phone's real price is rolled into the service plan you just purchased, and if you should try to get out of your service contract you will learn what the phone really costs! But it's nice to think of your cellular phone network provider as some benevolent aunt instead of the malevolent Ma Bell depicted in the movie *The President's Analyst* from days gone by.

Cell Phone Features

Even inexpensive cell phones come with numerous features these days to make them both easier to use and more powerful. It's impossible in a chapter this size to go over every feature that cell phones offer, but this section covers the most useful features that you might want to consider when you purchase a phone. Let's also cover a few of the features that are the most fun.

Two essential features top our list when considering any phone for purchase. The first is the connection quality and the second is reliability. Connection quality is the more easily assessed of the two. You can listen to the phone at the sales location; in practice the phone should sound at least that good when you are in range of a cell. Given a choice, choose a phone that offers multiple bands and modes.

Reliability is harder to assess, although you can ask which phones are returned less often. Every so often a rating service like Consumer Reports will rate cell phone models, which is useful — but not as useful as you might think. The problem is that cell phone technology is advancing fast and models are often obsolete in less than a two-year period. The build quality of the phone and its case are sometimes a guide to reliability.

Many people find size an important feature, and certainly the size of the display and keypad is also important. You can get a tiny phone, but you will have to compromise on the size of your display and keypad if you do. We recommend that you buy a clamshell design cell phone because it maximizes the size of the display and keypad, minimizes the size of the phone, and offers some additional protection to the display. Even long-time clam holdout Nokia is now making clamshell-type cell phones.

In the next section we describe smart phones in more detail, but you don't need to buy a smart phone to get a number of very useful features. Among the ones we particularly like are the following:

- Phone directory
- Speed dial or one-button dialing
- Last number redial and automatic redial (also called demon dialing)
- Recent calls
- Volume control
- Speaker phone
- Mute and hold
- Ringer control and a vibration setting

You'll find those features on nearly any cell phone that you purchase these days. Depending on your service provider you may also find that they offer services similar to the ones that you can get for your home phone, including:

- Caller ID
- Message forwarding
- Conferencing
- An answering service

We find an answering service to be particularly valuable for a cell phone because it is backup when you are in a no-service area or when you are on the phone and can't get to the second call. The list doesn't really end there. Even in lower-end cell phones these days you can find calendars, games, and downloadable customized sounds. Move up in price and you can add voice activation, text messaging (also called SMS or Small Message Service), and Internet access, which is described a little later in this chapter.

SENDING TEXT AND PICTURE MESSAGES

Text messaging, or TXT messaging as it is often called, is a method of sending small text messages from one phone to another. TXT messaging is a cross between a truncated form of e-mail and instant messaging. You may also find this service referred to as SMS or the Short Message Service. There are normally restrictions on the number of characters you can send (typically around 200 characters or less), and both parties have to have phones that are both TXT-message capable and also subscribe to the service. This feature is amazingly popular in Scandinavia and in Japan, where it's ingrained in the culture.

Here's how you send a TXT message on a digital phone:

1. Select Messages.
2. Select Send To or Send New.
3. Enter either the recipient's mobile cell phone number, his e-mail address, or his AOL ID number, and then select Next.
4. Type your message (concisely) and select Next or OK.
5. Select Options and then click or select OK.

Messages can be received on your phone display when you are talking (for some carriers) and are stored in the system for several days if you are not connected to your service. Some services not only offer TXT services, but have fully implemented Instant Messaging Services as well. Often the IM service is part of your TXT service and the utility for sending to an MSN or AIM address is included on the phone or a free download.

With the newer phones that contain cameras, you may be able to send picture or video messages from your phone. This feature has gotten a lot of press recently because there are simply places that you shouldn't send pictures from — doing so is very naughty. So you may find that picture phone use (as well as cell phone use) is banned in a number of places.

If you subscribe to the picture/video messaging service you can send pictures and video messages to other subscribers on your network. At the moment the maximum picture resolution is VGA standard or 640 × 480 pixels. Even if your recipient doesn't have this service, she will still receive the picture and will be able to display it if she has the right utility on her phone.

RING TONES

Everyone's favorite feature on cell phones are ring tones. The number of Web pages and Web sites devoted to ring tones is truly amazing. Take for example the site Ringophone.com. This site lets you download literally hundreds of ring tones, anything from classical music clips to TV show themes, to you name it. You can purchase a ring tone for 59 cents and install it on your phone. Ringophone.com is not unique; you can find similar sites at Ringtone.net, Myringtones.net, Ringtoneparty.com, and others.

Not all cell phones or cellular networks support ring tones, and for those that do, the installation is a little different in every case, but here's the procedure for how it works in general:

1. Go to the site with the ring tone.
2. Purchase or download the ring tone(s) of interest.

3. Specify the cell phone number you wish to send the ring tone to.
4. When you complete Steps 1–3, the system will call you with a data call in a short time, and you will see something like "Ringing tone received" (for Nokia phones, for example).
5. Press Options, then Playback, and OK to hear the ring tone.
6. After you listen to the ring tone, press the Back button, and then scroll to "Save Tone" and press OK.

As a general rule, ring tones are either transferred using SMS or by an application that is included with the phone. Undoubtedly your manufacturer includes this information on its Web site for your particular phone.

About.com has a ring tone compatibility utility that you can search at `http://cellphones.about.com/library/bl_rf_ring tones_compatibility.htm` as well as a FAQ on the subject. Even if your model isn't compatible with the ring tones you want to download, you'll find a number of ring tone conversion utilities on download sites, as well as ring tone composing software. We don't understand what all the fuss is over ring tones, but we must admit that we are a long way past our teenage years.

CELL PHONE GAMES

Before we leave the subject of time-consuming and fun things you can do with your cell phone, we would be remiss not to mention cell phone games. Games have been a fixture on cell phones for quite some time, and they remain one of the most popular features that people look for when they purchase a phone. If you have a smart phone based on Windows CE or the Palm, then adding a game to your phone is the same as adding any other application to that phone.

However, phones without PDA operating systems can also have games, and they use a different method to get and play those games. Cingular, for example, lets you download a game like this:

1. Access the Internet on your phone.
2. Select the Games command.
3. Choose the game you want.
4. Hang up.
5. Cingular calls you back and the game is downloaded to your cell phone.

Or you can follow these steps:

1. Go to Cingular on the Internet from a computer and select the game to download.
2. Cingular calls you back and the game is downloaded to your cell phone.

Games cost $2.95 at Cingular and after you download them they are yours to keep. Keep in mind that different cellular networks offer different game installation procedures, costs, and availability based on the specific model phone you have.

You may find that your phone actually comes with games on it already. That was the case with many Nokia phones in the 1990s that came with a game called ***Snake***. Newer cell phones, many of which are sold to be "Internet-ready," are implementing a mobile version of Java into their phones (see "Internet Access and WAP," later in the chapter). The market for cell phone games could be significant, at least based on the experience that NTT in Japan has had with its i-Mode phones over the 3G DoCoMo network.

The most popular cell phone games are what are called SMS games. That may change over the next couple of years as Java games replace this older format, but at the moment it appears that SMS game download and usage is increasing in the marketplace. SMS games are text games, offering word puzzles, quizzes, trivia, and other SMS answerable questions.

Depending on your phone's OS, different sets of games are available. The Symbian OS requires large game files, so you find this OS on larger smart phones like the Nokia 9210. As with Palm and WinCE, you download those games to a PC and transfer the games to your phone.

Nokia also has a mobile game cell phone platform that is being very carefully watched in the cellular phone industry. The Nokia N-Gage series (see Figure 17-1) is meant to provide a sophisticated game platform akin to the Game Boy Advance, but with the phone integrated into it. Like the GBA, the N-Gage uses special game cards that you insert in the phone to play. The graphics and sound of the N-Gage are a significant step up from the current crop of cell phones. Among the games you'll find for N-Gage are ***Sims: Busting Out***, ***Ashen***, ***Crash Nitro Kart***, ***Spider Man 2***, and many more. You can find the home page for N-Gage at `www.n-gage.com/en-R1/home/home.html`. N-Gage is really a game console with a phone built into it, the very essence of the concept of digital convergence.

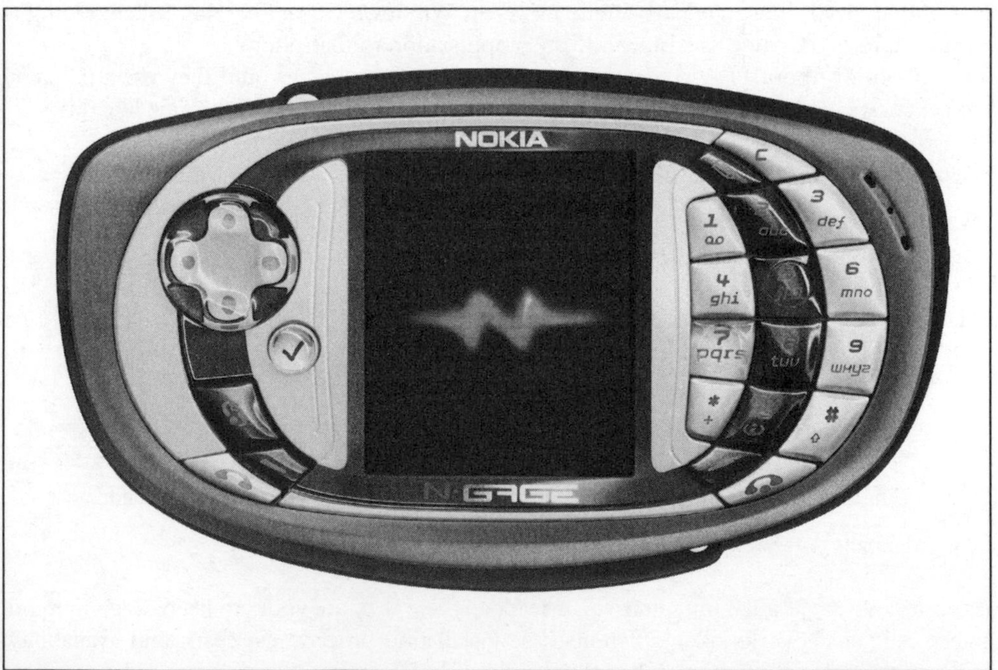

Figure 17-1: The Nokia N-Gage hopes to capture an audience weaned on PlayStation and Game Boy to the cellular phone market.

Of the phones that are Java-enabled, and there are many, the games tend to be large files that you download using your microbrowser. Among a sample of the games you can download are

- *Duke Nukem Mobile* for Cingular's Nokia 6100, Nokia 6800, Nokia 6200, Nokia 3300, Nokia 3595, Nokia 3100, Nokia 3200, and Motorola V400
- *Tom Clancy's Splinter Cell: Pandora Tomorrow* for the same phones listed in the line above
- *Precision Pinball* for Verizon Wireless's Motorola T720, LG VX4400, LG VX6000, and Motorola T730
- *Dell Magazine Crosswords* for Sprint's LG LX5350, Samsung SPH-A500, Samsung SPH-N400, Sanyo SCP-4900, Sanyo SCP-5300, Samsung SPH-A600, Sanyo SCP-8100, and Samsung VGA1000

This is only the start. We could spend the entire book describing cell phone games, but the book would be out of date before we finished writing it. You'll find numerous sites that list cell phone games, but here's a short list to get you started: `www.mobile-entertainment-guide.com`, `www.3gupload.com`, and CNET's cell phone zone at `www.reviews.cnet.com/wireless`.

Smart Phones

When is a phone not a phone, but a smart phone? And when is a PDA a phone and a phone a PDA? Strange as it seems, these questions are increasingly more difficult to answer these days. Here's how we define it (as of today): A phone is a smart phone when it contains an operating system that lets the phone engage in data-rich services. By data-rich services we mean things like Internet access, game play, and so on. It isn't necessary for a smart phone to run on an established PDA (personal data assistant) platform like the Symbian, Palm, or Windows CE, but when a phone does have that capability, it is undoubtedly a smart phone. That's the easy part.

A PDA is a PDA and not a phone when it has to have phone service added to it, and when the size and form factor isn't what's normally associated with a phone. For example, if you need to insert a phone modem add-on into the open slot on a WinCE PDA that's the size of a small brick, then that PDA is still a PDA. If the phone is built into the PDA, then it's a smart phone. Thus, we would argue that the author's (BAS) Kyocera 7135 (shown in Figure 17-2), a 3G phone with a Palm PDA, is a smart phone, but that the brick shape of the Treo 600 or the HP iPAQ h6315 PocketPC Phone Edition argue against their inclusion. Truthfully, this distinction is getting harder and harder to make, and if you're a PDA devotee you probably won't agree with this line of reasoning.

Internet Access and WAP

The problem with browsing the Web on a small phone is that there's very little real estate to work with. Graphical browsers convey a lot of information, including navigation, pictures, and other graphics, text, buttons, and so forth. Couple this with the fact that there are no standard screen sizes on phones and you have the recipe for a whole host of problems. You don't want to return to the world of text-only browsers, although some phones do, so you need an intermediate solution that lets you get the most out of the screen real estate that your device has.

Figure 17-2: The Kyocera 7135 is an example of a smart phone with the Palm V operating system built into it.

That's where the Wireless Application Protocol, or WAP, comes in. With WAP and the Wireless Markup Language (WML), pages can be composed that will work on a WAP-enabled browser or microbrowser. All of the browsers that you find on wireless phones — Blazer (see Figure 17-3), or Opera, or some other browser — are WAP browsers. The purpose of a WAP browser is to make as little demand for memory and processing on a device as possible. Therefore, WAP uses a reduced instruction set, and can be programmed with a reduced version of Java called WMLScript. Programs for a WAP browser are written with instructions that conform to the Wireless Telephony Application Interface (WTAI).

What WAP does is similar to what an HTTP service does with HTML — it takes pages composed in WML and renders them according to the instructions it gets from a browser. WML is a version of XML 1.0. WAP uses a very strict language specification and has its own language. In WAP parlance, pages are called DECKS, and each deck is constructed from parts called CARDS.

Figure 17-3: Handspring's Blazer is an example of a WAP-enabled browser. Notice how there's a sparse use of graphics and almost all content is either text or text links.

The WAP protocol is managed by an industry group called the WAP Forum (`www.wapforum.org`), formed in 1997 by Nokia, Ericsson, Motorola, and Unwired Planet. Today the group has membership from over 90 percent of the cell phone vendors. You'll find WAP running on all of the major cellular phone operating systems, and it is fully compatible with 3G networks, which are discussed in the next section.

3G Networks

Anyone who has ever popped a microbrowser on their cell phone can attest to how slow communications are over a phone line, even with the current data links in use, which are second-generation phone lines (digital networks). Voice communication just simply doesn't need that much bandwidth or throughput to be acceptable. However, a new type of network, dubbed "3G networks" or "third-generation networks," may change this situation and dramatically alter what you can do with your phone.

Plans to migrate the current 2G standards worldwide to 3G are underway. In Europe, Asia, and Africa, 2G GPS networks will be migrated to 3G GPS, whereas in the United States the current 2G CDMA standard will migrate to a 3G CDMA standard. The current definition of a 3G network by the International Telecommunications Union (ITU) is only that it meets a transmission speed of 144 Kbps, which unfortunately bodes ill for anyone who wants all the current wireless standards to merge into a single worldwide standard where you can go roam globally with the same phone.

3G networks offer much greater speeds, raising the current rate of around 10 Kbps to around 2 Mbps when the mobile phone is stationary. 3G phones operate over a frequency of 5 MHz. For mobile phones that are on the move, the connect speed drops to a maximum of 384 Kbps. A 3G connection is a shared connection, so in fact you won't normally achieve these maximum-rated speeds. If a large number of users are connected, your speed may drop down to 56K, that of a fast modem. Even at that speed, considering the smaller screens that have to be populated on phone browsers, Internet access will become much more palatable.

Here are some of the things that a 3G network will let a 3G phone do that is difficult, if not impossible, for the current generation of data phones:

- Video calling, where you see each other's image over the phone as captured by a camera in the phone
- Surf the Internet as if you were at your desktop
- Send and receive e-mail messages with large attachments
- Stream audio and video, and thus listen to your favorite radio or TV program in real time.
- Engage in videoconferencing
- Download MP3 audio
- Play an online game on your phone
- Couple a GPS function with a mapping database to download high-resolution maps and directions to your 3G phone
- Get electronic alerts and reminders from a network service

Essentially you have turned your phone into a broadband connected desktop computer. If you have bought theater tickets on your desktop computer, or logged onto your bank account to pay bills, or searched a reservation service to get a hotel or flight, then your phone will be able to do that too on a 3G network. It's a $50 billion gamble by the telecommunications industry, but one with a good chance of success. ***The Financial Times*** of London has a special report on 3G that you might want to look at online at `http://specials.ft.com/understanding3g/index.html`.

The first 3G network to launch in the United States was Verizon Wireless's Evolution-Data Optimized (EV-DO) Las Vegas network in January 2004, with roll out by August to Washington DC and San Diego, CA. Verizon Wireless's network is rated at up to 500 Kbps maximum throughput for connected users and costs users an additional $30 per month in fees. Other companies are also bringing 3G networks online in 2004, including both Sprint and AT&T. Within a year or so all of these companies will have full 3G coverage on their networks. Our best guess is that it may take an additional year or two, but that 3G service will be priced into the standard data cell phone package at a nominal cost increase.

To use a 3G network you need to either put a 3G-capable wireless card in your laptop or buy a 3G network–capable phone. Although a 2G phone can use a 3G network, it will be unable to achieve the desired throughput rates that this technology promises. In Chapter 19, we describe using PC Cards in your laptop to access a 3G network, including a description of the Verizon PC 5220 (Audiovox PC 5220) Card. Those cards give you data access, but not voice access on your laptop.

A 3G-capable phone may list that support on a label in the back of the phone. If you see something like Qualcomm 3G CDMA, then it *may* be compatible with 3G networks, but not necessarily. Sprint, for example, isn't compatible with the Sanyo SCP-4700, which is supposed to be 3G-capable, but the Sanyo 5150, Sprint TP5250, and Kyocera 2235 or 2255 are compatible. The upshot of all of this is that if you intend to use a particular company's 3G network, you need to check the compatibility of your intended phone before purchasing the service. The top listed phones on CNET.com for a search on "3G phones" in August 2004 were the Sprint Wireless Web Digital Link (a smart phone), Samsung LG LX5350, Samsung SPH-N300, Sanyo SCP-4700, Samsung SPH-A500, Samsung SPH-1300, Kyocera QCP-2235, and Verizon LG VX1—a list that will grow substantially longer and change over the next year.

Summary

In this chapter we took a look at one of the most important wireless markets, cellular phone technology. It's important because the telecommunications companies are building the mobile data networks of the future. As devices become more and more convergent, cell phones will become smart phones, and who knows where smart phones will take us next. Everything from your favorite games, to songs, radio, TV, and instant database access, along with communication can be enabled on the phones of the future. Necessary? Probably not, but they sure are a lot of fun.

In the next chapter, we examine the current state of personal data assistants, or PDAs, and what wireless networking can offer those devices.

Chapter 18

PDAs and Wireless Networking

The personal data assistant, or PDA, was meant to be a mobile device right from the start, so it wasn't long before the PDA was wirelessly linked to a network. The developers of early PDAs understood that if they could network their mobile devices, their PDAs could serve a myriad of functions, including data collection devices in hospitals, information distribution devices in libraries or schools, a limitless pad of forms that could be filled out and collected, input devices, output devices — an almost endless number of applications. But nearly all of them required network access.

This chapter looks at some of the wireless features of PDAs, including how you get yourself connected using hardware and software, transferring data from one device to another through beaming over IR ports. It also discusses some of the precautions you have to take and ways that you can improve the security of your data when it is wirelessly communicating with a network.

A Short PDA History

In 1993 Apple introduced the Newton MessagePad, a pen input computer the size of a small pad of paper. The Newton was a technological tour de force, but a commercial failure, because it was several years ahead of its time. The story of pen input tablets and personal computing devices is littered with many failures in the 1990s, as you can read about on Dan Bricklin's Web site (`www.bricklin.com/tabletcomputing.htm`). Momenta, GRiD, Slate, and Go are names now consigned to history. Michael Wolff's book ***Burn Rate: How I Survived the Gold Rush Years on the Internet,*** on the rise and fall of Go Corporation, is still one of the entrepreneurial classics.

In 1992 Jeff Hawkins and Donna Dubinsky formed a company called Palm, and were joined a year later by Ed Colligan. Palm Computing started out selling a $700 PDA called Zoomer that had the same form factor as the Newton, and was overwhelmed by similar products from multiple vendors. The PDA marketplace finally took its current form when the Palm Pilot 1000 and 5000 were introduced in 1996 to great acclaim. What made the Palm Pilot successful was its smaller size (it fit into a shirt pocket) and its much lower price. Suddenly there was a platform that the PDA marketplace could develop for, and with Newton struggling, many developers switched their efforts to the Palm.

In 1995 US Robotics bought Palm, and two years later 3COM bought US Robotics. Eventually Palm was spun out as its own company. By 1997, demand for the Palm was too great for the company to sustain and Palm licensed its OS to a number of companies, including IBM and eventually

Sony. The original founders of Palm went on to start Handspring and make a cheaper version of the Palm. In 1999, they introduced the Handspring, which was notable for its open card slot. That same year the first wireless Palm appeared in the form of the Palm VII. You can read an unofficial time line of Palm devices at www.jimthompson.net/palmpda/PalmHistory.htm.

While work on the Palm went on in the U.S., alternative PDA devices were coming to market in Europe and elsewhere. The Symbian operating system was introduced in 1998 when Psion and its EPOC software formed a consortium with Ericsson, Motorola, Nokia, Panasonic (Matsushita), and Siemens, who together controlled some 85 percent of the cell phone market at the time. The result was the appearance of the Epoc32 mobile computer and a whole host of smart phones based on Symbian from members of the consortium.

Today you'll find a number of alternative PDA operating systems, including everything from the Blackberry RIM OS used on Research In Motion's highly regarded smart pager to reduced forms of Linux.

The major competitor to the Palm platform is the handheld mobile Windows CE platform from Microsoft, which appeared in November 1996. Microsoft's introduction of the Tablet PC 2002 also represents a milestone, coming as it did some ten years after the original group of tablets and with ten years of research in pen computing for Windows.

PDAs and Wireless Technology

Although the first PDA to be wireless was the Palm VII (that is, if you don't count the cell phone market's entries), enabling a mobile device so that it can connect to a wireless network is no longer either an afterthought or an add-on. Chances are that if you have purchased a recent PDA, you may find that not only do they have the ability to communicate with other devices by IR, but many are Bluetooth devices or come with 802.11 Wi-Fi networking built into them, or both. Putting aside for the moment the issue of what it's like to browse on a microbrowser with WAP, many PDAs have much larger and higher-resolution screens than their cell phone counterparts. Thus, browsing the Web on a Handspring Treo, Sony Clié, or an iPAQ is an entirely different experience than browsing the Web using a browser on a typical phone.

If usability is more important to you than portability, then a PDA that has a phone capability is a better choice for you than a phone that has a PDA. For many people, that is a compromise that they are willing to make.

Wireless Networking on a Palm

Starting with Palm V, you could have wireless networking for your Palm. For later models that have Wi-Fi built in, here's how you would set up your wireless connection:

1. Tap the Wi-Fi setup icon on the Application Launcher.
2. Click Next and a list of available wireless networks will be built, as shown in Figure 18-1. Select your network from the list and then enter your encryption key (if required).

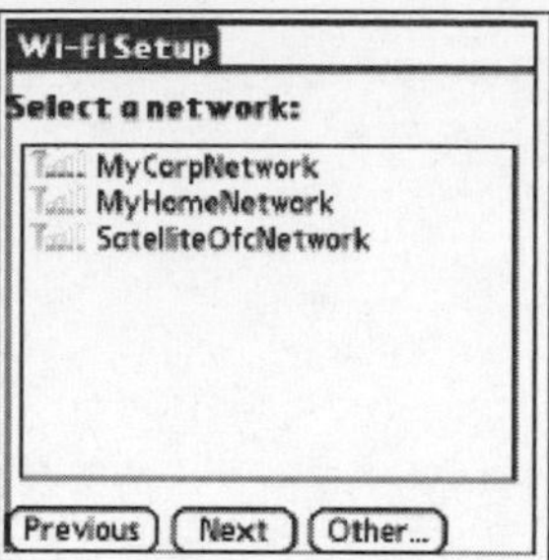

Figure 18-1: The Palm Tungsten C wireless utility automatically builds a list of available networks.

3. If you don't see your wireless network in the list, because the network doesn't broadcast its SSID or it isn't in range, click the Other choice in the list.
4. Enter the SSID name, and then click the box for WEP encryption and tap the unassigned box for the New network, as shown in Figure 18-2.

Figure 18-2: Creating a new wireless network connection.

5. Enter your WEP key into the screen shown in Figure 18-2. If your device is receiving an address by DHCP, you should close your settings and then be connected.
6. To manually set your wireless network address, click Preferences in the Wi-Fi utility, then Edit Networks, Select your network, and Details, and finally tap the Advanced tab, as shown in Figure 18-3.

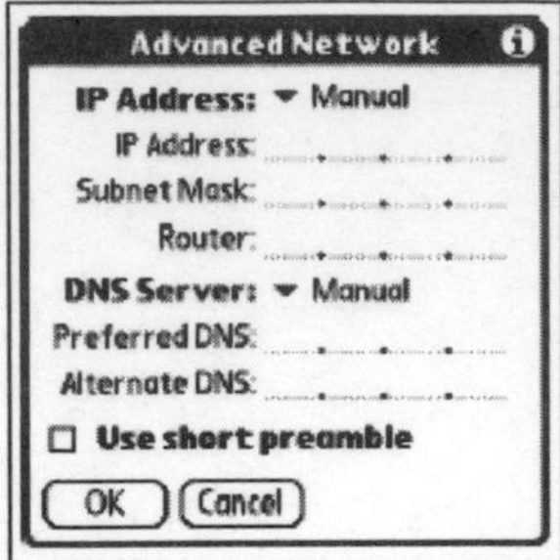

Figure 18-3: Enter your addresses in this screen when you are manually setting up a connection.

7. Enter your addresses and close the settings.

The Tungsten C is nice because it has wireless built into it. Sony Clié models NX and NZ also can be made wireless by adding Sony's Wi-Fi card to the Wi-Fi slot.

Wireless Networking on a PocketPC

Many PocketPC devices come with 802.11 already built into them. Those devices have a utility that will let you set up the built-in wireless network card. Click Start and then Programs to locate the utility. Often they have a name like *XXXX* Wireless Configuration, where *XXXX* is the name of your device. If you can't find that utility, click Start and then Settings to locate a similarly named icon. In either case, launch the utility to configure your device.

To use built-in wireless networking, you need to enter your settings and enable it. Do the following:

1. Open the Connection, tap Settings, and then click the Advanced tab.
2. Click the Network Card button, then the Wireless tab, and finally Add New Settings.
3. Tap the General tab and enter your SSID, if necessary.
4. Set the mode (Intrastructure or Ad Hoc), and in the Connects to box select Internet or Work.
5. Tap Authentication and enter your WEP settings, enable encryption (if desired), and then tap the Network Authentication (Share Mode) checkbox. Enter your WEP key into the Network key box, or click "Key is provided automatically."
6. Close your Settings.

For those PocketPCs without built-in wireless capability, you can add a Compact Flash Type II wireless card to them. Different wireless cards install in slightly different ways, but here is a general procedure on how you would add a card to a PocketPC that doesn't have built-in wireless capability.

To install a Symbol wireless CF card into a PocketPC, do the following:

1. Put your PocketPC into its cradle and attach it to your PC. Check that your version of the OS and of the Microsoft ActiveSync software supports this installation.
2. With the CF card slot open, put the installation disk for the wireless card into your PC and launch the setup program. Or, navigate to the card manufacturer's Web site and download the installation software.
3. Start the installation program on the CD or where you downloaded it. The program might be Setup.exe or some other executable file. The necessary drivers and software will be installed on your PC
4. Insert the card into the PocketPC. The card should be auto-detected and a network card and signal strength meter should appear at the lower right-hand corner of the PocketPC screen.
5. Click the icon to view the Properties dialog box.
6. Click the Mode tab (or something similar), as shown in Figure 18-4. Set the value of the ESSID, your wireless network's name, and the operating mode, which in most cases will be set to "Infrastructure" if you are connecting to an access point.

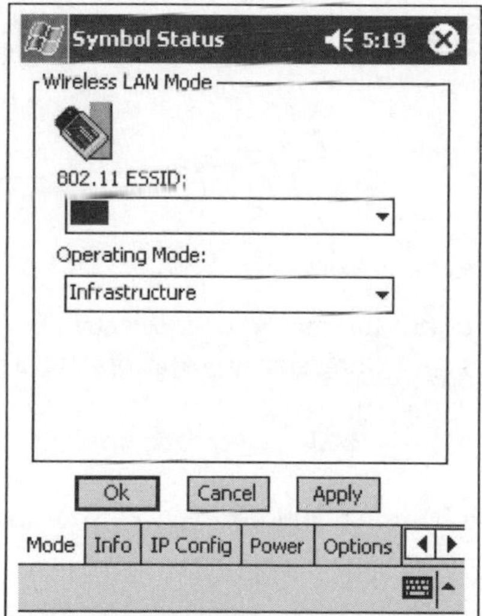

Figure 18-4: The Mode tab is where you enter your network and mode.

7. Click the IP Config tab (or something similar) shown in Figure 18-5 and enter whether you are using a static or DHCP address. Enter the addresses of your Gateway, DNS server, MAC address, and so on, as well as any assigned static address and click OK.

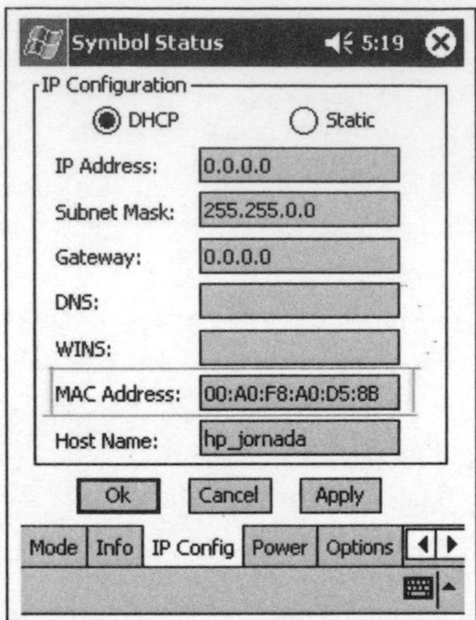

Figure 18-5: The IP Config tab is where you enter your addresses.

At this point you should see a signal from an available access point and be able to measure the signal strength. You'll probably want to save this particular connection as a named connection that you can use at a later time.

To save a wireless connection:

1. Click the Start button and select the Settings command.
2. Click the Connections tab, then click the Connections icon.
3. In the Settings dialog box shown in Figure 18-6 with Internet Settings selected, name the second setting Home settings, Work settings, or something similarly appropriate. The third "network connects to" setting should be The Internet.
4. Click OK and return to the Today screen.
5. Test your connection by opening a browser and by using Outlook to check your mail connection.

In rare instances, a PocketPC device doesn't come with built-in Wi-Fi, nor does it allow you to use a CF card. Some devices let you use a standard PCMCIA or PC Card, which is attached in a cover used to surround the device.

You may find that the instructions presented here, which work generally for PocketPC 2002, may not be required by your card if you are running PocketPC and you have the Zero Configuration feature turned on. With Zero Config enabled, the PocketPC will detect available network(s) and give you the opportunity to choose which one you want to connect to. You'll need to know any authentication keys if WEP is enabled on the network before you can connect, however.

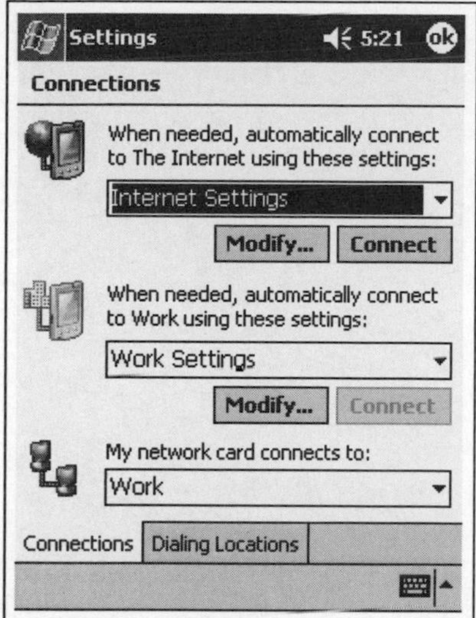

Figure 18-6: Saved settings for a wireless connection.

Beaming Data from One PDA to Another

PDA devices are meant to exchange data with desktop software, and synchronize new data between the two. Depending on the settings you set in each application, you either overwrite the desktop data with new PDA data, overwrite the PDA with new desktop data, or cross synchronize data, creating new records in each. However, to exchange data between one PDA and another, a more convenient method is required. That's where beaming comes in.

Starting with the very first Palm, these PDAs came with an IR transceiver to communicate with other Palms. You can beam

- An address card or an entire address book
- To do lists
- Memos
- Entire applications, especially games

Here's how you would beam a business card from your address book from one Palm to another:

1. Enable Beam Receive in your PDA preferences.
2. Point the two Palm devices so that the IR ports are aimed at one another.
3. Tap the application that will be beamed, as shown in Figure 18-7.

Figure 18-7: A list of applications in the Beam Application dialog box.

4. Open the Record menu and click the Beam Item command; or to beam all items select Beam Category.

That's all there is to it! Exchanging applications isn't much more difficult. Here's how to exchange an application between two Palms:

1. Turn on beaming and point the two devices so that their IR ports face each other.
2. Open the Application Launcher, and from the App menu select the Beam command.
3. Tap the application to be beamed and click the Beam button.

Beaming works for distances of from 6 inches to 3 feet (10 cm to 1 m) for most Palm models. If you are having trouble beaming, Palm recommends that you do the following: move out of direct sunlight, check your batteries, change distance or angle, check free memory, do a soft reset, and if necessary remove any system hacks. Not all applications can be beamed; you'll see the lock icon on the name of any application that can't be beamed.

Did I mention that you can beam games between Palms?

If you are attending a convention or trade show with your Palm you may encounter kiosks from a company called Bluefish or Wideray, similar to the one you see in Figure 18-8. Bluefish and Wideray allow you to have a database of information about the convention beamed into your Palm or PocketPC device that you can use while working the floor. The database application that you need is also installed by this process.

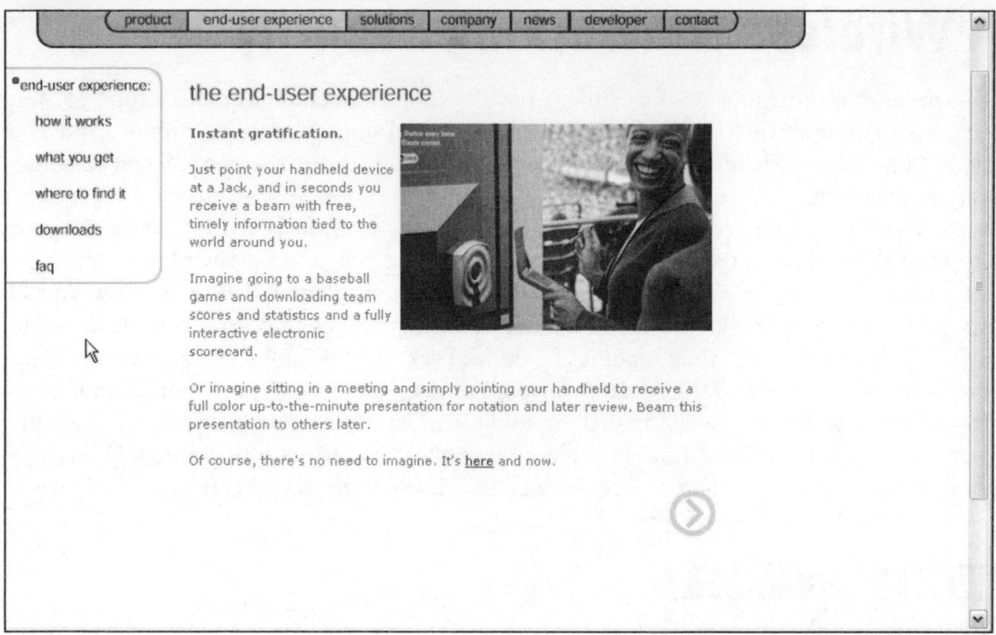

Figure 18-8: A person is shown here beaming information from a Wideray kiosk to her Palm.

Beaming is also a feature you find on the PocketPC, and it is equally as easy to do on that platform as well, as long as you are transferring the data between two PocketPC devices.

To beam data on a PocketPC:

1. Open the program that you want to send data from and then select the item to be sent.
2. Point the two devices toward each other so that their IR ports are in range.
3. To send contacts and appointments, among other things, tap and hold the item, and then tap Beam Item on the pop-up menu.
4. To send many other items, open up File Explorer, tap and hold the item of interest that you want to send, and then tap Beam File from the pop-up menu.

Finally, if you feel the need to beam information from a Palm or other device to your PocketPC, check out Peacemaker 1.2 from Conduits (`www.conduits.com/home.asp`). Conduits supports data transfer between many different IR devices.

Note

Many Palm and PocketPC devices have built-in Bluetooth capabilities. They are in fact ideal applications for Bluetooth. We don't cover using Bluetooth and PDAs in this chapter, however. For information on this topic, see Chapter 13.

PDA Wireless Networking Security

Since PDAs are meant to be mobile, they suffer from all of the vulnerabilities that laptops do. You need to protect them from theft, sniffing and password theft, data theft, data corruption, and to a lesser extent, from viruses. Theft is probably the most common threat, and the one you can most easily prevent with vigilance.

To protect against theft we recommend that you turn on the password security feature on your PDA. Both the Palm and PocketPC have security utilities that let you set a password in order to get access to the data on the device. Figure 18-9 shows this utility from a Palm V device. A password will protect your data from people with average computer skills; they will be forced to reset the device in order to eliminate the password, thus sending the device back to its default state. However, a password alone won't help you get your PDA back to you. For that, you need to have a method of identifying the device as yours. The single best thing to do is to have your name, address, and phone number engraved on the device. Although some utilities allow you to set a screen that shows this information, software is software and can be defeated or lost when the device is reset.

Figure 18-9: The Security application on a Palm V lets you set an access password, lock the PDA; and hide, show, or mask records.

More robust security applications are available that you can employ on PDAs. Some of these applications encrypt your data, password-protecting not only the device but individual applications and files, and passwords. Among this class of utilities are Applian's Pocket Lock and Virtual Wallet, Illium Software's eWallet, PDA Defense, PDASecure, TealLock, and others.

Although PDA viruses weren't particularly well known in the past, the inclusion of more Java and ActiveX applets and code on PDAs, particularly in browsing the Web, makes them much more vulnerable than they once were. It's worth mentioning that your chances of picking up a virus are probably greater when you are synchronizing your PDA than through a wireless connection.

The following vendors offer anti-virus software for PDAs:

- Airscanner for the PocketPC (`www.airscanner.com/`)

- Anti-Virus and FileCrypto from F-Secure (`www.f-secure.com/wireless/`)
- Avast! 4 for Palm and WinCE (`www.avast.com`)
- InoculateIT for Palm OS, Computer Associates (`www3.ca.com/Solutions/Product.asp?ID=171`)
- Karpersky Security for PDA (`http://antivirusi.com/kasp/kasperskypda.html`)
- PC-cillin for Wireless from Trend Micro (`www.trendmicro.com/en/products/desktop/pcc-wireless/evaluate/overview.htm`)
- Symantec Antivirus for Handhelds (`www.symantec.com/sav/handhelds/`)

Note

***PC Magazine* published an article called "PDA Protection" that appeared in 2003 with software suggestions for both the Palm and PocketPC. You can find this article online at** `www.pcmag.com/article2/0,4149,1267256,00.asp`.

As with any wireless networking situation, you can take steps on your own network to limit what outsiders can see. You can suppress SSID broadcasts and encrypt data using WEP, or better yet, WPA. However, you don't have those options when you are on the road connecting at a hotspot.

You may want to consider installing a VPN client such as Mergic VPN for Palm to protect your wireless communication on the road. A VPN will slow your transmission somewhat, but it will protect your data. Depending on who you are communicating with, a VPN may be a requirement for the connection. For home and small networks it typically isn't required. Most users of this type will find VPNs to be a little bit of overkill for PDAs, and for some underpowered devices the performance drag is too significant to be worth bothering with this feature. One nice feature of VPN client software is that it often comes with personal firewalls, something that isn't normally put onto the current generation of PDAs.

Strange as it seems, you may want to consider a physical device that shields your PDA from outside probing. Because PDAs are always on (even in a low-powered state), wireless transmissions can wake a device and provide access to it. You can protect your PDA by enclosing it in a shielded electrostatic bag (or better yet, a case) when you are traveling. One company, mobileCloak (`www.mobilecloak.com/mobilecloak/mobile.cloak.html`), sells an electrostatic PDA case that you can use for this purpose.

Don't forget that if your PDA has a flash storage card or device in it that stores the data you use, that card is just as much of a security concern as the handheld itself. You'll want to take measures to limit access to data on these cards, encrypt their data, or use a device with a personal identification method like biometrics.

Summary

In this chapter you learned how to connect your PDA to wireless networks. We focused on the Palm OS and Windows CE-based PocketPC devices because they are market leaders in this category in the United States. The principles, broadly applied, work with other types of personal data devices.

Many PDAs, particularly the newer ones, come with built-in wireless networking. You learned how to enable these services on the Palm as well as the PocketPC and how to create a connection, enter your network settings, and save the connection.

For devices that don't have built-in networking, you can add a wireless networking card. The process for setting up a wireless networking card is very similar to using the built-in capability.

Palm and PocketPC support a feature called beaming. The Palm platform is particularly well known for this data transfer mechanism. Beaming transfers data, data sets, and even applications from one device to another using their IR ports. Beaming is also of commercial interest because it allows the use of informational data kiosk appliances in public places.

Finally, security is one area of PDAs that doesn't get enough attention. Every year lost or stolen PDAs and the data they contain contribute to identity theft. Also, PDAs are becoming more susceptible to viruses and to wireless sniffing and intrusion. Various methods and a growing list of applications are available that will help you secure your device by hiding your passwords, encrypting your data, and checking for viruses.

In the next chapter we are really "going mobile" as we consider some of the wireless technologies that you can use in your car, van, RV, truck, or bus. So get ready and climb aboard the magic bus of wireless technology.

Chapter 19

Computing from Your Car

Your car is the ultimate mobile device; it is also probably the most complex computer you own. The automotive industry is the largest consumer of embedded processors in the world. In an age of convergence, it is not surprising that manufacturers are marrying one technology, the automobile, with another, wireless networking.

We are just at the beginning of this trend, but already the range of services is extraordinary. With a satellite-guided GPS system, you need never be lost again, and the necessary directions to your next destination is only a few buttons away. In place of AM/FM radio you now can choose satellite radio, which will narrowcast your favorite content in a way that only a premium service can. You can buy devices to broadcast your iPod's MP3s over your car's sound system, FM radio, and much more.

The automobile is a great platform for wireless computing because it is a controlled environment in a small space. Devices can be low powered, local, and controlled. One day you may see Bluetooth-enabled cars that provide a cushioning bubble around the car that prevents collisions, help you park, or communicate with sensors in the roadbed to help traffic planners route traffic efficiently. For now we have devices such as FastLane, which puts a transponder in your car that enables you to drive through a toll booth on the Massachusetts turnpike, or one in New York, New Jersey, or elsewhere and have the charges automatically billed to your account.

In this chapter you see some examples of what you can do in your own car using present-day technology. Although this chapter has an eye on the future, nearly all of the devices, tools, and technologies described here are devices that you can go out and buy today and install in your car.

Connecting Your Notebook to the Internet from Your Car

The idea of having Internet access in your car isn't new, but it is an idea whose time is coming, if it isn't here already. If you purchased a Mercedes-Benz starting in 2001 you could get an integrated cell phone in their COMMAND console. That console displays text with information from the Internet, displayed in the way that many cell phones with small screens do.

By 2003, vendors were introducing systems that provided Internet access directly for any device you wanted to connect to it. For example, one company called IP Wireless (`www.ipwireless.com/`)

demonstrated a wireless modem with speeds of 400 Kbps, with 3 Mbps promised. The beauty of the device is that it's entirely portable and can work wherever a cell phone works. IP Wireless used the CDMA cell phone standard, but boosted data throughput by synchronizing the different data streams and collecting them into contiguous packets. The system was put into demonstration that year, but awaits implementation from cellular providers.

IP Wireless's system brings us to the most important point about Internet in your car — it is most likely to be a cellular technology that connects you to the Internet, and your mobile phone company is the most likely provider. As phone companies introduce third-generation wireless networks, the so-called 3G networks, the switch from connected PDAs to connected laptops is just around the corner.

You can get access today from a number of companies through their cellular networks, but Verizon Wireless's entry in this category is a good example. With its NationalAccess plan and system you can connect from a data-enabled smart phone, or from a laptop with a PC Card to a VPN at a current rate of 40 to 50 Kbps average with bursts up to 144 Kbps. The cards currently recommended by Verizon Wireless for this system are the AirPrime PC 3220 Card, the Audiovox PC 5220, and the Sierra Wireless AirCard 580 PC type II PC card shown in Figure 19-1. These cards operate on the IS-95 networks that work with a dial-up connection over a cellular network.

Figure 19-1: The Sierra Wireless AirCard 580 card looks like an 802.11 card but is, in fact, a 3G cellular network PC Card that you can use to connect your laptop to the Internet.

Needless to say, because this system works with a cell phone in your car, it also works connecting your laptop to the same network. Figure 19-2 shows the VZAccess Manager software that you download from Verizon Wireless's Web site to install on a Windows PC. This is a connection manager and a dialer that helps you manage your NationalAccess sessions.

Figure 19-2: The Verizon Wireless VZAccess Manager is software that you can use to connect to an advanced (relatively speaking) cellular data network with connection speeds ranging from top of the line dial-up to near DSL quality.

Microsoft's Windows CE for Automotive, an initiative based on its .NET architecture, illustrates the potential uses of Internet technology for an automobile. Although your car already has sensors in it that report conditions to a car computer, manufacturers have yet to connect those computers to a central computer over the Internet. Doing so would allow the manufacturer to measure not only the time to replace fluids or perform a maintenance of some kind, but to consider your driving habits based on actual data and recommend specific settings and adjustments.

What Microsoft calls the "Connected Car" would offer a range of services including safety systems, routing, entertainment, diagnostics and monitoring, theft prevention, and computer access to the Internet. What Microsoft is providing developers is a Windows Automotive platform that will contain features such as speech and speech recognition, hands-free communication, A/V, mapping and graphics, and support for the wireless technologies of 802.11, Bluetooth, CDMA (Code Division Multiple Access — a cell phone protocol), and General Packet Radio Service (GPRS).

You don't really have to wait for an entire system to appear in a new automobile that you buy. You can add satellite radio, GPS systems, and cell phones with Internet access to a car today.

Telematics

Telematics is a term used to describe the convergent products that marry telecommunications with computers. Therefore, any dial-up service, wireless networking over cellular networks, and any network that uses a telecommunications system as its transport mechanism is referred to as telematics. GPS has also been lumped under this heading. As technology has advanced, telematics has come to be associated with the use of mobile technologies as enablers for telecommunication functions in automobiles. Every January, the Consumer Electronics Show (CES) in Las Vegas fills up the North Hall completely with automotive products. Although only some of these products involve wireless data transport, more of these products exist than you might imagine. In truth, this area has the potential to become a major industry by itself.

Satellite Radio

Wireless entertainment has proven to be a vibrant new area of technology for automobiles, and its introduction, while not overwhelming, looks like it can capture enough market share to be a viable product niche. The best example of wireless technology in the automobile so far has been satellite radio. To receive satellite radio, you need a special receiver that can capture SIRIUS, WorldSpace, or XM Radio, which are the three market leaders. Although the initial systems in the market were pricey, newer models have come in at price points under $100, which makes them more affordable to the average person and suitable for portable music devices. Each of these services requires a monthly subscription fee that averages about $10 to $12 a month.

What makes satellite radio, sometimes called digital radio, attractive to users is that it offers many stations, some with very specific content (narrowcasting), a high-quality sound, and is mostly commercial free. Whereas FM radio has a range of around 40 to 50 miles, the signal can be heard outside that range only when the signal goes through a repeater station. By contrast, a satellite signal can travel uninterrupted from far away in space, even halfway around the world. The net result is that you could travel vast distances and stay connected without interruption and at the same high quality level. Both XM Satellite Radio (`www.xmradio.com`) and SIRUIS Satellite Radio (`www.siriusradio.com`) specifically target the automobile market, and their receivers started to be offered in cars in 2001.

Satellite radio is available by direct reception on your receiver. In some areas of coverage satellite signals compete with many other similar signals. Satellite radio uses ground repeaters to extend the radio signal in dense urban reception areas in particular. Although the signal has wide coverage, it isn't a universal signal like GPS, which you can get anywhere in the world. You need to be in range of the satellite or one of the repeaters with your special receiver to make satellite radio work.

The satellite radio system uses a band around 2.3 GHz, also called the "S" band. That band is very close to the 802.11g band at 2.4 GHz. The satellite radio band was created by the FCC (Federal Communications Commission) in 1992 and two companies were licensed for broadcast: CD Radio (now SIRIUS) and American Mobile Radio (now XM). It's taken a while, but XM launched on September 25, 2001 and SIRIUS launched on July 1, 2002. Outside the United States a company called WorldSpace (`www.worldspace.com`) broadcasts in Africa, Asia, and South America.

The satellites being used by each company are different. XM Radio has two satellites in geostationary orbit, affectionately dubbed "Rock" and "Roll." General Motors and Honda are both investors in XM Radio, and have made big commitments to install their receivers in the cars they make. Alpine, Clarion, Delco, Motorola, and Sony, among others, make receivers for XM Radio, that offer 100 plus channels commercial-free as a subscription service.

The SIRIUS service uses three satellites in an elliptical orbit. The system has a satellite over the U.S. during all hours, with each satellite being in range 16 out of 24 hours a day. SIRIUS receivers can be converted to a lower frequency and with an adapter can play over a standard AM/FM car radio. That lets you add SIRIUS to your current automobile without having to replace your current sound system. XM Radio offers a similar add-on device. Figure 19-3 shows the Kenwood KVT-M700 in-dash TV-style receiver with motorized touch-sensitive screen set in a dashboard console.

Figure 19-3: The Kenwood KVT-M700 with SIRIUS Radio installed in an automobile console.

The company with the largest installed base in digital satellite radio is actually WorldSpace. It has three geostationary satellites: AfiStar for Africa, AsiaStar for Asia, and AmeriStar for South America and southern Central America. Its satellites went up between 1998 and 2000 and each carries 40 to 50 radio channels at the moment. Unlike XM and SIRIUS, WorldSpace uses the 1.4 MHz part of the L-Band, another area that has been designated for use by the digital broadcast industry. WorldSpace is not currently available in the U.S.

MP3 Players

You know the drill. You've got your musical life all ripped onto your MP3 player and now you want, no, you *need* to hear those great songs of yesteryear playing on your car's sound system as you lay rubber to the road and cut the night with your beams. If you haven't been so fortunate as to buy a new, expensive car with an MP3 playback capability, relax. Adding a wireless connection from your MP3 player (or any audio device) is one of the easiest things you can do. That's the hook used for the commercials offering iPods along with white Volkswagen Beetles. Figure 19-4 shows the Monster Power iCarPlay Wireless – FM Transmitter for iPods.

A number of vendors sell an FM radio car stereo transmitter that plugs into your device's audio or headphone output jacks and transmits a signal that your radio can tune into. The sending device can be any portable sound source, a DVD player for the kiddies in the back, your laptop, and others. You can adjust the frequency of the transmission to get the best sound from one of several, which in most cases gives really excellent results, the equal of any commercial FM station on your radio at its best. Radio Shack's model offers four frequencies, 100 hours battery lifetime, a 10- to 30-foot range, with a rated response of from 50 to 15 KHz with 45dB stereo separation and 0.5 signal distortions. That's near high fidelity, and about as good as you can do with almost any in-car stereo system. You'll find similar units from Monster Cable, Belkin, RCA, and others. These units go for around $15 to $35, with the main difference being the number of frequencies offered.

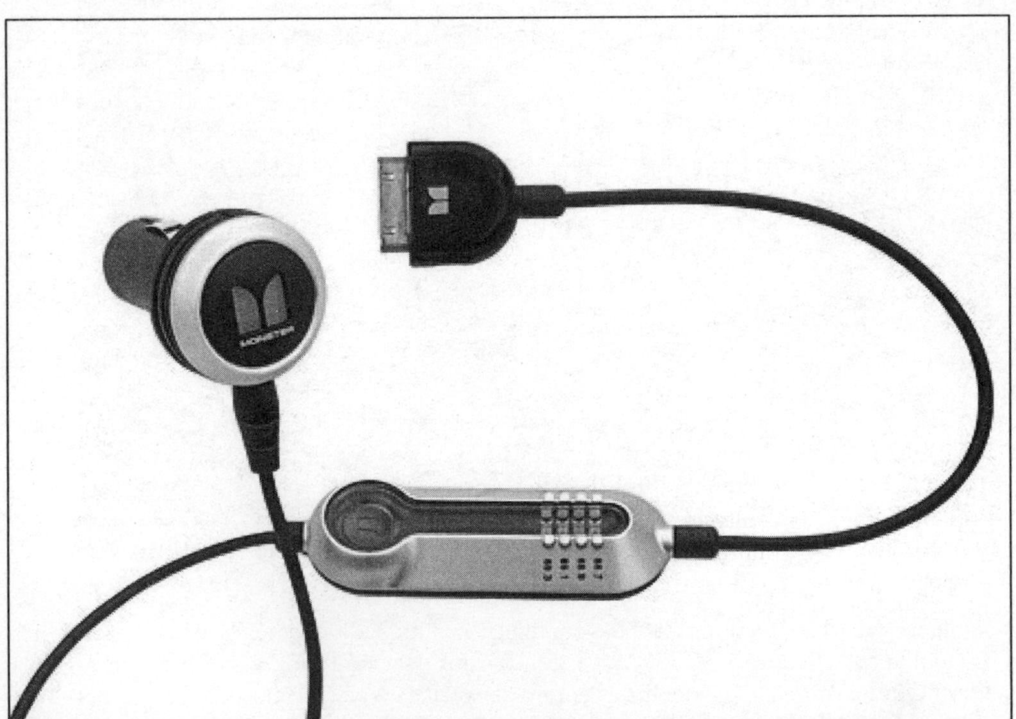

Figure 19-4: The Monster iCarPlay with Dock Connection Play lets you connect an iPod wirelessly through your FM radio.

GPS

As you probably know already, the Global Positioning System (GPS) is a satellite-based radio transmission system for locating any position on earth based on triangulation data obtained from three to eight satellites. With multiple measurements, GPS can calculate speed and direction as well as store the path you used to get to where you are so that you can make a return trip.

The system was launched for the U.S. military, and is still used for that purpose. GPS is a very sophisticated system, and can locate objects to within a few feet of their position. In the past the system was detuned so that precise location couldn't be determined to any better than 35 feet, but that restriction was lifted and now you can get positioning accurate to within 10 feet. A technology that gives you position and directions is a nearly perfect application for mobile devices.

We first encountered GPS in a Hertz car rental when we used its NeverLost system (shown in Figure 19-5). NeverLost uses a Windows CE device running Magellan software to store and process a database that contains location and mapping, points of interest, businesses, restaurants, hotels, parks, city halls, and a host of other things. As you travel, NeverLost speaks to you, telling you when to turn, how far to go, and in what direction. In the days when GPS was detuned, the NeverLost system retuned the device by using a gyroscope to measure the direction of movement and the miles traveled to extrapolate your current position from your last triangulated one. Thus you could go through a long tunnel and still be relatively accurately positioned when you emerged. NeverLost was and is remarkable, but more remarkable still is how low the prices and how much greater the capabilities of GPS devices are today.

You can very easily add GPS to any car by buying a GPS device from one of several different companies, such as Garmin, NAVMAN, and Magellan. These devices can be portable and are meant not only for cars but for backpacking as well. Devices run from around $150 to $2,000. What do you get for more money? How about 10-foot accuracy, multiple routes, hundreds of waypoints and track points, detailed color maps, locations of gas stations, rest areas, restaurants; data on the moon, sunrise and sunset; and up-to-date construction information. The highest-end systems offer instructions given to you by voice.

Adding GPS to a laptop is equally easy. If you have purchased a mapping program such as Microsoft Streets and Trips, Rand McNally's StreetFinder, or Delorme Street Atlas USA, you may have noticed that these packages can read the signals from GPS position locators. You can also find ample shareware and freeware in this category. A search on Download.com for the word "GPS" returns 37 listings.

For the most part, adding a GPS device to your laptop is as simple as installing the necessary drivers and plugging the device into your computer. Most GPS devices are USB connected, although earlier models were more often serial port devices. You'll probably find that the GPS device you purchase comes with one of the software packages mentioned above. When buying devices like these, try to make sure that they conform to the marine standard so that they are broadly compatible.

GPS is more than just a simple convenience; it offers us the potential for great efficiencies, and can and does save lives every day. You'll find GPS on your PDA, in your cell phone, on your laptop, in your car, in watches, and on handheld devices—just about anything that moves. Every year the technology gets cheaper and one day it will be ubiquitous, a true commodity.

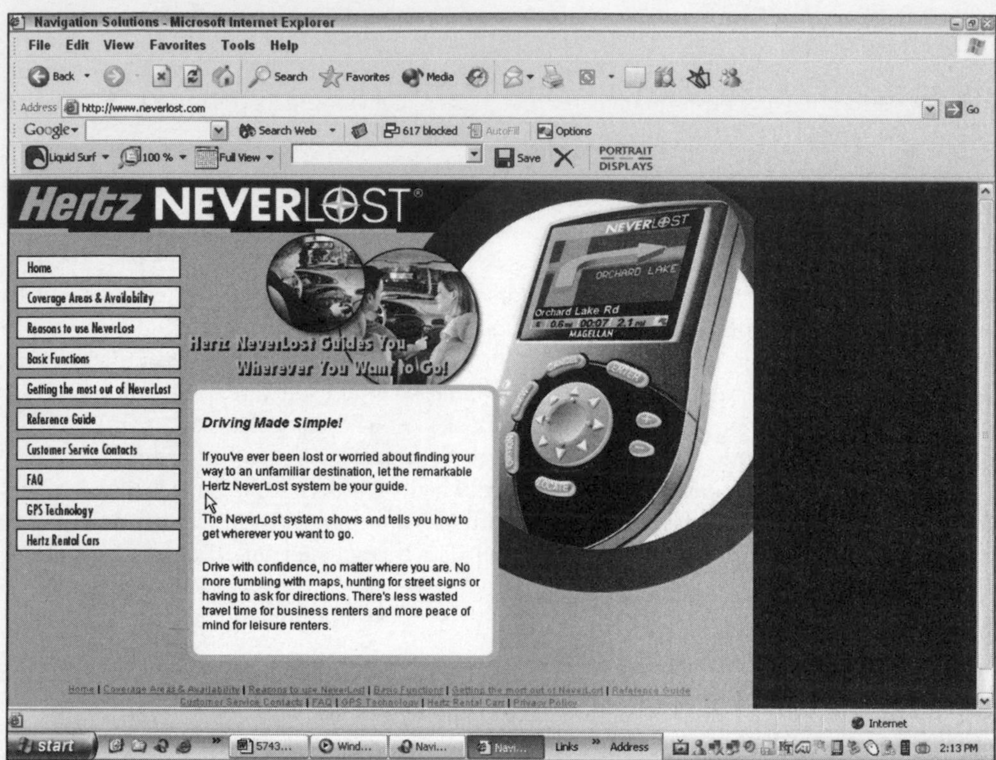

Figure 19-5: The Hertz NeverLost system is an intelligent GPS system with voice output that lets you draw on a large database of regional points of interests and attractions while guiding you from one point to another.

Traffic Transponders

A *transponder* is a small wireless radio transmitter/receiver with an identification code, a microprocessor, and memory. They've been used a long time in avionics (airplanes) to locate planes on radar and prevent collisions, but the technology has become cheaper and is now being used for automobiles.

You attach the transponder to your car, and as you go through the toll booth you are identified. Traffic transponders, as exemplified by the Fast Lane or EZ-Pass system in the northeastern United States, attach to the inside or outside of the front windshield and are used to pay tolls without actually having to stop at the toll both. The system is valuable because it saves the highway authorities money by allowing the toll booth to be automated, while allowing up to 2,000 cars to pass through a single toll booth during any specified hour. Anyone who has sat in long lines at the toll booths on the Massachusetts Turnpike or on the New York Thruway can attest to their value.

The system works when the car goes through a toll booth with a corresponding receiver connected to the authority's computer system. The two devices communicate over the 900 MHz frequency band, and the identification is used to record the number of the transponder and calculate the required toll. If the account is in good standing, the transaction is recorded in the vehicle's transponder memory and the light is changed from red to green. The actual read zone is only about 10 feet for Fast Lane, although it is larger for other parts of the system; and the rated accuracy is nominally rated at 99.9 percent. Figure 19-6 shows a Fast Lane transponder.

Figure 19-6: A Fast Lane transponder installed in the author's highly energy-efficient and politically correct automobile.

This initiative is part of a strategy called Intelligent Transportation Systems, or ITS, which is aimed at making travel safer and more efficient. The system's technology is meant to do three things:

- **Automatic Vehicle Identification:** Your car is registered in the system.
- **Automatic Vehicle Type Identification:** A toll is paid based on the number of wheels and axels as detected by sensors in the toll booth, and this is correlated to the vehicle you have registered with the system.

- **Violation Enforcement:** Improper use of the system and traffic through the toll booth can alert authorities; a camera takes an image of the vehicle and transmits it.

You can use Fast Lane and EZ-Pass on the following roadways:

- **Delaware:** Delaware Department of Transportation; Delaware River Port Authority; Delaware River and Bay Authority
- **Maryland:** Maryland Transportation Authority
- **Massachusetts:** Massachusetts Turnpike Authority
- **New Jersey:** New Jersey Turnpike Authority; South Jersey Transportation Authority
- **New York:** New York State Thruway Authority; Port Authority of New York & New Jersey; Metropolitan Transit Authority Bridges and Tunnels; New Jersey Highway Authority; Buffalo and Fort Erie Public Bridge Authority; New York State Bridge Authority
- **Pennsylvania:** Pennsylvania Turnpike Commission
- **West Virginia:** West Virginia Parkways

The Coming of Intel PCA

Pervasive computing, that is, the ability to use computers anywhere you are, is an industry initiative. From the Oxygen project at MIT to Microsoft to Intel, projects that need mobility are looking for a way to exploit wireless networking. Intel's particular initiative is called Intel PCA (Personal Client Architecture; see `www.intel.com/pca/developernetwork/overview/index.htm`), and the program seeks to create a framework that developers can use to enable data exchange and device control of applications over wireless links.

The aim, of course, is for Intel to sell more microprocessors in consumer products such as cell phones, and to have those devices interoperate together. It's a huge market, one that has a very high replacement percentage and a short product lifetime. If you want to know how powerful the cellular phone marketplace could be, consider this one fact: Sony has just discontinued its highly regarded Clié series (see `http://sonyelectronics.sonystyle.com/micros/clie/`) of Palm PDAs because the company feels that the market for these devices will be supplanted by smart phones. Indeed, we are at a point where many PDAs are being forced to become phones to compete in this market. The Handspring Treo is one good example.

PCA creates a framework for wireless mobile devices and separates the communications subsystem from the application subsystem. A hardware architecture model uses a set of common components and programming interfaces that binds the two modules together. Therefore, a developer of an application need only concentrate on the program itself using the PCA API (Application Programming Interface) to create the program; the details of how the application communicates with the device itself or another device somewhere else is abstracted away. From a hardware developer side this arrangement is also valuable because OEMs know that if they build a device that conforms to the architectural standard, there will be applications that will run on their system.

The situation with PCA is totally analogous to how operating system vendors such as Microsoft promote their products, such as Windows, to the developer community. However, Intel's initiative isn't an operating system per se, nor is it a virtual machine like Virtual PC. It is a programming interface with an associated set of program libraries that can be ported from one operating system to another. PCA is platform-, language-, and CPU/DSP architecture–independent. Therefore, you might see PCA technology show up on cell phones that run on a Linux kernel, the Symbian OS, the Palm, Windows CE, whatever. Similarly, the process for creating the necessary wireless interface can be done by the wireless providers for their particular network. Should a particular vendor such as Verizon Wireless, Sprint, or CellularOne upgrade its network, it can rewrite its connection code and know that all of the applications and hardware based on PCA will still function.

Intel sees the market for PCA devices as

- Entry-level PDAs
- Personal communicators
- Voice-centric handsets
- Web tablets

PCA is meant to be built on a series of processors based on what Intel has branded the XScale technology. XScale microprocessors are a new architecture that is compliant with the ARM version 5TE series of processors that are found in PDAs, cell phones, and other small computing devices. The application and operating system of a PCA system runs in the application subsystem. The communications subsystem is where one or more additional processors perform I/O and execute Layer 1, 2, and 3 operations in the communication stack. These additional processors can be a DSP (Digital Signal Processor) or an industry standard GPU or a general-purpose microprocessor.

PCA has a bus interface that can interface with Bluetooth, wireless USB, or a wired I/O component such as PCMCIA (CardBus). The memory in PCA devices can be either internal, external, stacked, or a combination of types. Applications can share memory or reserve it for use, and you can use SRAM, SDRAM, Flash memory, or an expansion card.

Summary

In this chapter you learned how wireless technology is changing the way you work, play, and travel in your car. Wireless connections for laptops are most often based on cellular technology, and you can connect via systems offered by major wireless phone providers. Cellular technology provides a broad range of coverage, similar to your phone, but is not a high-speed broadband connection. More typically it is a little slower than a DSL line, and a little faster than a modem line.

Many other wireless technologies offer longer range still. If you installed a digital radio or a GPS system in your car, those systems use radio signals from satellites that broadcast over entire continents. Sometimes these systems are supplemented by repeaters on the ground.

Finally, some technologies exist that work over a shorter range. Two that were discussed were the car transponder that pays tolls on highways and a wireless FM transmitter that will play your audio devices over the FM radio in your car.

In the next chapter you see what all of this mobile technology has wrought in the modern office. We consider how wireless technologies can be used to help you more easily create ad hoc meetings, get more use out of the different rooms in your office, give you more flexibility, and other related topics.

Chapter 20

The Wireless Office

In Chapter 14, you learned about some of the technologies you can employ to create an entertainment system connected by wireless networking. When you commit to establishing a wireless link, you provide your network with more flexibility and thus more choices in locating equipment where you want it instead of where it must be. Networks changed the way personal computers worked by allowing more efficient use of shared resources. Wireless networks further extend this advantage, making it even easier to share the kinds of resources that offices need. With a wireless office, you can connect to remote multifunction printers, better serve ad hoc meetings and presentations by beaming a PowerPoint slide show into the room that needs it, move people hither and yon without having to rewire an entire office (as many companies love to do), and have countless other conveniences as well.

SOHO, or Small Office or Home Office, has a counterpart called SOBO, or Small Office or Business Office. The distinction between the two is that (theoretically) the latter is not in your home, but more importantly there are several people working on the network for a business. Thus a small business network is much more likely to use a domain server, enforce security, and require shared business resources. Those differences argue for a different approach in setting up a wireless network, one that protects network traffic and that allows only authorized users to have access to those shared resources.

From your reading already you know how to set up a wireless network, and about many of the devices that can be used on a wireless network. This chapter looks at some of the recent developments aimed at making the office a friendlier place to work, how to enable employees to become unfettered by your wired network, and how to make sure that all of these important confidential communications are sufficiently safeguarded so that your corporate jewels are protected.

So give us your poor, your wired, your huddled workers yearning to compute free. We hold this access point up by this golden door. (Apologies are given to Emma Lazarus.)

Wireless Servers and Server Appliances

A wireless server can be a great convenience to your network because once you set it up correctly, there's not much more that you need to do to apply the service to any number of clients. In addition to unifying shared network services, a server or server appliance can lower overall costs by eliminating duplication of equipment, and allow access to a broader range of services than a network without a server. A server can be a simple appliance with a set of preconfigured services that limit what you can modify but lower the complexity involved in their setup, or it can be what is called a *General-Purpose Server (GPS)*. A GPS might be a Windows Server 2003, a Linux server, or a Sun

Server with a full range of services that you can install and configure. The advantage of a GPS is that it is almost infinitely configurable; the disadvantage is of course that you have to have expert knowledge to set it up properly.

We think that there are two very important reasons for setting up a network server:

- Improving security
- Improving performance

Your network server is used to authenticate a client, provide appropriate resource access, and offer other services such as directory services, certificate services, and even encryption and virtual network services. Because most of the processing for these services is removed from the client and onto the server where a single, more powerful (and perhaps specialized) processing engine is applied, a network server that provides wireless services will allow your network to be faster and your traffic to be optimized.

Using Windows Server 2003 as a Wireless Server

Windows Server 2003 is easily added to a WLAN, provided that it has a WLAN NIC or is attached to a wireless access point or another wireless transceiver. If the server detects a WLAN, you can add it to that WLAN very easily using the following method:

1. When you see the balloon appear in the Status area of the toolbar that says "One or more wireless networks are available," click that balloon.
2. Select the WLAN in the Connect to Wireless Network dialog box; then click the OK button.

When this method is used, the SSID, encryption key and encryption mode, as well as the authentication, are automatically transferred and you are connected.

Instances occur where automatic configuration won't be possible and you will be forced to configure the server (and other clients) manually. For a small network, that isn't an issue, but if you have a small office with 20 computers, manual configuration may be very tedious. Starting with Windows XP SP1 and Windows Server 2003, an addition was made to the Active Directory's Group Policy section to add a Wireless Network (IEEE 802.11) Policies Group Policy extension. That policy lets you create a domain Group Policy object that will set the preferred network and settings to any computer that you apply the policy to.

To set this group policy, do the following:

1. Open the Computer Configuration Group Policy snap-in and navigate to the Windows Settings/Security Settings/Wireless Network (IEEE 802.11) Group Policy branch, as shown in Figure 20-1.
2. Right-click the Wireless Network (IEEE 802.11) Policies object; then select Create Wireless Network Policy to start the Create Wireless Policy Wizard. When you create a policy, you name it and enter any of the settings that you want to be propagated to the Association and Authentication tabs of a wireless network device.

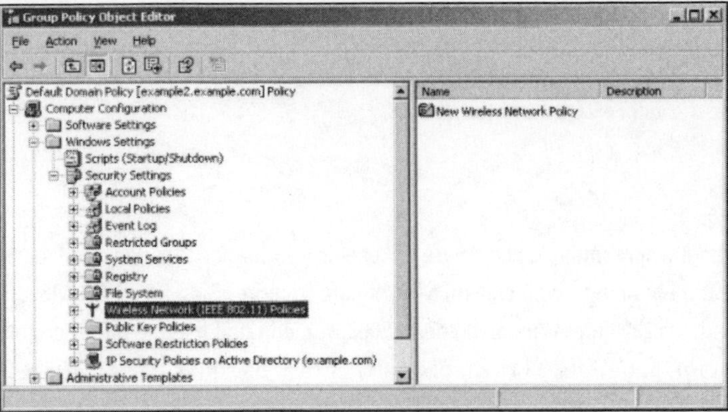

Figure 20-1: The Wireless Network (IEEE 802.11) Group Policy snap-in.

Note

The Wireless group policy can only be applied to Windows Server 2003, Windows XP SP1, and Windows XP SP2. Any computer running Windows 2000 (even SP4) or earlier versions of the operating system will not be able to participate in automated wireless configuration using a group policy.

3. Enter your settings in the General (shown in Figure 20-2) and Preferred Network tabs.

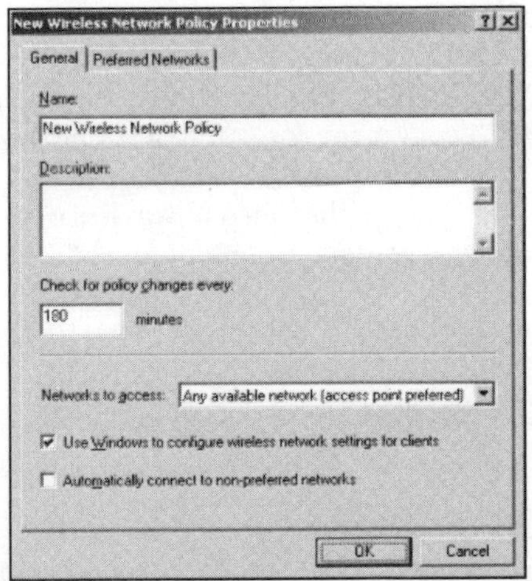

Figure 20-2: The General tab of the Wireless policy object.

4. Close all dialog boxes and the Policy console to save your settings.

Space precludes a full listing of all the settings in the Wireless Group Policy object, but you can get a description of them from Server 2003's help system.

Note

If you have a wireless environment where multiple clients are accessing information that you need to carefully protect, you may want to look into obtaining and installing a certificate from VeriSign for PEAP-MS-CHAP v2 wireless authentication on Windows 2000 and Windows Server 2003. You can find a white paper on this topic at `www.microsoft.com/downloads/details.aspx?familyid=1971d43c-d2d9-408d-bd97-139afc60996b&displaylang=en`.

The Wireless Network Setup Wizard

Windows XP Service Pack 2 ships with a Wireless Network Setup Wizard (WNSW), which is meant to provide an easy way to get your wireless connection up and running. This wizard assumes that the small business office doesn't have a central domain server or a dedicated professional or outside consultant who can help you set up a wireless connection. Many users have trouble turning on encryption and authentication. Therefore the wizard lets you pick options such as WPA with a Preshared Key (PSK) and Temporal Key Integrity Protocol (TKIP) encryption without having to know much about them. The use of WPA/PSK-TKIP is highly recommended whenever practical.

The wizard will let you set up an open network with WEP, although that isn't recommended. The best you can do with WEP is to select a strong WEP key; and the wizard walks you through this. As you might recall from Chapter 7, a strong key is one that can't be guessed from a dictionary of words or with numbers that identify you and the people or things around you. The strongest keys are the ones that are random hexadecimal numbers and letters, and have the largest number of characters that the particular protocol allows. So the wizard does a conversion for you to a strong key. It also makes sure that the same key is used on all other connected computers in your WLAN.

One of the most common issues users have is that the setup of the different wireless devices on a WLAN varies. Your access point might have a browser-based administration utility, while your NIC's settings are selected in the Network Connections dialog box. Windows XP SP2 unifies settings to a degree by allowing you to configure settings for both WEP and WPA-PSK using a new feature called the Windows Smart Network Key, or WSNK. Devices that have added WSNK will now register in the Wireless Network Setup Wizard. Some wireless devices that don't have WSNK support can add this support through software or firmware updates.

Here are the steps in the WNSW:

1. Launch the wizard from the Wireless Network Setup task or icon in the Network and Internet Connections folder.

2. Enter the wireless network name, also known as the SSID, as shown in Figure 20-3.

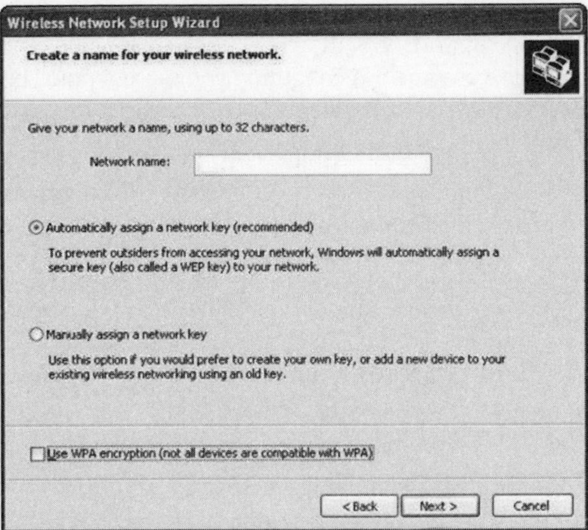

Figure 20-3: The Wireless Network Setup Wizard naming dialog box.

3. Set the authentication and encryption methods.
4. Create a strong WEP or WPA-PSK key.
5. Store the settings you just created into an XML file on a Universal Serial Bus flash drive, as shown in Figure 20-4.

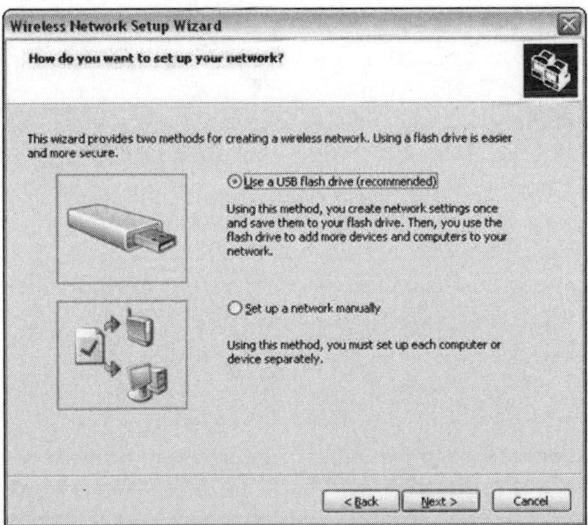

Figure 20-4: The wizard lets you create a settings key on a USB storage device.

Once you have a wireless configuration key on your USB storage device, plug that device as a key into any wireless device that supports WSNK, where it is read, copied, and installed. Microsoft recommends that you start by configuring your access point first, and then proceed on to configuring your network computers. You'll know that this system has worked because the USB drive will flash its status light three times.

6. Put the USB device into your WSNK-compliant access point or router. Configure that device, automatically if you can, manually if you must.
7. Put the USB device in your other network computers and install your settings on them. For computers, USB storage devices are supported in the Windows XP operating system automatically, and so when you put this device into any computer with Windows XP it is recognized automatically as a disk drive. Open My Computer and you will see it there. If you've set this up properly, the wizard will autorun on the computer you've just inserted the device into, ask if you wish to join the network you have set up, and copy the wireless configuration profile.
8. When you have completed all of the other device configurations, put the USB key into your starting computer and click Next to transfer all of those network settings to your computer. You will see a message that says that the wizard has successfully completed its task.
9. If you intend to configure more devices, leave the checkbox checked, otherwise click Finished.

Microsoft recommends that you reformat the USB device so that your settings are protected. To do so, right-click the icon of the USB drive in My Computer and then select the Format command from the context menu.

The only glitch is that your access point, router, or repeater has to have a USB port, and most don't, at this point. So to get these "legacy" devices to update and configure you will need to upgrade the firmware using their management software consoles, which unfortunately this wizard doesn't help you with. For those devices that can't be updated in firmware you are reduced to taking the printed settings and manually configuring the devices yourself, which in a way puts you back where you started if you are not knowledgeable about computer networks.

You can also use the wizard to configure any new WSNK-compatible device that you add at a later date. To do so, run the wizard again and it will re-create your settings on your flash disk so that you can then plug that disk into the USB port of your new WLAN device. If you want to, you can manually set up your WEP or WPA-PSK key, or change your existing WLAN network settings within the wizard. You might want to change the encryption keys on a regular basis as a security measure.

VPNs

A Virtual Private Network is an alternative method for securely communicating between computers. A VPN sets up a secured connection in much the same way that WPA does, but with many more required resources. With a VPN you need a special security system run on a server that encrypts and decrypts traffic. With a VPN server and a firewall that is set up to only allow VPN traffic, you have a very secure system over which to allow a wireless connection. The best setup places your wireless gateway in front of the firewall.

Many of the more sophisticated wireless gateways come with VPN built into them as a capability. You can also create a VPN in software as a service on a server. For very large networks or networks supporting many connections, a dedicated hardware solution is best because it contains specialized custom ASIC chips to encode/decode traffic quickly.

Windows Server 2003 VPNs

Windows Server 2003 and Windows Small Business Server 2003 come with two different VPNs built into them:

- Point-to-Point Protocol (PPTP) and Layer Two Tunneling Protocol with Internet Protocol security (L2TP/IPSec) connections
- Authentication Protocol-Transport Level Security (EAP-TLS) authentication

Setting up a Windows Server 2003 VPN is not for the faint of heart. At the minimum, to create a PPTP connection you'll need to do the following:

1. Configure a DHCP service to create a new scope for your VPN.
2. Open the Active Directory Users and Computers snap-in on your domain controller and install the Certificate Services component into the certificate authority on your network.
3. Create a new group of users for your VPN.
4. Configure an IAS server; that is a Windows Server 2003 that is providing RADIUS authentication to remote users.
5. Set up remote access policies, authentication methods, and your encryption policy.
6. Make sure that an IIS server (Internet Information Server) exists to provide Web and file services to your internal intranet clients.
7. Set up a VPN server, which involves creating an appropriate VPN network connection with the right addressing and properties (including RADIUS settings) on a Windows 2003 server.
8. Create a DHCP relay agent for your VPN so that incoming and outgoing traffic is directed to the correct server and nowhere else.

And that's just the server part. Now for the client to connect to a PPTP connection, you'll need to do the following:

1. Add the VPN user account to the local Administrators group.
2. Set an alternate IP configuration for a connection.
3. Create a new connection and set that connection to the VPN, entering the name and the host's IP address.
4. Connect to the VPN using a dial-up connection-type dialog box.

VPN Alternatives

The L2TP/IPSec-based remote access type of VPN connection relies on established credentials in the form of certificates. To set this up, you must configure certificates on your client and server. Normally you create this type of VPN when a public key infrastructure, or PKI, exists to provide the appropriate certificates. You would use L2TP/IPSec for high-security infrastructures, and really this type of VPN argues for dedicated IT staff. Finally, the EAP-TLS remote access VPN also uses a certificate-based authentication method, but usually uses smart cards in place of software certificates.

Does this make you want to throw your hands up and surrender? It isn't that any of these methods are particularly hard given a recipe, but you have to know more than most people are willing to learn to make them work. Microsoft makes it as easy as it can with a very detailed step-by-step procedure that you can follow at `www.microsoft.com/technet/prodtechnol/windowsserver2003/technologies/networking/rmotevpn.mspx`. Numerous shareware and freeware products are out there that allow you to set up your own VPN server, but most aren't any easier than Windows Server 2003 (albeit free), and at least Microsoft's service has tech support.

For a small office, it might not be worth the effort to create your own VPN service, and it might be cheaper to subscribe to a service than to buy an appliance. The fact of the matter is that you can subscribe to commercial VPN services that provide a secure network operations center for your traffic to flow through. The idea is that by having a secure connection from your client to the service's secure operation center, you are removing the ability of anyone to either sniff your traffic over your WLAN or on your wired LAN where your network traffic is unencrypted and most likely to be hacked. Two recommended providers of VPN services are Boingo Wireless (`www.boingo.com`) and WiFiConsulting (`www.hotspotvpn.com`). A list of commercial VPN providers exists at `findvpn.com/providers`.

Windows Provisioning Services and VLANs

Starting with Windows XP Service Pack 2, Microsoft added a feature called Wireless Provisioning Services (WPS) that is meant to make it easier for wireless clients to connect to a WLAN and use the Internet Authentication Service, or IAS, to validate their connection. Although this mechanism is most useful when connecting to a hotspot, it can also be used in an office when guest access to the Internet is provided.

When the provisioning service is created, it obtains the appropriate network settings, identifies the client to the WISP (either using a Virtual LAN [VLAN] identification code or through its IP address), obtains credentials to allow a connection, and then reconnects to the WLAN with a valid connection to continue working. A properly provisioned client computer could use this service to securely and easily access a small business office remotely from a supporting WISP.

Few small business networks will go to the trouble of setting up WPS unless the business is actually a WISP. To provide this service, you need an access point that supports VLAN or IP filtering, an access controller and a provisioning server, and you need to be running a domain controller with an Active Directory service. You must also have server(s) running the ISA and DHCP services, although depending on the number of connecting clients, you can consolidate these services onto a smaller set of servers. Figure 20-5 shows a simple network that conforms to these requirements.

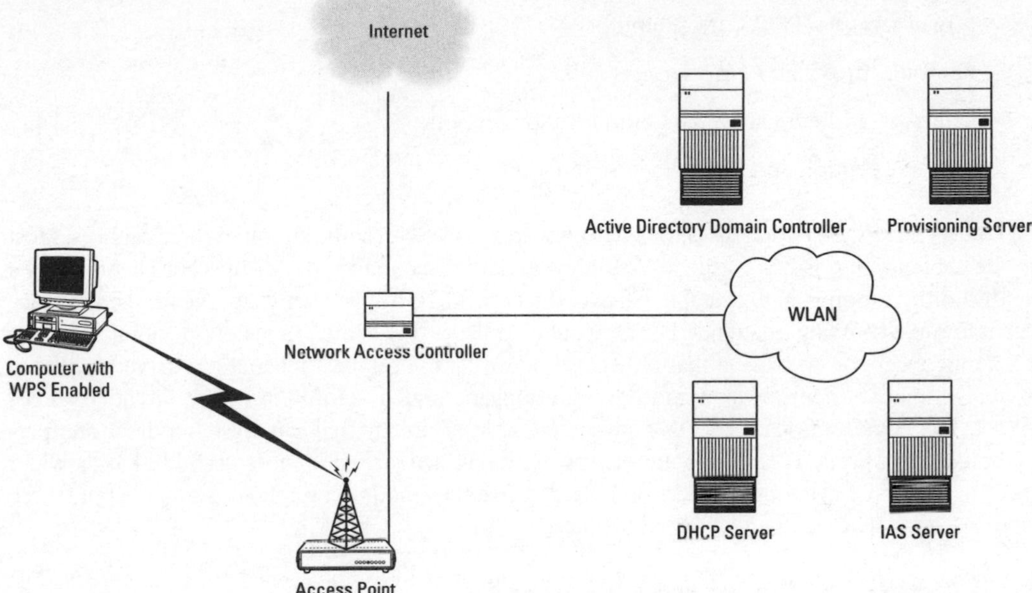

Figure 20-5: A small WLAN configured to allow Wireless Provisioning Services to mobile clients.

At the moment, you can connect to WPS-enabled networks with Windows XP Home Edition with SP2, Windows XP Professional with SP2, or Windows XP Tablet PC Edition with SP2. WPS would be simply a curiosity for the small office WLAN were it not for the consideration at Microsoft to add this feature to future versions of Windows 2003 Server. Indeed, if this happens, WPS will be one of the things we may see on small networks including future versions of Microsoft Small Business Server.

You can find a detailed description of the components of the Windows Provisioning Service and the related server components and their configuration on Microsoft's Web site at `www.microsoft.com/technet/community/columns/cableguy/cg1203.mspx`.

Server Appliances

We live in the age of appliances. Everybody and everything these days are specialists. A server appliance is a specialized device that provides shared network services, but only a specific smaller range of services with fewer configurations allowed than a General Purpose Server. The package is a hardware/software bundle with all the necessary applications already installed and configured or optimized. You simply plug it into your network hub, run a configuration wizard, and the appliance sets up a variety of services, including:

- Addressing services: DHCP and DNS
- Web services: HTTP and FTP, content caching

- File and print services
- E-mail services (POP3, IMAP, and/or SMTP)
- Firewalls, proxy, and NAT services
- Directory, authentication, and authorization services
- VPN, encryption and remote access services

Of course, most server appliances for small networks come with some subset of these services. Most often the configuration is done using a Web browser, and some make you set up your clients using a setup disk or by running an executable file over the network. Once you set it up, the server appliance is meant to run essentially unattended in what's often called a "lights out" mode of operation.

It's a misconception to believe that only small networks use server appliances. A server appliance need not be small or underpowered; indeed, many appliances such as InfoBlox's (`www.infoblox.com`) LDAPone, DNS One, and RADIUS ONE are special-purpose servers that can serve hundreds and perhaps thousands of users. From the point of view of a small network, it is more useful to have a wider range of services but have those services optimized so that the amount of work necessary to apply those services to your network's clients is greatly reduced.

Small Network Server Appliances

If you purchase a server appliance for the small office network such as the Toshiba Magnia, you may find that wireless networking is already built into that device. Not every small office server comes with wireless capabilities. If you purchase the less expensive Mirra Personal Server, that is the case.

Magnia is a Red Hat Linux 8.0 server that has a browser management utility. The average user wouldn't know or care that this appliance was based on Linux, just like TiVo users could care less. The Magnia SG10 (shown in Figure 20-6) is VCR size, and has a built-in hub of eight Ethernet Base 100/T ports with one of those ports meant to be connected to a cable or DSL modem. There's little to configure in the Magnia, and little that you can change if you wanted to. Mail is POP3 and SMTP but not IMAP4, and although you can set up a VPN and FTP server the Magnia doesn't come with a Web server, which is strange considering how popular Apache is in the Linux community. The 1.2 GHz Celeron, 256MB RAM model of the Magnia sells for around $1,400.

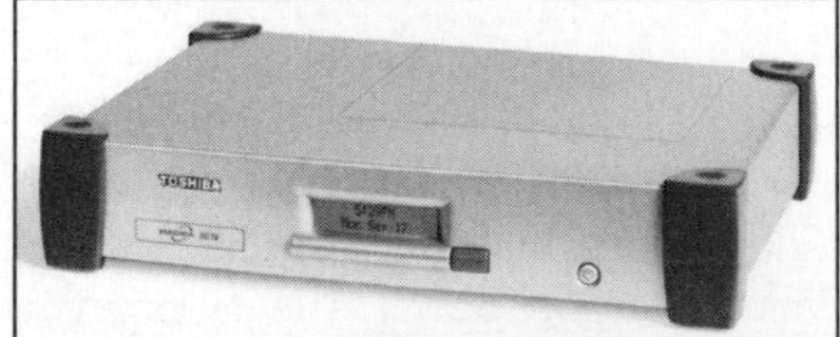

Figure 20-6: The Toshiba Magnia SG10 is a wireless 802.11b server appliance with a wide range of services.

A less capable, but much, much cheaper server appliance is the Mirra Personal Server. The 80GB model sells for $400 and the 120GB model sells for $500. The Mirra is meant for the home and micro business market and offers file and backup services. It's a no-frills product that comes in a PC case, but it performs the two functions it targets adequately.

This product category includes other more capable products, such as the following:

- IBM eServer xSeries 225
- Net Integrator Mark 1
- Dell PowerEdge 600SC
- Encanto Web Server
- Celestix Networks Aries Server 310
- PowerElf GreenComputer
- Sun Microsystems Qube 3 series
- MPC NetFrame 600

Most of these appliances are not wireless, but you can add wireless networking to several of them, in particular the IBM, Dell, and PowerElf systems. You'll find a comparison chart of products in this category at `www.iapplianceweb.com/apptable/iaw_soho_server.htm`.

Wireless VPN Appliances

It's for good reason that most people who choose to implement VPNs on their network do so on a dedicated device where almost all of this work has already been done by the device manufacturer. You've already seen how difficult setting up a VPN connection is on Windows Server 2003. It's a lot easier to set up a VPN on a dedicated device; indeed, all that may be involved is that you enter your client's ID or install a client utility.

Thus when you buy a firewall for a small office like the SonicWall SOHO TZW Wireless Firewall and VPN (shown in Figure 20-7) or one of its other products (see `www.sonicwall.com/products/vpnapp.html`), you get an appliance that is much easier and more convenient to configure. These appliances aren't particularly cheap, but they do come with a whole raft of additional features (many of which require additional purchases) such as intrusion detection, network anti-virus protection, content filtering, a Web-based network management system, and so forth. These devices are cheaper to install than Windows Server 2003, easier to configure, and once they are set up they can run pretty much unattended.

Figure 20-7: The SonicWall SOHO TZW Wireless Firewall and VPN is an example of a wireless server appliance that you can use to create and protect a WLAN.

Although SonicWall gets good reviews, other worthy candidates in this product category are available. Other products you might want to look at that will give you VPN capabilities for small offices are

- NETGEARProsafe Dual Band Wireless VPN Firewall (FWAG114)
- Watchguard's Firebox SOHO 6 (not wireless)
- 3Com OfficeConnect Wireless 11g Cable/DSL Gateway (wireless router)
- Linksys Wireless-G VPN Broadband Router
- Symantec FIREWALL/VPN 200 appliance (not wireless)

If you want a fully combined wireless VPN firewall network appliance, you have only a few choices in the small network market. However, if you are willing to separate the wireless part of the appliance away, you will find that a whole host of VPN firewalls are available that you can buy in a very wide range of prices. At the higher end are enterprise systems from network giants such as Cisco.

Summary

In this chapter you learned about some of the equipment you can use to create a wireless office. The chapter focused on setting up Windows Server 2003 for wireless networking, on server appliances, and on securing the WLAN using techniques such as VPN and VLAN. You also learned about some of the improvements offered to Windows XP clients with Service Pack 2. You'll likely find the Wireless Network Setup Wizard and Wireless Provision Service useful for getting started with a WLAN, or for automatically connecting to a hotspot while traveling.

In the next chapter you learn about the client side of connecting to hotspots.

Chapter 21

Hotspots and Other Connection Points

Hotspots are popping up all over, and this chapter describes how you can find and use hotspots. It gives you some information on connecting your laptop to the hotspot and provides some tips to help you get better throughput, make your session more secure, and troubleshoot some of the more common problems that tend to crop up when you are trying to connect.

Finding Connectivity Points

Public wireless LANs, or hotspots, are either free or fee-based. In either case, the hotspot provider has probably listed its hotspot in one of the online directories. If you have access to the Internet, the most convenient way to search for a hotspot is on the Web. The following are the best known hotspot locators:

- Intel's Hotspot Finder at `http://intel.jiwire.com/?iid=referrer_unwire+jiwire&`
- Boingo at `www.boingo.com`
- EZ Goal Hotspots at `www.ezgoal.com/hotspots/wireless`
- Free Networks at `www.freenetworks.org`
- HotSpot List at `www.hotspotlist.com`
- HotSpot Locations at `www.hotspot-locations.com`
- JiWire at `www.jiwire.com`
- Wi-Fi 41 at `www.wifi411.com`
- Wi-Fi Free Spot at `www.wififreespot.com`
- Wi-Find at `www.wi-find.com`
- WiFinder at `www.wifinder.com`
- Wireless Node Database Project at `www.nodedb.com`

All of the sites in this list are directory listing services. That is, hotspots are registered by their provider, or registered when someone sets up a hotspot with a wireless ISP, or WISP. There's a lot of duplication in these listings, and no listing dominates this field the way that Google does for search engines. Indeed, you may find that searching for a hotspot by location in a Web search engine is a useful approach.

Many hotspot network service providers and aggregators have listings on their Web sites of the nodes in their network. For example, if you want to find out where a T-Mobile hotspot is, you can go to its Web site and do a directory lookup. If you knew that T-Mobile was the provider for Starbucks coffee shops, you could also use this information to locate Starbucks with hotspots. Other providers such as Wayport (`www.wayport.com/locations`) can also be searched for locations in hotels, airports, and in other locations.

The problem with almost all of these commercial providers is that they don't list the free hotspots that are available in so many locations. Boingo is an exception to this rule in that a number of free hotspots are using its service. Boingo lists the free hotspots in its network, but doesn't list other free locations. You'll find that many communities have hotspots or open networks if you know how to find them. Often these communities advertise themselves in order to bring business into their area. Cities such as Portland (`www.personaltelco.net/index.cgi/WirelessCommunities`), Seattle (`www.seattlewireless.com`), and New York City (`www.nycwireless.net`) have networks like these. To find a community-based wireless network, search on the term "***cityname*** wireless network," where ***cityname*** is the city you want to search.

It's worth checking for a Wi-Fi connection anytime you are in a government building, a college, a convention center, or a library. Many of these locations may have open networks. If you find one, say with a Wi-Fi detector, it's a good idea to ask before connecting your system to the network. An open network may not necessarily be inviting you to join the hotspot; it may simply be a network that was left open by accident. Often when you are in a location that provides a commercial hotspot, such as a hotel, you may find that someone who has paid for the connection may have set up an ad hoc network and doesn't care if you use that connection.

The problem comes when you need to know about the location of hotspots, but you don't have an Internet connection. One possible solution is found in the software that Boingo supplies for its service, as well as those found from other providers. In that software is a database of Boingo hotspots that is stored on your laptop and that you can search when you are not connected. We'll look at Boingo's client in more detail later in this chapter.

Chances are that you'll find you're in a hotspot by encountering a sign that announces its presence. That sign might appear on the desk in your hotel room, on the door of a lounge in an airport or hotel, or at a coffee shop. Hotspot providers want you to know that their hotspot exists for your use; otherwise they wouldn't have gone to the trouble to install it. For example, you may see a WI-FI CERTIFIED WLAN Wi-Fi hotspot notice, which indicates that this particular hotspot supports Intel's Centrino campaign, or spot a sign with a commercial provider's name such as T-Mobile, Wayport, or Boingo.

Another way to connect to a hotspot in Windows 2000 or XP is to use software provided by an Internet service provider (ISP). Most hotspot providers will provide you with a utility that detects an available wireless signal and notifies you when you are in range. The class of software is commonly called a ***sniffer***, and it's possible to download other sniffers as well. Boingo's software is one example of a sniffer.

Getting Your Gear to Connect

Connecting your laptop to a hotspot isn't much different than connecting your laptop to your home network. Often you are using the same system dialog boxes and settings. Some differences exist, however, as well as some hidden concerns that you need to know about.

To begin with, your computer needs a wireless NIC to connect to a hotspot. In most instances, that means that either you have the capability built into your notebook using a preconfigured package such as Intel's Centrino brand, or you add a wireless NIC in the form of a PC Card (PCMCIA or mini-PCI). The trick is to have the right wireless technology to connect to the hotspot. Most of the current crop of notebooks are 802.11b devices, and more are being sold with dual protocol 802.11b/g added to them. You can't count on being able to connect to most hotspots with either 802.11a or 802.11g (although g is much more likely), but you can count on being able to connect to a hotspot by having an 802.11b capability. It's just that 802.11b has been around the longest, and that the second or third generation of access points with dual mode and tri-mode access points are just starting to replace the first generation.

Enable Automatic Addressing

Your network adapter should be set to "Obtain an IP Address automatically" and "Obtain DNS server address automatically." If you are a beginning user you can run the Network Connection Wizard in XP to specify a new connection. More advanced users can set these connection properties using the following procedure:

1. Select Network Properties from the Control Panel and open the Network Connections dialog box. If you right-click Network Neighborhood and select the Properties command, you get to the same place.
2. Right-click the wireless connection, and select Properties to view the Wireless Network Connection Properties dialog box shown in Figure 21-1 We recommend that you enable the "Show icon in notification area when connected" checkbox because it makes it easier to diagnose your wireless connection's condition.
3. Scroll down to the Internet Protocol (TCP/IP) property and select it; then click the Properties button.

Figure 21-1: The Network Connection Properties dialog box for a wireless connection.

4. Select "Obtain an IP address automatically" and "Obtain DNS server address automatically" as shown in Figure 21-2.
5. Click the OK button twice to accept the setting.

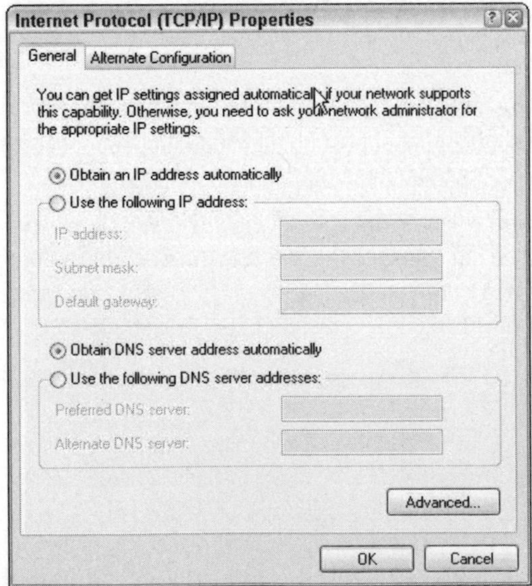

Figure 21-2: The TCP/IP Properties for a wireless connection.

You'll know you were successful in establishing a connection if you see an icon with two connected computers in the Status area of the taskbar.

Note

The icon for the two computers that each connection shows (if you enable it) gives you important information. Just like external modems, the two lights represent send and receive. The front icon is your computer sending data when it is lit up. The back icon is your computer receiving data when it is lit up. If you click the icon you open the Connection Status dialog box, which shows you how much data has been transferred.

Other operating systems may vary somewhat, but all of them let you set these settings.

Windows XP Wireless Client

Here are some instructions for connecting using the wireless client adapter with Windows XP:

1. Disable your proxy server. From Microsoft Internet Explorer, select Tools → Internet Options; click Connections, click LAN Settings, and disable the proxy server there, as shown in Figure 21-3.

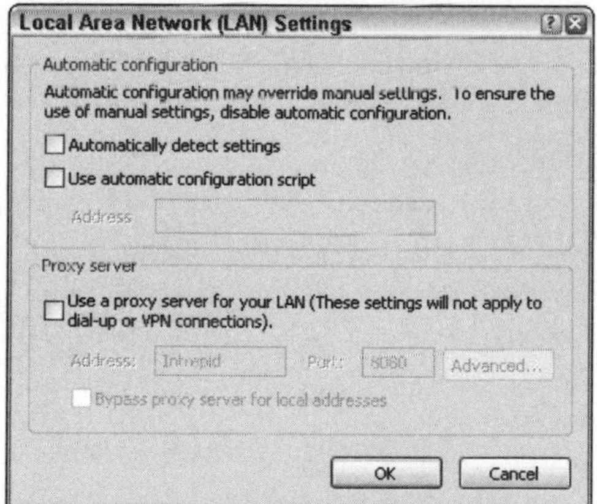

Figure 21-3: Turning off the proxy server in Microsoft Internet Explorer. Note the disabled settings for the Microsoft ISA server in gray.

2. With your wireless connection set for DHCP, and automatic DNS assignment enabled (which you did in the previous section), right-click the icon in the Status area of your taskbar and select Enable if your connection is disabled.

3. Turn on your firewall. If you are using Microsoft's personal firewall, enable that feature by checking the box on the wireless connection's Properties dialog box, at the top of the Advanced tab, as shown in Figure 21-4.

Figure 21-4: The Internet Connection Firewall in Windows XP SP1.

4. Right-click the icon for the wireless connection in the Status area of the taskbar and select View Available Wireless Networks.
5. In the Wireless Network Connection dialog box shown in Figure 21-5, find the name (SSID) of the hotspot's network and double-click the name.
6. For networks that don't have encryption enabled, the Connect button is disabled. Click the checkbox marked "Allow me to connect to the selected wireless network even though it is not secure" and click the Connect button.

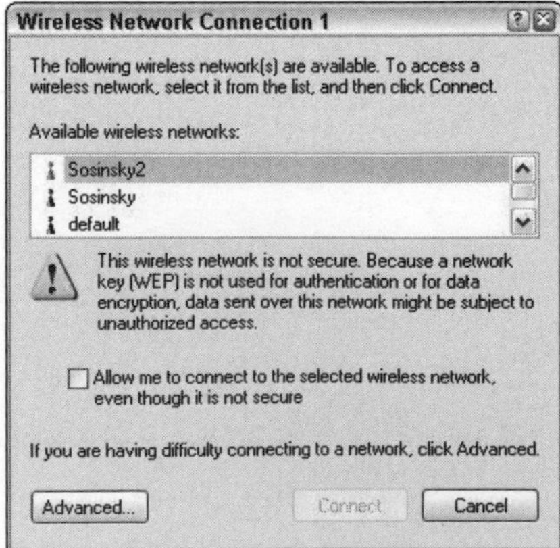

Figure 21-5: Selecting the available wireless networks using Windows XP's built-in wireless connection client.

For Windows 2000, a wireless connection isn't part of the operating system, which makes setting up a wireless connection a little more problematic, but no more complex than Windows XP. Your wireless PC Card should offer a connection client for Windows 2000 as part of its setup routine. If that is the case, you can either start the software in a control panel or by accessing the software using an icon in the Status area. Most wireless connection software for Windows 2000 lets you set up a network profile and select not only the wireless network, but also settings and which card to connect as well.

Boingo and Other Wireless Clients

In some instances the software provided by a hotspot provider is superior to the built-in Windows XP wireless connection, and you should use that software in its place. Boingo Wireless has an excellent software package, which is not surprising since it was among the first Wi-Fi service providers. Boingo's client stores location-specific profiles that you can use for your travel. You'll need to establish a Boingo account to use its client software, but at the moment establishing an account is cost free, although that may change. Figure 21-6 shows you the starting screen for the Boingo client.

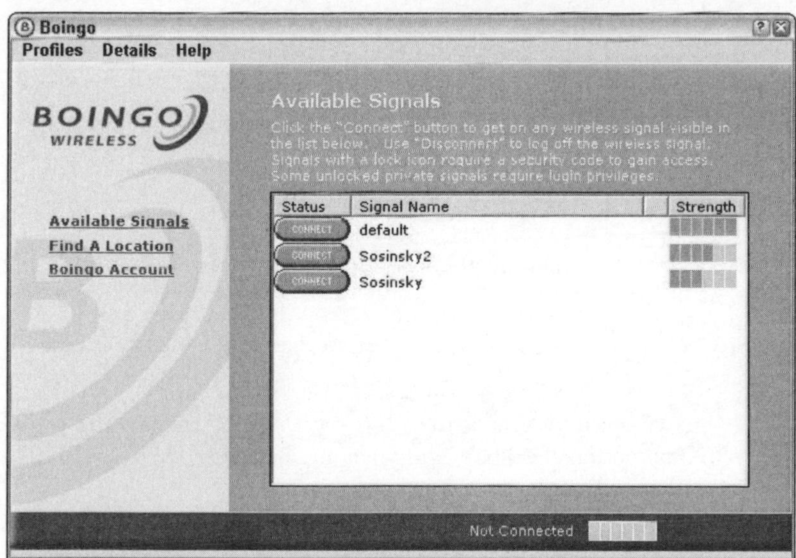

Figure 21-6: Boingo Wireless's client software is a refined alternative to Windows XP's built-in software.

As an example of a specific vendor's client software, let's take a look at what's involved in connecting with Boingo. Boingo creates and manages a set of profiles. The service offers a number of preset profiles, and you can change only the Auto Connect options for those kinds of profiles. You can also set up a profile for a connection completely.

Here's a synopsis of creating a profile with the Boingo client:

1. Double-click the Boingo icon, select Profiles ➝ My Signal Profiles, and then click the Add button to view the Profile editor, as shown in Figure 21-7.

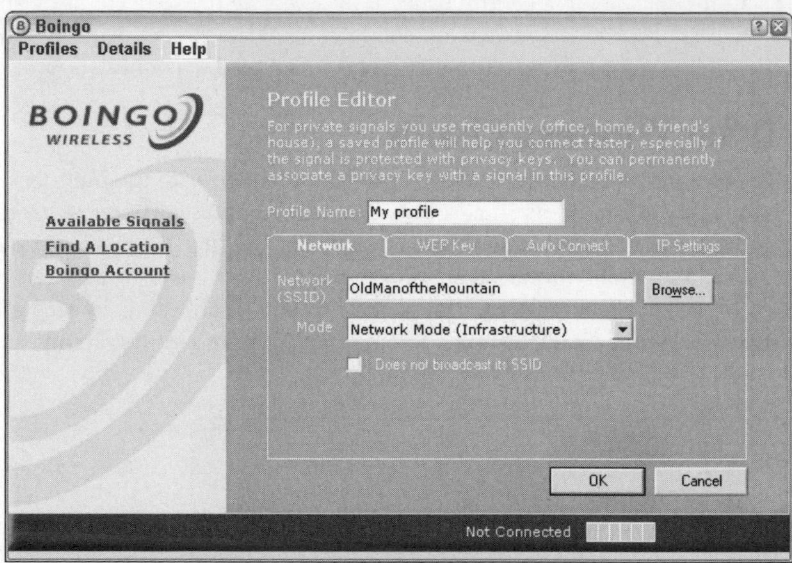

Figure 21-7: Adding a new profile to Boingo.

2. Enter the network name (SSID) in the field if you know it, or click the Browse button to see what hotspots are available in your location.

3. For any network that isn't broadcasting an SSID you'll need to click the "Does not broadcast its SSID" checkbox.

4. If encryption is enabled, you will need to provide the WEP key. Do so by clicking the WEP Key tab, checking the WEP Encryption checkbox, and selecting the "I Provide the WEP Key Data" radio button; then enter the key.

5. Set the method for connection on the Auto Connect tab, shown in Figure 21-8. You can choose to open the profile you are creating automatically, by offering it as an option, or by connecting automatically when the hotspot is detected.

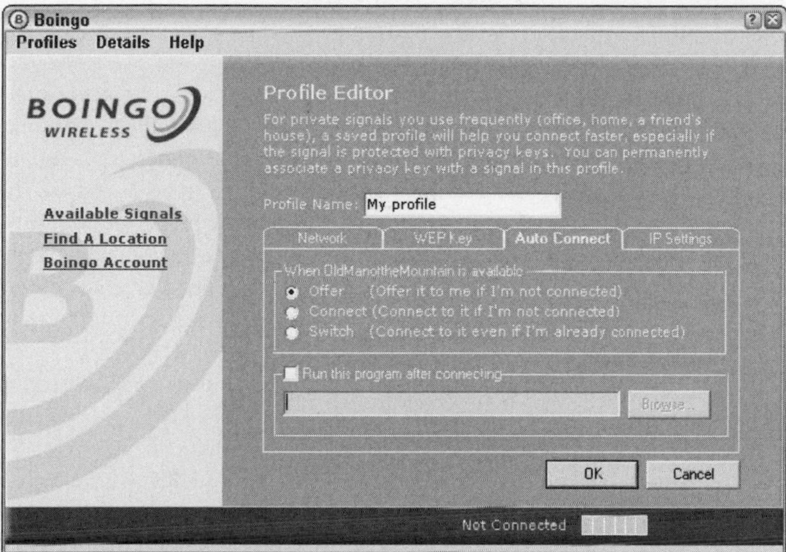

Figure 21-8: Boingo can auto-connect to your profile's connection when it becomes available.

6. If you haven't turned on DHCP and auto DNS, you can do so on the IP Settings tab in Boingo's software.
7. Click the OK button to create the profile and use it.

To connect in Boingo, click the Available Signals link in the starting screen, and then select the wireless network that is in your profile. That connection will be available if your wireless card can detect the network signal. Depending on your connection setting you may be automatically connected or be offered a choice.

If you are going to install Boingo's software, be sure to take advantage of its location database. The client comes with some additional utilities for troubleshooting connections. Among these tools are signal strength, connection history, signal details, and a system information screen that lists network details and information. Another feature called My VPN creates a Virtual Private Network or encrypted "tunnel" that runs from your computer to the server at the other end of the connection, which in this end is Boingo's connection server.

Boingo isn't the only provider with software that you might want to use. Another service that comes with software is iPass, called iPassConnect. iPass has both Windows and Macintosh clients available. Sprint's PCS software is derived from the iPass offering.

Hotspot Accounts

You shouldn't need a prior account with a free Wi-Fi hotspot, but there may be some registration feature involved if you don't have one. Even free hotspots may require that you register in some way in order to get their service. For commercial providers, having an account will save you some time getting connected but isn't generally necessary. Details on how you connect and either get an account or pay for a session should be available to you at the hotspot. For open hotspots where there is no SSID, you should be able to connect directly by enabling your wireless connection. For any hotspot that uses an SSID, you will find that either the SSID shows up in your list of available networks, or that it is not broadcasting its identification. For the SSID showing in your available networks, simply select that network. For a network that isn't broadcasting, you will need to find the name or ask for the name to connect to the hotspot.

In most instances, when you open your browser you are directed to the wireless Internet service provider's Web page, where you are asked to register. There should be instructions on that page as to the policies of the hotspot, as well as any fees associated with it. If you already own an ISP account for a hotspot provider network, after you sign in for the first time you will probably have a cookie dropped on you (if you allow it) and be automatically connected to the Internet. If you need to sign in, you will need your username or account name and security code or password.

Be careful to check the fees involved with a connection because they can be steep for commercial providers. If you need a credit card to pay to access the hotspot, make sure that you are providing that information over a secure connection. Secure connections are shown with two indicators: the use of "https://" in the address bar, and a locked lock icon in the status bar of your browser.

Mail and Server Settings

One of the problems you will encounter when you connect to a hotspot is that although your browser works properly, your e-mail no longer works. Most of the time it's your outgoing mail that's affected by the change in networks, but not always. There's an easy solution and a hard solution. Let's take a look at the easy solution first because it is, well, easy: Web mail. You can go to a number of places on the Web to get your e-mail from a browser. One that we like is Mail2Web (`www.mail2web.com`; see Figure 21-9).

In a Web-based POP3 server, you enter your e-mail address and your password and your mail is shown on the screen. You can view the mail, send a reply (with or without an attachment), and delete mail you no longer want. Many large service providers also maintain these services on their own Web sites. For example, with Earthlink that feature is called Webmail (`http://webmail.earthlink.net/`). It's important to make sure that whatever browser-based solution you use has secure connections. All of the three aforementioned services provide a secure logon.

Browser mail is fast to get to, but Web mail won't allow you to work offline, and is inconvenient when you are trying to maintain the kind of e-mail records that we all need to support our work, which brings us to the hard solution: finding the appropriate server settings.

The problem with outgoing mail is that many ISPs do not allow mail to be sent from unknown users on an SMTP port using the standard well-known port (number 25). The reason that ISPs block mail is that they are trying to prevent spammers from operating on their networks. You may find that setting your outgoing server to the SMTP server of your current network solves this problem. It often does, but not always.

You may find that some hotspots are configured so that you must first retrieve your mail from your POP3 account before you are allowed to send SMTP messages. You'll get a window, often for 30 minutes or an hour, in which you can send mail before the privilege is revoked. If you can't send SMTP mail, try waiting a few minutes to try again before abandoning a direct connection.

Figure 21-9: Mail2Web lets you access your POP e-mail from a browser over a secure connection.

Another workaround to the e-mail problem is to set up an authenticated SMTP connection. With an SMTP AUTH connection you give your name and password when prompted, and that allows you to send mail. This type of connection is a little slower than a standard SMTP connection, but it does have the advantage of being able to encrypt your outgoing message. Not all mail clients or ISPs support this feature, but when they do, it is very reliable. SMTP AUTH isn't a bad way to get around connection problems when your e-mail stops working at home.

Many hotspots restrict SMTP traffic at their firewall (period), thus preventing users from sending mail. In that case you may need to use the Web mail solution to send a reply. If you do send a reply using a browser, make sure you copy yourself on the message so a record of the transaction is stored in your e-mail program when you next retrieve your mail.

Hotspot Tips and Tricks

When you are connected to a hotspot, any protection that your home network afforded to you is missing for your new connection. It's essential that you use a personal firewall when you connect in a public location. Using your notebook without a firewall will make your notebook literally an open book; all of your files will be viewable over the Internet. You can turn on a firewall that is built into Windows by going to the Advanced tab of the Network Connection dialog box (shown in Figure 21-4 for Windows XP Service Pack 1) and checking the box entitled "Protect my computer and network by limiting or preventing access to this computer from the Internet." The feature is called the Internet Connection Firewall. In Windows XP Service Pack 2 this feature is substantially improved. If you aren't going to use Windows' built-in firewall, then by all means use a third-party firewall. The top three choices are Norton Personal Firewall, ZoneAlarm, and BlackIce, but others worth looking at include eTrust, McAfee, Panda, PC-cillin, and Sygate.

Note

Don't forget to turn off your personal firewall when you are done with your session. A personal firewall may interfere with your Internet connection when you try to use your home or small business network.

When you open your browser, you may not be taken directly to the hotspot provider's Web site and sign-up page. Depending on how you connect you may see your browser's normal home page in the browser window. That happens because your network settings direct you to that page, and the page is still in your cache. In that case you should click the Refresh button on your browser in order to force the page to reload.

If you can't connect at all to the hotspot, you should check your proxy server settings. If you have set a proxy server, you will need to turn that feature off. You saw how you can turn off the proxy server earlier in this chapter for Internet Explorer.

If your computer has a proxy server client, you may find that the client shows up in the Status area of your Start menu with an icon. For Microsoft ISA server, when you double-click the icon you will see the Firewall Client Options dialog box, where you can disable your firewall. Other firewalls have different methods for disabling them. However, it is still a good idea to go through the procedure shown earlier so that you've specifically turned off the proxy server.

Sometimes it is necessary to set a property called the ***preamble setting*** when a wireless NIC is unable to auto-detect the connection. To configure a preamble, follow these steps:

1. Open the Properties dialog box for the wireless connection.
2. Click the Configure button and then the Advanced tab.
3. Select Preamble Mode under Properties, and then for the Value settings, select "Auto Tx Preamble" (if that choice is available). The adapter shown in Figure 21-10 allows only a Long and Short and a Long only mode.
4. Click OK twice to accept the setting.

5. If the auto-detect doesn't work, try the value "long" and then try the value "short" to see if that lets you establish your connection.

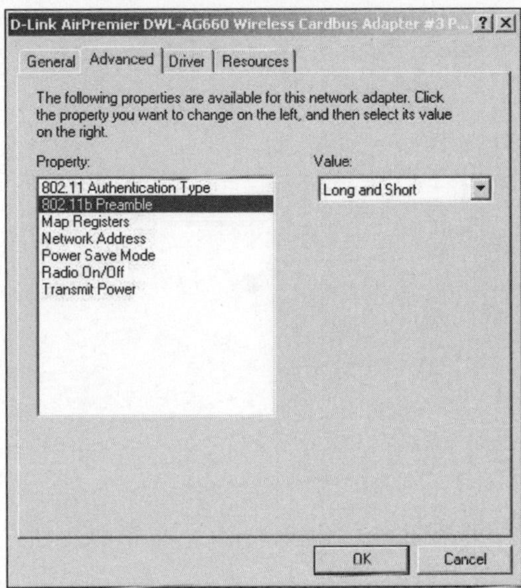

Figure 21-10: Try changing the Preamble mode of your wireless network card when you have trouble connecting to a hotspot.

In situations in which you are sure that a wireless signal is strong in your area, but you can't seem to detect it, always make sure that your wireless network card is enabled. The lights on the card only indicate that the card is detected and configured by your computer (in most cases), but they don't tell you if the card has been enabled or disabled. So right-click the icon on the Status bar and select Enable if it isn't already selected. Once you are sure that the connection is enabled, you may need to rescan to find the missing network. To rescan, do the following: open the Wireless Network Connection dialog box and click the Advanced button. On the Wireless Network Connection Properties dialog box, click the Wireless Networks tab, and then click the Refresh button. The network should appear and allow you to connect.

Summary

In this chapter you learned how to connect to a publicly available wireless LAN, also known as a hotspot. You can use your operating system's wireless client to connect to most hotspots, as well as software that some wireless ISPs offer. Connecting to a hotspot requires that you know where the hotspot is. You learned about different resources that you can use to locate hotspots in your current area as well as in locations you are traveling to.

You need to take into account a number of considerations when you connect to a hotspot. Number one on your list should be security: make sure that your computer is protected by a personal firewall. Also, if you run into problems connecting, check your proxy server. Many hotspots do not allow e-mail on them, and those that do may require special settings. This chapter also gave you some solutions to this problem.

In the next chapter, we move from the client side to the server side, and show you how to set up and run your own hotspot.

Chapter 22

Setting Up Your Own Hotspot

Few things are quite as nice as opening your laptop at a coffee shop, connecting wirelessly to a network, and enjoying a cup of coffee. A publicly available wireless network is called a ***hotspot***. Hotspots are popping up at bookstores, airplane terminals, hotels, and just about anywhere you might think to try to get some mail or do some work on your laptop. Many hotspots are free (so called *free-spots*) by intent and anyone is welcome to use them. Many more hotspots are free because people don't turn their wireless security on. No password and no encryption equals "free," and for some it is great sport to ride around "hotspotting" or "wardriving" in their cars detecting available hotspots to list on their Web sites. For a primer on warchalking, a related activity, see `www.jiwire.com/warchalking-introduction.htm`. Keep in mind that jumping on a wireless network uninvited is a form of hacking and an intrusion, so tread lightly.

In many instances it makes good business sense to set up a hotspot, and indeed for some companies setting up hotspots is a business in itself. If you own a motel and want to provide wireless networking to your guests, a hotspot is just the ticket. It can be a service that you charge for, which, if you have enough customers, more than makes up for the low costs involved in setting up a hotspot. Some companies will sell you a canned solution, a so-called "hotspot in a box." Other ISPs offer hotspot service as an option on your business account. Without too much effort it's straightforward to build your own hotspot as long as you know about a few of the hidden gotchas.

This chapter looks at how you as a small business owner can go about setting up a hotspot, making it a paying proposition (or not), and doing so safely and securely for all the parties concerned. We hope this chapter will answer the question "Is this a business for me?"

What Is a Hotspot?

That's easy! A hotspot is any publicly available wireless network that is available by intent. When you go into a Starbucks coffee shop, you'll find that it uses the T-Mobile wireless hotspot service as its hotspot provider. The way T-Mobile works is that a customer pays a monthly subscription fee to access T-Mobile's network, and then uses that account to connect to the service. T-Mobile is a large ISP in the hotspot market, but this is still a small market. What T-Mobile provides you is convenience. It does all the heavy lifting, you supply the cash. However, T-Mobile is a closed service meant for larger companies. It provides the hardware, the support, the billing, and the collection. You can elect to put a T-Mobile access point into your business, but you can't have your customers from other services connect via your hotspot with T-Mobile's network.

Plenty of other providers can offer you open solutions. From providers like these you get a conventional ISP business account relationship with pricing based on usage. Your customers get an account from any one of the services that honor each others' accounts, and that feature enables your customer to roam (which is, after all, what wireless is about). So setting up a hotspot can be as easy as making a phone call to a total solution provider, or as complicated as setting up any wireless network that is connected to the Internet. What you should opt for all depends on how much control over your services you want or need to have, and your intended use.

You need the following pieces to create a working hotspot connection:

- A high-speed connection
- An Internet service provider
- A Web server (yours or your service provider's)
- An authentication, authorization, and accounting (AAA) server
- A switch, router, or access point, preferably one that is meant for a business and not a SOHO
- Customers on a mobile device

Not all of those pieces need to be supplied by your business, of course, and a turnkey solution from a vendor such as T-Mobile won't require any of them. A simple setup for a small business's hotspot without a lot of connected users is shown in Figure 22-1.

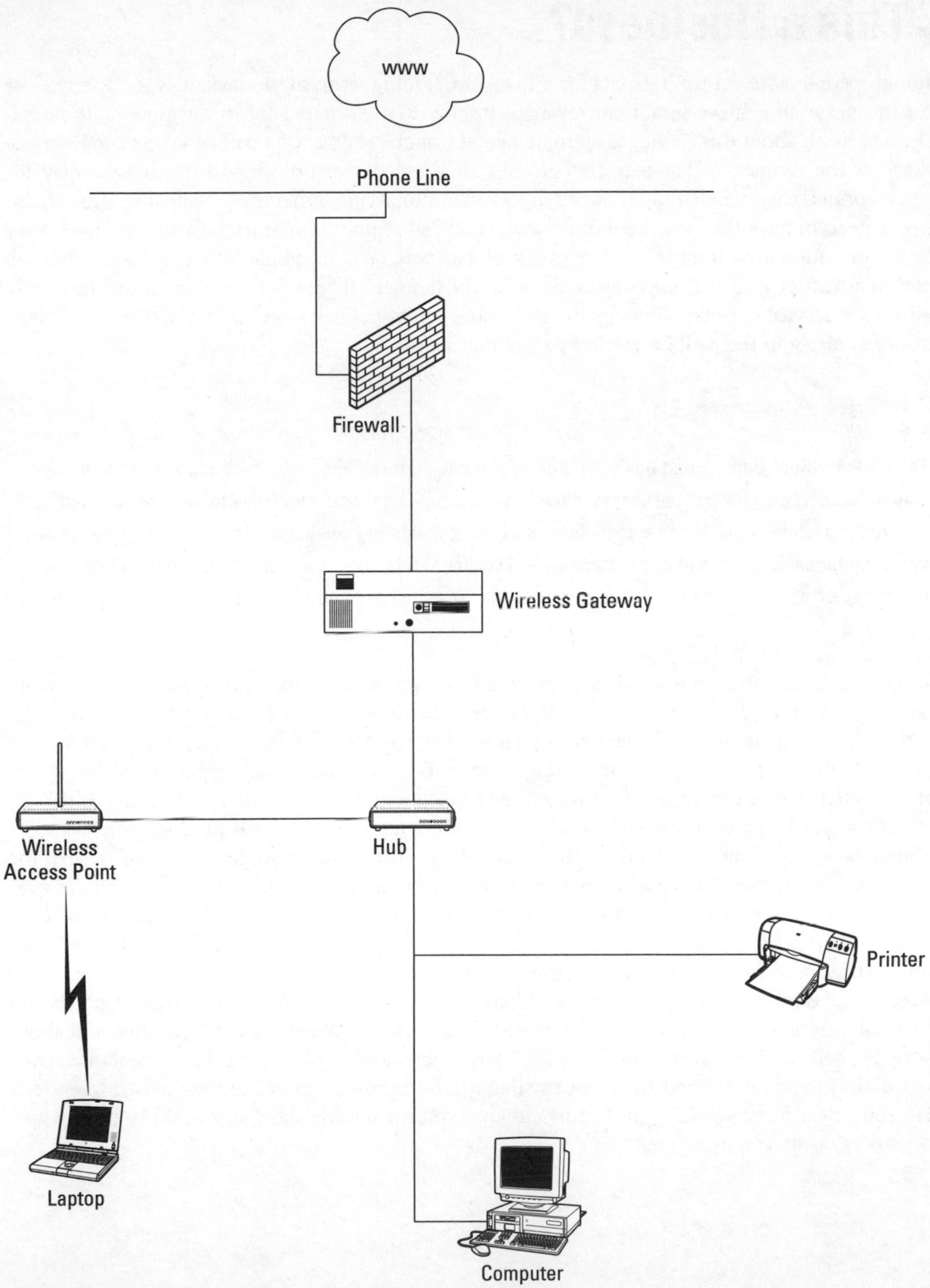

Figure 22-1: Network diagram for a small business hotspot.

Is This a Business?

Although people who set up hotspots for a living are finding work these days, it isn't entirely clear that a business can achieve significant revenues from an active hotspot for its customers. It's probably best to think about this service as an incremental revenue source, or a part of your overall service package at the moment. That may change over time as more people may be willing to pay for hotspot connectivity when that connectivity is ubiquitous and universally available. Essentially, hotspots need to have the same kind of coverage that cell phone companies provide. Because today there is no national or international network of hotspots, and no consistent pricing scheme, it's harder to attract paying customers for hotspots at the moment than it is to, say, get someone to buy a cell phone service contract. Perhaps the cell phone networks will become the wireless LAN connector of choice and this will be another part of that service.

Note

Intel's "Wi-Fi HotSpot Deployment Guide" is a great place to start reading about creating a hotspot. It contains specific scenarios for hotspot usage. Indeed, for Intel this is a product initiative for its resellers and its guide is really a white paper aimed at technical managers considering hotspot deployment. It's written in an easily understandable form, and at a technical level similar to this book. You can download the guide from `www.intel.com/business/bss/infrastructure/wireless/deployment/hotspot.pdf`.

If your business can be improved by providing Wi-Fi access to customers, perhaps you can avoid the headache of trying to audit and bill for service by adding the cost of service to your products. Any restaurant that is busy with few empty tables and requires multiple seatings throughout the evenings for meals to turn a profit isn't going to be helped by installing a hotspot. They don't want their customers just sitting around. However, any business with lot of empty tables and chairs or where the act of being on the premises adds sale volume due to additional product purchases is a candidate. The experience of others in your particular industry and in similar locations is often the best teacher. Remember, having a hotspot can be a differentiator that helps you gain advantage over your competition. A customer might choose your hotel over someone else's if you offer wireless connections. Chances are that your experience with hotspots will be tied to the kinds of customers your business attracts, and to your particular business model.

Among the establishment types that could benefit from a hotspot are airports, bus terminals and other public transportation; hotels and motels; Internet cafes, coffee shops, restaurants, and shopping malls; self-service and business centers; conventions and conference centers; schools; apartment buildings and offices; and any company that needs to provide guest access to network services.

Hotspots needn't be a permanent feature either. If you run a trade show you could be setting up a hotspot every time you move your "tent."

A Preliminary Checklist

Setting up a hotspot is very similar to connecting a wireless access point to any DSL or cable broadband connection. The major difference is that since your customers may generate significant network traffic on aggregate, most ISPs will require that you buy a business-class connection and establish a business account.

Here are some of the steps you need to take to implement a hotspot in your business:

1. Perform a site survey. Estimate the physical size of your desired hotspot and determine if your equipment has an adequate coverage area. Most access points offer coverage of about 300 feet in all directions. Walls can lead to significant drop off, and you may require additional access points and/or repeaters. See Chapter 9 for more details about structural impediments.

2. Determine the number of users that will connect on average and at the maximum level. If you figure that each user will require a throughput minimum of 100 Kbps to do e-mail as Intel suggests in its hotspot deployment guide, then more than five concurrent users requires at least a DSL line. You should also figure that each router can accommodate approximately 25 users. For more demanding throughput of larger file sizes (such as music files) you may find that your five users are using 1.0 Mbps and you will need a cable connection. In your calculation, keep in mind that not all connected users are generating traffic all the time, and make your estimates accordingly.

3. Test the equipment you are using for range, address provisioning features (such as DHCP, DNS, and gateway assignments), and for conflicts with other devices in the wireless range. To test your wireless coverage you can use a notebook computer, an RF analyzer, or an AP with a test standard feature. When you find a conflict, record the channel used, the MAC address, and the strength of their signal at several key locations.

   When you purchase your access point or router, you should get a guarantee from the seller. If your device conflicts with other devices, as is often the case for 2.4 GHz devices, you will need to exchange the item for a different device. You can get interference from microwave ovens, extended-range cell phones, wireless video monitors, metal walls, and most frustratingly from your neighbors using your same channel. Neighbors can be a problem if your business is in a dense location, less than 300 feet from other businesses. You'll need to test for conflicts, and be aware that metal walls do not show up in a site survey using an analysis tool. Perform your tests at different times of the day so that you locate intermittent but regular interference.

4. Draw your site and map out the range your access points will have. You should have enough cell size to have good coverage, but not extend out of your desired range. If necessary, add more access points so that they overlap and lower the power of your access points to get better coverage and serve more users, as shown in Figure 22-2. Your map should also indicate how many users will be in each zone so that you can design your overlap to accommodate the required connections.

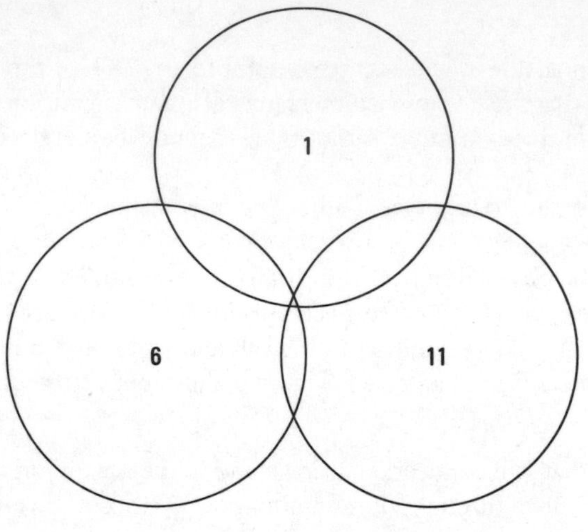

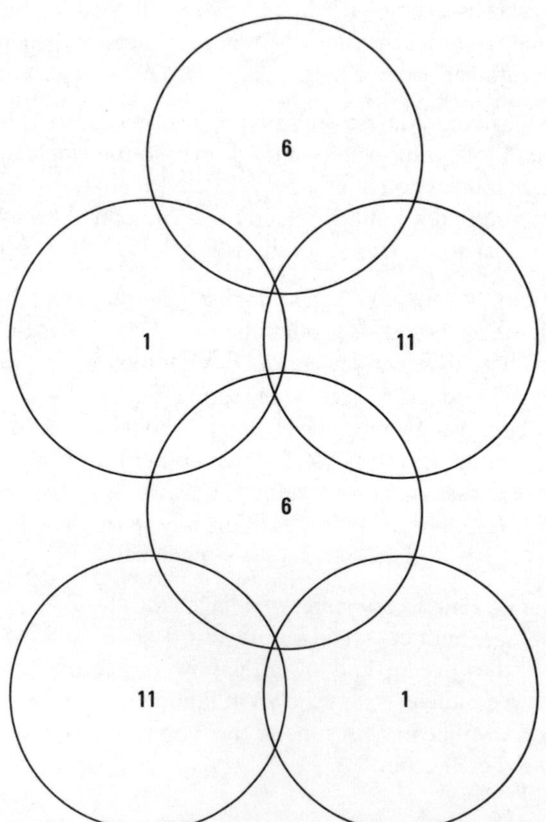

Figure 22-2: Overlapping lower powered access points can improve performance and coverage versus larger and fewer access points.

Note

Airmagnet, Airopeek, and Network Instruments Observer all offer RF analyzers. For software that you can use, consider NetStumbler (Windows), Mini-Stumbler (PDA), Airtraf (Linux), and Kismet (Linux).

5. Contact ISPs to get pricing and requirements and determine whether you are going to use a consultant or management service to help you with your hotspot. A consultant can be useful in setting up complex hotspots, measuring the quality of the connection, and in particular setting up security and billing software associated with a site.

In previous chapters you've been advised *not* to advertise your SSID. However, when you want the public to use your access point, it is a good idea for the network to advertise itself by broadcasting its SSID. It isn't absolutely necessary for a hotspot to broadcast, but it does allow someone in wireless range to connect without having to ask your staff for the SSID. If you don't advertise, your users will need to be told your SSID, which has some value in maintaining security. It's also a good idea to carefully manage the physical extent of your hotspot's broadcast to limit access to people who are not frequenting your establishment..

Selecting a Protocol

Any hotspot provider should assume that its customers are going to connect to its wireless LAN (WLAN) using different protocols and cards from different manufacturers. The greatest number of people will probably use the 802.11b protocol to connect. Smaller numbers of people will use 802.11a and 802.11g. The best you can do is to install an access point that offers tri-band support a/b/g, or install more than one access point to cover the different protocols in use.

Look for the following features in your access point/router because they are most likely to be useful to you:

- The ability to extend the range of your WLAN using repeaters and bridges
- Management software that shows you who is connected, what the throughput was, and other features
- Reliability and ease of use

The organization that certifies compliance of 802.11 devices is the Wi-Fi Alliance. It's a good idea to purchase equipment that carries the Wi-Fi Certified mark. That mark indicates that the access point or router has passed the Wi-Fi Alliance test suite. You can also post their network logo when you register your site with their directory found at `www.wifizone.org`. Both logos are shown in Figure 22-3. There is no cost for joining the Wi-Fi Zone.

Figure 22-3: The Wi-Fi Certified and Wi-Fi Zone logos.

Note

The Wi-Fi Alliance's Web site at `www.wi-fi.org` is a good place to begin an exploration of wireless technology in general and hotspots in particular. It offers straightforward non-technical explanations of terms and technologies as well as pointers to a large number of resources for further reading.

For more robust management, you may want to consider getting a Network Access Controller, or NAC. This gatekeeper device has smart filters, performs user authentication, and has management, logging, and accounting features. Two companies offering this type of device are BlueSocket and Nomadix.

Forget about features such as extended versions of protocols like ULTRA-802.11g or SUPER-802.11g because few if any of your customers are likely to benefit from the additional capabilities. The best hardware devices are the devices that are as broadly interoperable as possible. The fewer problems people have connecting to your hotspot, the less time your business is going to lose servicing your customers' computer problems and the more time you will spend on the business that your hotspot is meant to support. Whenever you have a choice, it's a good idea to sacrifice speed for reliability. Because most people either have 802.11b connections or have devices that are in theory backward-compatible with 802.11b, if you must choose a single protocol to get a really reliable unit you should choose an 802.11b access point.

Using Your ISP: The Acceptable Usage Problem

Not all ISPs encourage or want hotspots on their network. To some it's a security issue, but for most ISPs the issue is one of throughput: they don't want their network's bandwidth saturated by excessive traffic. Check your service contract and you will find a clause in almost all of them that allows service only under "acceptable use." The term *acceptable use* means that your ISP can pull anyone off its network that it deems to be doing something that it doesn't like. A spammer operating over a combination cable TV/broadband connection is going to get pulled (one hopes), as will any home that is serving up gigabytes per hour of music or porn on a peer-to-peer service.

What most ISPs don't tell their customers is that there is a threshold level of throughput that triggers the acceptable usage clause. Go beyond that level and you are going to get a letter warning you that you have exceeded your throughput quota. Service termination follows shortly thereafter. So if you are going to set up a hotspot that many people are going to use, you really have no choice but to call your ISP and tell them what you want to do. You'll probably do this before you know what traffic your hotspot generates, but this is the time to shop around for a deal. All ISPs are in business, and their business is selling bandwidth. With a business account and your ISP's rules on what you need to do to provide secure wireless access to the public, you will not run into this problem. Your only problem will be paying the bill, and many providers do what the phone company does—charge businesses a premium. So it pays to shop around.

Indeed, many ISPs do not allow e-mail to be sent over their network from a mail client when the person connecting to the network does not have an authorized account. Because most spam is sent using SMTP clients, and this mechanism could be launched to initiate a DOS (Denial of Service) attack through bandwidth saturation, this restriction makes some sense. It would not be possible to stop a user from sending mail from a browser client, but it is much less likely that bulk mail would be sent that way.

Hotspots in a Box

A hotspot in a box is a turnkey solution that you can buy and set up yourself. Typically you get a software package, instructions for configuring your system, and a support line if you run into trouble. Some vendors will sell you the hardware you need as part of the package; others just sell you the software and support. Any provider that sells you software, hardware, the connection, and manages it for you is really a commercial hotspot provider. We'll look at the commercial providers in the next section.

One of the advantages of a do-it-yourself package where you provide the hardware is that you can use newer technology and accommodate 802.11g users as well as implement a firewall, VPN, and other advanced security features that you might not get from a commercial hotspot in a box provider. If you use one of the latter type, it's worth asking about what it offers in terms of advanced and advancing technology. If a newer protocol comes along, such as 802.11i, will the provider support it and can you (or they) swap out your equipment to upgrade you? A good provider will update your software and hardware (if it supplies the hardware) with patches, firmware, and other upgrades.

One provider of free hotspot (free-spot) server software is Lessnetworks.com (`www.lessnetworks.com/index.php`). This Austin, Texas–based group, part of the Free Wi-Fi Movement, offers the Hotspot Server open source software that you can use to create your own free hotspot. When you run the software installation it creates a Linux system with the appropriate settings. Lessnetworks provides downloads of the software, sells its software on disk for a nominal cost, and even sells some preconfigured wireless servers on eBay that you can purchase as a package. According to the Lessnetworks folks, because of their software there are more free hotspots in Austin than there are paid sites.

Commercial Hotspot Providers

Several large commercial hotspot providers offer a turnkey and complete solution to hotspots. We've mentioned T-Mobile (`www.tmobile.com`) previously as a complete solution with its own dedicated and closed network; T-Mobile is Starbucks' and Borders' wireless hotspot provider.

Another large Wi-Fi service of this type that specializes in the travel market is Wayport (`www.wayport.com`). Wayport provides hotspots in hotels, airports, and retail locations, as well as providing wired high-speed services to businesses. Wander around an airport and connect through a Wayport 802.11b hotspot and it will charge you $6.95 for the connection. Packages of connections can be purchased at $25 for 3 connections, $50 for 8 connections, and $100 for 20 connections. You will also find Wayport as a high-speed wired connection in hotels, where they charge $9.95 for a 24-hour connection on top of your hotel bill. Monthly, annual, and corporate memberships can be purchased as well. Wayport currently has a pilot program going with 75 McDonalds restaurants in the U.S. to test hotspot commercial viability. Wayport does participate in roaming arrangements with other companies such as Boingo (mentioned later).

T-Mobile, Wayport, and a few others are aimed at large companies, and don't really serve the small business market. That may change over time as the market gets more competitive, or as these companies enter into agreements to let their users have roaming accounts on other networks. Surf and Sip (`www.surfandsip.com/`; Internet Café in a Box), FatPort (`www.fatport.com`—a Canadian provider), and others provide a commercial service that you are more likely to see adopted by a small business. You'll find that each service that caters to the SMB (small and medium business) market requires a setup fee, often monthly fees (they can be as high as $1,000/month), and will keep anywhere from 50 percent to 75 percent of the generated revenue. What you get from these companies is a monthly royalty check for the usage of their hotspot by your customers. They make your hotspot essentially a "lights out" operation for your business.

If you buy a commercial business class wireless router you may find that your wireless vendor has teamed up with another company to offer hotspot services. Boingo Wireless (`www.boingo.com/hso/hsiab/index.html`) has this arrangement with Linksys and will support devices like its Wireless-G VPN Broadband Router (WRV54G). When you connect that router to your ISP, you can create an account with the Boingo Hot Spot in a Box service. Currently there are 7,000 Boingo hotspots worldwide, and yours gets added to the list.

What Boingo provides is a Web-based management console. From its Web site you can monitor your hotspot traffic for one or more of your hotspots. Boingo makes its money the way all Wi-Fi hotspot providers do; it charges a monthly subscription fee to its users. When a new user connects to your hotspot you get $4 for daily use by someone who isn't a Boingo customer, $1 for each Boingo customer, and $20 for any user who signs up for the Boingo service through your hotspot. Boingo offers you co-marketing programs that include signs, tents, brochures, and a wireless hotspot listing in both its own directory as well as the Intel International Location directory. Better yet, Boingo provides end-user support, customer service, and customer billing.

Although Boingo calls its product a "hot spot in a box," it provides all aspects of hotspots with the exception of the connection. To my way of thinking, that makes Boingo a commercial provider. Boingo does offer what T-Mobile does not — the ability for users to roam on several dozen networks. In that sense Boingo is an aggregator, much like telephone companies that resell excess network capacity from telephone networks. Boingo's focus is on the small business market, and the aggregation of wireless networks is a plus in terms of providing you with paying customers.

Another offering along the lines of Boingo is the Surf and Sip Internet Café-in-a-Box, or ICAB for short (`www.surfandsip.com/ps_local.htm`). ICAB charges you a $300 setup fee to set up its hotspot. With its "Fee" plan you pay the lesser of $50 per month or 25 percent of your derived revenue to ICAB. It also offers a "Free" plan where you pay the setup but not the monthly fee and you get all the derived revenue. ICAB supplies the software, customer technical support, prepaid connection cards, marketing, and if you need them, the Wi-Fi access and managed computer stations. You supply your own broadband connection. ICAB has an interesting note on its Web site. It says "If you don't think you can increase sales by at least $100 per month by offering wireless Internet, you should be thinking about other ways to increase your revenue." That's probably good advice.

Airpath Wireless's WiBOSS Management Platform (`www.airpath.com/Products/wiboss/features.htm`) is yet another package provider. It will install whatever number of access points necessary to cover your business, all with a flat fee per location. It also offers a browser-based management console called the Provider Control Panel that lets you monitor usage and change your plan setup. Your package includes a customization feature (login and splash screen), an optional merchant gateway, free tech support, and a 24/7 branded customer care center.

The AIA Instant HotSpot (`www.instanthotspot.com/`) is a site where you can buy a standard package for a location of up to 2,000 plus square feet for $799 and an extended package for locations of 6,000 square feet or more. A premium package for $999 adds a credit card processing feature to the standard package, something that is also included in the extended package. What's nice about AIA's product is that even though it's a little more costly than some of the others, you get to keep the revenue you generate. AIA supplies everything except the broadband connection.

Almost all of these companies offer you a guarantee to decide if you want to keep their product and will refund your money if you don't. For AIA that guarantee is 90 days, whereas for Airpath the guarantee is 30 days. Use the guarantee period to thoroughly test your hotspot provider's technical support. If they aren't there for the trial, they won't be there to help you when you really need it further down the line. This is one of the most important reasons for signing with a provider. Test them both as your business network and as an end user would, if they provide end-user support.

Whatever platform you choose, one of the most important considerations is how large the pool of qualified users is. You'll find that organizations such as GoRemote (formerly GRIC; `www.goremote.com`), IPass (`www.ipass.com`), and others aggregate users. If your customer has an account on FatPort (`www.fatport.com`), DeepBlue Wireless (`www.deepbluewireless.com`), Wayport, and others then that account works on Boingo. So ask what networks participate in your vendor's roaming agreements and try to make some assessment of your likely audience.

Hotspot service contracts are a little like cell phone contracts. Providers want to sign you to a long-term agreement. The market is very fluid, however, and given how fast technology is changing in this area it is a good idea not to lock yourself into a long-term agreement if you can help it. You may find that your contractor also has savings it can pass along to you such as arrangements with ISPs for special low-cost connection packages, so ask about what additional benefits come with a long-term contract. You should be able to upgrade or downgrade a package based on the experience you have with your hotspot, and perhaps have a buyout clause.

Tips on Managing a Hotspot

First and foremost, make sure your hotspot is easy to use. As much as possible you want to avoid having to help your customers connect up. However, be prepared to offer assistance when someone has difficulty connecting — another good reason to keep things simple. You might want to consider printing up a connection guide.

Not all of your users are going to have a laptop or mobile device to make the connection they need when they show up at your business. Therefore you may want to consider adding a workstation or terminal for those types of users.

Management Software

Hotspot management software is an easily overlooked feature that is incredibly valuable. It's a significant differentiator between the different commercial providers and the Internet in a box packages. Good software can make security, billing, and other issues easy; bad software forces you to rely on log entries and other crude methods for analysis.

It's important to manage your hotspot for a number of reasons. Even if you don't intend to charge for its use you need to monitor what your users are doing. Any single user can bring your hotspot to its knees by saturating your bandwidth. It's not unheard of for a spammer to sit down with a cup of coffee and pump out thousands of e-mails. You also don't want users going to sites that will embarrass your other customers or perform illegal activities.

Even if you roll your own site, you should install and use a hotspot management package. There aren't a lot of choices at the moment in this category, but that will change with time. One product you can consider is called FirstSpot from a company called PatronSoft (`http://patronsoft.com/firstspot`). FirstSpot is a Web-based login that supports your hotspot configuration, security, auditing, and management. Some of this software's more desirable features include:

- Logon management, customization, and support for third-party password encryption routines
- Time accounting for both pre- and post-paid account activity
- Usage logs and reports, including connected MAC and IP addresses, time and duration of a connection, and other things
- Bandwidth throttling that lets you set the amount of bandwidth a user account or your site can use

FirstSpot requires a dual-homed (has two NICs) Windows XP, 2003, or 2000 server. You can dump your data out to standard SQL databases, or to any ODBC database. You can also deploy this software behind a NAT, PPPoE, or any static IP- or DHCP-assigned IP address network connection. PatronSoft offers a free trial for its software.

If you are using management software from a hotspot provider, you should also be managing security and user accounts in your software as well.

Hotspot Directories

Any hotspot really needs to be promoted in order to be successful. When people walk in the door they should see a sign that tells them that you have a hotspot and what kind of hotspot it is. You should also tell your customers how to connect to your hotspot and offer them a free trial. Mention your hotspot in ads for your business.

You'll want to get your hotspot listed in the hotspot directories. If your service provider doesn't do this for you, you should go to the following hotspot directories and do it for yourself:

- JiWire.com (submit to `data@jiwire.com`). Intel's hotspot list can be found at `intel.jiwire.com`.
- Google Wi-Fi Locator (`local.google.com/local?sc=1&q=wifi`)
- Wi-Fi HotSpotList.com (`www.wi-fihotspotlist.com`)
- Wi-Fi-Freespot (`www.wififreespot.com`)
- HotSpots-Free Directory (`www.hotspot-directory.com`)
- WiFinder Hotspot Locator (`www.WiFinder.com`)
- WiFi411.com (`www.wifi411.com`)
- WiFi Alliance WiFi Zone Directory (`www.wi-fizone.org/zoneFinder.asp`)

Some people recommend that you create a home page for your business that appears whenever someone successfully connects to your hotspot. That home page could be configured so that it is the starting point of an account-generation process. By having people create an account you can find out who your customers are for marketing purposes and track their usage. When they log in and out of their account you can track their usage and use that information to bill for the connection service.

Another good reason to create an initial Web page is that you can use that Web page to state the conditions of usage for your hotspot. If you have time limitations or restrict certain activities or visits to a certain type of Web site, you can use this page to state those terms. At the very least it's a good idea to remind your users that they are on an unsecured network connection, that they connect at their risk, and that their communications are not secure. You can also suggest what they need to do to protect their systems from outside examination.

Lessnetworks.com, mentioned earlier in this chapter, provides a solution that allows free hotspots to create just such a Web page.

Hotspot Security

The main thing to remember about hotspot security is that you probably won't use the encryption features or password authentication for users with your access point or any other fancy security features unless your hotspot is located in Japan (where encryption is required). Most hotspots use

"Open Authentication" (no encryption) instead of WEP, which is called a "Preshared Key Authentication" method. Keep in mind that WEP only authenticates a device, and it is assumed that if users know the key that they are allowed to connect. Other encryption methods, such as TKIP or AES, allow only Open Authentication. In all cases your hotspot will not be authenticating a user as is done on the network with a challenge/response mechanism (username and password).

The counter argument for enabling encryption is that it makes communication more secure and less easily sniffed by other computers. The extra difficulty connecting users with encryption and the reduction in throughput has to be weighed against the probability that someone may try and compromise your guest's communications. We feel that sensitive information sent to a non-secured site is something that is a problem in and of itself, and encryption won't help that. So we tend to opt for ease of use and count on users to implement their own security features. However, many other knowledgeable experts would disagree on this point.

Don't pay more to get a device that implements unusual security measures because you are going to leave them off so that the public can more easily connect.

Note

An alternative view suggested by others is that you should turn wireless data encryption *on*, so this is a matter of contention.

However, you should make sure that each of your users has a firewall set on their computer. If they don't have software such as Norton Personal Firewall, Zone Alarm Pro 4, or Black Ice (for Windows, for example), then at least remind your users to set the firewall that their operating system offers them. That firewall is turned on in the Advanced tab of the Network Connection properties sheet of a Windows XP connection, and is a checkbox called the Internet Connection Firewall that says "Protect my computer and network by limiting or preventing access to this computer from the Internet" (see Figure 22-4). In Windows XP Service Pack 2 the new Security Center will provide just such a reminder.

Although the current 802.11 protocols are not easy to make secure, we hope the release of 802.11i will offer some help. Until then there are some things you can do to help make your hotspot more secure:

- Make sure your network doesn't extend beyond your physical location.
- Don't broadcast your WLAN's router's network ID (SSID).
- Remind customers that unencrypted transfers can be read and that sensitive information such as personal information, credit card numbers, and passwords should be avoided on non-secure connections. Stealing information over a WLAN is not uncommon.

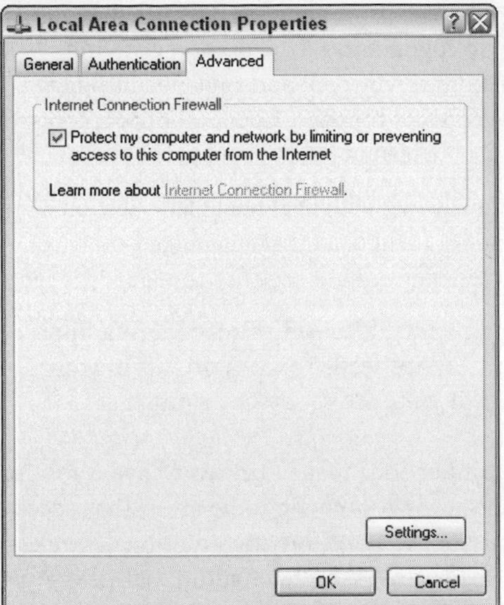

Figure 22-4: Turning the Internet Connection Firewall feature on in a Windows XP wireless network connection.

Note

Have your users look for the lock symbols in their browsers to determine the state of the connection, and have them use a secure SSL for e-mail. Most POP and SMTP accounts offer this kind of connection, as do most Web e-mail portals. You may want to recommend the use of client software such as HotSpotVPN (`www.hotspotvpn.com/`) for a more secure connection.

- Don't leave your router/access point's IP address, login name, or password set at the default. If your AP offers the username "admin" with no password, for example, change both of them. A bad guy only needs to look up your AP's manual online to know what the defaults are. Sometimes a router such as the Apple AirPort maintains an address that can't be changed.
- Use a strong firewall and put your wireless network on its own subnet.
- Do not allow your clients' computers to connect under a peer-to-peer network connection; that is, disable the "ad hoc" mode and enable the infrastructure mode on your router or AP.
- Make sure that connected computers are password-protected, both at a system and a shared file/folder level.

- Know your users. Make sure you have approved the people on your WLAN and that you monitor their activity to make sure that there are no rogue users. If you are registering users, you can enable the known MAC address feature of your AP and only permit known users to connect; something you can't do if your WLAN is meant for general public access without authentication.
- Turn off all wireless devices not in use, and that means *every night* if necessary. Test on a regular basis that when all of your wireless devices are turned off there is indeed no wireless signal that can be detected. Unauthorized access points are a security threat.
- Block TCP ports 135, 137, 138, 139, and 445 to directory, file, and printer sharing information to be transmitted. Disable NetBIOS over TCP/IP as well. You can do this in your firewall's software, in security software, and as part of your proxy server or router.

If your business network is going to use the hotspot connection, make sure you have a robust firewall or gateway between your LAN and your access point or router. Frankly, given that access points and routers are as cheap as they are these days you are better off buying additional wireless devices and keeping your network's wireless connection separate — why take additional risk? Any wireless connection on your business network needs to be encrypted and secured.

Auditing and Billing Usage

Billing is one of the more difficult aspects of managing a hotspot. Many different models are in use for billing customers. You can choose to

- Bill for each time or day that a user connects, thus avoiding having to monitor usage or collect user information.
- Charge a monthly or annual fee for an account, in which case you must create accounts.
- Bill on an hourly basis whether they are connected or not.
- Bill for actual usage time like cell phone companies do.

Most time usage management solutions use the login and logout times of users based on the logging capability of their wireless router/AP. When someone connects or logs into a connection, the MAC address is recorded in the log. Simple devices have difficulties measuring whether a user has logged off or has just been disconnected, and may not be able to check a connection using PING when a VPN session is launched or a specific firewall is in use. One of the advantages of using a more sophisticated solution like the Cisco Broadband Service Manager and the Nomadix HotSpot Gateway is that they have the capability to deal with VPNs and firewalls, as well as the added security features that they offer.

One company that sells a hotspot billing software solution is Alepo (`www.alepo.com/hotspot-billing-software.shtml`). Its RBS Hotspot software lets you monitor multiple sites and sign up subscribers to your network. You can sell one-time connections, prepaid connections, pay commissions to clients, and allow for roaming accounts. This software would be valuable for a larger business,

or for someone selling hotspot services and probably falls outside of the category of small business use. Another solution is LogiSense's (`www.logisense.com/billing_home.html`) engageIP Billing and DSS module, which is really also meant for a service provider.

Given the complexity of setting up an accounting solution (and the costs involved), it is probably better for small businesses to leverage this kind of software installed by their service provider rather than trying to duplicate that capability.

Summary

As you have seen in this chapter, setting up a hotspot is something that won't make you rich, but could be important to your business. If you compete in a market that offers this service such as a hotel or coffee shop, offering the service could be a deciding factor in getting and keeping business. After setting up other wireless networks such as your home or office, setting up a hotspot doesn't represent a significantly greater challenge.

However, there are things to keep in mind. You need to decide which ISP to use, find out what its throughput limitations (both quantity and type) are, and install appropriate equipment. Management software is one area that is difficult, so if you intend to bill by time or usage you will need to investigate your options. Luckily this is a growing area of service and you can find several canned or boxed solutions that you can use. If you don't want hands-on management you can simply make a phone call to a hotspot provider and have them do it all for you. It is satisfying to be able to manage this networking service, and doing so allows you to keep more of the revenues—with greater risks come greater rewards.

With this chapter we wind up the discussion of various product-related technologies and begin a section on troubleshooting. In Chapter 23 you'll get answers to your connection problems. Following that we'll first tackle security issues, and then device problems.

Part VI

Troubleshooting Your Wireless World

Chapter 23

Troubleshooting Connectivity

This is the first of three chapters on troubleshooting wireless networking. We look first at the common problems that you might encounter in establishing connectivity between your wireless device and the wireless network. Connection difficulties arise from any number of issues, including both hardware and software; even poor positioning of an access point or its antenna can be enough to significantly degrade a signal. This chapter presents these issues in a condensed FAQ (Frequently Asked Questions) format, which is a little different than the way previous chapters were organized, but is hopefully easier to read and will help you more quickly find the information you need to solve your problem.

My connection doesn't work. How do I find the problem?

The goal of any troubleshooting exercise is to isolate the problem so you know what you need to correct. Therefore, you need to start at either end of the connection and work toward the other end checking that hardware and software are functioning correctly. Most people tend to start at their mobile device end because the feeling is that an established server service is likely to be more reliable than a transient laptop network node. But in truth problems show up all along the connection route.

Most of the time you don't need to go component-to-component to diagnose a connection problem. If you have some idea what the problem might be, start with that factor and look at the components in hardware or software that impact that aspect of your wireless connection. For example, if your laptop gets a wireless connection, but that connection is very weak or transient and changes as you move locations, then you wouldn't start by checking the Ethernet cable between the access point and its hub. You might want to start by looking at the antennas and signal strength of your wireless components. In real estate, the motto is "location, location, location," but in troubleshooting, it's ***isolation, isolation, isolation***. So let's look at general areas of concern before moving on to specific problems. These are common areas of difficulty:

- Wireless access point or router's connection to the network
- Access point or router's condition, both hardware and software
- Physical positioning of devices and quality of signal
- Network interface card of client and settings

- Security mismatch or issue
- Client software or hardware problem

Because we take a more in-depth look at security issues in the next chapter (Chapter 24) and client devices in the chapter after that (Chapter 25), we will delay discussion of troubleshooting issues on those subjects until later.

My laptop can't connect to an access point, although other wireless clients in my office can. What should I do?

First make sure that it's not your location that's the problem. Try moving your computer to a known working location, or moving a working computer to your location. Another obvious thing to check is that you have seated the NIC in your computer correctly and that the adapter is getting power. That is, if it is a PC Card and it has lights (almost all do), do you see any lights on?

The fact that other wireless clients can connect to the WLAN means that the problem is specific to your laptop. You need to look at several factors: your laptop's network address, whether your NIC is functioning correctly, and whether you have the right software settings. Let's look at how you might diagnose this with a Windows XP laptop.

To check and fix your network address:

1. Click Start → Run.
2. Enter **CMD** and press the Enter key.
3. Type **IPCONFIG** and press Enter. `IPCONFIG` will return information about your network settings.

   Your wireless network connection should show as connected and have as an address a unique IP address in the same subnet as the access point the laptop is communicating with. That is, if your access point address is 192.168.0.1, the assigned IP address should be a valid and unique address in the range of 192.168.0.2 to 192.168.0.255. On some networks, laptops are assigned static IP addresses. A wrong address can be corrected manually by changing the settings in the Network Connection Properties dialog box for the TCP/IP property.
4. If your network address is dynamically assigned and the address is incorrect, you can force a reassignment by restarting your computer, or more conveniently by entering the `IPCONFIG /RELEASE ALL` command followed by the `IPCONFIG /RENEW` command.

   When you install Windows XP networking, you also install something called the Microsoft Loopback Adapter. This is a piece of software that lets you test your network card even when that card isn't connected to the network. If you see an address similar to 169.254.x.x/16, then your network card isn't getting an address from the DHCP server and you are viewing your loopback adapter address.
5. Enter **IPCONFIG** once again and see if you can establish a valid IP address and get a connection.

Sometimes having two or more DHCP servers can be the problem. If you are getting your correct IP address reset, check that there isn't a second rogue DHCP server. Many access points and routers let you enable this service, so it's easy to inadvertently establish additional DHCP servers without realizing it. If you can't establish a valid IP address, it's time to check your NIC and its settings.

My network address is correct, but I still can't connect my computer to a working WLAN. What's wrong?

The next two issues are NIC related: you need to determine whether the NIC is functioning correctly and whether the installed drivers are correct. That involves checking your device properties and perhaps swapping in a second NIC if possible. If this is a new WLAN you are trying to connect to, make sure that the protocol(s) the WLAN offers are one(s) that you can receive. If you have an 802.11a device, don't expect to be able to talk to an 802.11g network.

To check your NIC's device settings:

1. Right-click My Computer (either on your Start menu or your desktop) and select Properties.

Note

In Windows XP, the My Computer and My Network Places icons don't appear on the desktop by default. To add them you can alter the desktop properties by right-clicking the desktop and, on the Desktop tab, clicking Customize Desktop. The General tab is where you can select which items show up on the desktop. Also, some of the Start menu commands let you select a command from their context menu (right-click) called Show On Desktop, which also gets the job done.

2. Click the Computer Name tab and check that your system's name and workgroup or domain name is correct.
3. Click the Hardware tab; then click the Device Manager button.
4. Scroll down to the Network adapters section and click the + sign to open that section if necessary.

   If there is an X or a yellow caution sign next to the name of your wireless adapters, then the problem is your NIC.
5. Uninstall your NIC; then reinstall the card. Make sure that your driver software is the latest version and up to date.
6. If you still can't connect, try substituting a card that is known to work from another system and see if that solves the problem.

Not only is my network address correct, but my adapter card works properly too. What's next?

You've eliminated hardware as the probable cause of the connection problem, as well as the software that is driving your hardware. The next thing to check is the software in your computer. If you're connecting to a known working WLAN at a location where the signal strength is also known to be strong enough, your problem may be a function of incorrect network settings.

To check your network settings:

1. Open the Network Connections folder from the Control Panel, and check that the network connection is actually enabled. That is, the connection label should say Enabled. If there is a red X through the wire of the icon for the Connection, the connection is Enabled but unavailable. If you need to enable the connection, right-click the connection icon and select Enable. If that's not your problem, soldier on.
2. Right-click the wireless LAN connection and select the Properties command; then click the Wireless Networks tab. You can get to a similar location by right-clicking the connection icon in the Status tray (if you enabled that feature in your Network Properties dialog box for the connection) on the right side of the taskbar and selecting the Properties command.

Note

When you see the Wireless Networks tab in the Properties dialog box, that means that your NIC driver supports the Windows XP Wireless Zero Configuration protocol. If you don't see this tab, you may need to configure your card manually, consider replacing the driver, or replacing the card itself.

3. In the list of Available networks make sure that you not only see the WLAN, but also that you have selected its name. If you don't see the name, click the Refresh button.

   If you don't see your desired network, the problem is at the sending end, and you need to go to the next sections to check your access point.
4. If the network you are connecting to is a third-party WLAN, click the "Use Windows to configure my wireless network settings" setting. Otherwise, leave it unchecked.
5. With your desired WLAN selected in the Available networks section, click the Configure button to open the Wireless Networks Properties dialog box for that specific connection. Check that the following are correct: the SSID or name (it must be exactly right), and whether the Network Authentication and Data encryption settings are correct. More importantly, click the Authentication tab and check the settings there. Getting the network name or SSID exactly correct is particularly important in instances where the wireless network isn't broadcasting its name. Figure 23-1 shows you these settings.

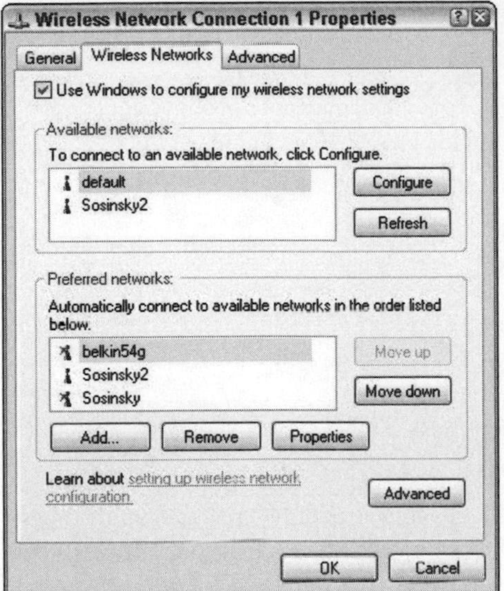

Figure 23-1: The Wireless Networks Properties box offers connection settings.

6. With your desired WLAN selected in the Preferred networks section, click the Advanced button to view the types of networks you can access. For your personal WLAN you should use either "Any available network . . ." or the "Access point . . ." choices. For an ad hoc connection, set that option. If you have the checkbox "Automatically connect to non-preferred networks" checked, uncheck that box if you are trying to connect to a preferred network.
7. Close the Properties dialog box.

Some settings in the Available Wireless Networks dialog box could also be a problem, so you should check there, too. To check the Available Wireless Network settings, do the following:

1. Right-click the connection icon either in the Network Connections dialog box or in the Status tray of your taskbar and select View Available Wireless Networks.
2. Your desired WLAN should be listed in the Available wireless networks list box and you should select it.
3. If the Connect button isn't enabled, perhaps your network doesn't encrypt its traffic and thus is not secure (see Figure 23-2). Click "Allow me to connect to the selected wireless network, even though it is not secure." If that enables the Connect button, click the button and test your connection.

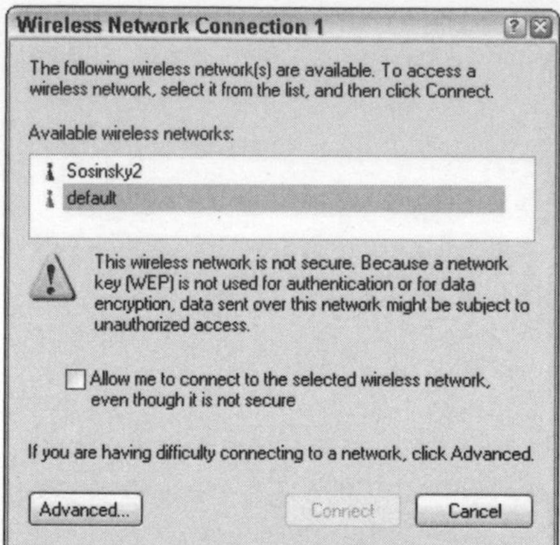

Figure 23-2: The checkbox that lets you connect to an unsecured network is one of those small things that often prevents you from establishing a wireless connection.

4. If enabling the checkbox in Step 3 doesn't fix the problem, even though you've clicked the enabled Connect button, then it's time to move on to diagnosing problems with your access point.

Rare instances occur where an entire TCP/IP networking stack becomes corrupted. That is, no matter what you do there is an error in the networking software in your computer. Windows XP is supposed to "self heal" and fix problems like that, but these issues are still possible, if unlikely. When you've eliminated all of the other possibilities you may want to remove your networking components and reinstall them. You can perform this operation from the Add/Remove Software Wizard in the Control Panel.

My NIC doesn't support Wireless Zero Configuration. What do I do?

You can still set your card up manually. Do the following:

1. In the Connection Properties dialog box, click Configure, and then click the Advanced tab.
2. Set the following parameters: your network SSID to the right value, WEP to Enabled or Disabled, the correct mode or network type, data rate to Auto or to a rate that is compatible with the protocol you are using (such as 11 Mbps for 802.11b), power save to Off or Disabled.
3. Close the Properties dialog box.
4. Click Start → Programs → Administrative Tools → Services.

If your computer doesn't have this item on it, you need to enable that option using the Advanced section of the taskbar Start menu properties, or get help from someone who can access this utility.

5. Disable the Wireless Zero Configuration service and set it so that it doesn't start up automatically.

My computer seems okay. What could go wrong with my connection itself?

Your wireless connection is exactly that, wireless, so it's unlikely that bad air is going to be the problem. The things you need to check are your antennas. If the location you're in is known to work with a similar system, then the antenna at the access point is not the problem, but the antenna for your NIC might be. For an external antenna (if you are lucky enough to have one — many PC Cards don't) perhaps you've neglected to connect the antenna to the card. Little things (unfortunately) mean a lot.

If your NIC has an internal antenna, as many of them do, you can't really check the card to see if that's the problem. The best you can do is to test another card and see if that card works. For your purposes, a broken internal antenna is the same as a broken NIC.

My computer's fine. What could go wrong at the access point?

Actually plenty, glad you asked. Access points suffer from many of the same problems that your computer does:

- They can lose their address if they rely on DHCP from another server for their address.
- They can have a problem with a wired network connection in the form of an Ethernet cable or hub.
- If the transmitter/receiver is a repeater or an access point repeating a signal, the device could have lost its wireless connection.
- The device itself could be malfunctioning or flaky.

How do I fix addressing problems?

Let's test some of the potential problems with addressing. First, open your management software for the device in question and determine whether the device is listed and has a correct network address. One problem you might run into is that your device loses its DHCP lease and can't reestablish it. Dynamic IP addresses are convenient, but in most cases they aren't really necessary for small home or small office networks. If you have an incorrect static address, fix it in the software.

Physically restart your device by either clicking the Restart button in the management console (which more often than not is browser based), pressing the device's restart button, or removing and then reinserting the device's power cord.

Strange as it seems, restarting can not only get you another DHCP lease for your AP's internal NIC, but it resets the small operating system inside the AP and that can often solve a troublesome problem — at least until the time when the same conditions occur to make the AP go silent again. For many DSL and cable modem customers, short DHCP leases can be a problem. For example, Comcast has a system where it issues 7-day or 1-week leases. But when network traffic and demand for leases are high, shorter leases are given out by the cable modem. The solution to this problem has been to restart the proxy server a few times until one of the longer leases has been obtained. This is trial and error, but the approach has proven effective.

You can also pull the power plug out of the device, count to 10, and then put the power connector back into the device. Software restarts are fine, but we recommend that you do a hardware reset prior to moving on to the next issue.

I can't locate my access point/router/repeater in the management software, or I can't log into it to view its settings. What do I do now?

Oh boy! You've misplaced your device's address or can't remember the password. If you can't remember, you have to start over with the device. Many wireless access points, routers, and so on have small holes that you can stick a pin or the tip of a paper clip into to reset the device. They may even say Reset on the outside. *This is a RESET button, and not a restart button*. When you press the reset button you are returning the device to its default conditions, default IP address, default network settings, default password (or no password), and so forth.

The good news is that now you know the password and IP address. The bad news is that now you have to return the wireless device to its former condition of grace. That means that you are going to have to change a computer's IP address to match the subnet of the default address, enter the name of the wireless network (SSID), select either DHCP or an appropriate IP address, pick the correct channel for the device, and set up encryption and other features. When you restart your wireless device, don't forget to change your computer's IP address back to something appropriate to your network, or you won't see the wireless device even if it is working correctly.

I know the password and address of my AP, but I still can't see it over the network. What's next?

The problem may be the network connection itself. Before testing that, however, try pinging the AP:

1. Open the Run dialog box (Start → Run or Windows key + R).
2. Enter the text **CMD** and press the Enter key.
3. Enter **PING** *XXX.XXX.XXX.XXX* in the Command Prompt window where the X's are replaced by the AP's default IP address.
4. If you get a response, move to a different computer to test the management software, or connect your AP directly to a computer to manage it.

   Don't forget that you need to ping from a system that can see the AP, one on the same hub or with the same subnet.
5. If you get no response, close the Command Prompt and proceed to the next tests.

Wired network connections are easily tested, and the problems fall into the following categories:

- Bad network cable (CAT5)
- Cable connection is not properly seated
- The hub's port is damaged
- The hub itself is damaged
- The hub has an uplink that is not functioning because the button has been inadvertently pressed changing the uplink to a simple port
- The link to the network from the hub is damaged

The best way to test these possibilities is in stages. You can eliminate the entire set of possibilities by plugging a working device like a laptop into the network cable end that was connected to the AP. If you can see the network, then none of the preceding possibilities is the problem.

If the physical connection is faulty, do the following:

1. Swap out the network cable; then check your connection.
2. Move the connection to another port on the hub; then check your connection.
3. Check the uplink button; then check your connection.
4. Replace the hub, or move the AP and testing computer to another hub and see if you can see the network.

If none of these issues are problems and you have a live wire connection to the network, but still can't see the access point, it is time to call technical support at the company that makes or sold you the access point. It's also probably time to replace the access point.

The truth is that some access points/routers/repeaters that are built for the consumer market (and particularly the ones that were introduced early on a year or two ago) were not well made and have high defect rates. If your access point is troublesome, cuts out, and you can't figure out why after you do everything that you can think of, it is time to replace it. Use the rationale that the newer model with the SuperUltraModulate HighGain 802.11! will be worth the extra cost and you are just trading up. Whatever rationale you do use, realize that your time has a certain value and that after you've invested the appropriate amount of time, it is time to move on. There's always eBay, right?

Sometimes the problem is that you have a connection, but for some reason that connection is either slow, transient, or doesn't allow you to actually view systems on your network. Following are some common reasons and methods for addressing problems of those types.

My wireless network connection is really slow. What could be possible causes?

The good news is that you have a connection. The bad news is that while you wait for your e-mail everyone else in the office went home long ago. There are several reasons why you could be getting a poor data throughput from your connection. First, check that your wireless network is the correct

and active network connection. If you have more than one network interface, such as a wired and wireless connection, older systems tend to have trouble managing that. If that's the case, disable your wired connection.

Interference is another reason why connections become slow. Check to see that there aren't any competing radio sources interfering with your connection's signal. Beyond turning off any microwave ovens, wireless phones, baby monitors, cordless game controllers, and wireless radios, make sure that none of these devices is within 25 feet of your system.

Also, check to see if your wireless setup has one access point interfering with the signal of another. That is, if you have two access points with the same channel, they can reduce the signal from each other where they overlap.

I'm connected and my throughput is good, but I can't find any of the computers on the network. What's wrong?

You may need to enable file and print sharing. In Windows XP, open the Wireless Network Connection Properties dialog box shown in Figure 23-3, click the General tab, and make sure that the section entitled "This connection uses the following items" has File and Printer Sharing for Microsoft Networks checked and enabled. If this checkbox isn't present, do the following:

1. Click the Install button.
2. Select Services.
3. Click the Add button.

Figure 23-3: The File and Printer Sharing for Microsoft Networks setting in Windows XP.

4. Select File and Print Sharing for Microsoft Networks.
5. Click OK, enable the service, and close the Network Connection Properties dialog box.

In Windows 2000, the procedure is a little different. There the service is enabled as follows:

1. Open the Network and Dial-up Connections control panel and click Local Area Connection.
2. Click Properties; then under the "Components checked are used by the connection" section select the File and Printer Sharing for Microsoft Networks checkbox (if necessary).
3. If that checkbox is missing, click Install, Service, and click Add.
4. Select the File and Printer Sharing for Microsoft Networks and click OK.
5. Close the Local Area Connection Properties, then close the Local Area Connection Status dialog box, and finally close the Network and Dialup Connections window.

Summary

This chapter presented probably 95 percent of the problems you are likely to encounter when you are having problems connecting to a wireless network. Network connection difficulties are troublesome and can waste a lot of time until you figure out what is wrong. Often it's not just one thing, but two or more problems and they are also often quite basic in nature. Be systematic, be thorough, and try to eliminate possibilities by isolating different parts of your network connection. When you can, substitute things that you know are working in place of something that isn't working to help eliminate one or more possibilities quickly. If you have knowledgeable people around you, ask for help because sometimes other people working with fresh eyes can spot things that you can't.

Although troubleshooting connectivity isn't entirely unfamiliar to people with basic networking skills, wireless security has features unique to wireless networking technologies. In the next chapter you see some of the more common problems people run into, and how to go about solving those problems.

Chapter 24

Troubleshooting Security

Security is unfortunately a major issue on a wireless network. The basic problem is that the current wireless standard doesn't authenticate users in the same way that a domain security database does. A user has to know the SSID name and the key to gain access to the network, but the system doesn't demand that users identify themselves to the network. That important task is left to your network's authentication authority, which is most often your domain server. The reason for the pass-through is that authentication at the wireless access point adds an additional layer of complexity that the designers of 802.11 wanted to avoid, and also limits access to the network for anyone who doesn't have an account.

Also, it's harder to set up a wireless network security scheme than it should be for the average user, and unfortunately it's also easy to make mistakes. Mistakes have consequences, anything from someone you don't know or want to allow on your network jumping on for a joyride to someone stealing data, or worse, your identity. It's best to catch these problems before they occur rather than after the fact. If you troubleshoot your wireless security before problems arise, you may save yourself considerable grief later on.

Security is a little like buying an insurance policy: you don't know if you'll ever need it, but when you need it, you really need it. In this case, with the lack of an intrusion, you may never even know whether or not you needed it because the lack of a security breach doesn't mean that people aren't trying. You only have to open a port scanner and monitor the traffic coming in from the Internet to know that someone is trying to access your network every few minutes. If your network has a firewall or a proxy server, and you have the security logging feature turned on, perusal of that log will likely be an eye opener.

With all this in mind, let's take a look at the problems involved with wireless network security and how you can go about diagnosing and fixing them before they really become problems.

I'm on a public access point; the network is open and unencrypted. How do I best secure my laptop?

When you are connected to a hotspot, some of the wireless network security tools such as WEP and WPA may no longer be available. Therefore you need to consider other means for securing your laptop and the data that is transmitted and received. The two main methods for securing a laptop are enabling a personal firewall and encrypting traffic.

For Windows, either enable the Internet Connection Firewall feature for a network connection, or turn on a program such as Norton Personal Firewall or Zone Alarm to prevent outside access. A personal firewall is a barrier that prevents outsiders from scanning your data and file system. Some packages, like ZoneAlarm Pro, examine the nature of the traffic and let you accept or decline an access.

Turn off file sharing, and unshare any network shares that exist on your system.

My e-mail doesn't work on the hotspot. How can I get my e-mail securely?

For some mail servers and ISPs, it is possible to encrypt your e-mail password. You can also use an Authenticated POP or APOP to create a session token from your password that is used to authenticate you to the POP server. APOP tokens are secure and are unique per session, so they can't be guessed or reused. However, APOP doesn't encrypt your message traffic, so it is really only moderately useful.

Another technique for protecting e-mail is to use SMTP AUTH. The SMTP Authorization protocol was described more fully in Chapter 21, but the technique involves using SMTP commands to authenticate yourself to an SMTP server so that you can send outgoing mail. If you are having trouble sending mail on a hotspot you may have to use this technique anyway. The problem with SMTP AUTH is that it protects only your password, and doesn't protect your traffic.

To best protect your traffic, you should consider using your own personal encryption program. The software that is the current standard for encryption is the program PGP, or Pretty Good Privacy. PGP uses public key/private key cryptology to encrypt traffic so that only the person with the correct private key at the receiving end can use the public key in combination with his or her private key to encrypt the communication. To download PGP go to `www.pgp.com`.

Other methods used to protect data in transmission work by encrypting traffic. You can use technologies such as Secure Sockets Layer (SSL), Secure Shell (SSH), and Virtual Private Networking (VPN) to protect you data in transit.

How do I turn the Windows firewall on?

The Windows XP firewall was one of the enhancements that you paid to get when you upgraded to XP. With Service Pack 2, the firewall has been enhanced.

To turn on the Windows XP firewall, do the following:

1. Open the Network Connections dialog box either from the Control Panel folder or by right-clicking My Network Places and selecting the Properties command.
2. Click the connection you will be using for wireless networking.
3. Click the option Change Settings of this Connection in the left pane, or right-click the connection and select the Properties dialog box.
4. Click the Advanced button.
5. Enable the checkbox "Protect My Computer by Limiting or Preventing Access to This Computer from the Internet."
6. Accept the setting and close all dialog boxes.

What other things should I turn on and off to improve security?

Here is a list of 12 services and settings that you should consider changing:

- Install antivirus and anti-spyware software.
- Turn off the ad hoc mode for your wireless network unless you are in a secure location.
- Separate your wireless network from your wired network with a firewall.
- Secure access points so that they can't be physically accessed (remember that they come with reset buttons).
- When you change an access point's settings, do so by using a direct connection from the wireless device to the computer you are using to access the management software to limit the path the data travels.
- Turn off the SNMP (Simple Network Management Protocol) service because that service allows users to auto-discover devices on a network.
- Use static IP addresses in place of dynamic DHCP addressing; turn off DHCP on your network.
- Use MAC filtering on small networks. On larger networks MAC filtering is troublesome.
- Pick strong passwords that can't be broken, especially for the administrator password.
- Always disable a wireless NIC connection when it is not in use.
- If you detect a security breach, change your settings and access passwords and systems to your network.
- Always change any default settings you find, and document your changes in a safe location.

What is a strong password?

A strong password is one that is not easily breached by a password generation program. The following are some suggestions, from most to least effective:

- **Random Sequence:** In a perfect world, your best password is a truly random sequence of numbers and letters in mixed case that form as long a string as the system allows. However, remembering a random sequence such as "AeECa2B311aD" is hard if not impossible: "aA1C3dbB2cD4" would be easier to remember, because although it isn't random, it is at least not meaningful and it is a sequence.
- **Abbreviation and Substitution (Acronyms):** Next best is a sequence of numbers and letters that have some meaning and are added together to form a composite. For example, "G0R3DS0XG0", where 0 substitutes for o and 3 substitutes for e might make for a winning combination.

- **Combined Words:** This is what you get on those pesky AOL disks, things like "wirelesslover", "802.11ordie", and the ever favorite "badhairday" are used to get initial entry for an AOL log on. Cracking programs use word lists to generate combinations, so eventually these kinds of passwords are vulnerable.
- **Single Words:** A single meaningful word such as your cats' names "Stormy" and "Shadow" are easily cracked. If they are personal items that are meaningful to you that others know, they are easier still. People who know you don't need a cracking program to guess a password like this or a password like 062093 or 1140, which might be the birthday of your kid or the ending of your phone number. Passwords such as these are simply an invitation to others to "come on in."

How do I disable my wireless connection?

You can disable a wireless connection by either changing a setting in your network connections Properties dialog box, or by physically removing your network card. In Windows XP, here's how you disable the adapter:

1. Open the Network Connections dialog box.
2. Right-click your wireless connection and select the Disable command. The label will state that the connection is disabled. When the connection is unavailable but is still enabled, you will also see a red X through the connection line as, shown in Figure 24-1.

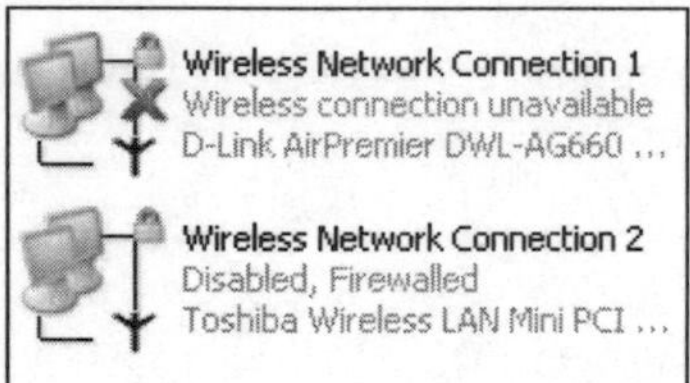

Figure 24-1: A disabled network connection icon.

3. To enable the connection again, repeat Steps 1 and 2, selecting the Enable command. This is also a good time to check to see if your firewall is turned on.

To remove the NIC adapter from your laptop if you have a NIC adapter that is a PC Card:

1. Right-click the Safely Remove Hardware icon in the System tray, and then click the Safely Remove Hardware command.
2. Click the NIC adapter's name in the Safely Remove Hardware dialog box (see Figure 24-2), and then click the Stop button.

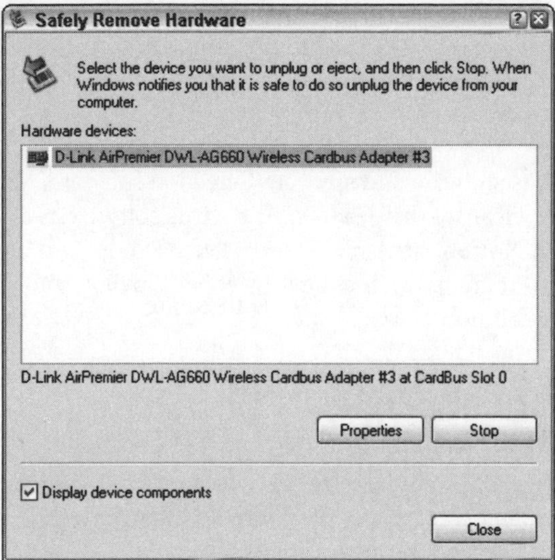

Figure 24-2: The Safely Remove Hardware dialog box.

3. When XP informs you that it is safe to remove the card, do so.

Not all laptops offer the Safely Remove Hardware feature, but most newer models do. For those that don't you can often download an appropriate utility after the fact from your OEM vendor that will allow this feature.

Does the software I run on a wireless network make a difference to my security?

The answer, unfortunately, is yes. Some operating systems and some programs are more prone to attack than other software. The Windows operating system and Microsoft Internet Explorer are popular targets because hackers can create more havoc and get more exposure by attacking them than they can by attacking Linux or the Macintosh. Although you will get an argument from many people, Windows is probably as well written as either of those other operating systems, but is simply the object of more attention.

Other common targets of attack are Windows applications such as Internet Explorer, Internet Information Server (IIS), Microsoft Outlook, Exchange, and the Office programs — all for the same reason as Windows itself: they're more popular. Changing browsers to something like Netscape or Opera will lower your risk, but isn't always possible for many people. Microsoft Office is particularly vulnerable because it allows scripts to run. You can disable the execution of scripts or require that a script ask for permission before it runs, which is prudent.

The reason that Microsoft went to the trouble to create Windows Update for users is to plug security holes quickly. Access to Windows Update is one of the best reasons to pay for a licensed copy of Windows, and you should always be up to date on the software offered for your system by that Web site. The Office version of Windows Update, called Office Update, is also one that you should check frequently. In versions of Windows where you can enable automated notification and updating, it's a

good idea to do so. We recommend that you enable automated notification, but do ***not*** enable automated download and installation. The reason that we make this recommendation is that if something goes wrong with your update, or your system changes in some way that you don't like, knowing what was done to your computer will better help you revert your system back to the past state at the point just prior to the change.

We also recommend that you use anti-virus software and spyware-detection software. Many good anti-virus packages are available, with some clear market leaders. Anti-virus software is a relatively mature market and you can't go wrong with Norton, McAfree, Trend Micro, Panda, and others. On the spyware side the choices are less clear. Programs such as Spy Sweeper, SpyBot, and Adaware, along with others, seem to offer only partial solutions.

What's the biggest mistake I can make when it comes to wireless network security?

There are two features that you need to attend to for any wireless network device that transmits and receives radio signals. The first is not changing the default password for the device in question, and the second is not enabling some form of encryption on your network.

Don't kid yourself; anyone who is determined to gain access to your wireless network knows the default administrator's account name and the default password (which is most often left blank by most vendors). As soon as they know what the device is, they can often go to the manufacturer's Web site and download the manual. The manual will have all the information they need.

It's that initial entry that you want to prevent because that entry can provide a means for delivering a Trojan horse, worm, a backdoor program such as BackOrifice, or a custom program that dials out of your network and provides settings and access.

Someone has gained access to my wireless network. What can I do to stop a second access?

The short answer is ***change things***. Start with the password that allows access to your network settings. If you have encryption enabled, change the key that encrypts the traffic. For small networks such as a home and small business, it isn't that much extra trouble to rename the network's SSID. For larger networks, changing the SSID is going to be more trouble than it's worth because you will have to visit all the individual access points, routers, repeaters, and other devices to reset the network name.

Is WEP secure?

Yes and no. WEP encryption uses what is called a ***shared key*** to encrypt traffic. When you turn WEP on, you can enable up to four of these shared keys. WEP keys are esoteric beasts; most are entered in hexadecimal (some are in ASCII). It's not unheard of for someone to write down the shared secret encryption password key on a Post-it note and stick the note on the wall. Keys need to be physically protected.

WEP can and has been cracked, putting this security mechanism into the category of useful but not foolproof. An intruder has to be knowledgeable to crack a WEP-encrypted wireless network, so for almost all users WEP will be enough to stop entry to almost all people.

The larger the WEP standard used (256-bit versus 56-bit) the harder it is to break a key. If you are using a larger key size, make sure that all of your wireless equipment supports this standard. That includes not only access points, repeaters, routers, and gateways, but NICs as well.

With a program like the Linux AirSnort (`www.airsnort.shmoo.com`) or with WEPCrack, crackers can listen to network traffic and analyze it to guess the key. If you find that it takes less than an hour to crack your key, then your encryption is not secure. If you find that your key requires weeks to be decrypted and sequenced, then WEP is probably sufficient.

Actually it isn't that easy to crack a WEP encryption scheme if the key is well designed and strong, and it requires a very concerted effort on the part of the cracker to overcome. In order to figure out the parts of a key and then put them together in sequence, the intruder would have to spend many days to get the needed information. If your network traffic is light, then the amount of time required can be on the order of weeks. So for a small network and one that isn't transmitting sensitive data, WEP can be sufficient.

How can I prevent cracker programs from defeating WEP?

On small networks the single best thing you can do to keep intruders from gaining access to a WEP-enabled network is to change the encryption keys on a weekly basis. Because a strong password can require that a sniffer program see as many as 16.8 million frames of data to crack a key, changing the key frequently defeats this. Just doing this one thing provides very strong protection for a small network.

Key rotation isn't easily done on larger networks with WEP because you have a lot of overhead when it comes to key distribution. However, key rotation is part of WPA, as discussed in the next section. Every time you log on with WPA, a temporal or session key is generated.

What's better than WEP?

The WPA or Wi-Fi Protected Access encryption is part of the new 802.11i security protocol. WPA also uses a shared secret key system, just like WEP, with one to four keys. Unlike WEP, WPA keys are plain-text passwords and are called preshared keys, or PSK (see Figure 24-3), or sometimes pre-shared passwords. What differentiates WPA is that the PSK isn't actually used as the encryption key; an algorithm uses the PSK to create a second key that won't allow network access. With the WEP security mechanism the password key itself is used to generate the encryption key. So if someone cracks the encryption, he has your key. However, in WPA, if the intruder gets the PSK, then he still gets access to your wireless network but he can't extract the PSK from network traffic.

What devices offer WPA?

Although WPA is attractive, only newer devices have this feature. If you have an old 802.11b access point you probably don't have WPA on that device. Sometimes this feature is added through a firmware upgrade, so check with your vendor and look on its Web site to see if you have any additional options. You'll find WPA on almost all 802.11g devices made after 2003.

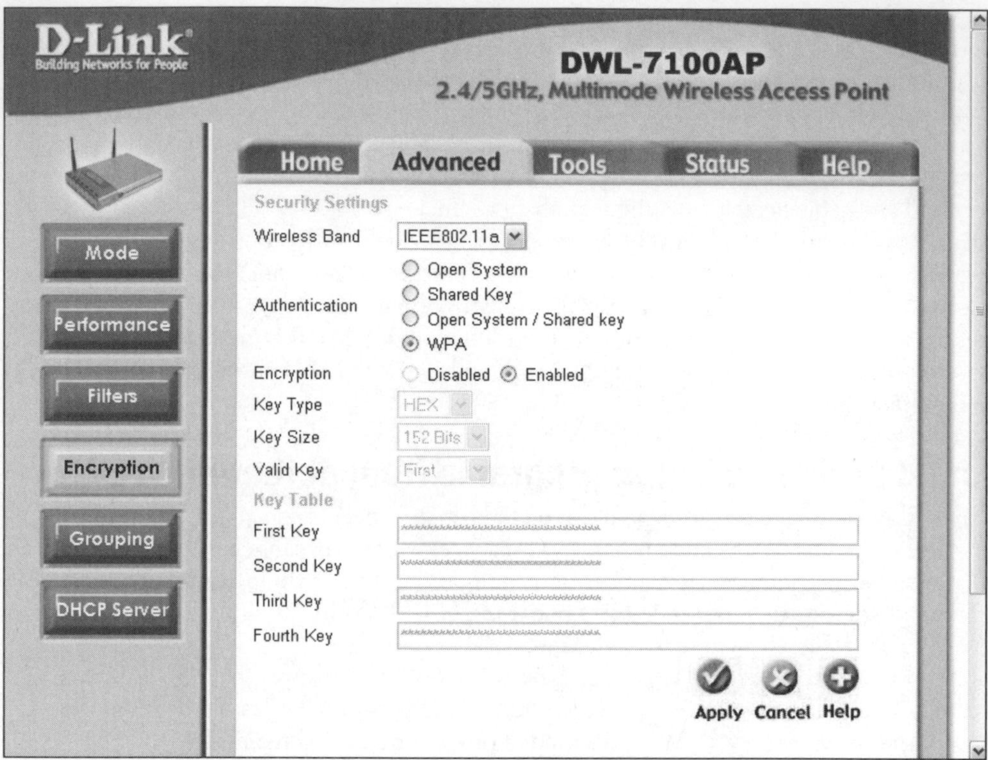

Figure 24-3: The WPA encryption system generates temporal or session-specific ID keys that make it harder to crack than the WEP protocol. Shown here are the WPA settings for a D-Link D WL-7100 access point.

When anyone opens their notebook they can see my wireless network as an available network. How can I keep my network invisible?

A wireless network appears in the available wireless network list when you broadcast the SSID of the network. So if you turn off the broadcast feature in your access point's security screen, the name will no longer appear on the list. Some access points refer to a disabled broadcast as a "closed network"; whereas one that broadcasts its name is referred to as an "open network."

Turning off broadcast doesn't really improve security if people know what the network name is, but for anyone who doesn't know the name, it's one more obstacle that an outsider must surmount to gain access to your network.

You should also keep in mind that although a network name doesn't get broadcast and you can't see it in Windows operating system dialog boxes, there are plenty of software programs, some commercial and others shareware, that people can use to see the network name. So turning off the broadcast won't stop an advanced user from gaining access. Therefore you need to balance the value of hiding a network name from view against the inconvenience of not being able to automatically see the network name and use it without having to enter it.

I've turned on the MAC filtering feature in my access point. Does this prevent outside access to my wireless network?

MAC filtering is a feature where you specify the MAC addresses of the NICs for computers that you trust. It would seem to be a foolproof method for limiting access because the MAC address of every NIC in the world is unique. However, anyone who can listen to your network traffic, especially if the traffic is unencrypted, will be able to see the MAC addresses of the computers on your wireless network, and can use the information to spoof a MAC address and gain access to your wireless network.

The situation with MAC addresses is even less secure than you might imagine. Many routers and access points allow you to change their network adapter's apparent MAC address in order to allow that device to connect to an ISP where a particular network adapter MAC is required for a connection.

As with suppressing SSID broadcasting, filtering MAC addresses is only going to make it impossible for the average computer user to gain access. Hackers working with easily available software can get past this security feature.

How can I limit people outside my building or floor accessing my wireless network?

One way to limit access is to make sure that your wireless signal doesn't extend out beyond the physical limits of the space you are trying to cover. In other words, define your coverage area.

The best way to determine your coverage is to test it with a Wi-Fi detector and with a wireless notebook. Be sure that you are using a sensitive wireless NIC, one that has very good reception when it's in range. You don't want someone to come along with a better NIC and detect a signal that you couldn't.

Numerous ways exist to limit the amount of area that an access point, router, repeater, or gateway covers. You can use directional antennas to aim the signal, as well as barriers to stop the signal. It's not foolproof, but it does offer some level of protection. However, limiting the signal range does not preclude the need to encrypt traffic, to suppress SSID broadcasts, and to do MAC filtering (in that order).

Don't forget to turn off wireless access to your network after hours. The incidents of mischief being done are higher on nights and weekends when there are few if any people around to monitor activity.

When I'm in my office, I can see many available networks of other businesses in my building. What should I do?

Consider a situation in which your small business is in an incubator building with many other businesses. Each business has a wireless network, and none are far enough away from one another to limit the signal reception. When you or your coworkers open the available wireless networks dialog box, several other networks are listed. If you log onto another network, you might not notice that you're not connected to your own network because you have browser access to the Internet. You'll notice that your e-mail doesn't work, and that network services aren't available, but an average user might not know why. Then there's also the consideration of that computer being a possible security breach if it hasn't been protected well enough.

You can do a few things in a situation like this. First, make sure that your network comes up first in the list of names and set up client access so that it logs onto the first name in the dialog box.

Better yet, pay a visit to other network owners in the building and explain to them the situation. Get those other networks to suppress their SSID broadcasts. The other security mechanism such as encryption and MAC filtering on their networks doesn't affect you. If one or more of the networks are set up as hotspots, such as the coffee shop on the ground floor, you may not be able to get them to suppress their SSID. For commercial hotspots there are probably some user validation methods in place that limit entry; but for free hotspots there won't be any validation and you will just have to live with the problem.

Summary

In this chapter we discussed some of the common problems that you encounter with security on wireless networks. Turning on WEP or WPA encryption is the single best thing you can do to secure your system. You can also make your system more secure by choosing strong passwords and changing defaults on the hardware you purchase.

In truth, any network can be broken over time, either through software methods such as installation of a rogue program, or by hardware methods such as lifting someone's computer or copying down a password that's left posted on someone's office wall. If you protect your network proactively by employing methods such as key rotation, suppressing SSID broadcasting, and limiting your wireless network's range and availability, you can minimize your exposure. Indeed, if you are a small network, then given the smaller amount of traffic that flows over your network, your task is much easier than it would be on a large network.

In the next chapter we'll take a last look at some more troubleshooting issues, those that are related to the wireless devices that you use.

Chapter 25

Troubleshooting Mobile Devices

A number of issues come up frequently with mobile devices that affect their ability to connect to wireless networks and use their services. In the two previous chapters, we looked first at connectivity issues and then security issues. In this chapter you see some of the problems that occur with a variety of mobile devices, including NICs, antennas, Palms and PocketPCs, cell phones, Bluetooth, wireless USB, and IrDA devices, to name but a few.

My laptop's new NIC won't connect to a working access point although the settings seem correct. What should I look at to correct the problem?

If you don't get a signal where you know a signal exists and the lights on the NIC seem operational, you need to check your settings. Once you are certain that your wireless network settings are correct, you can move on to checking hardware. The wireless network settings that need to be correct are those for

- SSID (these names are case-sensitive)
- Enabling the connection
- Selecting the right channel
- Providing the correct WEP/WPA key
- Selecting the correct access mode (infrastructure or ad hoc)

If these settings are correct, check that your equipment is correctly installed in the Device Manager. You should see the NIC listed without an exclamation mark or yellow triangle next to it. If there is a yellow exclamation mark, it indicates that there is a resource or IRQ conflict. Uninstall the NIC and reinstall it with the most up-to-date driver. Do not simply reinstall the adapter software because that will leave the current driver active on your system again.

If none of this works, try swapping out for another network card.

My current Centrino notebook doesn't support 802.11g. How do I get that standard in my computer?

The original Centrino notebooks came with built-in 802.11b wireless networking. Some of the current generation of laptops enable you to swap out the wireless card to go to the next generation. Most do not. The easiest way to add enhanced wireless capability is to add an additional wireless PC Card or wireless USB adapter to your computer.

With two different wireless transceivers in your notebook you run a minimal risk of creating a looping situation. You also want your notebook to choose the fastest adapter for throughput. Therefore, the best thing to do is to disable the on-board wireless NIC and use your faster card whenever possible. The nice thing about 802.11b is that it is broadly compatible. If your upgraded PC Card can't seem to connect, you can disable it and enable the on-board capability. However, most of the faster cards come with multiple standard support, and almost always support 802.11b.

Why can't my laptop get a strong wireless signal in one specific location of my house even when I move an access point close to that location?

The most probable cause for a poor 802.11 signal is radio interference. The first thing to determine is whether this is an intermittent or constant problem because that will determine the type of device that might be responsible. Interference occurs when two devices try to send packets over the same radio frequency as one another, resulting in timeout errors or data loss.

For intermittent interference, check the following devices:

- Wireless phones
- Microwave ovens
- Wireless radios
- Bluetooth devices

For 802.11g networks, any device broadcasting in the 2.4 GHz range may cause a problem. For 802.11b networks, you may find a problem when you try to use a 900 MHz range.

You need to move your access point at least 10 feet away from a microwave oven at a minimum; 25 to 30 feet would be better. So moving the access point may be a simple solution to this problem.

For constant interference, consider these possible causes:

- A nearby wireless network
- Overlapping access points with the same channel number

Actually these are both essentially the same problem, and they have the same solution. Try changing the channels of adjacent radio transceivers so that they don't overlap. If this is your neighbor's network, you will have to seek some cooperation from them or try to alter your settings to compensate. Do a site survey to see where you can see other networks or multiple access points, as well as their settings, and make appropriate changes.

Another way of working around the problem of interference is to strengthen the power of your signal in the problem location. The stronger signal essentially overwhelms or swamps the weaker signal, allowing devices to lock onto it. This may not make you popular with your neighbors, but it is effective.

Also try changing the configuration parameters. In addition to changing the channels you can also use a different frequency hopping pattern. The newer standards support 5-GHz signals, and there is less interference using this frequency. You will also find that upcoming 802.11e standards offer avoidance algorithms that help prevent RF signal interference.

Why is it that when I add an antenna to my wireless device the signal strength doesn't change?

Assuming that your wireless device is compatible with the antenna, the most likely reason is that the antenna you added is not positioned correctly or is not of the correct type to provide you with the needed gain to notice a change in signal strength. If you are located in the center of an access point's range, adding an omnidirectional antenna would help your signal strength. However, if you are off to the side of a building, you may need a directional antenna to get the boost you need.

Antennas and wireless devices are very sensitive to orientation. That is, the characteristics of an antenna's transceiver most often qualify the device as a horizontally or vertically oriented device. Small changes in both the antenna and the mobile device can make a large difference in signal strength. Try changing the orientation of both devices as well as their positioning to see if it makes a difference. The chances of an antenna being broken, particularly a non-powered antenna, are small; however, if you have a powered antenna you should check that it's getting its required amount of power.

My laptop can't receive a signal from my access point, although I'm well within the advertised range of both devices. What could be the problem?

Several reasons exist for why a laptop's NIC may not be able to detect an access point. The most important limitation is the number of intervening obstacles between your laptop and the access point. Walls, ceilings, and even metal doors can dramatically reduce the signal strength. Also, the effective wall thickness is greatly enhanced by the angle of the wall between your laptop and access point. A 2-foot wall would appear 4 feet thick to a radio signal at a 45-degree angle, and over 52 feet thick at a 2-degree angle. What the obstruction is made of makes a big difference as well. Metal and concrete have higher stopping power than does wallboard and glass.

Check also that your radio signal isn't being interfered with by other radio transmitting devices. The common problems involve appliances operating on a similar frequency, for example 2.4-GHz cell phones interfering with an 802.11g network. Other possible sources of interference can be access points set up with the same channel number that overlap.

Experiment with positioning your mobile device and its antenna to improve your signal strength.

My NIC advertises that it supports an enhanced version of 802.11a or 802.11g, but I get nowhere near that throughput. What is wrong?

All of the enhanced versions of different 802.11 protocols are based on proprietary tweaks in the software or chip set used by a particular vendor. In order to get something like D-Link's Super G or Super AG mode to work, you need to have devices on both ends that support it. In most instances that not only means devices from the same vendor, but devices in the same series from the same vendor.

How do I find the MAC address for the NIC in my laptop?

Often the MAC address is located on a label on the card itself. If you need to locate the address while the card is in the laptop, there are several methods you can use. Perhaps the easiest one is to use `IPCONFIG /ALL` to obtain the address, as shown in Figure 25-1. The Toshiba Portege 3505 shown in Figure 25-1 contains a 10/100 wired Ethernet connection, a built-in internal Intel modem and the Toshiba Wireless LAN Mini PC Card (internal), and a D-Link AirPremier PCMCIA (PC Card) external NIC.

To get the MAC address in Windows XP, do the following:

1. Click Start → Run.
2. Type **CMD** and click OK.
3. Type **IPCONFIG /ALL**. Look down at the section for your wireless adapter for the line starting "Physical Address." That line contains your MAC address.

To perform the same procedure in Windows ME/98/95, do the following:

1. Click Start → Run.
2. Type **winip.cfg** and click OK. The IP Configuration dialog box appears, with the MAC address listed as the Adapter Address, as shown in Figure 25-2.

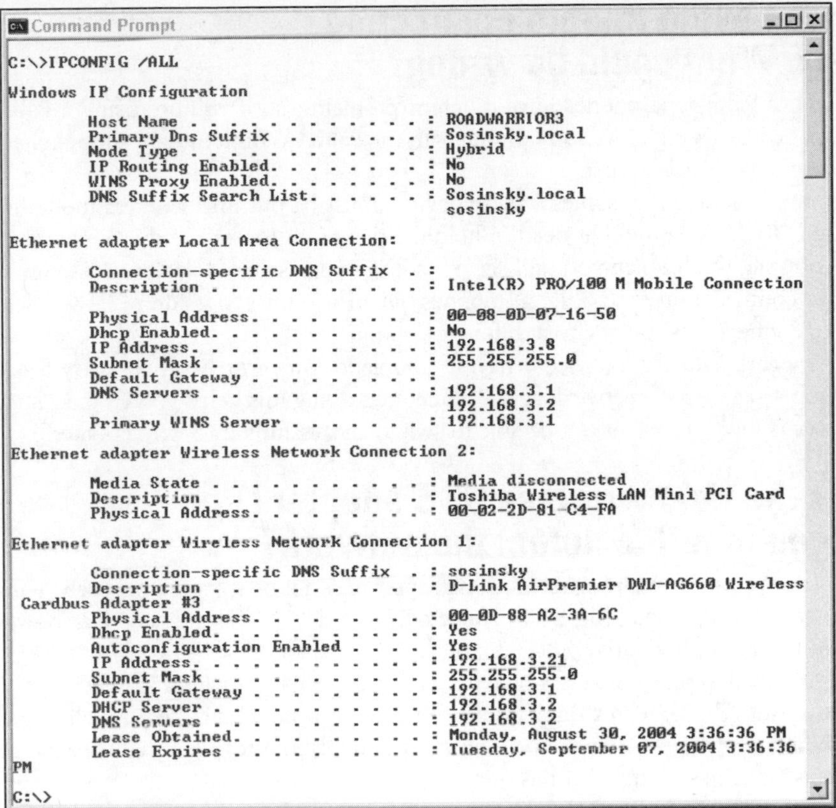
Command Prompt
C:\>IPCONFIG /ALL
Windows IP Configuration
Host Name . . . . : ROADWARRIOR3
Primary Dns Suffix . . . . : Sosinsky.local
Node Type . . . . : Hybrid
IP Routing Enabled. . . . . : No
WINS Proxy Enabled. . . . . : No
DNS Suffix Search List. . . . . . : Sosinsky.local
sosinsky
Ethernet adapter Local Area Connection:
Connection-specific DNS Suffix . :
Description . . . . : Intel(R) PRO/100 M Mobile Connection
Physical Address. . . . . : 00-08-0D-07-16-50
Dhcp Enabled. . . . . : No
IP Address. . . . . : 192.168.3.8
Subnet Mask . . . . : 255.255.255.0
Default Gateway . . . . :
DNS Servers . . . . : 192.168.3.1
192.168.3.2
Primary WINS Server . . . . : 192.168.3.1
Ethernet adapter Wireless Network Connection 2:
Media State . . . . : Media disconnected
Description . . . . : Toshiba Wireless LAN Mini PCI Card
Physical Address. . . . . : 00-02-2D-81-C4-FA
Ethernet adapter Wireless Network Connection 1:
Connection-specific DNS Suffix . : sosinsky
Description . . . . : D-Link AirPremier DWL-AG660 Wireless
Cardbus Adapter #3
Physical Address. . . . . : 00-0D-88-A2-3A-6C
Dhcp Enabled. . . . . : Yes
Autoconfiguration Enabled . . . . : Yes
IP Address. . . . . : 192.168.3.21
Subnet Mask . . . . : 255.255.255.0
Default Gateway . . . . : 192.168.3.1
DHCP Server . . . . : 192.168.3.2
DNS Servers . . . . : 192.168.3.2
Lease Obtained. . . . . : Monday, August 30, 2004 3:36:36 PM
Lease Expires . . . . : Tuesday, September 07, 2004 3:36:36
PM
C:\>

Figure 25-1: Using IPCONFIG /ALL to locate a wireless NIC's MAC address in Windows XP.

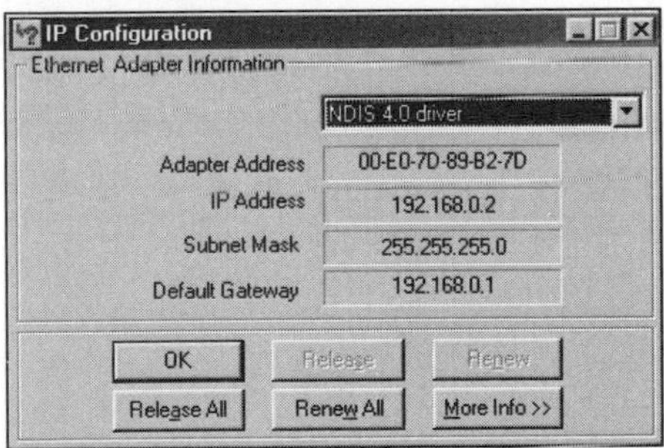
IP Configuration
Ethernet Adapter Information
NDIS 4.0 driver
Adapter Address
00-E0-7D-89-B2-7D
IP Address
192.168.0.2
Subnet Mask
255.255.255.0
Default Gateway
192.168.0.1
OK
Release
Renew
Release All
Renew All
More Info >>

Figure 25-2: Using WINIPCFG to locate a wireless NIC's MAC address in Windows ME/98/95.

My Palm is having trouble connecting wirelessly. What could be wrong?

Different models of Palm-type phones have different problems, so if you are using a Palm or Treo PDA as a phone, or a Samsung or Kyocera phone with the Palm OS built in, you should check for the problems specific to your model first.

One common problem is that some of these devices must be put into wireless mode first before they can be used. To do so you might need to hold the power button or the disconnect button for a certain length of time, after which you will see an icon on your screen for a wireless connection or you might get a confirmation tone. Like all phones, when a Palm is outside of its wireless area, it won't be able to connect. Try moving to a different location.

For locations where your Palm device is having trouble locking onto a network, try restarting the device and letting it search for a network again. Sometimes doing this helps you connect successfully.

If your battery is low, you might not be able to switch successfully into wireless mode.

Why does the new wireless USB adapter I just plugged in fail to detect the network?

A number of reasons exist for why a wireless USB adapter may not be working properly. The first and most obvious reason is that the plug isn't connected properly; or if the device is a powered USB device, that you forgot to plug in the power adapter.

Sometimes you need to plug a wireless USB device directly into a powered USB hub. Try plugging the device directly into the USB port that's located on your computer itself because all of those ports are powered. When the wireless USB device is properly connected, the power light should be on and you may see data lights flash if the unit has them.

Another reason why a wireless USB adapter might not work could be that the software isn't installed properly. Uninstall the device, and then reboot and reinstall the device. Wireless USB is plug and play in Windows XP, so the new hardware should be detected and initiate the setup program. If the install fails to solve your problem, go to the vendor's Web site and look for a more up-to-date driver to install. Use the Device Manager to open the device and then install the new driver in place of the old one.

If your wireless USB adapter can receive a signal from an access point in the infrastructure mode but can't log on, check its settings. The two devices must

- Be set to the same broadcast channel
- Be set to the same SSID
- Be set to the same security options
- Be part of the same workgroup or domain, and each computer have a unique name
- Have TCP/IP enabled, be on the same subnet, and have a unique address

I can't seem to get my IrDA device to work properly. What are the issues?

IrDA devices are really pretty simple serial communication devices. The number one problem with getting them to work is having a COM port conflict or having set the COM port incorrectly. The first thing you can try is to alter the COM setting for the IrDA device. If that doesn't work, change the COM port setting for your mouse or modem if those are serial devices on your system. Doing this may allow your IrDA device to work properly at its default settings. You change these settings in the Mouse or Phone and Modem Options control panels. You can also change the COM settings in the Device Manager for each of these devices.

Not all motherboards support IrDA natively. If yours doesn't, you will need to pick an IrDA device that doesn't need motherboard support. IrDA drivers are part of the Windows operating system, although some vendors supply their own drivers.

If your IrDA device is installed properly, but doesn't seem to actually control the device it's intended to control, check that the two devices are within the effective range of one another. You can also try lowering the rate at which data is exchanged and seeing if that improves the communication.

Finally, check that your IrDA device is compatible with the device you are trying to control. Several different types of IrDA devices are on the market, and each one can work with only a subset of the TVs, printers, computers, phones, and other devices that accept IR signals.

My two Bluetooth devices don't connect. What could be the problem?

If you expect to make a connection between Bluetooth devices, the first thing to check is that Bluetooth is actually installed on the devices in question and that you've turned the Bluetooth service on. The service is turned on in software.

After that, the next most likely thing is that the profiles are missing on one or both devices, or that the two profiles don't match. For example, if you want to connect a mobile phone to a headset, both devices must have the same profile, which in this case is the headset profile. To connect a Palm or PocketPC that is Bluetooth-enabled to that same phone, you would need a dial-up networking profile; and should you wish to print from your PDA, you would have to have the Basic Printing Profile (BPP) on both devices. These profiles are specific to each manufacturer and model. With devices that have Bluetooth built into them, chances are that the service is on and has the correct profiles to find companion devices.

A Bluetooth profile is rather specific for the kind of device being used. If you have a Bluetooth keyboard or mouse, those devices are supported by a profile called the Human Interface Device, or HID, profile. Because a mobile phone wouldn't come with this profile, you shouldn't expect Bluetooth keyboards or mice to be able to connect to one another.

Another issue is that the two devices might be out of range of one another. If you figure that Bluetooth has about a 30-foot bubble, that range could be lower if the two devices are separated by a wall. Try moving the devices closer.

What does the Bluetooth message "Devices not found" mean?

The pairing or bonding process works by passing a protected passkey from one device to the other over an encrypted link. Depending on the security settings, you may not be able to make a direct connection. For example, you wouldn't normally leave on a device-to-device connection for personal address book or contact exchange. When you wanted to exchange the data, you would turn security off for the short time you were in range.

If you see a message like "Devices not found," device discovery may not be enabled. On some Bluetooth devices, depending on the manufacturer, there is a setting that turns on device discovery. If that setting is turned off, you will not be able to make that connection. Some Sony and Ericsson mobile phones have this feature on a discoverable menu.

What does the message "Pairing unsuccessful" mean?

The fact that you got this message means that the two devices engaged in a handshaking operation but didn't have the correct information to proceed in establishing the connection. Most often this means that there was a wrong password or PIN presented.

It's possible to also create a pair and still not have the two devices work in the way they should. The usual reason for this to happen is that the devices are trying to use different profiles. Check the manual for the two devices or the online Web site of the manufacturers to see what profiles are supported.

What different Bluetooth devices does the iPAQ support?

The iPAQ hx4700 series Pocket PC supports the following Bluetooth profiles:

- Basic Printing Profile
- Dial-Up Networking Profile
- File Transfer Profile
- General Access Profile
- Generic Object Exchange Profile
- Hard Copy Replacement Profile (printing)
- LAN Access Profile
- Object Push Profile
- Personal Area Networking Profile
- Serial Port Profile
- Service Discovery Application Profile

Any device with one of these profiles can connect to, transfer data to and from, and be commanded by this particular iPAQ.

What is bluejacking and how can I prevent it?

Bluejacking is the unauthorized access of one Bluetooth device by another. It's relatively easy to do, and for phones and other devices it can have consequences. To bluejack another person's phone, the intruder uses Bluetooth on his phone to discover any available phones in the vicinity. When the handshake completes and the devices are paired, the two phones are linked and information on one phone can be seen on the other. Most often, the other person will be doing this as a prank or be using the method to communicate something to you anonymously, but in some instances the practice is much more insidious.

There are reports that once the pairing is complete, it is possible to suppress the display of the intruder's device on the target phone. Once the trust is established, anything in memory can be backed up to the intruder's phone. The stealing of contacts in this manner is called bluesnarfing. Worse still, once a phone is bluejacked, the trust relationship stays in the memory of the cell phone until all the memory is erased.

The easiest way to eliminate the threat of bluejacking is to turn off your autodiscovery feature. If an intruder can't see you, he can't pair up with your phone. Also remember that if your phone is bluejacked, the person doing the bluejacking must be nearby because the intruder is using Bluetooth for a transmission mechanism.

For more information on bluejacking, go to `www.bluejackq.com/`.

Why do I hear static or cross talk on my mobile phone?

Several reasons exist for why you might get static on your cell phone. If you are operating on a low battery, there may be sufficient charge in the device to make the phone call and connect, but not enough charge to lock the signal. If your battery is low, try changing it or using a car charger.

If you are hearing constant static, you may be in an area with electronic interference. Move away at least 25 feet from powered devices such as microwaves, blenders, or other mobile phones, and your reception may improve. Constant static also occurs when your phone has a defective antenna, or if your phone is damaged in some way. Make sure that your antenna is pulled all the way out because an antenna that is partially retracted can be a cause of static and dropped calls. If the static isn't constant, but varies from one location to another, the most likely reason that static exists is that you are in a poor reception area. You should move to a better area. You'll also get static when there are electrical storms in your area.

Under most conditions, a digital phone is less susceptible to static than an analog one. You may also find that if you have an analog phone, you experience cross talk. Cross talk is when you can hear other peoples' conversations in the background of your own. It more often occurs in land lines inside buildings with multiple lines carried over wires that are near to one another. The signal leaks from one line to the other.

The simple solution to cross talk is to switch from analog to digital if your cell phone allows this. You should also report the problem to your service provider because they may be able to correct it.

Summary

This chapter concludes the discussion of wireless devices by considering the common hardware problems that these devices encounter. The focus of the chapter is on the components and settings that are responsible for the wireless networking. Because each device type has a very specific set of parameters and software settings, a detailed discussion of each wouldn't be as valuable to you as a visit to your product's manual or the manufacturer's Web site to get the detailed information you need.

Index

Numerics

A

D

G

H

I

J

K

L

M

N

continued

O

P

Q

R

S

X

Y

Z